Imitations of Life

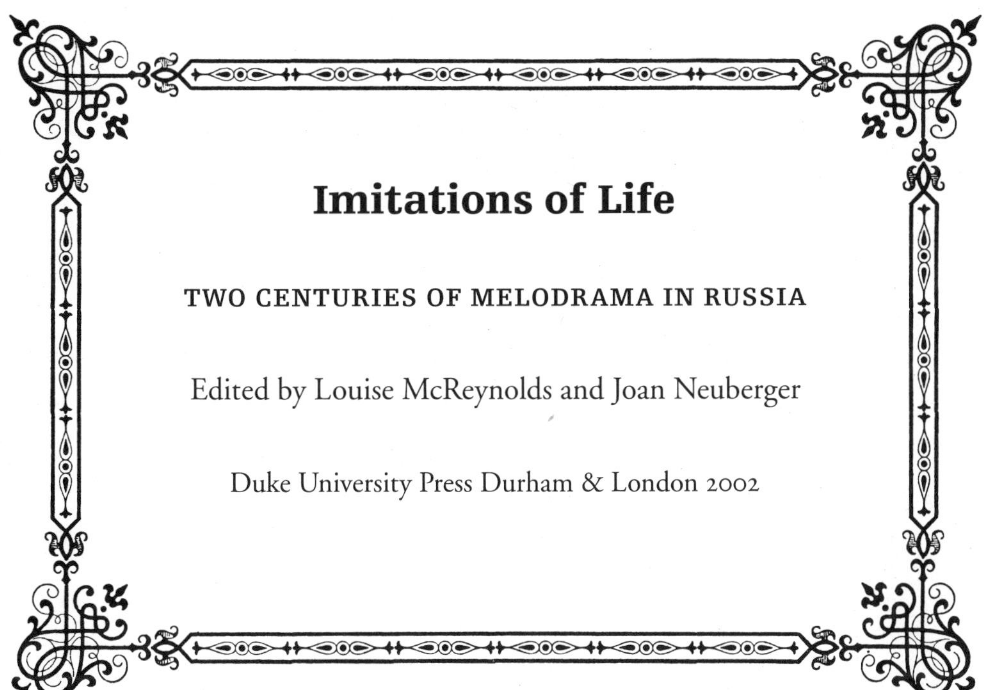

# Imitations of Life

## TWO CENTURIES OF MELODRAMA IN RUSSIA

Edited by Louise McReynolds and Joan Neuberger

Duke University Press Durham & London 2002

Printed in the United States of America
on acid-free paper ∞
Designed by C. H. Westmoreland
Typeset in Adobe Garamond with Egyptienne
display by Tseng Information Systems, Inc.
Library of Congress Cataloging-in-Publication
Data appear on the last printed page
of this book.

To the incomparable Tania Pavlenko,

our mutual friend

## Contents

## Acknowledgments

This volume on melodrama, the most traditional of genres, was born on the Internet. Daily e-schmoozing about our favorite movies eventually led to academic questions about the peculiarities of Russian melodrama. We solicited answers from our other Webmates and, instead of holding a conference, came together @style. Fear not, though, that technology rationalized relations and factored out feelings. The Web turned out to have the same fundamental structure as melodrama, a crisscross of private and public concerns, coincidental twists of fate, some excess emotions, and several crossed paths.

We thank all of those who deepened our appreciation of Russian melodrama. There would never have been a book in the first place if not for two filmmakers who inspired our passion for melodrama, Evgeny Bauer and Douglas Sirk, and two actresses who made it unforgettable, Vera Kholodnaia and Dorothy Malone.

Our contributors inspired us with their creative answers to our original questions, and they did so with extraordinary efficiency and good cheer. We are sincerely appreciative of the institutions that have come to respect the importance of popular culture in academics and supported our research: the International Research and Exchanges Board (IREX), the Kennan Institute for Advanced Russian Studies, and the University of Hawaiʻi and the University of Texas Faculty Development Programs. In Honolulu, Linda Engelberg actively collected sources of prerevolutionary popular culture, especially movie melodramas, and Matthew and Michael Kunihara assisted with the illustrations. In Austin, the University Cooperative Society generously awarded the volume a Robert H. Hamilton subvention grant. We thank our editors at Duke University Press: Valerie Millholland, Miriam Angress, Jonathan Director, and Jean Brady.

We thank our friends, the heros and heroines of our lives: Laurie Bernstein, Judy Coffin, Margot Henriksen, Val Kivelson, Lynn Mally, Dan Orlovsky, Don Raleigh, Jim von Geldern, Bob Weinberg, and Reggie Zelnik. Our families deserve far more than thanks: these protagonists of our private lives offer us, their captive audiences, an embrace of excess and ambiguity that keeps us engaged in every scene; to Charters, Max, and Joel Wynn, and to Alice, Betsy, and Rebecca McReynolds, infinite gratitude.

Above all, we thank each other for the years of performing supporting roles in the melodramas of each other's life.

# Imitations of Life

*Louise McReynolds and Joan Neuberger*

# Introduction

> Not one of the books that later made Nikolai Nikolaevich famous was yet written. . . . He passionately sought an idea, inspired, graspable, which in its movement would clearly point the way toward change, an idea like a flash of lightning or a roll of thunder capable of speaking even to a child or an illiterate. He thirsted for something new.
> —Boris Pasternak, *Doctor Zhivago*[1]

> Sirk has said: you can't make films *about* things, you can only make films *with* things, with people, with light, with flowers, with mirrors, with blood, in fact with all the fantastic things that make life worth living.—Rainer Werner Fassbinder[2]

Enter the world of Russian filmmaker Evgeny Bauer and you enter a world of *things.* Each of his popular turn-of-the-century melodramas is crammed with objects: clocks, telephones, gadgets, and statuettes clutter his desks; rooms overflow with sofas, chairs, and tables; long, deep-focus shots create corridors of fashionably dressed, swirling figures who occupy spaces that seem to stretch infinitely toward an interior horizon; and planes of empty space are broken up by so many artificially placed architectural columns that contemporary critics ridiculed him for it. Bauer's cult of the object, his romance with things, signified more than a Victorian cliché of accomplishment and acquisition. It was an antidote to the Russians' nineteenth-century cult of the *idea,* a string of

The protagonist's study crammed with objects in Evgeny Bauer's *Child of the Big City* (A. Khanzhonkov and Col., 1914).

garlic worn to ward off the diabolical Red Domino stalking the pages of Andrei Belyi's *Petersburg.*

As the incarnation of the sacred *idea,* the alluring Red Domino makes a remarkably effective trope in modern Russian history, where the intelligentsia mounted the most articulate opposition to the autocracy and designated themselves a political elite.[3] In a country where intellectual exchange had to substitute for political action under an autocracy stubbornly opposed to popular expression and participation, Belyi's symbolism in *Petersburg* accentuates the dominant role that culture played in Russian politics, while warning of the danger implied in Pasternak's personification of the intelligentsia's faith in ideas. During the course of the nineteenth century, artists and intellectuals across the political spectrum refined their uses of the *idea,* the singular weapon they possessed in their struggle against autocracy and backwardness. By century's end, they had endowed thought itself with the power to resolve Russia's perennially "accursed questions," to integrate its warring classes into one harmonious society, to change the world, and ultimately to transform humankind.

In essence, the prerevolutionary intelligentsia believed that culture, as they understood it, could resolve social inequities by constructing a single shared national identity. Not surprisingly, the intelligentsia also believed that by virtue of their part in possessing and creating ideas, they merited the leading role in society. Faith in the *idea* was not restricted to one or another political party but was shared by people as diverse as the ultraconservative Konstantin Pobedonostsev, the historian and liberal spokesman Paul Miliukov, and Bolshevik leaders Vladimir Lenin and Lev Trotsky. Historians and literary scholars, by and large, have accepted the intelligentsia's aspiration to power as the driving force in the narrative of the imperial period, and they have constructed the era as a teleology, leading fatalistically toward revolution as the only event capable of realizing the *idea*. In the end, their aims turned out to be as furtive as the Red Domino.[4]

Among the cultural elite, Belyi and his percipient Symbolist colleague, poet Alexander Blok, although they were great proponents of the transcendent powers of abstractions and ideas, understood the seductive power of material desire and earthy entertainment. Belyi and Blok acknowledged the temptations of the marketplace and recognized that the existence of those whose desire for *things* would challenge the utopianism rooted in the cult of ideas. Belyi and Blok watched the crowds that surrounded the Red Domino on the boulevards of St. Petersburg: the growing population of peasants, workers, and bourgeoisie whose own cultural traditions and thirst for innovation had equally deep roots in Russian cultural life, and whose consumption of commercial culture was already transforming public discourses, political as well as cultural. And these crowds did not disappear in 1917, or for that matter in 1991. Commercial culture in general and melodrama in particular remain a central, if underappreciated, force in Russian society. As an alternative to the old intelligentsia's valorization of reason, propriety, and public and political commitment, melodrama offered its audiences a world of feeling, sensation, and private moral dilemmas. But for all its emphasis on the interior landscape, melodrama was by no means detached from the real world of transformation and conflict. In every age, setting, and medium, melodrama explored the social issues that preoccupied its audiences and offered models of behavior for changing times. Both before and after 1917, as shifting lines between private and public were being drawn and the public invasion of the private was being justified on new ideological, economic, and political grounds, melodrama helped people negotiate new boundaries in social life.

The Russian cult of the *idea* and a privileging of political thought and revolutionary ideology have obscured the genuine diversity of Russian cultural production and consumption. Just as the boundaries separating classes had become more porous by the end of the nineteenth century and social identity had become more complex, artists of the period intentionally mixed genres that had previously been associated with specific classes. Painters, architects, and musicians, for example, incorporated folklore and commercial motifs into their work. At the same time, commercial artists often larded their entertainment with social and political commentary, a device monopolized previously by belles lettres.[5] In social terms, the consumers of culture were themselves becoming highly heterogeneous.[6] The survival of this culture into the soviet period, when political circumstances should have written its death sentence, testifies to its power and underscores the historical significance of commercial alternatives to the utopian cult of the *idea*. The popularity of commercial culture in the nineteenth century indicates at least one overlooked historical path that Russia might have taken.

The collection of essays in this volume examine one of those alternatives by looking at Russian and soviet melodrama, a genre perennially popular with consumers of commercial entertainment but long held in contempt by those distrustful of popular tastes. The essays presented here address the questions raised by the seeming paradox of a bourgeois cultural form in an ostensibly hostile environment. The marginalization of commercial culture, both before and after the revolution, the idealization of abstract thought over materialism and consumption, and the widespread suspicion of bourgeois, western individualism, would suggest at the very least a peculiar reception for melodrama in Russia. On the other hand, the characteristics of excess, sensation, spectacle, and affect, so closely associated with melodrama, are also deeply ingrained in Russian cultural history, suggesting conversely fertile ground for the reception of melodrama there. The essays in this volume explore the uses of melodrama by Russian writers, artists, filmmakers, and playwrights in the nineteenth and twentieth centuries to ask, in part, whether there was a uniquely Russian melodrama.

The modern history of melodrama in Russia stretches back to the genre's earliest days following the French Revolution. From its origins in France in the 1790s as a specific form of staged drama, melodrama has been adapted to every artistic genre and has entered everyday life as a distinct mode of behavior. Despite its resulting diversity of forms and uses, common formulaic properties continue to give it recognizable integrity. As Peter Brooks argued in *The Melodramatic Imagination,* the classical study of the 1970s that rescued the genre from two centuries of intellectual condescension, melodrama is best understood as "a mode of conception and expression, [and] as a certain fictional system for making sense of experience."[7] The particular features of this "fictional system" consist of an aesthetic of excess and a Manichaean narrative structure, which pits good against evil in what seems today to be almost satirical extremes. Brooks understood that "melodrama has the distinct value of being about recognition and clarification," a capacity that allowed it critical perspective on the issues of its age, from national politics to gender, class, and consumption.[8] Simply stated, melodrama exaggerates the circumstances of time and place in which it is produced, and as a result it offers a uniquely accessible mode of analysis for audiences to perceive the interaction among politics, art, and everyday life. Because melodrama is self-consciously about its own present, it offers scholars a new perspective on the dominant ideologies—political, cultural, social—in which each story is set. But because the cultural elites routinely denigrated melodrama, its doubtful status made it a guilty pleasure for those who indulged in its production and consumption. In order to place Russian melodrama in a historical and international context, it is important to review the history of melodrama alongside its contemporaneous critique. Both contexts were extensively shaped by the cultural politics of their times, and shaped in turn the evolution of melodrama and of its reception.

The genre's association with the disreputable crowd dates from its inception in France following the revolutionary upheavals that began in 1789; its perseverance derived from its continued ability to make the contemporary world, especially in times of transformation, comprehensible to audiences who lacked the ability to articulate many of the ambiguities and contradictions that social change brought into their lives. Although philosophe Jean-Jacques Rousseau coined the term *melodrame* to underline the musical element he added to his theatrical dramas, it was his fellow countryman René-Charles Guilbert de Pixérécourt, from a significantly different intellectual background, who produced the first corpus of plays to be recognized as representative of this new theatrical genre.

A writer with little taste for revolution but with great sensitivity to the profound changes he observed in the 1790s, Pixérécourt referred to his works as "spectacular prose dramas" written "for those who do not know how to read."[9] Because the official censorship forbade spoken dialogue on the nonofficial stage, Pixérécourt pioneered a new type of production that drew on traditional popular culture and the drama unfolding in the streets of France.[10] He introduced special sight and sound effects to engage his audiences on a fundamental sensory level, which complemented the intense emotionalism of the situations that entangled his characters. This primal sensationalism led to the accusations of escapism that have always tarnished melodrama's successes, by those who would reduce it to its simplest elements. From the French stage the genre spread briskly across Europe and to the United States, and it spread into new media as well, especially with the advent of cinema at the end of the century.[11]

Melodrama raced into new territory in the wake of dissemination of ideas of the Enlightenment. One of the underlying tensions that had prompted revolution in France produced what would become a central motif in melodrama: the conflict between identities in the private and public spheres. The *private* individual, conceived during the Enlightenment as an autonomous agent, struggled to find appropriate *public* identities in the emergent spheres created by new social, political, and economic institutions. The narratives of melodrama aimed to resolve these conflicts through emotion and happenstance rather than logic. Providence and coincidence replaced reason and social institutions as the narrative motor in these stories, which were served up in an aesthetic of excess: inflated emotion, stylized sets and acting, and wildly unbelievable plots. In political terms, however, excess did not generate subversion. However wild the plot, the existing order was restored at the end. This apparent stability gained western melodrama a reputation as a fundamentally conservative genre. Melodrama resolved conflicts by reaffirming rather than challenging contemporary hierarchies and was presumed, therefore, to leave its audiences satisfied with the status quo.[12]

Assumptions about the composition of the audience further supported a conservative reading of melodrama. Contemporary critics and retrospective scholars believed that its fans came from the political periphery: women and workers who had not yet developed a secure political identity derived from either gender or class. Presumptions about the political naïveté of the audience impelled these critics to implicate melodrama in a cultural debate that had explicitly political ramifications about the relationship between high culture and low, and the relative social value accorded to each. For social critics, the image of the disenfranchised spending their meager earnings and their few leisure hours reincorporating themselves vicariously into the system that denied them access to power suggested an ignorance that bordered on complicity. The aesthetics of emotion, sensation, and excess appeared to render melodrama an irrational, escapist entertainment, prompting critics to charge the genre with undermining the rational justifications for an enlightened legal and political order.

Melodrama's reliance on coincidence to move the action toward climax also encouraged charges of political conservatism. Stories structured by forces over which the protagonists exercised no control, it was thought, could not encourage audiences to take charge of their own lives. Enlightened intellectuals' faith in agency in the early nineteenth century, central to both representative and revolutionary politics, was drowned out by the sensationalist spectacle on the stage.

Small wonder that early opponents of melodrama despaired of a genre that appeared to bolster dominant power structures and the complacency of the subordinate multitudes.[13] In large measure, however, the political complexion of the audience was read backward from critics' stereotypes about popular tastes. Melodrama's subtle but pointed challenge to gender and class hierarchies and its engagement with public issues of morality and power eluded early critics. Indeed, over the decades changing conditions had transformed the composition of melodrama's public as well—ticket prices, literacy skills, and the media themselves all complicated the audiences for melodrama. Nor, for that matter, were the plots as predictably uniform as critics charged. Despite formulaic aesthetics and excesses, melodrama's makers often used the genre's formulas in innovative ways to explore social identities and social change.

Early critics misunderstood melodrama because they saw it as a debased form of the theatrical genres that they knew: tragedy and realism. However, as Peter Brooks has persuasively argued, melodrama originated as a response to the limited capacities of these two forms to address the conflicts ordinary individuals faced in post-Enlightenment society, where moral certitude, shaken by industrial and cultural revolution, was defending itself against the heavy artillery of secularization.

Brooks pointed out that the distinction between melodrama and the familiar forms of tragedy and realism was paramount at first, when melodrama offered audiences a fundamentally modern theatrical mode for experiencing the changes connected with industrial and political revolution. Unlike tragedy, which for dramatic tension relied on forces that individuals could not control and, therefore, ended in inescapable ruin, melodrama mired its characters in adverse situations, but provided resolutions that restored order to their worlds. Brooks noted that in contrast to realism, and despite melodrama's grounding in the secular and familiar, the genre fostered self-indulgent emotional expressionism over rational discourse. Generations before modernism received credit for shattering the surfaces of realism, Pixérécourt's innovations in sensory experiences soon led artists to use an *aesthetic* of emotional excess to explore the *content* of emotions lying repressed beneath the surface rationality of realism. Melodrama, popular with those unable to articulate their own needs clearly, came to depend on nonverbal means to convey what words were inadequate to communicate. Hence the performance techniques of a heightened style of acting, with its exaggerated gestures and mannered characterizations, became synonymous with the genre.

In creating a new mode for perceiving modernity, melodrama borrowed heavily from Romanticism, the initial reaction against the Enlightenment. Appealing to the visceral rather than the cerebral, melodrama drew from romantic obsessions with feelings and the occult, and from gothic novels with their dark secrets and mistaken identities. Elucidating what Brooks termed "the 'moral occult,'—the domain of operative spiritual values, which is both indicated within and masked by the surface of reality,"—melodrama helped its audiences sort out the ethics of a secular world.[14] The characters' inability to express themselves in words remains central, as they negotiate their conflicts through repression and sublimation. Because their private anxieties are rooted in public policies, the melodramatic expression of their anguish reflects something about the larger edifices that structure their lives. As Brooks noted, melodrama anticipated the two philosophical strains that emerged in the course of the nineteenth century to address the effects of both social structure and the unconscious: first Marxism and then Freudianism.[15] Like psychoanalysis, melodrama became increasingly preoccupied with the return of the repressed; significantly, it did so in forms that linked it directly with social and political life.

One of melodrama's essential properties lies in its engagement with contemporaneous social issues.[16] In Patrice Petro's words, the genre offers "a heightened and expressive representation of the implications of everyday life."[17] Originally, the limited scope of such presentism contributed to its cultural marginalization because, as critics argued, melodrama located social stress within specific sets of circumstances instead of advancing universal truths about the human condition. What was intended as a reproach, however, reflected characteristics of melodrama's audience and its cultural function, which historical perspective casts in a more positive light. Melodrama proved to be a medium for cultivating cultural self-awareness and self-expression for the social groups emerging from the upheavals associated with the industrial revolution.[18] As Thomas Elsaesser noted, the genre was integral to the development of bourgeois identity because it provided these new classes with a "particular and socially conditioned *mode of experience.*"[19]

This presentism, however, also constitutes an obstacle to analyzing melodrama; the typical plot's reliance on specific moral contexts has not served individual texts well. Individual melodramas aged quickly when situations that appeared life-altering to one generation came to seem ridiculous to the next, after past conflicts had been resolved or became irrelevant. In the late twentieth century, historical melodrama becomes most readily accessible through the camp sensibility that has reconstituted one era's moral occult in terms of its own.[20] Paradoxically, however, presentism has proven to be melodrama's most enduring advantage for cultural and social historians by providing documentary evidence of the social traumas of the past. As the wrenching changes of the French and industrial revolutions gave way to technological and political revolutions in the twentieth century, melodrama continued to offer emotionally cathartic probing beneath the surfaces of new ideologies, and it provided dramas of identity formation to audiences eager to consume them. In so doing, these aesthetically remote texts bring the burning social and cultural issues of the past within the reach of scholars in the present.

By the end of the nineteenth century, melodrama had left behind its origins on the bourgeois stage to enter many other forms of popular culture, especially literature. Literary melodrama borrowed from both the supernatural of the gothic novel and the "glistening tear" inspired by sentimental fiction. It also increased the audience base for the genre, attracting more educated women and creating a unique space for them, a psychological "room of their own."[21] On the stage, the music of the "melo" lost its importance once the censorship relaxed controls over spoken dialogue, but the use of theatrical spectacle to intensify the action remained. Music would return as an integral element at the very end of the century with the emergence of the silent cinema, a medium particularly well suited to melodrama because of its own capacity to dramatize emotion and its immediate popularity among women and the urban poor. As the movie industry advanced technologically in developing sound and color, film melodrama remained popular by utilizing its uniquely sensational visual elements to amplify the emotional impact of its images. By the end of the nineteenth century, melodrama had already proven its durability as a prism of contemporary culture by adapting both form and content to suit changing times.[22]

From the very beginning, melodrama's orchestrated appeal to the broadest public guaranteed rejection by intellectuals. In the 1960s, though, when academics began to revise their understanding of popular culture and recognize the powerful role it could play in mediating political and social conflict, melodrama won recognition as an important source of cultural commentary. Douglas Sirk, a refugee Weimar intellectual who found his way to Hollywood and directed the most extravagant of the 1950s movie melodramas, played the determining role in the elevation of melodrama to a critically acceptable art form. One of technicolor's first masters, and one of the first to bring Berthold Brecht's influence to film, Sirk consciously turned some of Hollywood's biggest stars into Freudian simulacra for the angst of repressed sexuality and irrational passions underlying the surface complacency of the 1950s. Sirk's cinematic portrayals of glamorous middle-class women trapped in the false security of the domestic economy demonstrated an extraordinary capacity to serve both the priests and the rabble. He became the darling of both crowds and critics with films that offered moralistic examinations of postwar conformity through characters who inevitably violated the norms of middle-class morality in lurid, melodramatic excess.[23]

Sirk's movies about women frustrated with bourgeois life made natural texts for the nascent field of feminist studies in the 1970s, when feminism joined forces with film criticism to redress the inferior status of melodrama.[24] Together they reimagined the female viewer, formerly construed as passive and marginal, by endowing her with critical agency.

The opulent sets characteristic of melodramatic mise-en-scène were no longer disdained for cultivating bourgeois values but rather were appreciated for their use of contrast and extravagance to expose social inequalities and tensions among genders, classes, and cultures.[25] The new scholarship acknowledged the complexity of the audience, and it replaced assumptions about melodrama's Manichaean morality with a sophisticated appreciation for its capacity to render dichotomies ambiguous. In a key revisionist point, Laura Mulvey recognized the ambiguity in melodrama's conventional restoration of the status quo. In most melodrama, the same problems that had generated conflict in the opening scene still simmered below the surface calm as the curtain fell or the last page was turned.[26] Once it was understood that melodramas could problematize hierarchies as much as they reinforced them, the genre could offer a significant new category of cultural analysis.[27]

This critical reappraisal, initiated by Sirk's reinvention of an ambiguous melodrama and the feminist discovery of its capacity for a submerged challenge to underlying cultural, sexual, and class conflicts, has expanded possibilities for revealing readings of melodramas in other times and contexts.[28] In Russia, audiences for melodrama experienced the industrial revolution under significantly different social and political circumstances from those that spawned the genre in the West. Yet melodrama was as popular in Russia as in the West, from its inception at the turn of the nineteenth century through the collapse of communism. Was there, then, a uniquely Russian melodrama? Yes and no. Sharp differences are readily apparent between Russian and western melodramatic texts, but their cultural functions are remarkably similar. In short, what made Russian melodrama unique was Russia, not melodrama. Throughout this volume, individual authors show repeatedly that melodrama as a genre followed the same historical trajectory as its counterparts in western Europe and the United States. Peter Brooks's conceptualization of the genre's prescriptive functions applies to Russian melodramas of every type and period. Literary authors, playwrights, and filmmakers used melodrama to address issues of social identity in times of transition, to explore the shifting boundaries between public and private, and to both challenge and reaffirm existing hierarchies, but they did so to explore specifically Russian or soviet versions of those issues.

As the studies in this collection will show, melodrama in Russia was a malleable form, as useful for the radical intelligentsia as it was for the middlebrow. Melodrama offered a counternarrative to challenge the intelligentsia's view of itself as the country's sole conscience and primary cultural authority. The private pleasures and passions on the domestic palette of commercial melodrama encompassed a social world as large and varied as any represented in the radical cultural narrative, or even in the works of renowned novelists. By dramatizing class tensions, urban-rural transformations, marriage politics, struggles over national memory, the nature of heroism, and the conflict between the worship of ideas and the accumulation of things, melodrama had the capacity to explore the most important cultural conflicts at the heart of the construction of both national and individual identity.

In Russia, melodrama was useful even for some of its harshest critics among the intelligentsia. The Freudian notion of the repression of sexuality found a Russian political analog in the repression of the Russian people. Even more significant, radical narratives, both political and literary, plotted revolution in melodramatic terms: good battled evil; ravished innocence and virtue were restored by moral action; and radical male heroes defended the honor of the (female) motherland. From the intelligentsia's point of view, Russian society before the revolution was a Manichaean world where an evil government defiled an innocent people and where educated heroes—and heroines—intervened on their behalf. Despite the communalism of nineteenth-century socialist theory, the intelligentsia's view of itself as the "conscience" of the nation revealed at least one strain in radical thought to be an individual affair, preoccupied with choices about individual values—honor, sacrifice, commitment, morality.

During the revolutionary era and into the postrevolutionary reconstruction, when Bolsheviks adopted melodrama's moral purity for the deceptively simplistic political narratives of socialist realism, the genre was less useful for exploring transformations and revealing the repressed than for establishing new categories of good and evil and opening up the private to the purgative glare of public, politically charged morality. The rich tapestry of prerevolutionary urban cultural life was badly burned by the Bolshevik revolution, but it was never entirely destroyed. The Bolsheviks' efforts to tame private passions and expose the hidden arenas of private life deprived the revolutionary-reconstruction melodrama of its century-long fascination with everyday complexities, thereby forcing artists, filmmakers, and writers to seek new ways of stretching the limits and plumbing the depths of the permissible. As tensions increased between official discourse and everyday experience—between the public and private, the collective and individual, and the idea and the thing—artists found abundant material for melodramatic treatment.

In socialist realist works of the 1930s and 1940s—in the boy/girl/tractor/machine-gun melodramas—domestic passions were never far from the surface. After Stalin's death, the recovery of private life offered melodrama a new role as a self-reflexive, at times ironic, genre for exploring the legacy of revolutionary culture (well before the collapse in 1991, it should be noted). The revival of private life as a legitimate subject for the arts raised questions about the impact of public values on domestic ones. By exploring basic human relations, post-Stalinist melodrama offered insights into the survival of the individual after the assault of the collective. Despite their differences, the long history of affinities between melodramatic and revolutionary modes of thought, despite their differences, made melodrama an especially apt tool for exploring the individual *within* the collective, the private morality *underneath* the strictures on public performances, the tensions resulting from political manipulations of both public and private morality. Issues that lay at the heart of melodrama's staging of the conflict between public and private life were also central to Russian political culture throughout the modern era, when social responsibility turned into coerced conformity and demands for a right to privacy became an excuse for greed and hedonism.

Rightfully identified as a chorus from below, melodrama offers escape not from political reality but from a social and moral certainty imposed from above. The essays in this volume examine the uses of melodrama within Russian political culture to rethink several features of Russian and soviet historiography. They bring the middle classes back to a status long denied them, for example, because melodrama examines attitudes toward the status quo without assuming a direct connection between the bourgeoisie and electoral politics. Gender roles, a central preoccupation of melodrama, are examined for their ability to focus moral dilemmas and reveal hidden strengths as well as hidden weaknesses of identity. Both the power and the limitations of the pervasive soviet state become apparent in its blatant manipulation of the genre, and a subtext of resistance allows melodrama to provide its fans with one means to circumvent the predations of that state. As an authentic reflection of popular sentiments, melodrama contains all the ambiguities, contradictions, and ironies implicit in such a mediative cultural idiom. Furthermore, the Russian example suggests possibilities for a deeper and broader understanding of melodrama as a genre across cultures. The study of Russian and soviet melodramas shows, for example, that the presumed audience for propaganda enjoyed an alternative source for simplified social and political discourse. Moreover, these studies provide evidence that the political elite considered the genre useful for state purposes as well.

In the first essay in this volume, Richard Stites identifies the Russian audience for early melodrama as socially diverse. In so doing, he expands Pierre Bourdieu's argument that culture provides a form of capital, by suggesting that cultural taste can also supply a marker of social identity distinctly different from that prescribed by class. Contrary to common assumptions about melodrama's middle-to-lower-class audience, Stites finds a significant element of the audience for melodrama in the more elevated populace at the Winter Palace, and he reveals an international constituency for plays performed in radically different political climates, from New York to St. Petersburg. The specific plays he discusses star one of melodrama's most celebrated characters, the vulnerable female whose return to patriarchy is ensured, but only after sufficient tears have been shed. Because these early plays established patriarchy as the site where social conflict could be reconciled, Russia's autocracy shows an often overlooked cultural affinity with bourgeois capitalism. Furthermore, Stites's concluding discussion of Alexander Herzen's revolutionary adaptation of one of the era's most popular melodramas demonstrates both the underlying affinities between revolutionary and melodramatic modes of constructing social reality and melodrama's inherent challenge to convention, which Sirk brought to the surface a century later.

The different cultural uses to which Russian and western writers put melodrama are explored by Julie Buckler, who looks at how "Russia" became at once a location and a character in several important western melodramas. Such writers as Victorien Sardou and Oscar Wilde utilized melodrama's Manichaean dualism to emphasize the political differences between Eastern and Western Europe, identifying eastern autocracy as the villain that made western liberalism look "good." From the western viewpoint, the "evil" Other portrayed by Russia had two equally odious sides: autocratic oppression and revolutionary socialism. Western melodramatists resorted to a familiar trope, the power of female love, to redeem unsavory politics. The melodramatic "Russia" that appeared on western stages, however, enacted western rather than Russian anxieties. True love could redeem the western heroic versions of Russians, but tsarist audiences who lived in genuinely oppressive circumstances were less impressed by love's redemptive potential.

Wilde and Sardou drew their Russian heroines straight from contemporary stereotypes of revolutionaries. Placing their women in a melodramatic conflict within a western, liberal context, those women had little choice but to take their own lives in order to demonstrate the primacy of true love over political action. At first glance this might evoke favorable comparison with the heroines created by Russian authors. But, as Beth Holmgren shows in her portentously subtitled essay, "Why She Died," there were stark differences between western and Russian women's motivations for suicide. These, together with differences between the meanings death imparted to conflict resolution, demonstrate the conflicting cultural uses of the generic conventions, just as Herzen had suggested earlier. The western heroines committed suicide in order to dramatize their marginalization in society. The women created by the authors in Holmgren's study—one Polish and the other Russian, both female—make political statements with their deaths, but the stakes are reversed. The West's idealized Russians, as described by Buckler, reaffirm patriarchy and the capitalist status quo; on the other hand, the authentic Slavs die questioning capitalism, not autocracy.

The suicidal Russian heroine in Holmgren's essay, Mania Eltsova of *The Keys to Happiness,* found her fate recast by the prolific moralist Count Amori, the pen name used by "boulevard" author Ippolit Rapgof, who rewrote some of the most sensational novels of the fin de siècle. As Otto Boele points out in his essay, the way in which melodrama sets up the conflict between good and evil made it an appropriate medium for identifying some of the tensions that beset society as the old regime tottered toward its collapse. Amori included Mania in a cast of decadent fictional characters, but he erased the suggestive ambiguities that her creator, Anastasia Verbitskaia, had raised about her self-indulgent, self-fulfilling lifestyle. More to the point, by calling on readers to accept his own unequivocal righteousness, he was emulating the moral certitude of the old intelligentsia and trying, unsuccessfully, to subvert the very power of the genre he employed.

Amori tried to redraw the moral world in black and white, an agenda he did not carry over into the scripts he wrote for the emergent black-and-white world of early cinema. Movies and melodrama were made for each other. From the acting styles that played on emotional rather than verbal expression to its ability to hide hollow morality beneath glamorous or virtuous surfaces to their socially heterogenous audiences, cinema was able to refract as well as reflect cultural mores. More than in any other mass medium, the vision of Russia that flickered across its silver screens showed a country that had lost its moral compass as a direct result of the disarray in the national domestic economy. The weakening of tsarist authority was represented metaphorically in Russian melodrama as a troubled and problematic head of the household. As Louise McReynolds argues in "Home Was Never Where the Heart Was," her essay on the enormously popular silent cinema, the familiar melodramatic trope of domesticity appeared repeatedly in Russia as a home without a patriarch. As figures more than simply incompetent in running their households, melodramatic fathers were prone to violate the vulnerable young ladies left in their care. In a significant departure from generic convention, these movies ended without closure or resolution. A rickety status quo remained in place but, unlike in western melodrama, it was hardly restored.

The last shot in a prerevolutionary movie melodrama, in which the possibilities for reconciliation lay dead literally as often as figuratively, contrasts sharply with post-1917 melodramas, equally popular and made manifestly political by the new regime. Commissar of Enlightenment Anatoly Lunacharsky recognized the power of melodrama to reach the unsophisticated audiences whose support was critical to the new regime. As Julie Cassiday argues in her study of the temperance drama, another conventional melodramatic scenario, the genre provided a familiar cultural site for identifying good and evil and negotiating an individual's banishment from and return to the community. An alcoholic who drinks away his family's chance for happiness wrenches our tears for those defenseless against his weakness, and in the early soviet temperance drama such a drunk could just as easily personify a public issue as a private grief. Unlike such classic western plays as *Ten Nights in a Bar-Room,* in which drinking marked specifically individual behavior, the soviet temperance drama mobilized the audience into judging the drunk's behavior for its impact on the collective. For a government determined to heal the wounds left by civil war, the activist temperance drama depended on reconciliation and return in order to lay the foundations for what would become the new status quo. Most significant, it also set into motion the uniquely soviet melodramatic tendency to privilege public over private concerns.

Temperance dramas put citizens on trial for unethical behavior that tore the social fabric, and the juxtaposition of alcoholism with sobriety made an especially easy contrast of good and evil. Stalin, however, found the most radical political use for melodrama since Pixérécourt's initial questioning of the French Revolution. Lars Lih uncovers the melodramatic structure underlying the show trials of 1936 to 1938, where life imitated lowbrow art with devastating results. The trials deployed classic melodramatic tropes to illustrate political good and evil and to villainize political threats. The evildoers singled out for exposure and banishment in these real-life melodramas were the "waverer," an individual who still had doubts about the new community, and the *dvurushnik,* one who hid his hatred of the virtuous soviet community under a mask of surface loyalty. The emotion that these melodramas played on was fear, a categorically public fear that worked to transform the very nature of privacy into a threat to public order and thereby justify the exposure of all private life to the state's gaze.

Stalin's brilliant manipulation of melodramatic structures could not, however, sustain a status quo that derived so much of its authority from exhausting, debilitating fear, nor could soviet society maintain its excessive intrusion into the private sphere. The versatility of melodrama proved itself once again during the "thaw" that followed Stalin's death in 1953, when artists reclaimed private life as a legitimate, if contested, subject. Susan Costanzo's study brings us yet another public trial about private life, but this one staged in an experimental theater at Moscow University in 1957. Director Rolan Bykov used the innovative staging of a Czech melodrama to highlight the potential for ambiguity that had been in decline under Stalinism. Like his contemporary Douglas Sirk, Bykov had been influenced by Brechtian uses of form to evoke psychological moods. At the same time that Sirk was questioning the American ideals of consensus and conformity during the cold war, Bykov was raising comparable doubts about conformity under soviet socialism.

Although Bykov used the conventions of melodrama to challenge the moral certainty of Stalinist public values, Mikhail Kalatozov used similar conventions to rework the central trope of late Stalinist culture, the Second World War. One of the signal cultural events of the period, Kalatozov's film *The Cranes Are Flying,* undermined sacred icons of soviet wartime heroism. Comparing *The Cranes Are Flying* to a war-era movie melodrama *Wait for Me,* Alexander Prokhorov argues that in the late 1950s Kalatozov fulfilled people's need to reconcile the public memory of national victory with their devastating personal losses. As the action shifted from the external battlefield to the domestic and internal one, Russian men and women replaced the Nazis as the sole source of evil during the war. And again, like Sirk in the United States, Kalatozov used melodramatic conventions to raise questions about the private individual held captive by public ideology.

In the 1970s, director Nikita Mikhalkov took cinematic melodrama a step further into moral ambiguity and a subtle questioning of the late soviet status quo. Joan Neuberger's discussion of *Slave of Love,* Mikhalkov's complex melodrama within a melodrama, shows this film to be much more than the "retro-chic" costume drama that critics branded it. Setting his story in the final days of Russia's old regime, Mikhalkov used the world of bourgeois filmmaking to explore the affinities between revolutionary and melodramatic approaches to life's basic questions. By collapsing categories usually seen as mutually exclusive, Mikhalkov uncovers the the moral interdependency of public and private life. In *Slave of Love,* Neuberger argues, Mikhalkov used the old-regime setting to challenge the revolution's repression of private life, while at the same time decry the seductive dangers of private self-absorption, a pointed reflection on the revived private sphere of his own time. Ultimately the film represents choices between good and evil as primarily individual affairs, but also as ambiguous and difficult in the renewed (and remembered) soviet private life as they had been in the heroic and conformist soviet public sphere.

Helena Goscilo brings this volume to a fitting end by connecting prerevolutionary to postsoviet society with her analysis of celebrity funerals. Structured like melodrama, these public rituals accentuate the presentism of the genre, as the urgencies of the present determine celebrity status. The first funeral she discusses, that of silent film star Vera Kholodnaia, recalls both the popularity of the silent movies themselves and Mikhalkov's calculated use of a Kholodnaia-like heroine in *Slave of Love.* The funerals of Stalin and of the dissidents who spoke out against the soviet privileging of public over private remind us that Stalinism never entirely erased opposition, and they illustrate some of the particularly Russian forms that opposition took. Melodrama in the soviet period assumed a heightened political function precisely because so little was permitted to be said out loud. In a society where reason struggled against impossible conditions, emotions ran persistently high. The last funeral Goscilo discusses shows that melodrama will continue to play an important function in postsoviet culture, as the terms of good and evil and public and private again undergo redefinition: these funeral melodramas mark the death ritual of the monopoly of the *idea.*

Whether electrifying from beneath the proscenium arch of the legitimate stage, springing to life from the pages of a romance novel, flickering on the silver screen, or lying in funereal repose, the heroes and villains of Russian melodrama interpreted their audience's contemporary worlds, and they did so in terms that illuminate the writing of Russian history. The story of melodrama would be worth telling even if the essays here simply recreated images of the past. As fragments of a story heretofore deemed unworthy of analysis, the essays in this volume fill an important blank spot in the historical record. The now-established field of cultural studies, however, suggests ways that melodrama can isolate stress points in social and political structures that are not otherwise visible. These studies of melodrama in Russia restore a limited agency to groups long regarded as the passive pawns of oppressive political systems, autocratic and communist. They reveal a lively, ongoing negotiation over issues of morality, power, and identity. And they show how such subjects could be approached in ways that were both aesopic and quotidian in times when direct speech about the everyday was impossible. Most important, though, these studies of Russian and soviet melodrama reaffirm Belyi's Red Domino as an apocalyptic and tragic symbol of old-regime, Enlightenment culture in decay, and they offer a corrective to the dangers of the Russian cult of the *idea.*

Such postsoviet fare as Masha Gessen's *Dead Again* and Andrei Siniavsky's *The Russian Intelligentsia,* which hold the intelligentsia responsible for the successive failures of attempted democratic transformations, underscore the continuation of the belief that high culture plays a uniquely important role in Russian politics and history.[29] Although they reverse the intelligentsia's own judgment of itself as tragic heroes and *blame* the intelligentsia for the current crisis, Gessen and Siniavsky are still taking the view from the top and obscuring the rest of the Russian world. Observers who would look instead for the culture that was actually, and voraciously, consumed at the end of the soviet era would find melodrama in a prominent place. No television program before or since, and perhaps no cultural product, has matched the popularity of the imported, outdated Brazilian *telenovelo The Rich Also Cry,* which dominated the airwaves during the first year after the failed coup of 1991 elevated Boris Yeltsin to power. Horrified critics reverted to stereotype and denounced the soap opera as "escapism." Without giving serious thought to what else viewers might be gleaning from the long-running saga of Marianna, the beautiful heroine who raised her son in secrecy from the father who never knew of his birth, intelligentsia critics missed the essential appeal of the addictive serial.

Of all the melodramas imported by Russian television studios, including the American *Santa Barbara* (which enjoyed greater success in Europe than at home), *The Rich Also Cry* generated the most devoted following along with a cottage industry of spinoffs, including a Russian-language novelization. The original show contained the classic ingredients of melodrama: a self-sacrificing mother, the concealed identity of a son, the threat of incest when the boy meets his younger and unknown sister, and a father forced to negotiate the oedipal conflict with the son he never knew he had. Douglas Sirk would have appreciated the richly exaggerated aesthetics of its spike heels, big hair, tight skirts, and hot tempers. In the 1990s, as in revolutionary eras past, Russian audiences appreciated a narrative that reflected the everyday turmoil in their lives far more coherently than they did the reigning political figures and ideologies.[30] The Brazilian melodrama "worked" because it was grounded in the moral dilemmas of the everyday and it was structured to dramatize the complex issues its viewers understood implicitly but could not yet articulate. The millions of Russians who glued themselves to the television to follow Marianna's exploits tuned in for the show's most obvious value, entertainment. But if they watched obsessively, they did so with considerable irony and self-reflexivity—the funniest joke in Moscow at the time was that "the poor also cry." Marianna's fate was more than simple escape from political reality; the soap opera helped people to configure and comprehend the essential elements of the new national melodrama that began its run in 1991. As this book goes to press, the Russian government has just announced a rise in vodka and bread prices and the return of the second most popular soap, *Santa Barbara.* Canceled following the economic crisis of 1998, *Santa Barbara* returns to the broadcast schedule during a particularly desultory presidential campaign and, according to the *Moscow Times,* the program matters to Russian voters as much as the economic crisis or the war in Chechnya.[31] Like earlier audiences who enjoyed Kotzube, Verbitskaia, Bykov, and Mikhalkov, or who sat anxiously through show trials and temperance dramas, Russians needed and still need the contemporary melodrama to make sense of their lives in times of change.

## Notes

1 Boris Pasternak, *Doctor Zhivago,* trans. Max Hayward and Manya Harari (1958; New York: Pantheon Books, 1986), 7.

2 Quoted in David A. Cook, *A History of Narrative Film* (New York: Norton, 1981), 613; Fassbinder refers here to the great director of postwar Hollywood melodrama, Douglas Sirk (born in Germany as Detlef Sierck), whose work is discussed below.

3 Among the many works that conflate the two, up to and including Richard Pipes's mammoth two-volume *A History of the Russian Revolution* (New York: Knopf, 1990) and *Russia under the Bolshevik Regime* (New York: Knopf, 1993), the textbook example remains Franco Venturi, *Roots of Revolution: A History of the Populist and Socialist Movements in Nineteenth-Century Russia* (New York: Gosset and Dunlap, 1966).

4 As John Bayley points out: "An idea in Russia exists to be implemented by the means of power, even though it may have been conceived in abstraction, barren argument, apparent helplessness. . . . Russia has always presented itself as a perfect paradise for the historian of ideas" (Bayley, "What Follies and Paradoxes!," *New York Review of Books* 45, no. 18 [November 29, 1998], 37).

5 Among many other examples, see Anna Povelikhina and Evgenii Kovtun, *Russkaia zhivopisnaia vyveska i khudozhniki avangarda* (Leningrad: Iskusstvo, 1991); Joan Neuberger, "Hooliganism and Futurism," in *Cultures in Flux,* ed. Stephen Frank and Mark Steinberg (Princeton: Princeton University Press, 1994); and James von Gelden and Louise McReynolds,

eds., *Entertaining Tsarist Russia* (Bloomington: Indiana University Press, 1998).

6 On changing audiences, see Yuri Tsivian, *Early Cinema in Russia and Its Cultural Reception* (London: Routledge, 1994); Richard Stites, *Russian Popular Culture: Entertainment and Society since 1900* (Cambridge: Cambridge University Press, 1992); and Jeffrey Brooks, *When Russia Learned to Read: Literacy and Popular Literature, 1861–1917* (Princeton: Princeton University Press, 1985).

7 Peter Brooks, *The Melodramatic Imagination: Balzac, Henry James, Melodrama, and the Mode of Excess* (New Haven: Yale University Press, 1976), xiii.

8 Ibid., 206.

9 Quoted in Lynn Hunt, *The Family Romance of the French Revolution* (Berkeley: University of California Press, 1992), 181.

10 Ibid.

11 Jacky Bratton, Jim Cook, and Christine Gledhill, eds., *Melodrama: Stage, Picture, Screen* (London: British Film Institute, 1994). See also Frank Rahill, *The World of Melodrama* (University Park: Pennsylvania State University Press, 1967).

12 Julia Przybos, in *L'enterprise melodramatique* (Paris: Librairie Jose Corti, 1987), takes a similarly conservative stance on melodrama, but adds an interesting perspective based on the anthropological studies of Victor Turner, who believed that popular culture maintained social stability by offering sites for conflict resolution.

13 On the historical critique of melodrama, see Christine Gledhill, "The Melodramatic Field: An Investigation," in *Home Is Where the Heart Is: Studies in Melodrama and the Woman's Film,* ed. Christine Gledhill (London: British Film Institute, 1987), 5–39. On the conservatism of female-oriented popular culture, see also Ann Douglas, *The Feminization of American Culture* (New York: Avon, 1977). Andreas Huyssen discusses some of the fundamental politicized associations in "Mass Culture as Woman: Modernism's Other," in *Studies in Entertainment: Critical Approaches to Mass Culture,* ed. Tania Modleski (Bloomington: Indiana University Press, 1986), 188–208.

14 Brooks, *The Melodramatic Imagination,* 5.

15 Ibid., 201. See also Wylie Sypher, "Aesthetic of Revolution: The Marxist Melodrama," in *Tragedy: Vision and Forum,* ed. Robert Corrigan (New York: New York University Press, 1965).

16 As Gledhill argues: "Melodrama addresses us within the limitations of the status quo, of the ideologically permissible. . . . If melodrama can end only in the place where it began, not having a programmatic analysis

for the future, its possibilities lie in this double acknowledgment of how things are in a given historical juncture, and of the primary desires and resistances contained within it" (Gledhill, "The Melodramatic Field," 39).

17 Patrice Petro, *Joyless Streets: Women and Melodramatic Representation in Weimar Germany* (Princeton: Princeton University Press, 1989), 34.

18 David Grimsted has pointed out that "the ties between melodrama and the great democratic-bourgeois revolutions of the last quarter of the 18th century are self-evident truths" (Grimsted, "Vigilante Chronicle: The Politics of Melodrama Brought to Life," in Bratton et al., eds., *Melodrama,* 199).

19 Thomas Elsaesser, "Tales of Sound and Fury: Observations on the Family Melodrama," in Gledhill, ed., *Home Is Where the Heart Is,* 49.

20 Susan Sontag, "Notes on Camp," in *Against Interpretation* (1961; New York: Farrar, Straus, Giroux, 1966), 275–92. Sontag notes that "pure examples of Camp are deadly serious" (282), as are melodramas.

21 Janice A. Radway, *Reading the Romance: Women, Patriarchy, and Popular Literature* (Chapel Hill: University of North Carolina Press, 1984). Chapter 3, "The Act of Reading the Romance: Escape and Instruction," discusses the significance of melodrama's seemingly fraternal twin, the Harlequin novel, to its female readers.

22 For melodrama outside of popular culture, see Stuart Cunningham, "The 'Force-Field' of Melodrama," *Quarterly Review of Film Studies* 6, no. 4 (1981): 347–64.

23 The abundant literature on Sirk has been collected and analyzed by Barbara Klinger in *Melodrama and Meaning: History, Culture, and the Films of Douglas Sirk* (Bloomington: Indiana University Press, 1994). Sirk's classic movies include *Magnificent Obsession* (1954), *Written on the Wind* (1957), and the Lana Turner version of *Imitation of Life* (1959).

24 Although Betty Friedan did not discuss Sirk in her pioneering analysis of the unfulfilled woman, *The Feminine Mystique* (New York: Norton, 1963), both essentially address the same social problem and the same social character.

25 Elsaesser, "Tales of Sound and Fury," 62. See also the epigraphs at the end of the collection (365).

26 Laura Mulvey discusses the problems of melodramatic closure in "Notes on Sirk and Melodrama," in Gledhill, ed., *Home Is Where the Heart Is,* 75–79. See also Bratton, Cook, and Gledhill, eds., *Melodrama,* 3.

27 Gledhill, "The Melodramatic Field," 5–39, especially part 2, "Historicising Melodrama."

28 In addition to the numerous works cited throughout this collection, see Sarah Maza, "Stories in History: Cultural Narratives in Recent Works

in European History," *American Historical Review* 101, no. 5 (December 1996), especially 1510–12.

29 Masha Gessen, *Dead Again: The Russian Intelligentsia after Communism* (New York: Verso, 1997); and Andrei Siniavsky, *The Russian Intelligentsia,* trans. Lynn Visson (New York: Columbia University Press, 1997).

30 Fredo Arias-King, in "Is It Power or Principle? A Footnote on Clinton's Russia Policy," discusses the residual effects that the stars of this extraordinarily popular show might have had on the 1993 elections to the Duma, and potentially thereafter. This article appeared first on the Web, in Johnson's Russia List, no. 2475 (13 November 1998); it is scheduled for publication in the spring 1999 issue of *Demokratizatsiya,* which the author edits.

31 "The Voters Also Cry . . . for Help," *Moscow Times,* 22 February 2000.

*Richard Stites*

# The Misanthrope, the Orphan, and the Magpie

## Imported Melodrama in the Twilight of Serfdom

### O, So Melodrama!

Traditional soviet readings of melodrama were not much different from the older, simple ones written in the western world. The *Theater Encyclopedia* of thirty years ago offered an elitist and politicized discussion of melodrama—barely admitting the genre's existence in Russia. Melodrama's cardinal sin was that its alleged concern for the poor and the weak was offset by an affirmation of the "bourgeois" order and a preachy message of class peace. The genre thus masked real, systemic social evils behind a war between abstractions of good and evil.[1] In actuality, the opposite may have been the case: Russian audiences who regularly saw legally permitted productions about the struggle of the poor and the weak against the rich and the strong in a secular setting may have become as attuned to social evils as did the far fewer readers of antiserfdom novels and essays. In any case, there is no denying melodrama's enormous popularity in the last half century of serfdom when it flourished on the Russian stage.

Today's viewers come equipped with a well-established antimelodrama lexicon bulging with as many clichés as are found in the genre itself. In a world where horse opera has been with us for a century and soap opera for seventy years, it is not hard to be "sophisticated" about melodrama. Even some of its avid consumers utter the word as a sneer. Original melodrama as it emerged out of the French Revolution, the storm and stress of early romanticism, and "bourgeois sentimentalism" had its instant critics, but not a long history of dismissal. Melodrama was born on stage—a story in dialogue spoken by actors, visually decorated, and accompanied by music. The European public enthusiastically devoured vaudevilles and melodramas along with operas—many of which had melodramatic story lines. All evidence shows that audiences enjoyed the wonderfully outrageous plots. They identified with characters, wanted a certain plausibility, and accepted colorful exaggeration of that plausibility. When the genre was young, consumers of all classes were able to suspend disbelief. One did not have to be a gruff merchant or a poor clerk to immerse oneself in the toils of Pixérécourt or Kotzebue or Scribe.

In melodrama, certain character types and situations recur constantly.[2] A useful typology, although not rigorous or unfailing, suggests the melodramas of the grotesque, the adventure, and the family setting. The first drew on gothic novels of the eighteenth century, ruled in the "bloodbath theater" of London, and culminated at the turn of the twentieth century in the Paris Grand Guignole. The "cape and sword" adventure journeyed out to exotic places and back to historical times imagined. The family or domestic melodrama differed, and still does, from these two. In fact a more basic division lies between the melodrama of effect (or action) and that of affect (or emotion)—or, more bluntly, that of blood and that of tears. The gender appeal for the latter seems clear, and the playwrights of the age were fully aware of the growth of female audiences everywhere. Of the three works I will discuss, the Kotzebue domestic melodrama is of the second type and the two French pieces are of the first. Each partook of the other's modes; and all employed sensational devices. These devices were especially effective—because unexpected—in the family or domestic play, whose finale was often acted out in a wild place—from the mountains of Savoy in Pixérécourt's *Coelina* (1800) to the rushing ice floes of D. W. Griffith's film *Way Down East* (1920). The sensation could also be provided in the gritty urban version of domestic melodrama by a contrastive visit to back alleys and slums.

Melodrama is replete with much-scorned coincidences, with deus ex machina, and with the tricks of switched babies, mistaken identities, and the stirring moment of reconnaissance, or discovery of true identities. Such features are also found in classic drama, but in melodrama, justice—usually poetic—triumphs, wrongs are righted, and villains are punished. Tragic catharsis, the property of high art, never occurs. In the moral sphere, early European melodrama effected a transfer of revolutionary virtue and justice and populist values to the stage. Added pathos arose from inflicting evil on the already afflicted—the poor, the female, the weak, the child, the orphan, the blind, the deaf, the slave, the convict. The villains could come from outside the law—bandits and pirates; or they could emerge, slimy and unambiguously wicked, from respectable social milieux. A recurring conflict was that between a maiden ready to sacrifice her life to preserve her purity and the villain who falsely denounces her after his sexual advances are rebuffed. This surely resonates with Christian hagiography: Saints Agatha, Lucia, Margaret, and many others were martyrs not only to their faith but to the frustrated lust of men who brought about their deaths.

Scholars of great drama enjoy the advantage of being able to supplement textual study with live performance, however different the present versions are from the originals. It is now almost impossible to see melodramas of bygone days on stage. There is no market in the theater, and no interest in the academy. Historians must thus be doubly alert to what audiences might have seen and heard when melodramas were performed, including the setting, the seating, and the theater building itself. Stage effects in the more successful houses played for sensation: exotic locales and elaborate machinery imitating warships, fortresses, grottoes, alpine crevices, jungles. When the taste for historical, biblical, and mythological themes declined, more weight was given to urban contemporary settings, particularly in the 1840s in France under the influence of Eugène Sue's novel *Mystères de Paris.* Acting styles are hard to imagine even when we have script notes: the story was told by declamation, exaggerated gestures, coded movements, tirades, soliloquies, and asides—in which, for example, the villain would confide to the public his evil designs. A feel for the style may be gotten by watching the silent film melodramas of the 1910s.[3]

Music is often overlooked in theater history, and it is all but gone today on the drama stage where it was a vital component in the nineteenth century. Beethoven's incidental music to Goethe's *Egmont* and Mendelssohn's to Shakespeare's *Midsummer Night's Dream* was the fruit of a common practice even in high drama. Melodrama always used music, not only in the overture to get people seated but to signal entrances, exits, and dramatic moments; and as a means for emotional and character underlining—a plaintive flute for the innocent heroine, growling double basses to announce the villain, a lively tune for the comic. These devices were drawn straight from German musicological doctrine of the eighteenth century, a code known as *Affektenlehre* according to which minor slow meant elegiac; major slow, majestic; major fast, vigorous and triumphant; minor fast, menacing. This code guided composers of nineteenth-century melodrama music (and opera) and, later, of film scores.[4]

What follows is an attempt to delineate the experience that Russians had with European melodrama in the early nineteenth century, those last decades of serfdom when Russian theater was in fact a theater of war—a war of classic and romantic, state and private, elite and popular, capitals and provinces, declamatory and "natural" acting. The Russian experience of culture—what people saw and heard—is as important as Russian cultural production itself. This is particularly true for the melodrama of this era, which was largely imported. As in all other arts, when Russians came late to a genre they consumed what was available—in this case the French and German products. I offer in this essay a triptych of European melodramas that were popular everywhere in Europe and became an integral part of the Russian stage. Russian histories of theater usually dismiss them scornfully, yet without some understanding of these and similar works, what can we ever understand about the people in the theater itself—the cast, the writers, the translators and adapters, and those who outnumbered everyone else: the audience?

### Mellow Drama: Kotzebue's First Hit

August von Kotzebue (1761–1819) is a name known—if at all—to students of European history as the German playwright in the service of Tsar Alexander I who was stabbed to death by a German nationalist student in 1819—a deed that launched Prince Metternich's infamous Carlsbad Decrees. But to hundreds of thousands of theatergoers in places ranging from the United States to Siberia, Kotzebue was a household name. Better known than Goethe and Schiller in his day, Kotzebue wrote about 230 plays and boasted of being able to write one in a three-day period. All but forgotten now, his plays were translated into French, Russian, Danish, Swedish, Spanish, Romanian, Italian, Dutch, Greek, Bulgarian, Serbian, and English. In the German states, they made up one-fourth of the repertoire of plays performed in the years 1795 to 1825;

in New York, fifty-two of the ninety-four theater performances in 1799 were of Kotzebue's plays. A student of his work has called Kotzebue "a phenomenon of literary and social history."[5] In Russia, Kotzebue effected a reorientation of theater taste as surely as did Beaumarchais in France a few decades earlier. His characters populated Russian stages in the capitals and in the provinces and helped launch the careers of well-known actors during the reign of Alexander I and Nicholas I.[6]

The great appeal of Kotzebue's works lay in their stageability, spectacle, immediacy of sentimental expression, and in their sense of empowerment and agency that was wholly absent in the neoclassical genre based on Greek models where the gods were in charge. Kotzebue wrote crisp dramatic material in plain language. His success—and his badge of shame to critical scholars—arose partly from his willingness to cater to a public weary of the tirade in rhymed verse of French neoclassical drama and comedy. The entertainment quotient of his work was provided by exotic settings in South America, the Near East, and on the ocean. Viewing his comedies, operas, one acts, farces, adaptations, and melodramas, audiences gaped at the animated impersonations of pirates, Gypsies, slaves, Peruvian Indians, uprooted Asians, rebels, impoverished nobles, and misused women—to say nothing of kings, sultans, and innumerable pseudohistorical figures attired in colorful costumes and backed by elaborate sets. Interwoven into the spectacle was the open expression of "naturalistic" feeling, with an occasional hint of sex and a down-to-earth sentimentalism. The socially expanding Russian audiences who were surfeited with—in Beaumarchais's scorching words—"the death of a Peloponesian tyrant or the sacrifice of a young princess of Aulis" could readily identify with his works.[7] People reared in the late eighteenth and early nineteenth century could relate more easily to everyday dramatic situations and to heroes who could triumph over evil than they could to exalted ancients locked in an uneven battle with the gods.

Kotzebue was a well-traveled bourgeois man of the world who claimed no depth of intellect. He skillfully played the strings of a sentimentalism that was already in literary vogue, and he spiced it with high adventure. Born into a family of Weimar petty officials in 1761, he moved in the environment of Schiller and Goethe, studied law, and became entranced by theater. He took up a minor post in St. Petersburg under Catherine II and began his dramatic career there with *Demetrius the Impostor,* one of many plays on this theme penned by European writers. Settling in

Estland in a judicial post, Kotzebue immersed himself in amateur productions and founded the first theater in Reval (Tallin). For two decades from 1781 onward he lived on and off in the Baltic or in other parts of Russia before settling most of the time in Germany. Arrested under Tsar Paul in 1799, he was sent to Siberia on an unfounded suspicion of radicalism. Pardoned after a few months, Kotzebue returned, made his peace with Paul, and later became a favorite of Tsar Alexander I.[8]

An enlightened conservative, with a humanist outlook at least in his youth, Kotzebue in his works frequently criticized abuses of privilege and even of monarchical power. But in later years, like many of his contemporaries, he became an apologist of the Restoration and a keen foe of liberalism, democracy, constitutions, student rights, and a free press. Although not exactly a "spy" for Tsar Alexander I, he was certainly on his payroll as a nominal state councilor and supplied him with political intelligence, mostly in private correspondence. For all these reasons, Kotzebue was assassinated by Karl Sand in 1819. And this dramatic demise obscured Kotzebue's importance in history as a successful dramatist who dominated the stages of two continents for decades in all genres of melodrama.

*Misanthropy and Repentance* (1788), Kotzebue's first international sensation, premiered in Reval and then opened in Berlin where it was acclaimed by audiences composed of, in Oscar Mandel's words, "kings, lords and ladies, wealthy merchants, humble spectators—everyone except disgruntled intellectuals."[9] European readers and playgoers had been steeped in sentimentalism for decades before this play opened. As a "melodrama of affect" it was designed to appeal to popular sentiment, especially to female audiences. *Misanthropy and Repentance* was the ultimate gusher melodrama—both dialogue and stage directions are soaked in tears. It contains no villain and no violence, only the emotional turbulence in the finale when an errant wife repents to her husband in a lengthy dialogue and is forgiven. Baron Meinau, the male protagonist known as the Stranger, has spent three years of bitter hatred of self and of the human race as a result of the aberrant infidelity of his young wife, Eulalia. Repentant, she has gone into humble service to atone. The reunion is coincidental, their reconciliation organized by noble friends. The play presents an affecting dramatic treatment of the utter desolation of the two protagonists. Meinau, "an ice-cold man of clever mind" in the words of his servant, is an ancestor of those hard-faced, harsh-talking heroes with a soft heart who later inhabited westerns and crime melodramas on film. Eulalia, whose "heart bleeds and [whose] tears flow" at her fate, was an early model for heroines endowed with kindness, charity, and chaste modesty. In the very final moment of the play, after extended speechifying suspense, the afflicted couple are reunited in the presence of their children.[10]

The extraordinary impact of this play, and especially its heart-warming and eye-wetting finale, was conditioned not only by the sentimentalist literary movement of the time, but probably also by liberal life-affirming philanthropic currents among the bourgeoisie—the mainstay of Kotzebue's European and American audiences. This ideology encapsulated the antislavery crusade (Kotzebue wrote *Negro Slaves* [1796] on that theme) and other reformist movements. Eulalia was a perfect stand-in for the repentant convict so beloved of the penal reform movement of the time in many countries—especially in the Anglo-Saxon ones where Kotzebue flourished luxuriantly.[11] Having fallen afoul of the moral law, Eulalia has "paid the penalty" by years of separation from her loved ones, is now ready to "re-enter society" (family), and is given "a second chance." The emotional interplay of *Misanthropy* has direct analogies in prison literature. Meinau's friend and comrade-in-arms describes Eulalia in terms of her underlying virtue, her momentary lapse, her prolonged penance, and her worthiness of pardon. Eulalia, in the dialogue with Meinau, emphatically contrasts her own remorseful and atoning posture with that of "a hardened criminal," the unredeemable element in progressive penological discourse.[12]

*Child of Love* (1796), which dealt with illegitimacy, was the first Kotzebue play performed in St. Petersburg. By the late 1790s, he was well known in the Russian provinces, and dozens of his plays had been translated into Russian, with *Misanthropy and Repentance* in the lead. Of the many versions of the play, a partial list includes two published in St. Petersburg (1792), two in Moscow (1796, 1801), one in Smolensk (1812), and two in Orël (1824, 1826). As early as 1800, during his brief sojourn in exile in Siberia, Kotzebue met people in Moscow, Kazan, and Tobolsk who knew his name and work. A friendly governor of Tobolsk province offered the playwright a chance to stage one of his new short comedies. On his way out of Tobolsk to his place of exile in remote

Kurgan, Kotzebue was accosted by a Russian actress from an itinerant troupe asking him costume details about a play of his in which she was about to perform, *Virgin of the Sun.*[13]

On returning to St. Petersburg after his pardon, Kotzebue served at Tsar Paul's court theater. Kotzebue's complaints about the stringent censorship are well known and often quoted. Less known was the reaction of the iron disciplinarian Tsar Paul—he was "deeply moved" to the staging in 1800 in French by French actors of *Misanthropy and Repentance* at the Hermitage Theater. Kotzebue's popularity thereafter grew apace: in the years 1800 to 1820 up to half of the plays in a season in Moscow and St. Petersburg were his. In 1806, a German correspondent in St. Petersburg reported that "the name of Kotzebue in the [theater] announcements is here always the surest magnet for a full house."[14] Within a decade Kotzebue was fully established in Russian provincial stages, serf theaters, and amateur productions. At Kazan University, his works inspired an amateur student theater in which Sergei Aksakov played the role of Meinau. Aksakov soon became known as a theater critic, long before his other reputation was made as the poetic memoirist of the Orenburg steppe or as the father of two Slavophiles.[15]

Audiences in Russia adored Kotzebue for what he delivered, whether in German, French, or Russian. Directors and theater entrepreneurs loved him for the full houses. And certain actors found in his work a natural vehicle for their talents. Kotzebue's plays required acting gifts untapped by the classical repertoire. Pavel Mochalov, Peter Plavilshchikov, Alexei Iakovlev, and "a whole series of major Russian actors" made their name in Kotzebue roles. Mochalov, the icon of the "Moscow" emotional style (contrasted with the classical demeanor of the St. Petersburg players) found his first stage success in Kotzebue's plays. A memoirist recalls that when Mochalov played Meinau in *Misanthropy and Repentance,* "he would begin [his tale of woe] calmly, almost indifferently; but little by little his emotion rose to a pitch that seized the audience. Every added word expressing the accumulated bitterness of his soul moved their hearts more strongly, till finally they were unable to suppress their tears." Plavilshchikov's best role was Meinau, but Aksakov, while a student in the newly opened Kazan University, was thrilled by his performance in *Child of Love.* A. S. Iakovlev (1773–1817), the son of a Kostroma merchant, was a shop clerk when his talent was discovered. On stage, he privileged emotion over reason and when he played

Pavel Mochalov as Meinau in August Kotzebue's *Misanthropy and Repentance.* From Robert Leach et al., *A History of Russian Theater* (Cambridge: Cambridge University Preess, 1999), 108.

Meinau, not even "a heart of stone" could withstand his acting. Iakovlev turned on a "faucet of tears" in the audience and could bring tears to his own eyes at certain moments. A contemporary Russian critic, Stepan Zhikharëv, comparing various well-known actors of the 1810s, observed that although they all played Meinau with merit, none could compare to Iakovlev who "made you cry."[16]

At the coronation of Tsar Paul in 1797, Alexandra Karatygina played Eulalia opposite Iakovlev as Meinau in *Misanthropy and Repentance.* She was noted for the "feeling and tenderness" of her style. It was, in the view of one scholar, the role of Eulalia that brought her talent to perfection. By contrast, the most famous actress of the age, Ekaterina Semënova, daughter of a serf, initially played the Kotzebue *emploi* but found her true line of business in classical and neoclassical plays. Her electrifying performance in *Medea* was as far from the Kotzebue genre as any could be. And it is Semënova who is canonized in theatrical history, although both her declamatory style of acting and her repertoire were on the verge of decline when she reached the peak of her career.[17]

A well-known soviet scholar of the 1920s called the Kotzebue oeuvre *meshchanskaia drama* (lower middle-class or philistine drama) and repeated the familiar Marxist cliché that melodrama, along with other popular forms, deflected popular passions away from the terrible reign of Nicholas I, just as it was doing in the France of Louis-Philippe. He also quoted contemporary classicists who called Kotzebue's plays *kotsebiatina* (Kotzebue trash). Those writing from an aesthetic perspective fixed on the playwright's simplicity and lack of art. Kotzebue frankly admitted that he was a second-rate writer—but one who wished to give pleasure to the masses of theatergoers. Pleasing audiences, to certain critics then and now, can be considered pandering—a cheap and ultimately immoral act.[18] The Decembrist V. K. Küchelbecker (Kiukhelbekker), for example, detested the "sentimental-German" drama of Kotzebue "which gave the ladies of the Zamoskvorechie District [of merchant Moscow] much to rave about."[19] Here the resentment is leveled not only at the creator but at the very audience he serves, an audience that allegedly has been hoodwinked and is thus worthy of contempt.

But let us listen to a different voice, that of Rafael Zotov, novelist and dramatist, author of over one hundred plays, including melodramas and historical pastiches. He spoke for the seatless *parterre,* where stood teachers, journalists, youth, and officers who, he believed, came for the "theater" as opposed to the seated public who came for the "show." "The *parterre,*" he wrote, "is a crucial element in the theater. Without it, the passion of the middle classes [*srednoe soslovie*] would not develop. The life that is imparted by the *parterre* encourages actors and makes them fear the stern and educational judgement that is located there." Elsewhere he wrote that "our audiences were raised on exclamations, shouts, and turgid phrases. But as soon as they were shown a domestic environment, the joys and sorrows of ordinary life, as soon as they saw verisimilitude and naturalness, as soon as they heard the voice of natural feelings—they joyfully jumped off the high horse of Sumarokov [the eighteenth-century classical dramatist] and with all their hearts attached themselves to the plays of Kotzebue."[20]

Kotzebue's numerous "cape and sword" plays, replete with nasty villains and exotic locales, also did well on the Russian stage, but none had the resonance in Russia of *Misanthropy and Repentance.* This is probably because the French imports in the "action" subgenre of melodrama were better and more timely (as will be discussed below) or because it was easier in Russia to translate them fast. *Misanthropy* appeared early and won patronage at court and in the German theater of St. Petersburg and elsewhere. It could be heard in three languages, sometimes in the same city. Although no detailed evidence of audience reaction is available, we do know that this melodrama gained instant popularity. It would be tempting to ascribe some peculiarly soulful element in the play that had special appeal for Russians. Were Russians especially sympathetic to the "agency" of a Eulalia or forgiving of her sin? Was there operating a moral equivalent of the European prison reform movement, a tendency to pity the wrongdoer? One thinks of the peasant habit of lining the road to Siberia and praying for convicts; and of the enduring tenderness in Russian literature to "fallen women."

The evidence allows no more than speculation. Like their European counterparts, Russian critics of the time differed over the pivotal moment in *Misanthropy and Repentance:* the moral propriety of forgiving an unfaithful wife on stage. But accounts of its public reception—in Russia and elsewhere—almost aways focus on the favorable impression made by the final scene of reconciliation, clearly indicating that the key ingredient of the play was forgiveness and redemption, enduring features of New Testament Christian theology and ecclesiastical practice. In spite of the secularism launched by the French Revolution and the preceding Enlightenment, the deep wells of religion (and of Freemasonry) still offered sustenance to the public, perhaps all the more so when decked out in simple domestic fiction and acted on stage. Russian audiences who flocked to and wept through *Misanthropy* were cosmopolitan not so much in the sophisticated sense, but rather as sharers of that transnational collective surge of philanthropic emotionalism and charitableness that at this time was being exhibited—and constantly violated as well—all over the European continent.

### An Orphan on the Provincial Circuit

Kotzebue has been compared to Guilbert de Pixérécourt (1773–1844), the "father of French melodrama."[21] The "melodrama of effect" in Pixérécourt's work and that of his Parisian rivals, Caigniez and Ducange, ruled the day. In the backdrop of melodrama hung the French Revolution with its own melodramas of violence, betrayal, pathos, rescue, and a world reversed. Pixérécourt fought on the side of both royalist emigrés and Jacobins, and he met real prototypes for the stock villain that he virtually invented for Parisian audiences who frequented theaters located on what was called the Boulevard of Crime. Pixérécourt wrote about 120 plays, half of them melodramas, that were performed thousands of times in the first half of the nineteenth century. After the appearance of his first full-formula melodrama, *Coelina, or, The Child of Mystery* (1800), at the very moment of the transition between the inward turmoil of the Revolution and the outward spectacles of Napoleon, Pixérécourt was hailed as "the man who made all France weep."[22] Not far behind him came Victor Ducange, famous for breaking all the rules of drama by putting three generations of life on stage in *Thirty Years, or, The Life of a Gambler* (1827), a play about a compulsive gambler who kills a fellow train passenger for money to feed his gaming frenzy and subsequently discovers that the victim is his son. *Thirty Years* was very popular in Russia where the table and the deck could also be a lethal occupation (the well-known composer Alexander Aliabev was convicted of murder over a card game in the 1820s). But it was Ducange's *Theresa, or, The Orphan of Geneva* (1821) that achieved world acclaim.

The plot of *Theresa* is crucial in providing clues to audience reaction. Like *Misanthropy and Repentance,* it deals with high-born people. Kotzebue's cast resided in a castle; Ducange's characters live in the Swiss château of the widow de Sénange and her son Karl. The mysterious young woman who has been taken in by the châtelaine is Theresa, disguised as "Henriette," and she is about to be betrothed to Karl. The back story, slowly revealed, is her early life as an adopted (although in fact biological) daughter of a high noblewoman. When her mother dies, Theresa is revealed as the beneficiary of her vast fortune until the swindler Walther falsely accuses her of malfeasance and has her sent to jail. While she is out on bail, Walther concocts a plan—as he informs the audience in a long aside—to force her to marry him and thus get his hands on the fortune by revealing the truth about the will. But Theresa flees and finds shelter first with the kindly Pastor Egerthon and then with the de Sénanges. Walther appears at the engagement party and reveals Theresa's shameful arrest. At this point the plot accelerates into high, but still verbose, action. Theresa flees in shame to a hiding place arranged by Egerthon. Madame de Sénange and Walther learn of her whereabouts and both arrive when Theresa is absent. In the dark, Walther, now resolved to murder Theresa, mistakenly kills the older woman. When Theresa returns and discovers the body, she is suspected of murder. In court, however,

Egerthon accuses Walther without telling him who the victim really is. The pastor confronts the killer with the live Theresa, and he is so frightened by what he takes to be a ghost that he breaks down and confesses. Theresa is absolved of all criminal activity.[23]

French melodrama flooded into Russia in the 1810s and 1820s. St. Petersburg and Moscow repertoires in the years 1813 to 1825 contained ten melodramas of Pixérécourt. (His works were so well-known that his *Pizarro, or, The Conquistador of Peru* was satirized by Dmitri Lenskii in Russia's most durable stage comedy, *Lev Gurych Sinichkin* [1839]). In those years, the capitals saw four plays of Caigniez and several of Ducange, including *Theresa,* which by then had already played around the world. Imperial Theater actors had to take the roles assigned to them and shift from serious tragedy to melodrama or vaudeville and even to opera and ballet. The classical star Semënova in St. Petersburg played de Sénange, with her sister Nimfodora Semënova as Theresa and Iakov Brianskii as Walther. Detailed sound effects and music are marked in the margins of a Moscow copy of the script. Many of the silent scenes demanded very expressive mimicry and clarity of movement in order to motivate the plot; as obvious as it sounds, we must remember that there are no closeups in theater. Stage movement was carefully taught by dancing masters, ballet being a mandatory part of the training of all dramatic actors in this era.[24]

I have no data on the reception of *Theresa* in the two capitals, but the experience of the provincials throws some light on the levels at which people saw melodrama. Frequent assertions to the contrary notwithstanding, theater flourished in the Russian provinces during the pre-emancipation era. The Imperial Theater system held a monopoly in its half-dozen houses in St. Petersburg and Moscow but was little concerned about what went on in the provinces. There, close to two hundred serf theaters operated at the apex of their development (ca. 1770s–1820), mostly on estates but also in provincial and district capitals. To these must be added commercial theaters owned by nobles, merchants, and other classes in the towns, and traveling troupes that crisscrossed the country in a permanent caravan of troikas and carriages, rattling with musical instruments, sets, machines, and costumes. At almost every one of the thousands of fairs one could find some kind of theatrical performance—not only puppet and folk entertainments but also *King Lear, Wilhelm Tell,* and Russian tragedies, comedies, vaudevilles, operas, and melodramas. Out of this circuit came some of the finest actors on the Moscow and St. Petersburg stages—including the most famous of all, Mikhail Shchepkin, a serf.

All three of the plays discussed here played this circuit. At the high end of the scale stood the once famous provincial theater of Nizhny-Novgorod, which flourished during the reign of Nicholas I. One of its standbys, borrowed from the capital stages, was *Theresa, or, the Orphan of Geneva.* For the highest-paid star of this theater, Anna Vysheslavtseva, Theresa was a bread-and-butter role. In her production, the murderer Walther used arson rather than the knife in order to enhance the spectacle.[25] At the lower end of the scale—fairground performance—we have the comments of the musician Iury Arnold from about 1835. While in Kharkov at the time of the Kreshchinskaia Fair, Arnold saw *Theresa,* disliked it, and conceded, rather sourly, that it was at the time a very popular melodrama.[26]

The comments of I. I. Lavrov, later an actor at the Maly and the lead singer at the Bolshoi in Moscow, offer a different perspective. Lavrov began life as the son of a petty merchant in Tambov province, worked as a peddler, a factory worker, and other menial occupations. In 1844 he began acting in a provincial repertoire that included Shakespeare, vaudevilles, operas, and melodramas. Lavrov's account of the provincial years—about sixty engagements in about thirty towns, villages, and fairs—is richly descriptive of theater life, including conditions of employment, audiences, managers, patrons, interfering officials, sudden dismissals, money matters, and backstage romances. It is also brutally frank about brushes with the police and about drunk and disorderly actors who were run out of town. How did Lavrov become an actor? During visits to the fairs along the Volga, while still a peddler, he became enchanted with carnival entertainment. The turning point of his life occurred in Astrakhan where in 1844 he saw his very first play, *Theresa, or, The Orphan of Geneva.* Lavrov was so captivated by the play and its performance that he was permanently hooked to life in the theater. In the pages of his memoirs, Lavrov pauses to give a plot summary of *Theresa* and to admit, after many years, that he wept for Theresa and felt a deep hatred for Walther.[27]

Lavrov recounts another incident at this performance. In the scene where Walther denies his guilt of the murder, a spectator cried out from the audience: "You lie, you son of a dog, bandit. You killed [her]. Look at these good folks [in the theater]; they are witnesses. Am I right, friends."[28] The public in the stalls and in the loges laughed and the police removed the spectator. This episode was fairly typical of audience behavior in the theater—and not only in Russia. According to an anecdote, at the premier of Rossini's opera *Otello* in Naples in 1816, when the singer playing Othello approached Desdemona in her bed, the audience shouted to the actress: "Watch out, he has a knife [*sic*]!"[29] Another example, related in Herzen's "Magpie," was the "old joke" about a good German viewer at a performance of *Don Giovanni* who shouted to those chasing Don Juan: "He fled down the alley to the right." If opera could induce this kind of belief, how much more could melodrama evoke such reactions, despite its artificial music and stylized gestures.[30]

The evidence on the reception of *Theresa* is thin and anecdotal, but certainly it can indicate its durability for at least three decades, and it can attest to its wide trajectory—from the imperial houses of the capital to commercial theaters at important Volga towns to the barns of the Kreshchinskaia Fair in Ukraine. What caused the classical composer and violinist Iury Arnold to curl his lip in scorn also drove a budding actor to tears (and to a career) and at least one spectator to near intervention. As in the other plays discussed here, the central figure *Theresa* is an agonized and finally redeemed or rescued woman. Theresa's status as an orphan doubtless had its own resonance; a Russian melodrama titled *The Lunatic Orphan Susanna* was playing the circuit during the same period. According to detailed topographical studies of Russian towns, virtually all of the towns possessed an orphanage and benefit performances for the support of orphans were common in provincial theaters.[31] Judging from what I have read of reactions to melodrama and related genres all over provincial Russia (and in the capitals as well), audiences delighted in both "pity and terror"—Aristotle's vaunted description of tragedy. But they also wanted agency, action, spectacle, and thrill. A murder plot twisted around the fate of a victimized young woman fit this formula to perfection.

## The Flight of the Magpie

The origin of the story of the "thieving magpie," who unwittingly sent a young woman to her death, is obscure. One source on its genesis

Title page from *The Magpie, or, the Maid.* From Isaac Pocock, *The Magpie, or, the Maid* (London, 1816).

refers to a medieval legend, another to "a curious French legal case," and a third to a (probably the same) real event in which an innocent peasant girl was wrongly hanged for the theft of an article by a magpie.[32] This story was fashioned into a French melodrama in 1815 and adapted for Rossini's opera in 1817. Both won popularity in Russia. Alexander Herzen used the motif as the core of his famous story "Soroka-vorovka" (1848).

The melodrama, *The Thieving Magpie, or, the Maidservant of Palaiseau* is often attributed solely to L.-C. Caigniez, author of *The Judgement of Solomon,* which is the first use in melodrama of a courtroom and of a biblical subject. In fact, the original author was J. M. T. Baudouin d'Aubigny, who submitted his play to a Parisian director. Unread, it was found by the director's child and given for rewrite to the already established melodramatist Caigniez. With music composed by Alexandre Piccinni, *Magpie* was staged in 1815 in the midst of Napoleon's Hundred Days, an event that had no effect on the box office. In fact, the director made such a huge profit from its many performances that he eventually retired on his earnings to a country place, aptly named the Hamlet of the Thieving Magpie.[33]

The action of *Magpie* turns around two linked problems, both involving the maidservant Annette. First, she is accused of having stolen her mistress's silver plate, which has actually been pilfered by a magpie attracted by its glitter. Second, she has, quite independently, sold one of her own cheap plates in order to help her old father who has deserted the army because of mistreatment and is fleeing his pursuers. The witnesses against Annette include an honest Jew who truthfully recounts his purchase from her of a plate, and, more important, a villainous magistrate who falsely accuses her because she has rebuffed his advances. Annette is found guilty and is sentenced to death. The audience knows the truth and the tension is generated, as in so many melodramas, by the fact that the innocent heroine cannot reveal the truth out of fear for her father's fate. The authors of the melodrama intervene to avoid the miscarriage of justice that apparently ended the original version, but the intervention is not immediate: after the tribunal renders its verdict, a march to the scaffold is staged, adding to the suspense. Annette, in a final act of sacrifice, sends a servant to deliver money to her father who is in hiding. As the comic servant counts the money, the magpie reappears and steals one of the bright coins. The man follows the bird to its nest and finds the stolen plate. Annette is cleared and her father pardoned.

Like *Misanthropy and Repentance* and *Theresa, Magpie* was an international success. It remained popular in France for a half century and was adapted in the United States and in Britain where one performance opened in London in 1815 at Covent Garden. The Russian version, *Soroka-vorovka,* premiered in Moscow in December 1816 as a benefit performance, which was followed by three more performances that month. In 1817 it played nine times—a record run for that era. For the 1816 St. Petersburg performance, Annette was played by M. I. Valberkhova, the daughter of the ballet master who also translated the play.[34]

The most enduring treatment of the magpie was the delightful opera *melodramma* of Gioacchino Rossini, *La gazza ladra,* which premiered at La Scala in Milan in 1817. The libretto by Giovanni Gherardini was adapted from the French original in 1816 for the then well-known Italian composer Giovanni Paisiello, who died that year. It was taken over by Rossini. His *Gazza* is an *opera semiseria,* a light melodrama with comic elements set against a continuous background of menace. Some names and character types were changed; for example, the villain in Gherardini's libretto is the mayor of the town. The cleverly wrought scene in which Ninetta (Annette) deliberately misreads to the mayor the description of the deserter in a letter of warrant for the hunted father was apparently copied for *Boris Godunov* by Alexander Pushkin, who saw the opera in Odessa during the 1823–1824 season. Rossini's music is charming—full of melodious arias yet occasionally darkened as in the prison scene, the trial, and the march to the scaffold, which introduced the novel (and to some objectionable) use of snare drums. *La gazza ladra* became a favorite vehicle for Giuditta Pasta, Maria Malabran, and Rossini's wife Isabella Colbran. It opened in St. Petersburg in February 1821 in Russian as *Soroka-vorovka,* with Nimfodora Semënova, who was also a singer, again in a melodrama lead, as Aneta (the Russian translation used the original names), and with Elizaveta Sandunova as the landowner's wife. Like its model, *Gazza* had a long stage life in Russia.[35]

Thus for about three decades, and perhaps longer, the thieving magpie flew around Russia as *La pie voleuse* in the French theater; as *Soroka-vorovka* in Russian theaters; and as an Italian opera. In both town and provincial estate theaters, the role of the wronged female was played by serf actresses, themselves subjected to all kinds of mistreatment and false accusations in their everyday lives. Although the irony is striking, it is difficult to say just what linkage audiences and performers made between the unjust system that undergirds all the magpie stories and their own social vulnerabilities. But the specific analogy was made by Alexander Herzen in his famous tale of serf abuse and sexual harassment, "Soroka-vorovka." To the theatrical inspiration of the story Herzen added historical material screened through a serf actress and a serf actor, and then he fictionalized it into an enduring critique of a particular aspect of serfdom that everyone knew of at the time but which is often downplayed in histories of that institution: house serfs as creative artists under the control of their owners. Herzen drew his tale from an episode in the life of a serf actress.

The villain of the true story was Count S. N. Kamenskii, a noble landowner and theatrical entrepreneur of Orël province. Orël was far from being a cultural backwater; on their estate, the Iurasovskii brothers in 1828 put on serf ballet, variety shows, and choral music. Another half-dozen landowners ran estate theaters, including the Turgenevs and the

Taneevs, the latter offering opera, ballet, and drama performed by serfs and free provincial actors. A. A. Pleshcheev, a cellist and friend of Nikolai Karamzin, maintained a serf orchestra on his estate that was held to be the musical center of Kaluga, Orël, and Tula provinces.[36] Kamenskii possessed a serf theater on his estate and a commercial theater in the town of Orël, which lasted from 1815 to 1835 (the writer Nikolai Leskov recalled seeing it as a child). As one-story wooden structure occupying an entire block in Cathedral Square, Kamenskii's theater was as large, according to a contemporary, as Moscow's Apraxin Theater at the Arbat Gates. The interior consisted of stalls, *baignoire,* two upper circles, and a gallery—with tickets priced accordingly. Printed posters advertised productions, and one of the earliest provincial newspapers, *Drug rossian* (1816–1818) reviewed them.[37]

Kamenskii hired some actors, transferred serfs from his estate, and bought some from other serfowners. He purchased the Kravchenkos, an acting couple and their six-year-old tap-dancing daughter, for 250 male serfs. He also tried to acquire the then budding actor Mikhail Shchepkin, but without success. An officer serving in Orël in 1827–1828, M. D. Buturlin regarded the theater as a refuge from garrison life in what was otherwise a monotonous town. Kamenskii spared no expense on lavish sets and costumes, a German ballet master, and a large, well-trained serf orchestra.[38] But he was a rank amateur of theater and most of his actors were deficient in acting and singing. The eccentric owner, wearing his Turkish war decoration, the Order of St. George Second Class, would sit in the box office and sell tickets. Once a prankster officer friend of Buturlin bought his seat with a huge bag full of small coins in order to hold up the line. During performances, Kamenskii, armed with a stick and a script, sat in the first row, his family like royals, placed in a center box. The repertoire was the familiar one for provincial theaters: *comédies larmontes,* melodramas—including *Soroka-vorovka*—vaudevilles, ballet, and operas by Cherubini and Boiledieu. And even with all the unevenness of performance, the theater was rarely empty,

Kamenskii ran his home and his theater like a regiment. Lackeys and actors were uniformed in different colors and given court ranks, changing colors as they were promoted. The actresses were isolated and locked up at night in a harem-like complex in the courtyard. When two sisters in the company became the object of flirtation among local officers, one of them, caught in a correspondence, was flogged. Into this environment fell the victim of the real-life melodrama; she was one of Kamenskii's actresses who not only played Annette in *Soroka-vorovka* but acted out the role in real life as a women falsely accused by a powerful man whose sexual overtures she rebuffed. The actress Kuzmina (or Kozmina; no other name is given in the sources) was originally a serf member of the landowner P. V. Esipov's estate theater about thirty miles from Kazan. When he opened a theater in the town of Kazan in 1803–1804 with a cast drawn from his estate theater, Kuzmina was brought along. Although Esipov apparently kept his actresses in a harem, Kuzmina's brief account of her life recalled him as a kindly master and made no reference to sexual relations. Esipov gave her an education, training, foreign travel, and exposure to a broad culture—but not her freedom. He promised to bequeath her emancipation at his death, but failed to do so. An improvident man, Esipov went broke in 1810 and died in debt in 1814. His troupe was dispersed and Kamenskii bought Kuzmina in 1814 or 1815. She first appeared on the Orël stage at its official opening. Her skills in roles such as Cordelia in *Lear* and "Edelmona" in *Othello,* as well as roles in the lighter genres, were much admired by the public and the press.

By 1822, the man who was to hear and tell Kuzmina's tale, Mikhaïl Shchepkin, arrived in Orël. Shchepkin, a serf actor also enmeshed in a struggle for manumission, was already widely known on the provincial circuit and would soon be drafted by Moscow's Imperial Theater. Kamenskii hired him as a guest actor to play in Mikhail Zagoskin's popular *Gospodin Bogatonov, or, A Provincial in the Capital* (1817). While there, Shchepkin saw Kuzmina play Annette in Caigniez's *Soroka-vorovka.* Greatly affected by her performance, he was determined to talk to her and, after much pleading with Kamenskii, interviewed her for her story. Kuzmina had learned French, German, and English and had been happy in Esipov's service. Kamenskii, who she claimed had no understanding of theatrical art, had purchased the troupe for three hundred thousand rubles and paid her well. Then came the insinuations and flirtations. Puzzled when Kuzmina did not respond to his advances, Kamenskii made an open proposition. Kuzmina refused him and he retaliated by denying her good roles and costumes (a critical expense item for an actress all through the century). When the actress found money to buy her own dresses, Kamenskii insulted her, implying that she was selling her body to purchase clothing. She then told him that, although

Mikhail Shchepkin, ca. 1850 (daguerreotype). From Laurence Senelick, *Serf Actor* (Westport, Conn.: Greenwood Press, 1984), 187.

innocent of the charge, she would spite him by having a baby in a loveless match.

Kuzmina's account was in fact commonplace for actresses of the era—and not only among serfs. She may have exaggerated the events of her story; and one must wonder why Kamenskii, who could have an actress flogged for a slight indiscretion, would limit his revenge to a mere insult. But what made her tale so famous in theatrical discourse is the dual treatment it received at the hands of Shchepkin and Herzen. As early as 1839 the actor began recounting the story of Kuzmina to his friends, and it allegedly brought tears to their eyes. He retold it many times before and after Herzen's story was written. The man who recorded Shchepkin's tale from dictation was the famed folklore collector Alexander Afanasev, who put it to paper in 1861. In the 1960s, his transcription was found in the archives by a soviet scholar, but Afanasev's version contains errors and shows signs that he had read Herzen's story before hearing it from Shchepkin.[39]

The most famous Russian radical of the age, Alexander Herzen, immortalized and fictionalized Kuzmina's experience in the short story "Soroka-vorovka" and also brought the ancient legend of the magpie full circle, ending his tale with the death of an innocent woman. Herzen took the main theme from the lips of Shchepkin himself in one of their many conversations. He wrote the story in 1846 and it was published in *Contemporary* in 1848 (with some of its language about serfdom and power toned down). The outer frame of Herzen's "Soroka-vorovka" is an ironic and amusing debate between a Slavophile and a westernizer, the former upholding the submission and silence of women and arguing that "Slavic" women—being modest creatures—were not suited to the stage where people disport themselves and rant their lines before the public. The westernizer refutes these and other arguments and then tells the tale; the teller is modeled on Shchepkin, and his account is also a frame within which the actress tells her own story.[40]

The villain of this prose melodrama, Skalinskii (Russian for crag), is modeled on Count Kamenskii (Russian for stone). He resembles in some ways the vindictive magistrate in Caigniez's *Magpie*—a powerful figure, rejected and vengeful. But the French villain is abstract, he could be almost any blackguard, whereas Herzen's figure, like the original, possesses concrete contours and colors. He is a landowner, a serfowner, whose power does not depend on his credibility in a court of law; he is deeply embedded in the social and political system of serfdom and seigniorial authority. Skalinskii, like Kamenskii, brooks no dallying among the actors; he imprisons one for sending a note to an actress. The fictional version of Kuzmina has ended up under Skalinskii's roof through an illegal trick added by Herzen to the Kuzmina tale: the suppression by relatives of her former benefactor's will granting her freedom. When Skalinskii's advances to the fictional version of Kuzmina fall flat, he voices his power over her with the ugly words: "You think you are an actress. You are my bonded property."

In Herzen's tale there are no upper-class sympathizers to help and rescue a blameless young woman, as in the plays of Ducange and Caigniez. The heroine-victim breeches the chaste rules of true melodrama by her own defiant act of sexual expression. But the reader is intended to find her deeper virtue in the courage and sense of fair play of that act. She is a powerless innocent devoted to her art who becomes her own "delivering hero" with the aid of a meaningless lover whom she takes as an act of vengeance on the count. There are no surprises or coincidences in Herzen's melodrama; it is a dark "society tale" rather than the melodrama of the original *Magpie.* And, to give his work more pathos and sharper social commentary, Herzen has the actress die from complications after childbirth.

Herzen's story and its layered sources offer an unusually complex study in intertextuality. A possibly real event from the European past had been clothed in legend, adorned, and then woven into a melodrama that was immediately plotted as an opera. A real-life Russian actress in servitude played on stage the role of the fictional servant wrongly accused. The serf actress was herself wrongly accused by her master of a different act—"stealing" her own body from him. Her version of the episode then emerged for a limited public as a sentimental morality tale recited in salons by a former victimized serf actor. Herzen fused the stage role of Annette with the real role of Kuzmina into an ideologically framed abolitionist tract. His magpie story is shorter and simpler in plot than the stage melodrama that partly inspired it, but its greater moral complexity lies in its three levels of villainy.

One level is outright testamentary fraud by the heirs of a master who had bequeathed manumission, an illegal act but hard to rectify in practice. To paraphrase Peter Brooks, this kind of act betrayed the "rules" of serfdom, which is itself a betrayal of the cosmic moral order.[41] The dominant villainy is the institution of the serf theater harem, a familiar although not endemic feature of the system. Law and custom were ambivalent on the practice and only rarely were abusive examples punished, usually at the local level. The third level of villainy was the wholly legal practice of promising, without delivering, freedom to serfs. This was a common custom among owners of serf painters, musicians, and actors. Some masters found it psychologically useful (although hardly necessary) to deflect offers of purchase of star artists by other landowners or by the Imperial Theater system. Others used the promise to keep their artists at least minimally happy and able to perform or create. Esipov, the benign first owner of Kuzmina, was a well-meaning villain by default. Because the victim is a woman, the emerging discourses on serfdom and on women's lot are melded. Herzen's melodrama adds a deus ex machina in the form of dishonest relatives, a device that actually vitiates the larger impersonal and systemic functioning of juridical unfreedom.

Abolitionist literature in the reign of Nicholas I—a subject not fully investigated by scholars—was sporadic and heavily constrained. Fictional references to the plight of bonded artists and the human degradation it could entail were episodic and couched in oblique language.[42] On the other hand, conversations and correspondence among nobles and between nobles and state artistic institutions abounded with entreaties, threats, negotiations, and contracts dealing with purchase, transfer, and manumission of serf artists. Societies composed of magnates and art patrons were formed precisely for these purposes.[43] Herzen's "Soroka-vorovka" was part of this discourse, a particularly clarifying tale that points up the issue of dependence, subordination, and abuse of power in the world of performing arts. To avoid the appearance of writing a tract, he employed the clever ruse of fiction and he invoked the plot from a popular genre that had great resonance. The tale was riveting, entertaining, full of pathos, and capped by the unhappy ending that punctuated the lives of so many real-life serf artists. The term for "villain" in French melodrama was either *tyrane* or *traître.* Herzen inserted both kinds of villains into "Soroka-vorovka"—the serfowner-tyrant and the falsifier-traitor—thus adding melodramatic effect to the social drama. After emigrating to western Europe in 1848, Herzen's pen was free to engage in the exposure of the arbitrary treatment of those serf artists who suffered the particular psychological agony of arrested development or the enchainment of talent.

Herzen's treatment of the victim theme suggests another process at work in the twilight of serfdom. Studies of late imperial reading tastes and popular fiction have described how news items sometimes fed into that genre, thus mediating the real event with the literary product.[44] No mass-circulation press was available to story-weavers of prereform Russia. But "media" sources from which they could draw certainly existed: the aforementioned epistolary discourse on abuse and liberation, salon or circle anecdotes such as Shchepkin's, and the villain-victim melodrama. Thus a distinctly entertainment genre could, as I suggested at the outset of this chapter, contribute not so much to popular consciousness of injustice as to the continuing formation of elite sensibilities about the evils of serfdom.

The experience of imported cultural products cannot be divorced from native production or creation, because adaptation, translation, setting, and performance are themselves acts of creativity. The imported melodrama—not in spite of but because of its foreign themes, characters, and locales—found wide acceptance in Russia as entertainment. It might be tempting to say that these imported works were "Russianized" in their performance, but it would be more accurate to say that they were subjected to several local influences. Upper-class travelers from the capitals often found performances they had seen at home unrecognizable in the provinces. One ought not to postulate the unique popularity of melodrama. Everywhere in Russia until mid-century, when training began to bifurcate into drama and music roles, the same actors played in all genres, from tragedy to opera to vaudeville; and audiences consumed them all with apparently equal enthusiasm. Just as Shakespeare, performed with adaptations and adjustments, could thrill spectators of the Old West in early-nineteenth-century America,[45] so could Schiller enchant dwellers in the outreaches of the Russian empire. Melodrama played a prominent but not exclusive role in entertaining the theater public. It is a well-established fact that, in previous times, certain works that are now canonized often lived vitally among the "low." The masters were loved by audiences of various classes; they were often adapted and performed in accordance with local audience expectations that bordered on entertainment. Even their best and truest translations commonly shared the stage with vaudevilles and comic interludes.

It is hard to speak about the moral or mental impact of melodrama on audiences, not the least because of the tremendous variation among audiences in terms of wealth, position, estate, geography, gender, and age. It is doubtful that many of those theatergoers who wept over the reconciliation of Meinau and Eulalia and who rejoiced over the deliverance of Annette and Theresa were ever aware of Herzen's adaptation of the form in his prose story, and it is doubtful also that those scenes on stage changed their lives. But theater events were certainly part of their lives, a part that is not often considered in recovering and reconstructing the sensibilities of the Russian people—and other peoples of the empire as well. This is especially true of provincial life, a subject still rather weakly developed in Russian historiography. The study of melodrama offers only a few peeks into it; broader exploration of all genres provides much more. But it is virtually certain that melodrama was the key viewing experience of most provincials. It was the genre they could best relate to, and probably the one that helped them "read" other more complex theatrical texts.

The biggest impact of melodrama on Russian theater was in stagecraft itself: costumes, sets, and especially acting. Acting did not become "realistic" overnight. Every generation, it seems, smiles at the "realism" of previous ones. This can only mean that every generation in turn had its own realism; that is to say that they experienced verisimilitude in the same way later ones did and do. But there did occur a clear divergence between the high-style declamatory method of neoclassical verse drama and the more earthy conversational delivery of melodrama. Melodrama sought illusion rather than stylized quasiballetic performance in order to drive the story and heighten suspense and sensation. Asides and soliloquies were reduced in number in favor of more "naturalistic" interaction of the players. The methods required to perform imported melodramas successfully were also those that made the plays accessible to audiences from increasingly broad social origins. Even actors on the capital stages found—or reinvented—themselves by acting melodrama. In the provinces, where stage rules and customs were relatively fluid, styles sprung from melodrama flourished more quickly. As Russian theater began to stage more works on contemporary Russian themes, the practice amplified of drafting provincial actors onto the imperial stages to play roles requiring special Russian inflections and sensibilities. And this practice laid the groundwork for the masterful performances of Russian theater in the second half of the nineteenth century.

## Notes

1 *Teatralnaia entsiklopediia,* vol. 3 (Moscow, 1961–7), 787–88. For dates and performances, see A. I. Volf, *Khronika peterburgskikh teatrov s kontsa 1826 do nachala 1855 goda* (St. Petersburg, 1877).

2 See Vladimir Propp, *The Morphology of Folktales,* 3rd ed. (Austin: University of Texas Press, 1971); and Joseph Campbell, *The Hero with a Thousand Faces,* 2d ed. (Princeton: Princeton University Press, 1988).

3 Frank Rahill, *The World of Melodrama* (University Park: Pennsylvania State University Press, 1967), 83; Paul Ginisty, *La mélodrame* (Paris,

n.d.) offers pictorial evidence of specific gestures and movements. For some modern perspectives on melodrama, see Jacky Bratton, Jim Cook, and Christine Gledhill, eds., *Melodrama: Stage, Picture, Screen* (London: British Film Institute, 1994); Daniel Gerould, ed., *Melodrama* (New York: New York Literary Forum, 1980); Michael Hays and Anastasia Nikolopoulou, eds., *Melodrama: The Cultural Emergence of a Genre* (New York: St. Martin's Press, 1996); and Peter Brooks, *The Melodramatic Imagination: Balzac, Henry James, Melodrama, and the Mode of Excess* (New Haven: Yale University Press, 1976). Brooks's volume, although it applies dramatic and affective structures of melodrama to the later novel form, contains interesting insights on the plays as well.

4 On *Affektenlehre,* see Don Michael Randel, ed., *The New Harvard Dictionary of Music* (Cambridge, Mass.: Harvard University Press, 1969), 16.

5 Oscar Mandel, *August von Kotzebue: The Comedy, the Man* (University Park: Pennsylvania State University Press, 1990), 30.

6 Ibid.

7 Quoted in John Lough, *Paris Theater Audiences in the Seventeenth and Eighteenth Centuries* (Oxford: Oxford University Press, 1957), 237–78.

8 For discussion of the Russian years, see Gerhard Giesemann, *Kotzebue in Russland: Materialien zu einer Wirkungsgeschichte* (Frankfurt, 1968).

9 Mandel, *August von Kotzebue,* 35.

10 August von Kotzebue, *Menschenhass und Reue: Schauspiel in fünf Aufzogen* in *August von Kotzebue: Schauspiele,* ed. Jürg Nathes (Frankfurt/Main, 1972), 46, 72. I thank Dr. Hubertus Jahn for securing this text for me. The earliest Russian translation I found is *Nenavist' k liudiam i raskaianie,* 4th ed. (Orël, 1826).

11 *Menschenhass und Reue* was staged as *The Stranger* in London every year from its debut until 1842 and many times after that.

12 Kotzebue, *Menschenhass und Reue,* 115, 122.

13 Ira Petrovskaia and V. Somina, *Teatralnyi Peterburg: Nachalo XVIII veka-oktiabr 1917 goda* (St. Petersburg, 1994), 83; Giesemann, *Kotzebue in Russland,* 73–74; Avgust von Kotsebu, *Dostopamiatnyi god moei zhizni,* vol. 1 (n.p., 1879), 107, 128–31, 161–64; this is the Russian translation of *Das merkwürdigste Jahr meines Lebens* (1803; Munich, 1965), 136–37, 139–40, 170, 172.

14 Kotzebue, *Dostopamiatnyi god,* vol. 2, 74–76, 84–86, 99–100; *Das merkwürdigste Jahr,* 261–62, 272.

15 Simon Karlinsky, *Russian Drama from Its Beginnings to the Age of Pushkin* (Berkeley: University of California Press, 1985) 191–92; Giesemann, *Kotzebue in Russland,* 175, 119.

16 Sergei Aksakov, *Sobranie sochinenii,* vol. 1 (Moscow, 1895–1900), 321;

V. Vsevolodskii [Gerngross], *Istoriia russkogo teatra,* vol. 2 (Leningrad, 1929), 29, 58–59, 64–65; P. A. Karatygin, *Zapiski* (Leningrad, 1929), 91–92; Giesemann, *Kotzebue in Russland,* 104. On Iakovlev, see also Leonid Grossman, *Pushkin v teatralnykh kreslakh: Kartiny russkoi stseny, 1817–1820* (Leningrad, 1926), 88. Boris Varneke, *History of the Russian Theater,* trans. Boris Brassol (New York: Macmillan, 1951), 255.

17 Petrovskaia and Somina, *Teatralnyi Peterburg,* 84; Irina Medvedeva, *Ekaterina Semënova: Zhizn i tvorchestvo tragicheskoi aktrisa* (Moscow, 1964), 11, 16, 31, 37.

18 Giesemann, *Kotzebue in Russland,* 181; Vsevolodskii, *Istoriia,* vol. 2, 29, 33.

19 Küchelbecker is quoted in *Istoriia russkoi dramaturgii XVII—pervaia polovina XIX veka* (Leningrad, 1982), 258.

20 Zotov quotations from Grossman, *Pushkin,* 19; and Vsevolodskii, *Istoriia,* vol. 2, 30.

21 This comparison is made by Hans Schumacher in August von Kotzebue, *Die deutsche Kleinstädter* (1803), ed. Hans Schumacher (Berlin, 1964), 106.

22 Rahill, *The World of Melodrama,* 40, 44.

23 Viktor Diukanzh [Victor Ducange], *Tereza, ili zhenevskaia sirota, melodrama* (Moscow, 1833), translation of *Thérèse, ou l'orphéline de Genève.* Lynn Hunt, discussing melodrama in *The Family Romance of the French Revolution* (Berkeley: University of California Press, 1992), makes much of mistaken identity in the genre, although in fact it is an ancient and continuous device in many genres of fiction and drama.

24 *Istoriia russkogo dramaticheskogo teatra* [hereafter *IRDT* ], vol. 2 (Moscow, 1977–87), 140, 280, 286; Medvedeva, *Ekaterina Semënova,* 267.

25 On Vysheslavtseva and her roles, see A. S. Gatsiskii, *Nizhegorodskii teatr (1798–1867)* (Nizhny-Novgorod, 1867), 1–60.

26 Iury Arnold, *Vospominaniia,* vols. 1 and 2 (Moscow, 1892), vol. 2, 101. Arnold as a child had played in amateur theatricals in Kotzebue's *Misanthropy and Repentance* and *Child of Love* (vol. 1, 26).

27 I. I. Lavrov, *Stsena i zhizn v provintsii i v stolitse* (Moscow, 1889), 40–56.

28 Ibid., 50.

29 Charles Rosen, *The Romantic Generation* (Cambridge, Mass.: Harvard University Press, 1995), 602.

30 A. I. Gertsen [Herzen], *Sochineniia,* vol. 1 (Moscow, 1955), 337. Lawrence Levine cites similar instances in *Highbrow/Lowbrow: The Emergence of Cultural Hierarchy in America* (Cambridge, Mass.: Harvard University Press, 1988), 30.

31 S. P. Gagarin, *Vseobshchii geograficheskii slovar* (Moscow, 1843).

32 The legend source is in Rahill, *The World of Melodrama;* the legal case in

Herbert Weinstock, *Rossini: A Biography* (New York: Knopf, 1968); the real event in Richard Osbourne, *Rossini* (London, 1986).

33 L.-C. Caigniez and J. M. T. Bandouin d'Aubigny, *La pie voleuse ou la servante de Palaiseau: Mélodrame historique* (Paris, 1815). The title page also indicates a ballet as well as the music by Piccinni. Commentary in Rahill, *The World of Melodrama,* 56–63; and Ginisty, *La mélodrame,* 121–38, 219.

34 The Russian translation by Valberkh is *Soroka-vorovka ili palezosskaia sluzhanka* (St. Petersburg, 1816). See also *IRDT,* vol. 2, 280, 288. The British adaptation "translated and altered from the French" by Isaac Pocock is *The Magpie, or, The Maid? a Melo Drame* (London, 1816). I thank Professor Abraham Ascher for securing a copy for me.

35 David Kimball, *Italian Opera* (Cambridge: Cambridge University Press, 1991), 358, 563; Osbourne, *Rossini,* 198–201; A. Gozenpud, *Opernyi slovar* (Moscow, 1965), 389–90; Weinstock, *Rossini,* 498, 77.

36 E. S. Kots, *Krepostnaia intelligentsiia* (Leningrad, 1926), 144–45, 148; Thomas Hodge, *Mutatis Mutandis: Poetry and the Musical Romance in Early Nineteenth Century Russia* (Ph.D. diss., Stanford University, 1992), 208.

37 My reconstruction is drawn from many accounts that largely overlap and conflict only on minor details. These accounts include Priscilla Roosevelt, *Life on the Russian Country Estate* (New Haven: Yale University Press, 1995), 139–41; N. Chernov, "Krepostnye aktrisy orlovskogo teatra," *Teatralnaia zhizn* 4 (1961): 28–29; M. D. Buturlin, "Teatr grafa Kamenskago v Orle v 1827 i 1828 godakh," *Russkii arkhiv* 7, no. 10 (1869): 1707–11; V. Putintsev, "Krepostnaia aktrisa Kuzmina," *Voprosy literatury* 9 (September 1963), 190–95; Lawrence Senelick, *Serf Actor: The Life and Art of Mikhail Shchepkin* (Westport, Conn.: Greenwood Press, 1984), 10, 48–49; T. S. Grits, "K istorii 'Soroki-vorovki,'" *Literaturnoe nasledstvo* 63 (1965): 655–60; and *IRDT,* vol. 2, 288, 423–26, 528. Leskov's much later story about brutal treatment of serfs "The Toupée Artist" (1883) was inspired by the murder of Kamenskii's father; see Hugh McLean, *Nikolai Leskov: The Man and His Art* (Cambridge, Mass.: Harvard University Press, 1977), 438–41.

38 For information on serf orchestras, see Kots, *Krepostnaia intelligentsiia;* and Richard Stites, "The Domestic Muse: Music at Home in the Twilight of Serfdom," in *Interactions and Transpositions: Russian Music, Literature, and Society,* ed. Andrew Wachtel (Evanston, Ill.: Northwestern University Press, 1998), 187–205.

39 For the Afanasev text, see Grits, "Kistorii 'Soroki-vorovki.'"

40 Gertsen [Herzen], "Soroka-vorovka: Povest," in *Sochineniia,* vol. 1, 327–50, 502–7.

41 Brooks, *The Melodramatic Imagination.*

42 One of the several streams of abolition thinking, the sporadic if never-dead reform discussion under Alexander I and Nicholas I, has been laboriously reconstructed from the record by a number of historians who all agree that very little came of government efforts. Most draw on the pioneering work of V. I. Semevskii, *Krestianskii vopros v Rossii v XVII i pervoi polovine XIX veka,* 2 vols. (St. Petersburg, 1888), see especially vol. 1, 316–17, 396–97. See also Peter Kolchin, *Unfree Labor: American Slavery and Russian Serfdom* (Cambridge, Mass.: Harvard University Press, 1987); and Jerome Blum, *Lord and Peasant in Russia from the Ninth to the Nineteenth Century* (Princeton: Princeton University Press, 1961). For the literary side, see William R. Dodge, *Abolitionist Sentiment in Russia, 1762–1855* (Ph.D. diss., University of Wisconsin, 1950).

43 P. N. Stolpianskii, *Staryi Peterburg i Obshchestvo pooshchreniia khudozhestv* (Leningrad, 1928); G. Komelova, "Peterburgskoe Obshchestvo Pooshchreniia Khudozhestv i ego deiatelnost v 20-40-kh gg. XIX v," *Soobshcheniia Gosudarstvennogo Ermitazha* (1958): 34–36; E. Golubeva, "Iz istorii Obshchestva Pooshchreniia Khudozhnikov," *Iskusstvo* 10 (1961): 67–72.

44 For a superb introduction to this, see: Louise McReynolds, *The News under Russia's Old Regime: The Development of a Mass-Circulation Press* (Princeton: Princeton University Press, 1991) and Jeffrey Brooks, *When Russians Learned to Read: Literacy and Popular Literature, 1861–1917* (Princeton: Princeton University Press, 1985). For further enrichment, see Joan Neuberger, *Hooliganism: Crime, Culture, and Power in St. Petersburg, 1900–1914* (Berkeley: University of California Press, 1993) and Laura Engelstein, *The Keys to Happiness: Sex and the Search for Modernity in Fin-de-Siècle Russia* (Ithaca: Cornell University Press, 1992).

45 For comparison, see Levine's classic account, "William Shakespeare in America," in his *Highbrow/Lowbrow,* 11–81.

*Julie A. Buckler*

# Melodramatizing Russia

## Nineteenth-Century Views from the West

"Melodrama" is rarely evoked as a critical category for thinking about Russia, because there has never been an interest in claiming melodrama as part of Russian cultural history.[1] Both western and Russian sources on Russian stage works from the nineteenth century almost entirely elide the category of melodrama. Even dramatists who might reasonably lay claim to the term—for example, Alexander Ostrovsky, whose plays treat social and moral problems within a shifting economic landscape—have been shielded from suspect melodramatic affiliation by scholarly precedent that favors the realist aspects of the Russian dramatic tradition.

Russia's problematic relationship to melodrama arises from social and historical circumstances. Melodrama as a form parallels the ascendance of the bourgeoisie in France and the working classes in England and America, coinciding with the expansion of the "illegitimate" nonaristocratic theater in the western world. Following the French Revolution, melodrama thus spearheaded another sort of revolution, when new theaters on the Boulevard du Temple opened to entertain the urban working class. But no such sudden liberation of the Russian theater public occurred. Russian translations of French melodramas played on the stages of the St. Petersburg Bolshoi and Aleksandrinsky theaters during the first half of the nineteenth century, when the aristocracy dominated the Russian theatergoing public. And ironically, as the lower orders of Russian urban society began to frequent the theater in greater numbers during the second half of the century, melodrama continued to cater to upper-class audiences with society dramas by writers such as Alexandre

Dumas *fils* and Victorien Sardou. In nineteenth-century Russia, melodrama largely represented an imported western delicacy, rather than a theatrical form that gave voice to a new social majority.[2]

In spite of nineteenth-century Russia's problematic relationship to melodrama's role in negotiating social hierarchies, western nations used this aesthetic mode to conceptualize Russia for themselves. Russia as an imagined nation appeared in several French and English melodramas: Guilbert de Pixérécourt's 1819 *The Outcast's Daughter;* Eugène Scribe's libretto to Giacomo Meyerbeer's 1854 opera *The North Star;* Oscar Wilde's 1880 *Vera, or, The Nihilist;* and Victorien Sardou's 1882 *Fédora* reincarnated as Umberto Giordano's 1898 opera by the same name. These fictional, melodramatic Russias served as a site for playing out western cultural fears and fantasies. But this is precisely how various "Easts" came into being in the imperial context. This essay takes as a departure point the premise of, in the words of Laura García-Moreno and Peter Pfeiffer, "the . . . notion of national identity as an ongoing process of negotiating identity and difference that takes place both within and beyond the borders of single nations."[3] As Homi Bhabha declares: "The 'other' is never outside or beyond us; it emerges forcefully, within cultural discourse, when we *think* we speak most intimately and indigenously 'between ourselves.'"[4] The four western stage works discussed in this essay do not simply represent Russia by means of melodramatic convention. Pixérécourt, Scribe, Wilde, and Sardou rely on melodramatic convention to manifest Russia within the western cultural landscape, to make Russia visible. The more spectacular and exotic this melodramatized Russia appears on stage, the more familiar it seems, evoked by means of established generic formulas and traversed according to well-worn narrative roadways. These four melodramatic works about Russia offer a provocative counterpart to the melodramatism with which the female domestic sphere would be infused in twentieth-century western film and television. Instead of magnifying an enclosed, private space, these "Russian" melodramas expose a vast imaginary expanse to the collective gaze of western theatergoers.

J. H. Amherst's *Napoleon Bonaparte's Invasion of Russia, or, The Conflagration of Moscow (a Military and Equestrian Spectacle)* from the 1820s offers a striking illustration of how Russian cultural identity could be negotiated through melodrama. The most spectacular scene in Amherst's melodrama transpires on a main street of Moscow, during the famous fire of 1812:

> Houses falling.—WOMEN and CHILDREN burnt to death, borne along. Conflagration—alarm bell ringing—shrieks and cries from right and left—crash continually going—crackling of sparks and embers—dreadful explosions—many of the INHABITANTS half naked with blankets or carpets about them—a cart of half burnt furniture drawn by the INHABITANTS—the PATRIOT YOUTHS assist those FEMALES who are brought on fainting—one very aged MAN is assisted through the flames in a chair.[5]

Along with the requisite melodramatic fireworks, Amherst's work stages the conquest of Russia by Napoleon and the French troops. The Russians may be victorious at the end, but the invasion of Moscow by foreign troops remains the most dramatic scene in the work, the scene most often invoked by critics and spectators, and referred to by the title of the play itself. During the course of Amherst's stage work, Russia has been colonized, generically speaking, and opened up for melodramatic conquest by the West. In the melodramas by Pixérécourt, Scribe, Wilde, and Sardou, western aesthetic and social structures similarly invade such an imagined Russia.

The four melodramas of Russia examined here manifest palpable anxiety over the power of the sovereign ruler, the plots and plotting of national history, and the possible threats to Russian national autonomy and integrity.[6] And yet, this very autonomy depends on Russia first being enabled and constituted as an "actor" in a general cultural conversation, as characterized by Judith Butler: "Whereas some critics mistake the critique of sovereignty for the demolition of agency, I propose that agency begins where sovereignty wanes. The one who acts (who is not the same as the sovereign subject) acts precisely to the extent that he or she is constituted as an actor and, hence, operating within a linguistic field of enabling constraints from the outset."[7] Butler refers here to hate speech, in which one voice exercises a ritual form of subordination over another, but her remarks can also apply to other kinds of constitutive speech. "Interpellation," an address that constitutes a body by giving it a social existence, marks and inaugurates a subject. Interpellation is conventional and performative; it is an illocutionary act that signifies while literally enacting this signification. The four melodramas of Russia discussed in this essay all perform a kind of melodramatic interpellation, whereby a western artistic discourse intended for the public stage constitutes Russia.

Russia was not only the product of such interpellations, of course, but also engaged in calling forth similarly interpellated cultural subjects. Russia's literary and theatrical depictions of itself took shape against Russian views of the West, and in response to southern and eastern imperial subjects: Circassians and Chechens, Georgians and Armenians. The gradual annexation of territories by the Russian empire occurred in conjunction with the representation of these peoples through the use of "rhetorical postures, symbolic diction and tropes" in Russian literary works by Pushkin, Bestuzhev-Marlinsky, Lermontov, and Tolstoy.[8] Such characterizations of imperial Russia in recent scholarship take as their inspiration what Edward Said calls the "*geographical* notation, the theoretical mapping and charting of territory that underlies western fiction, historical writing, and philosophical discourse" of the nineteenth century.[9] But it is not the purpose of this essay to explore Russia's attempts to represent itself within such cultural discourse or to chart Russia's responses to western interpellations. Indeed, the four melodramatic works treated here had little or no stage life within Russia. This article seeks rather to illustrate the ways in which a highly performative, spectacular genre such as melodrama renders startlingly visible the interpellative acts constituting imperial Russia from outside.

The three most prolific national producers of melodrama—France, England, and America—were also the most important producers of literature with a "peculiarly acute imperial cast," most notably in the form of novels.[10] Said's influential work on Orientalism as discourse, which he characterized as a largely British and French cultural project involving "orientalized" locales such as Egypt, India, and the Far East, has since been extended and modified for the West's view of Russia. Larry Wolff has shown that the idea of eastern Europe was indeed related to that of a mythological Orient: "It was western Europe that invented eastern Europe as its complementary other half in the eighteenth century, the age of Enlightenment . . . and civilization discovered its complement, within the same continent, in shadowed lands of backwardness, even barbarism."[11] This gaze toward the East came to define the map of modern civilization for western Europeans, particularly for France and Britain and often through literary works, travelogs, visual art, and stage works. In this way, exoticized "eastern" melodramas such as Moncrieff's *The Cataract of the Ganges* and Fitzball's *Thalaba, the Destroyer,* as well as the earlier-mentioned Amherst piece, became fashionable during the Romantic 1820s. During the course of the nineteenth century, such stagy representations of the East displayed an increasingly knowing awareness of their orientalizing effects, a development that complicated the model for such seemingly imperialistic depictions.

The four western stage works treated here constitute Russia in all its fierce, autocratic glory using established melodramatic convention. Inscribing melodrama's own features within the performed space of Russia conquers this alien empire by means of the West's own aesthetic discourse. Because these melodramatized depictions of Russia must invariably enact ritual submission to western forms and conventions, melodrama itself may represent a form of cultural imperialism. But, true to form, melodrama's productive ambiguity carries the day, and all four melodramatized Russias prove to be unsettling places, despite their ostensibly familiar contours.

### Pixérécourt: Conquering Russia

In his landmark study *The Melodramatic Imagination,* Peter Brooks makes Pixérécourt's "historical" melodrama *The Outcast's Daughter* emblematic of the melodramatic form, an identity that the play explicitly stages through the recognition and admiration of virtue, the aesthetics of astonishment, the signs and proof of virtue as pure "spectacular" signifiers, and the repetitions and final understanding of the message.[12] Pixérécourt's play introduces elements invoked repeatedly in western stagings of Russian cultural concerns: exile, political intrigue, revolution, and national identity. As Pixérécourt's heroine traverses the Russian empire from East to West, she masters this space in generic terms. In the final scene, Russia declares its final allegiance to the melodramatic principle.

Pixérécourt based his 1819 classical melodrama *The Outcast's Daughter* on Madame Cottin's novel *Élisabeth,* which traces its eponymous heroine's journey across Russia. The melodrama opens in Siberia, where Elisabeth's parents, the Polish Count and Countess Potoski, have been living in exile for sixteen years, four thousand versts from St. Petersburg. Germany is approximately three thousand miles away, and the would-be traveler faces all manner of natural obstacles: foaming torrents, mountains of snow, deserts full of wild animals, avalanches, and vast forests. "Europe is lost to us forever," remarks Potoski sadly.[13] The Russian seat of government represents the closest thing to Europe in this melodrama, located far to the west of the story's starting point.

An ambitious rival had falsely accused Potoski of plotting against the crown, and only a personal pardon from the tsar can restore the family to their former life. But the Potoskis' status as exiles prohibits them from writing letters, and they have no other way to communicate their plea to the tsar. But then it is discovered that through an official oversight women are allowed to travel out of the territory of exile, because their perceived physical feebleness seems not to warrant a formal prohibition. Women are thus possessed of a melodramatic efficacy denied to male subjects, a fact that will be asserted in each of the four stage works discussed here.

Elisabeth resolves to undertake the journey to St. Petersburg and throw herself at the tsar's feet. She believes that her noble mission will communicate itself to the semicivilized peoples of the Russian territories, from whom she must solicit help along the way. Elisabeth also expresses her conviction that she will find expressions sufficiently eloquent to obtain a pardon for her parents from the tsar. In simple terms, Elisabeth's mission is to cross Russia and make herself understood, thereby to render her family seen and heard. Elisabeth's mother, Phedora, presents Elisabeth with a cross, a gift from her own mother, instructing her daughter to "never part with this sign, so revered throughout the entire expanse of this empire."[14] Of course, Phedora is misinformed because the non-Russian peoples inhabiting these eastern territories were not Christian. Also of significance, Pixérécourt does not specify whether this is a western or eastern cross, which is to say whether the cross asserts a Russian Orthodox identity or a Polish (western Catholic) one. If it is the latter, Elisabeth's journey represents a conquest only masquerading as supplication, an attempt to annex Russia to Europe.

The second part of Pixérécourt's melodrama takes place on the banks of the Kama River and features a view of the mountain range that separates "Europe from Asia." Elisabeth has reached the halfway point of her journey from Saimka to St. Petersburg. The exhausted heroine arrives at the cabin of Ivan, who reveals himself as her father's old enemy, a former Livonian nobleman. Touched by Elisabeth's willing forgiveness, Ivan offers to provide written proof of Potoski's innocence. Pixérécourt's melodrama ostensibly insists on the superiority of writing over other forms of communication but actually privileges showing over telling, in true melodramatic fashion.

Ivan defends Elisabeth against a band of marauding Tartars, whom she quiets by displaying her cross, a gesture that serves as a prelude to an unambiguous moment of melodramatic conquest. When the Tartars hear Ivan's story of Elisabeth's courage, they prostrate themselves before her, transformed by her example into noble, civilized beings, converted into subjects of the melodramatic empire. But, as Elisabeth and Ivan prepare to leave, a terrible storm gathers force. As the waters rise around her, Elisabeth kneels on a plank and embraces Phedora's cross. The waters float Elisabeth over to the European side of the river, but separate her from Ivan, who manages to scribble the necessary few lines about Potoski before expiring. Villagers of non-Russian origin witness this miracle, watching raptly as the play crosses the border between East and West. Pixérécourt's melodrama pretends to stage the affirmation of Russian imperial identity, but instead it makes the play's subjects swear an aesthetic allegiance to the West.

The third and final part of Pixérécourt's melodrama opens outside the Moscow Kremlin walls. This part of the melodrama specifies groups of non-Russian extras, as did parts 1 and 2, "who give themselves to the effervescence of their joy. They perform original dances from their lands," providing the requisite exotic window dressing.[15] The new tsar's coronation will take place on the following day. The future tsar has learned of Elisabeth's heroic journey and awaits her arrival. But the lord marshall, anxious to conceal long-standing abuses of authority, plots to foil Elisabeth's interview with the tsar and prevent her entrance to the Kremlin.

After various delays, Elisabeth finally enters the throne room and stands before the magnificent courtiers and the tsar. But Pixérécourt's melodrama fails to deliver what was promised to its audience. Elisabeth need not tell her story nor plead eloquently for clemency, because the tsar already knows all and has been expecting her. There is no spectacle of revelation. The tsar tells her that long before her arrival the pardon of Count Potoski had been signed, and a courtier had been dispatched to Saimka to inform her parents. At these words, Potoski and Phedora appear and prostrate themselves joyfully before the tsar as artillery fire outside signals the beginning of the coronation ceremony. The tsar declares that he will reinstate Potoski's riches and dignity, but "it is not in my power to elevate Elisabeth; placed above her sex by her sublime action, she has become at once its glory and its model."[16]

The Potoski family has been pardonned by a tsar not yet crowned, and the play has made no reference to the preceding ruler who banished Potoski.[17] The "revolution" in the melodramatic plot occurs from above, and the peoples of the Russian empire seem too contented with their new ruler to revolt. Elisabeth never gets her chance to perform before the tsar, to be seen and heard. Instead, the tsar silences Elisabeth by sanctioning and canonizing her revolutionary act. He transforms her preemptively into a national symbol and a feminine ideal, somewhat akin to the way that the four western stage works discussed here imagine and constitute Russia as a familiar, unthreatening melodramatic space.[18]

The plot of Pixérécourt's melodrama traverses the vast expanse of Russia, moving from East to West. The Polish heroine Elisabeth undergoes many trials to extend her reach toward Europe. The point is the annexation of new peoples and territories to the growing melodramatic empire, and the real spectacle is the command performance of "Russian" obeisance to melodramatic convention.

## Scribe: Claiming Russia

Giacomo Meyerbeer's 1854 opera *The North Star* (libretto by Eugène Scribe) offers a melodramatic Russian respinning of Meyerbeer's earlier opera called *A Military Encampment in Silesia,* based on an episode in the life of Frederick the Great. Meyerbeer himself functions in music history as an "assimilative" figure, his work a popularizer's blend of German, Italian, and French operatic techniques and staging devices. Scribe is known for writing vaudevilles, comedies of manners, and *opéras-comiques,* as well as political and historical dramas, melodramas, and grand operas. The impressively implausible *North Star* revolves around political and amorous plots. Catherine, a village girl who makes her living selling liquor to laborers, disguises herself as a boy to fight in the Russian army. She loves a carpenter named Peter, who is really the Russian tsar. Catherine informs the tsar of a conspiracy planned by mutinous soldiers, and at the end of the opera she is triumphantly crowned empress of Russia.[19]

Historical melodrama as a subgenre existed from Pixérécourt's time onward, drawing on precedents and motifs from Kotzebue, Schiller, Shakespeare, and others. Real historical incidents could serve as the basis for a melodramatic plot, and the setting might be historically removed or colorfully foreign. Scribe's libretto blends together a pastiche of motifs from eighteenth-century Russian imperial history. The carpenter-tsar Peter is Peter the Great, the founder of St. Petersburg, who presided over the initial phases of the city's construction and took an interest in ship building and technological advancement. Peter the Great actually worked as a carpenter in the west. The character Danilowitz, a pastry cook who becomes a colonel close to the tsar, resembles Alexander Menshikov, who was reputedly promoted by Peter from pie seller to the titled nobility. And during the first decade of the eighteenth century, the Don Cossacks did rebel and try to join forces with the Cossacks of the Ukraine under the leadership of Mazeppa, who was secretly corresponding with the Swedes.

The heroine of *The North Star,* the village maiden Catherine, recalls Peter's wife Catherine I, a woman of nonnoble origin from the Baltic region. Catherine in this way resembles Pixérécourt's Elisabeth, in that she is not Russian but from a proximate country annexed to the Russian empire but closer culturally to the West. In *The North Star,* Catherine quells marauding Kalmucks, Bashkirs, Tartars, and Cossacks by donning "the costume of a Bohemian soothsayer" in memory of her mother, Vlasta, a priestess revered throughout Ukrainian lands.[20] Catherine sings and dances with the rebellious tribes and in this way convinces them to join the tsar's army. Here Catherine's role seems suspect: she induces the non-Russian "savages" to enlist, using theatrical means to secure their allegiance. The Kalmuck and Cossack men must shave off their beards as a prerequisite to military service; this detail makes reference to Peter's decree that his courtiers shave their beards and effect a more western appearance, a fitting requirement in the project of constituting Russia melodramatically.

Like Pixérécourt's *The Outcast's Daughter,* Meyerbeer's opera moves toward the seat of imperial Russia. The three acts transpire in a Finnish village near Vyborg, at a Russian military camp, and in the tsar's

St. Petersburg palace. In act 2, the evil Colonel Yermoloff plots against the tsar, spreading a rumor among the military officers that the knout can be used on officers as well as enlisted men. The men vow to resist this barbaric practice or die. Peter pretends to be an army captain, investigating the possible rebellion among his forces. From her sentry post, Catherine, dressed as a man, watches the tsar drinking and flirting with the vivandieres. Incensed with jealousy, she swims across a river, is shot at as an escaping insubordinate, disappears, and is presumed dead. Catherine manages to leave a piece of paper for the tsar that names the conspirators, and Peter learns that the traitors' plan is to surrender the camp to the Swedes as soon as they hear the signal, the sacred march of the tsar. The tsar's anthem will thus ironically herald Russia's annexation to the West. But at the critical moment, Peter unmasks himself and the soldiers fall at his feet, ready to fight the Swedes instead of joining them. The "conquered" Russian troops march out to meet the western enemy. But this particular struggle for sovereignity is just a decoy; Russia will yield to the seductive strains of western operatic arias in the last act.

Act 3 opens in the tsar's palace in St. Petersburg, one month later. Peter mourns for his lost Catherine, and declares himself willing to relinquish his crown if only his happiness might return. He confesses that carpentry work helps to relieve his tumultuous emotions, and reveals to Danilowitz that he has even constructed a workshop just like the one in Finland, and has summoned the Finnish workers to his palace. Peter has literally transformed the Russian capital into a western site.

Peter suddenly hears Catherine's voice singing, and Danilowitz reveals that Catherine has been found, but that she has tragically lost her reason from the traumatic events at the encampment. Catherine herself appears, dressed in white and clearly ready for a mad scene à la Lucia. But the sight of the familiar workshop and workers, who obligingly call for her to bring them drinks, partially returns her reason. Peter shows himself and Catherine falls fainting into his arms. Before she returns to consciousness, Peter's courtiers dress her in a royal mantle and crown, placing a marriage bouquet in her hands.

The ending of *The North Star* seems almost parodically consistent with melodramatic convention, in which "the body of persecuted virtue is at first expressionistically distorted, as in a hysterical conversion, then is rewarded, feted, married, and emblazoned with all the signs of the public recognition of its nature."[21] The spectacle ends as all cry "long live the empress!"; western-style singing and dancing have quelled any possibility of rebellion. But *The North Star* has staged a real revolution whereby a peasant girl is crowned empress, quite literally as a dream, while the heroine sleeps. But instead of considering this denouement a defeat, Scribe's drama celebrates the democratic aspects of melodramatic love, which conquers all.

### Wilde: Plotting Russia

Oscar Wilde's play *Vera, or, The Nihilist* displayed bad timing in both generic and thematic terms. Between the completion of the play's first version in 1880 and its unsuccessful 1883 premiere performance in New York City, history more or less guaranteed that *Vera* would fail. In March 1881, Tsar Alexander II of Russia died in St. Petersburg from an assassin's bomb, and the Russian revolutionaries in Wilde's play suddenly seemed in the worst possible taste. Sensing as much, Wilde postponed the London premiere planned for late 1881. America seemed to offer a more appropriate climate for Wilde to stage his drama, and he publicized *Vera* by displaying the costumes for his play in the windows of Lord and Taylor's department store.[22] This display of theatrical objects proved prophetic, because Wilde's play now haunts the periphery of his dramatic oeuvre and is included in his collected works as a mere museum piece and historical curiosity.

Wilde's Vera joins a circle of nihilists after her brother Dmitri is sent to Siberia for revolutionary activities. Dmitri implores Vera to avenge him and compels her to take the nihilists' oath: "To strangle whatever nature is in me, neither to pity nor to be pitied, neither to show mercy nor to take it, neither to marry nor to be given in marriage, neither to love nor to be loved. . . . To stab secretly by night, to drop poison in the glass, to set father against son and husband against wife, without fear, without hope, without future, to suffer, to annihilate, to revenge."[23] Wilde's nihilist credo resembles a melodramatic villain's code of dramatic conduct. This is a difficult oath for Vera to live by, because love and personal loyalties govern all of her choices. But unlike Elisabeth and Catherine, this heroine will not be rewarded or raised to the throne for her efforts.

Vera falls in love with Alexis, a young revolutionary who turns out to be the tsarevitch, a noble republican who has repudiated his father's tyrannical rule. After the evil tsar is assassinated, the nihilists order Vera to kill the tsarevitch. She infiltrates his sleeping quarters in the Winter Palace, but instead of executing her mission she fatally stabs herself so that Alexis can escape the nihilists and live to liberate Russia. Vera's death cannot be seen as tragic, however, nor is it a garbled, debased form of conventional high-style dramatic tragedy. Her death is an explicitly melodramatic act, one that valorizes personal, individual emotion over political agency or, more accurately, one that attempts to remove the heroine from her participation in radical politics. What is more, in staging such melodramatic affinities as late as the 1880s, Wilde's Vera affirms essentially conservative values in politics *and* art.

Wilde's Vera is the descendant of two real-life Russian female revolutionaries: Vera Figner and Vera Zasulich. But although Wilde gave his dramatic heroine a name resonant in nineteenth-century Russian revolutionary culture, the Russia of his play is a strange, hybrid creature that corresponds to the hodgepodge nature of its melodramatic form.[24] *Vera* stages an indigestible mixture of cultural referents, using the familiar and the exotic in unlikely combination. The "Russianness" of Wilde's play establishes itself with insistent invocations of bears shot during the great winter and neighbors freezing to death in their sleighs during snowstorms. Nevertheless, this melodramatized Russia seems a very familiar place, to judge by its generic signposts.

In Wilde's *Vera,* Russianness is stagy, inherently theatrical. Russianness draws additional attention to itself by dressing outlandishly. The nihilist conspirators in their secret garret wear yellow cloaks and scarlet masks. They use an elaborate system of passwords, which they exchange while standing in a semicircle. Vera attends the grand duke's masked ball in a gorgeous gown, desiring to see the tsar and his "cursed brood" face to face. The tsar, "whose soul is black with his iniquity," is the "cleverest conspirator" of all, claims Vera.[25] When the tsar's soldiers burst in on the nihilists, the conspirators don their masks. Vera declares them to be a "company of strolling players travelling from Samara to Moscow to amuse his Imperial Majesty" (27). To save his friends, Alexis removes his mask and reveals himself to the soldiers (and simultaneously to the nihilists) as the tsarevitch. He explains that he left the palace to amuse himself with the players and to flirt with a pretty Gypsy girl. But the cynical courtier Prince Paul assures the tsar that the tsarevitch poses no threat: "The Prince is a very ingenuous young man. He pretends to be devoted to the people, and lives in a palace; preaches socialism, and draws a salary that would support a province. Some day he'll . . . cut up the red cap of liberty to make decorations for his Prime Minister" (42).

Prince Paul predicts that Alexis unmasked actually represents business as usual. After the tsar's assassination, Prince Paul acts quickly, sending for the crown, scepter, and robe of state and proclaiming Alexis the ruler of Russia. It is precisely for his acceptance of the crown—the key prop—that the nihilists deem Alexis a traitor. But Prince Paul's remark renders the ending of Wilde's play ambiguous. Each character wears multiple disguises and plays several standard melodramatic stage roles.

Act 4 opens with one of the oddest developments in the play. Prince Paul infiltrates the nihilist circle and asks to be admitted to their number, because Alexis has stripped him of his powers. Prince Paul provides the nihilists with a map of the Winter Palace and the keys to Alexis's private apartments. Paul assumes that after Alexis is dead he can return to the palace and continue to stage manage the monarchy. "This is the ninth conspiracy I have been in in Russia," says Prince Paul. "They always end in a trip to Siberia for my friends and a new decoration for myself" (61).

To the end, the nihilists remain true to their vow of theatricality: they draw lots from a skull bowl and mark the regicide's lot with a bloody sign. The president of the nihilists formally offers Vera a choice of the dagger or the vial of poison to do the deed, and she chooses the former. She is to throw the bloody dagger out the palace window at the precise stroke of midnight, to let her fellow conspirators know that the false traitor Alexis is dead. She sets off for the palace in the requisite black cloak.

Alone, Alexis muses on the crown lying on the table: "What subtle potency lies hidden in this gaudy bauble that makes one feel like a god when one wears it?" (67). Melodrama often points to its props and symbols in this way. When Vera appears, he offers her the crown and his hand in marriage. Alexis wants to lay "this mighty Russia" at his beloved's feet and rule the people with her "by love, as a father rules his children." "Tomorrow," he promises, "I will crown you with my own hands as empress in that great cathedral which my fathers built" (70–71). They will rule the melodramatic empire together. But Vera refuses: "I am a Nihilist. I cannot wear a crown." Her final gift to Alexis is a last theatrical trick. "See!" she cries, "The bloody man behind you!" (73). When Alexis turns to look, Vera flings the dagger covered in her own heart's blood out the window to appease the conspirators below and to save the young tsar from their wrath.

The melodramatic nihilism of Wilde's play overturns the conventions of political drama. Love supersedes all. Revolutionaries assassinate themselves. The will of a single individual assures Russia's republican future. The real survivor of Wilde's *Vera* is the tsar's sophist advisor Prince Paul, whose western-style "urbane witticisms" prefigure Wilde's mature dramatic works.[26] Once again, western theatergoers can feel at home in a melodramatized Russia.

### Sardou: Playing Russia

Like Wilde's *Vera,* Victorien Sardou's 1882 play *Fedora* uses political intrigue to structure a melodramatic love story. Sardou's *Fedora* belongs to a subcategory of melodrama seen from the second half of the nineteenth century: detective melodramas of murders and government spies. This trend began earlier with works such as the 1829 *Vidocq, the French Police Spy,* and grew with the spreading influence of Edgar Allan Poe, Charles Dickens, and Wilkie Collins.

Political intrigue and rebellion recall melodrama's very origins in the fall of the Bastille and its aftermath. The site of the new popular theaters in Paris, the Boulevard du Temple, eventually came to be known as the boulevard du Crime. Early melodramas featured evil tyrants and noble brigands. The secret policeman of the French Terror, Fouché, became a favorite melodramatic villain in *Secret Service* (1834) and *Plot and Passion* (1853). This evolving melodramatic subgenre made central the device of an incriminating scrap of paper, originally a lover's note, that falls into the wrong hands. This paper now represented "political documents, plans of fortifications, blue-prints of inventions, sealed orders and rough drafts of international treaties, to be lost, stolen or mislaid, sold, traced or photographed."[27] Sardou chose the well-heeled types of the drawing room as protagonists for his melodrama of political machinations in order to overlay amorous and political intrigue. Fittingly, it is that hackneyed melodramatic device, the incriminating letter, that brings about the heroine Fedora's demise. The most convincing characters the play has to offer are its numerous working professionals, those who do their jobs to keep the show moving along: police, doctors, diplomats, and private house servants, all with given names.

The plot of *Fedora* revolves around the death of Vladimir, son of police chief General Yariskin. Count Loris Ipanoff fatally shoots Vladimir to defend his honor as a husband, because Vladimir had been carrying on an affair with Loris's young wife, Wanda. In the aftermath of Vladimir's death, Loris flees to France. In Russia, General Yariskin arrests, tortures, and kills Loris's brother to punish Loris, whom he claims is a dangerous nihilist. But General Yariskin wreaks his vengeance for entirely personal reasons: to avenge the death of his son. Vladimir's fiancée, the wealthy Princess Fedora, is distraught at her beloved's loss; she has no knowledge of Vladimir's perfidy and believes his death to be a political assassination. Fedora moves to Paris and pretends to be a nihilist in hopes of delivering Loris to the Russian authorities, and she sends information about Loris to General Yariskin. But Fedora falls in love with Loris and ultimately uses her covert operations to establish his trustworthiness as a lover. He tells her his story and she relinquishes all thought of revenge.

Loris and Fedora enjoy a lovers' idyll, marred only by Loris's unstinting efforts to discover the person responsible for his brother's death. Loris never suspects that the party responsible is his own true love, until a letter telling him so arrives in response to his inquiries. Fedora despairingly takes a fatal dose of poison before confessing to Loris that she had once schemed to destroy him. When the dust clears, there is not one genuine revolutionary element among the cast of *Fedora,* but many that are reactionary. The Russian expatriates in Paris play at being revolutionaries, but instead enact the antiquated plots of the early nineteenth century from classical melodrama and the society tale. Ostensibly about the dread disease of nihilism that improbably infects the flower of Russian aristocracy and relatives of the Russian imperial family, Sardou's play only concerns the betrayals and half-truths of lovers. Regarding forms of proof, a veritable obsession that the play displays, *Fedora* politicizes the personal, and makes the political highly personal.

Although *Fedora* invokes a melodramatized Russia, the play points unambiguously toward the West. The action of the play moves from St. Petersburg to Paris; the opera stages the final act in the Bernese Oberland. The Russia of Sardou's play is literally imagined, the object of its characters' gaze from abroad. And the most famous Fedora ever was the actress who originally realized the role: Sarah Bernhardt, not the fin de siècle Russian actresses who emulated her.[28] In conversation with a

French diplomat, Fedora declares herself to be barbarous, inhuman, and nonwestern in her thirst for revenge. But Fedora is only half a Slav, because her mother was Greek. Sardou's play stages a failed search for Russianness in melodrama itself, staging a chain of unmaskings and identifications that, as in Wilde's *Vera,* ends inconclusively. The search for Russianness fails, precisely because the play stages the failure of such a project. Sarah Bernhardt herself allegedly made the following statement during rehearsals for the play's first run:

> For me, Fedora is like a second creation of Woman. Eve, God's creation, is Woman. Fedora, Sardou's creation, is *all women.* At least this is how I understand the role. Fedora represents the incarnation of all feminine charms and faults. In order to properly render the author's conception, she should be at once coquettish like a Slav, fierce like a Spaniard, amorous like an Italian, refined like a Frenchwoman, and thoroughbred like an Englishwoman: a fallen angel with white wings. I endeavored to be all this, and it helped that I have traveled a great deal, since I could take all these diverse types from real life.[29]

Woman in Sardou's play, as Bernhardt sees it, resembles the melodramatic form itself, an admixture from all manner of artistic genres and national traditions.

Everything about Sardou's *Fedora* is familiar, but made slightly strange by disguise. *Fedora* abounds in the conventional props and gestures of melodrama: shooting, a trail of blood, incriminating letters, revenge, confession, and poisoning. Even the heroine's last name, Romazov, hovers at the edge of memory, evoking the Russian imperial family, the Romanovs. The play's ostentatious signs of Russianness, the ubiquitous samovar and the huge, bejeweled Byzantine cross in which Fedora conceals poison, are implicated in the eventual collapse of the pretense and the end of the spectacle itself. When she realizes the part she has unwittingly played in the death of Loris's relatives, Fedora poisons herself by emptying the fatal powder from her cross into a teacup and drinking the brew in Loris's presence.

A perpetual confusion of identity for the play's characters emphasizes the elusive nature of Sardou's fictional Russia. *Fedora* actually consists of two parallel dramas; one is played out between the ghostly Fedora and Loris, and one transpires between the "real" lovers. Fedora has a ghostly double, because Loris speaks of a woman "spy" who dogs his movements. Fedora herself speaks in the third person of the woman responsible for the death of Loris's brother. Loris also has a double: the evil nihilist who shot Vladimir to revenge himself on General Yariskin. But the true hero and heroine of *Fedora* are not the ill-fated lovers Loris Ipanoff and Fedora Romazov. The real stars of the show are Count Vladimir and Countess Olga, who best exemplify the slippery play with identity that shapes *Fedora*. These two characters can best be described as not existing at all.

Countess Olga amuses herself in Paris by playing the political exile, declaring politics her current passion. Olga had previously disguised herself as a man in St. Petersburg to assist at the hanging of the nihilist Presniakov. She tried entering a convent but found it dull, and decided to sample international politics. During the final scene of the operatic version, Olga appears in black, having renounced the world after being dropped by her Polish lover Lasinski, himself a spy for the Russian government. But when Olga receives an invitation to go bicycling, she rushes off happily to don bloomers, a famous moment in Giordano's opera when opera meets the coming twentieth century. The comic deflation of Olga's endless costume changes literally makes a farce out of Russian political concerns.

Even more remarkably, Count Vladimir manages to play a central role in the plot of *Fedora* without ever actually appearing on stage. Vladimir is the son of the ruthless General Yariskin, another powerful but never-seen presence in the play, who pursues suspected nihilists and other enemies of the Russian government. But neither Sardou's play nor Giordano's opera actually list Vladimir as a character in the drama. In a complicated bit of stage business described in detail by stage directions, the fatally wounded Vladimir is conveyed into his St. Petersburg home and into his bedroom by the police detective Gretch and by servants, without being seen by the audience. Throughout the first scene, characters go in and out of Vladimir's room through a door on the main part of the stage. The spectator, like Fedora, catches tantalizing glimpses of the doctor and servants ministering to an invisible Vladimir, who is pronounced dead at the end of act 1. We learn of Vladimir's true nature only in act 3, when Loris shows Fedora a letter that proves Vladimir's ignoble intentions regarding their marriage. In both play and opera a photograph of Vladimir is kept on hand so that Fedora has a focal point for her grief and bitter reproaches. Vladimir actually serves as a self-conscious marker for what is promised but never truly manifested in this melodrama about Russia. For all of melodrama's spectacular features as a genre, *Fedora* is a play without a visible center, much less a Russian center. Or, perhaps more accurately, *Fedora* stages the fearful *idea,* not the reality, of a threat to an already indeterminate national integrity (whose?).

It is true that, through Vladimir, the evil General Yariskin's reach extends throughout the work, ultimately responsible for the deaths of Fedora and Loris's brother.[30] Still, the play contemplates Yariskin's machinations from the comfortable distance of its European vantage point. As far as Sardou's play is concerned, Russianness is a purely conventional matter, because Russia has long since joined the melodramatic league of nations. Fedora's suicide takes on an almost sacramental quality when she imbibes the poison from the Byzantine cross in a cup of Russian tea.

The melodramatic inspiration for these four western stage works derives from the internal divisions within imperial Russia. Pixérécourt and Scribe evoke nations with western orientations that were subsumed into the nineteenth-century Russian empire: Poland, Finland, the Baltics. In *The Exile's Daughter* and *The North Star,* non-Russian subjects traverse Russian national and cultural territory, and are honored by the Russian monarch. In *Vera, or, The Nihilist* and *Fédora,* the result is more ambiguous. These two melodramas end in a stalemate, whereby the heroine kills herself rather than serve either nihilist radicals or cynical government reactionaries. In taking their own lives, both heroines seem to choose the middle, western way, to point hopefully to a path between the two barbaric "Russian" alternatives. The two heroines' suicides, largely the product of overplotted misunderstandings, emphasize their identification with a middle, western aesthetic mode such as melodrama, associated with commerce, capitalism, and hybrid forms. Melodramatized Russias, in the person of their female protagonists, are cultural mixtures, unable to lay claim to either high national tragedy or authentically to low national folk forms. Romantic love serves as the engine of these two stage works. The personal is not political, but rather the political is reassuringly personal in such a melodramatized Russia.

In the melodramas by Wilde and Sardou, political "nihilism"—the principle that allows a society to re-create itself through self-negation—resembles melodrama in its overturning of established social and cultural hierarchies. In Russia during the second half of the nineteenth century, nihilism developed out of "Left Hegelianism" and strove for a dialectical development toward social justice through the efforts of powerfully willed individuals who rejected existing authority. The most fanatical Russian nihilists were the anarchists, who saw even their own annihilation as part of the creation of a new world. Although the nihilist wave merged to a great extent with the larger populist movement in the 1870s and 1880s, the term "Russian nihilist" lived on outside of Russia as a popular catchphrase for western writers to refer to various Russian populists, radicals, revolutionaries, anarchists, and terrorists. Although the stage nihilists created by Wilde and Sardou are absurdly theatrical or oddly absent, the nihilist notion does serve, unexpectedly, to remake Russia in the West's image.

The very notion of nihilism, like the vast expanse of Russia staged in these plays, opens up a representational space for evoking the cultural Other, particularly an Other that is gendered female.[31] This is why the melodramas of Pixérécourt, Scribe, Wilde, and Sardou use female protagonists to chart the imagined Russia with their movements and to amplify its meanings with their bodies. This use of the feminine form in itself is not unusual, because national representations often draw on the familiar "trope of the nation as woman," and melodrama has always been associated with the travails of a virtuous heroine.[32] But in the particular cases of Pixérécourt, Scribe, Wilde, and Sardou, the iconic figure of the nineteenth-century Russian female revolutionary superimposes itself on the customary disenfranchised melodramatic female subject given voice by the hyperbolic, gestural language of the genre. More precisely, in the words of Jacky Bratton et al., "Rather than displacing the political by the personal, melodrama produces the body and the interpersonal domain as the sites in which the socio-political stakes its struggles."[33]

The female nihilists of 1860s Russia were fashion guerrillas, rejecting the enslaving frills and charms of conventional femininity. Peter Brooks claims that the "revolutionary moment" (meaning the French Revolution) represents "the origins of what we might call an aesthetics of embodiment, where the most important meanings have to be inscribed on and with the body."[34] The body becomes the "site of signification," and by means of "an active semiotic process" such as melodramatic theater "the body is newly emblematised with meaning."[35] The female revolutionaries of the 1870s and 1880s placed themselves in physically dangerous situations to write vengeance on the bodies of their autocratic oppressors. Some of them participated in the literacy movement and worked as typesetters for the underground press, spreading seditious writing by means of their physical, as well as moral and intellectual, commitment. Others worked in factories and fields.

The trial of Vera Zasulich, after her failed 1878 assassination attempt on the governor-general of St. Petersburg, cast the female revolutionary as a noble, martyred heroine in the eyes of many Russians and resulted in Zasulich's acquittal. But after the March 1881 assassination of Tsar Alexander II, Russian women radicals were put to death publicly. During the 1877 Trial of the Fifty and Vera Figner's 1884 trial, female revolutionaries had the opportunity to explain themselves to the Russian nation with public statements before they were locked away in prison or sent to Siberia. The Russian female revolutionary, armed with her pistol and bomb, must have suggested herself to the West as a promising melodramatic subject.

But western melodramas raise the problem of the female revolutionary only to dismiss her as a threat. In the melodramas of Wilde and Sardou, the female revolutionary uses a dagger and poison to kill *herself*, not to assassinate others. In the melodramas by Pixérécourt and Scribe, the heroine is willingly subsumed into the imperial power structure. Quintessentially melodramatic excess and "special effects" in Wilde and Sardou divert the viewer from the purely personal dramas masked by social and political spectacle. And the revolutions staged by Pixérécourt and Scribe bring Russia into the western fold. All four plays seem in this respect less consistent with the current view of melodrama as "an agent of modernity" than with the old disparaging view of melodrama as a "bourgeois and quietist form," at least as far as Russia is concerned.[36]

The connection between melodrama and revolution is a confused one. Following the French Revolution, according to J. Paul Marcoux, melodrama in the theaters offered a way to "re-establish an hierarchical order," to present "an idealized model of behavior," and to provide "an antidote to the dissolution of society."[37] The notion of melodrama is not incompatible with that of revolution, although the "melodrama of revolution" has been a "minor strain, often passing unnoticed within the vast expanses of conformist plays," as noted by Daniel Gerould.[38] On the other hand, melodrama took on itself the dramatic task of depicting the trials of the unjustly oppressed. During the periods of political freedom in nineteenth-century France, melodramatic stage productions regularly featured rebellious crowds and depraved rulers. America produced self-righteous political melodramas in the form of mid-nineteenth-century "vigilante chronicles," in which the common man takes justice into his own hands and punishes the villainous rich bourgeois.[39] In Soviet Russia of the early 1920s, the cultural establishment recognized melodrama as a useful vehicle for populist propaganda. Soviet melodramas often took the failed Paris Commune of 1871 as their subject, the "first true proletarian revolution" to which the 1917 Bolshevik revolution could be connected.[40]

Like melodrama, nihilism now serves cultural historians as "a central concept in the diagnosis and critique of modern civilization," according to John Goudsblom.[41] Some twentieth-century cultural critics have considered nihilism, much like melodrama, an encroaching aesthetic and social disease that bequeathed itself to the twentieth century in new pernicious forms: terrorism with modern weaponry, soap operas, and made-for-TV movies. But nihilism and melodrama also share the potential to bring about a revolution in cultural values, valorizing what has been previously underrepresented or invisible. The melodramas discussed here contribute to just such a project. None of Russia's assertions of its western affinities can match the revolutionary claims to likeness made by the melodramatized western representations of Pixérécourt, Scribe, Wilde, and Sardou.

Melodrama is simultaneously a progressive and conservative artistic mode, turning the world upside down while ensuring that nothing changes, serving the stage that mounts it. In this way, the melodramas of Pixérécourt, Scribe, Wilde, and Sardou bring about revolutions to draw an imagined Russia generically closer to the West.

## Notes

1 The entry on "melodrama" in the 1967 *Kratkaia literaturnaia entsiklopediia* (Short literary encyclopedia) invokes prominent western figures such as Rousseau, Monvel, Pixérécourt, Ducange, Dumas, and Hugo, but notes only briefly that during the 1820s to 1840s, Russian dramatists Rafael Zotov and Nikolai Polevoi produced a number of didactic, politically conservative melodramas. Polevoi's melodramatic affiliation refers

to his early sympathies for the "third estate" (in the Russian cultural context, this term refers to the merchantry) and his fondness for bathetic effects in historical drama. Zotov was one of the most prolific translators of western theatrical pieces from French, German, and Italian for the St. Petersburg Imperial Theater Directorate, including French melodramas of the 1820s such as Ducange's hugely popular *Thirty Years, or, The Life of a Gambler.* Zotov also composed his own comedies, vaudevilles, and melodramas, whose texts and titles are rarely invoked in biographical accounts and histories of the Russian theater. During the later half of the nineteenth century, melodrama occupied a place "at the far periphery of the literary process" (*Kratkaia literaturnaia entsiklopediia,* 754) in the plays of little-known writers Viktor D'iachenko and Pyotr Nevezhin. Dramatic works acknowledged as melodramatic rarely receive even a cursory mention in Russian literary history.

2 For a more nuanced view of Russian audiences and reception for three particularly influential melodramas from the early nineteenth century, see Richard Stites's essay in this volume, "The Misanthrope, the Orphan, and the Magpie."

3 Laura García-Moreno and Peter C. Pfeiffer, eds., *Text and Nation: Cross-Disciplinary Essays on Cultural and National Identities* (Columbia, S.C.: Camden House, 1996), vii.

4 Homi K. Bhabha, ed., *Nation and Narration* (New York: Routledge, 1990), 4.

5 J. H. Amherst, *Napoleon Bonaparte's Invasion of Russia, or, The Conflagration of Moscow* (London, 1822), 25.

6 The conspiracy play (for example, *Julius Caesar* and *Richard III*) was a standard form of historical drama, because "conspiracies provide a kind of metaphor for the dramatic action within the historical process" (Herbert Lindenberger, *Historical Drama,* 31). Tyrant and martyr plays also represent major subcategories of western historical drama from the Renaissance and neoclassical traditions.

7 Judith Butler, *Excitable Speech: A Politics of the Performative* (New York: Routledge, 1997), 16.

8 Susan Layton, *Russian Literature and Empire: Conquest of the Caucasus from Pushkin to Tolstoy* (Cambridge: Cambridge University Press, 1994), 8.

9 Edward W. Said, *Culture and Imperialism* (New York: Knopf, 1993), 58.

10 Ibid., 63.

11 Larry Wolff, *Inventing Eastern Europe: The Map of Civilization on the Mind of the Enlightenment* (Stanford: Stanford University Press, 1994), 4.

12 Peter Brooks, *The Melodramatic Imagination: Balzac, Henry James, Melo-*

*drama, and the Mode of Excess* (New Haven: Yale University Press, 1976), 24–28.

13 Guilbert de Pixérécourt, *La fille de l'exilé, ou Huit mois en deux heures* (Paris, n.p. 1819), 14.

14 Ibid., 34.

15 Ibid., 61.

16 Ibid., 96.

17 Madame Cottin's novel *Élisabeth* makes it clear that the new tsar is Alexander I and the coronation is taking place in March 1801. Elisabeth's father Potoski describes his crime as defending his native Poland against the dominion of Russia and plotting to free his countrymen. He would have been imprisoned by Catherine II in this case.

18 For a treatment of silenced and overwritten female characters in the Russian literary tradition, see the chapter "Misogyny and the Power of Silence" in Barbara Heldt, *Terrible Perfection: Women and Russian Literature* (Bloomington: Indiana University Press, 1987).

19 In 1855, Scribe composed a play titled *La czarine,* also historically based on the relationship between Peter the Great and Catherine I. *La czarine,* unlike *L'étoile du nord* presents its heroine as an adulteress involved with Menshikov, but not as a schemer or a spy.

20 Eugène Scribe, *L'étoile du nord* (Paris, 1854), 18.

21 Peter Brooks, "Melodrama, Body, Revolution," in *Melodrama: Stage, Picture, Screen,* ed. Jacky Bratton, Jim Cook, and Christine Gledhill (London: British Film Institute, 1994), 19.

22 Frances Miriam Reed, "Introduction" in Oscar Wilde, *Vera, or, The Nihilist* (Lewiston: Edwin Mellen Press, 1989), xxxi.

23 Wilde, *Vera, or, The Nihilist,* 12.

24 The play's topography initially specified Moscow, while actually describing St. Petersburg (the Winter Palace, St. Isaac's Square, the tower of St. Nicholas).

25 Wilde, *Vera, or The Nihilist,* 23. (Hereafter, citations appear in the text in parentheses.)

26 Reed, "Introduction," xlii.

27 M. Wilson Disher, *Melodrama: Plots That Thrilled* (New York: Macmillan, 1954), 56.

28 For a discussion of the professional lives of actresses Lidia Iavorskaia ("Little Bernhardt") and Vera Kommissarzhevskaia ("Russian Duse"), see Catherine A. Schuler, *Women in Russian Theatre: The Actress in the Silver Age* (New York: Routledge, 1996).

29 Gaston Sorbets, "*Fédora* au théâtre du Vaudeville," in Victorien Sardou, *Fédora* (Paris: L'Illustration Théatrale, 1908), 33.

30 Sardou's 1887 drama *La tosca,* which served as the basis for Puccini's opera in 1900, stages the connections between drama, opera, and social surveillance. *La tosca* depicts the relationship between an opera singer, the police, and a group of revolutionaries. Puccini's opera links singing and torture, featuring a faked execution within the opera story that turns out to be real—within the frame of the opera story. Tosca's famous aria "Vissi d'arte" (I lived for art, I lived for love) is meant to be sung by an operatic soprano who should be able to say the same about herself.

31 This essay did not treat Russia's own tradition of fictional nihilism—prose works (often novels) by Turgenev, Chernyshevsky, Dostoyevsky, Goncharov, Leskov, Pisemsky, and others.

32 Andrew Parker, Mary Russo, Doris Sommer, and Patricia Yaeger, eds., *Nationalisms and Sexualities* (New York: Routledge, 1992), 6. Such representations include Marianne, the increasingly domesticated symbol of French revolutionary liberty, and other female national symbols such as Germania and Britannia.

33 Bratton et al., *Melodrama,* 1.

34 Brooks, "Melodrama, Body, Revolution," 17.

35 Ibid., 18.

36 Bratton et al., *Melodrama,* 1–7.

37 J. Paul Marcoux, *Guilbert de Pixérécourt: French Melodrama in the Early Nineteenth Century* (New York: Peter Lang, 1992), 7.

38 Daniel Gerould, "Melodrama and Revolution," in Bratton et al., *Melodrama,* 185.

39 David Grimsted, "Vigilante Chronicle: The Politics of Melodrama Brought to Life," in Bratton et al., *Melodrama,* 200.

40 Gerould, "Melodrama and Revolution," in Bratton et al., *Melodrama,* 193.

41 Johan Goudsblom, *Nihilism and Culture* (Oxford: Basil Blackwell, 1980), ix.

*Beth Holmgren*

# The Importance of Being Unhappy, or, Why She Died

The nightingale trilled, shrilling out individual notes that sounded like some wistful prelude to the rhapsodies of the Angels.

When the sun's fire lit Stefcia's bed with all its radiant power, the heavenly scout rustled its wings and blazed a golden trail as it flew from the room, bearing away the absolutely pure soul of—Stefcia.

The azure messengers carried her off undefiled as their feathers spun above her an enchanting halo of invisible brilliance. And, flying into the blue, to the feet of the Almighty, the entire angelic choir and the girl's clear new soul sang out a religious trumpet call—*Salve Regina.*
—Helena Mniszek, *The Leper*[1]

Farewell! The door has opened slightly, and I'm standing on the threshold. I glance back and I see only you at my side on all the intricate paths. I'm taking your portrait from the desk and kissing your brows, your eyes and lips. You, who gave me so much earthly joy, you, who have loved me so selflessly, most noble of people, remember me in your faithful heart! I know that it won't beat again for another love. I know that you won't have long to roam alone in the twilight. And the night that will also finally bring peace to you, exhausted by love, is near.

One final request: bury me beside Yan—beside the beloved bench on which you and I sat that radiant morning when my heart first

> started to beat for you. And while you live, close the house and park, lock them up. Let the paths along which you and I walked to meet joy become overgrown! Let no one's laughter sound within the walls where I cried in your arms, where you loved me. Don't let the empty chatter of strangers disturb my final sleep beside Yan and frighten off the radiant shade of our past happiness.—Anastasia Verbitskaia, *The Keys to Happiness*[2]

Thus exit the heroines of two of the biggest blockbusters in the Slavic world. In *The Leper,* a Polish novel penned by Helena Mniszek in 1909, the pure and lovely Stefcia Rudecka dies on her wedding day of an attack of brain fever provoked, literally, by poison-pen letters ostracizing her as a "leper." The anonymous letter writers thereby succeed in preventing the misalliance of Stefcia, a child of the homey middle gentry, with the scion of a great magnate family, Lord Waldemar Michorowski. *The Keys to Happiness* (1908–1913), the serialized Russian bestseller by Anastasia Verbitskaia, characteristically allows its heroine, Mania Eltsova, the last word before she commits suicide and follows her lover into death. Throughout the fourteen-hundred-page novel Mania has been discovering the titled keys to happiness, achieving creative and professional fulfillment as an Isadora Duncanesque dancer and freely pursuing her sexual desires with a series of lovers, including the Jewish radical tycoon Mark Steinbach, and the reactionary, anti-Semitic Russian nobleman Nikolai Nelidov. But her unhappy love for Nelidov ultimately dooms her to a slavish "femininity" and joint annihilation, as her last testament to Steinbach makes plain.

Why did these popular heroines die? Or, rather, what might it mean that they had to? Elsewhere I have analyzed both texts as variations on the popular romance—a subgenre evolved in the West that privileges the presumed virtues and desires of middle-class women.[3] Specifically, the popular romance scripted a successful misalliance: the middle-class heroine's tempestuous courtship by and eventual marriage to a wealthy aristocrat.[4] My typology necessarily stopped short before the difference of these novels' unhappy endings. Death and unhappiness have no business at the close of a popular romance. The romance's focalizing heroine, always an empathetic model for readers, is to live and love on very well. Yet the promising, sensitive heroines of *The Keys* and *The*

*Leper* ultimately give the reader the slip, passing abruptly from model to monument, eliciting first empathy and then grief. In this essay I want to explore what melodrama does in these texts, for I think it is precisely the interaction of melodrama with the romance that rendered these heroines so compelling and so significant for their fin de siècle readers. The admixture of melodrama at once elevates the popular heroine and connects her meaningfully with a changing society conflicted about gender and class identity.

This interaction between two popular artistic forms also must be read in relation to "serious" fin de siècle Russian and Polish culture, because both novels, like many other "popular" works of their day, negotiated between the "serious" and the "popular," between what we would term highbrow and middle- to lowbrow culture, in their address and message. In fact, the absence of a clearly designated middlebrow product and audience in late tsarist Russia and its subject territory of the kingdom of Poland exacerbated the tension and increased the cross-fertilization between "serious" and "popular" art forms.[5] Urbanization, industrialization, improved education, and mass-production technology had shaken fixed class boundaries in these late-nineteenth-century societies, increasing literacy, facilitating the entrance of most classes into the professions, developing a mass-circulation press and new consumer markets, and encouraging a new consumer awareness.[6] During this period, the Russian and Polish intelligentsia, with their deep commitment to social service and "serious" culture, came to exercise a more attractive than controlling influence on the publishing market, because the growing and disparate educated "middles" in these societies still aspired to intelligentsia prestige even as they pursued more individualized professional goals and embraced the material blandishments of the market. Their resistance to a bourgeois identity, as writers and readers, prevented the development of a western-style bourgeois culture, at least in name. It fell to the writers to devise a satisfactory nonmiddlebrow middle product for this burgeoning audience.[7]

Both Helena Mniszek (1878–1943) and Anastasia Verbitskaia (1861–1928) stepped boldly into the breach. Both quickly realized that their success did not depend on a qualifying education, special contacts, or critical approval—traditional stumbling blocks for women in high culture. Ensconced on her family estate, the aristocratic Mniszek debuted with *The Leper* and capitalized with like successors on its extraordinary popularity. Born into a middle-gentry family, Verbitskaia trained as a singer, but eventually forsook music teaching (and other less-desirable jobs) for full-time writing in the 1890s. Her works, largely focused on women's creative, social, and sexual liberation, garnered her enormous popularity and the financial largesse to launch her own publishing firm. To the great consternation of highbrow critics, who had dismissed their writings as derivative and formulaic, both Verbitskaia and Mniszek could and did flourish as bestselling authors—more specifically, as women writers of women's novels. Once they had proven their success and secured a clientele with their first bestsellers, both Mniszek and Verbitskaia continued to churn out large novels, demonstrating the ability and tendency, if not the explicit intent, to serialize after the fashion of other twentieth-century commercial artists.

Yet, facing the cultural no-man's-land of the middle, Verbitskaia and Mniszek aspired to the status of the "serious" writer and attempted the moral and spiritual effects of such a position in their respective societies. Verbitskaia's recognition by and self-maintained association with the leftist darling Maxsim Gorky (1868–1936) and his *Znanie* (knowledge) band of critical realists strongly indicated her self-conception as a "serious," even activist, author.[8] Her "new woman" heroine, most fully realized in *Keys,* combines socialist sympathies with a singular feminist campaign for professional fulfillment and sexual freedom. As if to double guarantee Verbitskaia's high-culture pedigree, *Keys* boasts a modernist orientation as well, manifested in Mania's insistence on self-expression, devotion to her esoteric Dionysian art, and disdain for the demands and capacities of her affluent audience. *The Keys* contributed at great length to the politics versus art debate that absorbed educated Russian society in the decade separating the revolutions of 1905 and 1917.[9]

Mniszek drew from a similarly conscience-stricken poetics—the sharply observant, problem-solving realism of Polish positivism—and she too sought endorsement from one of its founding fathers, the novelist Aleksander Głowacki, who wrote under the pseudonym Bolesław Prus (1845–1912).[10] Positivism, born out of the ashes of the failed 1863 uprising against the tsarist authorities, banished romantic nationalism for the pragmatic goals of general education and local economic development. Positivist heroes typically were either efficient professionals who both made money and did good or dispossessed aristocrats who had learned their political and economic lessons and were rebuilding Poland as an apolitical economic power.[11] Mniszek's *The Leper* self-righteously seconded the positivist goals of morally rejuvenating and successfully professionalizing a recalcitrant Polish aristocracy.

### Melodrama and the Heroine

Coupled with this "serious" orientation, however, was the potent blend of popular romance and melodrama that was the real force behind sales of *The Keys* and *The Leper.* The psychological and consumer appeal of the romance has been well documented on late-twentieth-century examples. Although we lack similar documentation on fin de siècle readers, we can use the twentieth-century analysis to identify similar affective features in the works of Verbitskaia and Mniszek.[12] Like their twentieth-century cousins, these novels envision the heroine's emotional and sexual fulfillment through a liaison with a providing hero (or heroes), her special social distinction as the true beloved of a seemingly superior man, and her initiation into a refining materialism.[13] *Keys* and *The Leper* were especially equipped to allure audiences of fledgling consumers: the popular romance's heroinic plotline showcased incessant costume changes, sumptuous dinners, opulent settings, and maybe a European tour or a tennis match.[14] Yet in both novels melodrama periodically disrupts and eventually defeats the romance heroine's delectable progress. The class provenance of the melodrama is more elusive or perhaps elastic than that of the popular romance, precisely because of its conflicts and reversals.

Moreover, its form is not as defined as that of the romance, although Christine Gledhill asserts that its characteristic plot "turns on an initial, often deliberately engineered misrecognition of a central protagonist," whose requisite victimization ultimately resolves in "public recognition of where guilt and innocence really lie."[15] But melodramatic effects are quite distinct in Mania's stormy encounters with love, sex, and art and in Stefcia's sexually disturbing and socially provocative relationship with Michorowski: the reliance on stylistic excess (visual, gestural, emotional), the venting of scandal scenes and character outbursts, the dramatic reversals in character mood and plot, and the juxtaposition of extremely polarized good and evil—what Peter Brooks interprets as the manifestation of a "moral occult" in a desacralized age.[16] Above all, melodrama in these texts delivers the surprise knockout of "stark ethical conflict" to the romance's comfortable, happy end—the heroine's final conflict and transcendent death.

But what melodrama denies the romance heroine in terms of material and domestic reward, it amply returns in socially approved charismatic power. Melodramatizing Stefcia and Mania, Mniszek and Verbitskaia tapped into a theatrical tradition that had proved wonderfully fortuitous for women as subjects and actors. The melodrama performed on stage or in real life afforded the female artiste a most positive and affective public role, especially on the background of fin de siècle theater. Throughout the nineteenth century the stage had attracted Russian and Polish women with at least the illusion of a public profession and financial independence. Despite women's gradual admission into other professions, the attraction to the stage had intensified by the century's end, as actresses gained social prestige, and were imitated as fashion plates and heeded as media personalities.

Yet this did not mean that the actress was at last dissociated from the prostitute.[17] Such decontamination demanded a specific repertoire and the cultivation of a specific public reputation. The melodramatic heroine appealed to actresses and audiences alike as an accessible artistic "disinfectant," a role redolent of religious drama and experience in its agonies, ecstasies, and clear moralizing.[18] One characteristic example is the remarkable Russian actress Liubov Nikulina-Kositskaia, who rose up from serfdom to inspire and star in Alexander Ostrovsky's dramas. She first encountered the stage through melodrama (specifically in *The Red Veil* [1840s] and *Maiko* [1841]) and she discovered in it a sanctifying passion, an emotional intensity that matched her own religious-ecstatic temperament:

> The play ended and we went home. I was sick at heart and spent two days in bed. What musings, what desires, what hopes thronged my head! Fever and chills alternated by the minute, ravings were torn from my lips—how I suffered! But I was no longer living that life, I had already passed entirely onto the stage and saw myself playing Maiko. Slowly I came to my senses with the conclusion that the theater was my life, but my mother's words appeared before me like a living icon: "The theater is a sin." So I decided that even if you, theater, were a sin, I would be yours and got out of bed as if nothing had happened.[19]

The "sin" conventionally ascribed to the theater was expiated by just such performances.

Born into a theatrical matriarchy a half century later, Verbitskaia insisted even more vehemently on the sanctioning power of melodrama. Her memoir sketches of her grandmother and mother positively embrace melodramatic temperament and behavior as *family values.* Her grandmother, the professional, earns glowing reviews for her formal performance: "She *lived* on stage: she suffered and deceived, she blushed and paled, she wept hot tears, she made the whole theater weep, she could strike terror into the audience with a single movement of an eyebrow, a single flutter of her lashes, a burning glance, a single motion of her hand."[20] Verbitskaia enthuses even more over her mother's melodramatic personality, "that complicated soul who cannot be judged by ordinary standards" and who "insisted that we 'display' our feelings and, somewhat strangely, valued the form more than the substance."[21] An amateur actress, this beautiful, passionate, tyrannical, extravagant, artistic mother serves, not at all coincidentally, as the first reader of Verbitskaia's books and as one of her recurring heroinic types.

Russian theatergoers thoroughly approved of this sort of melodramatic performance, provided that the actress remained sexually discreet. In her study of the Russian actress in the Silver Age, Catherine Schuler discerns the actress's leading role in testing the public's notions of proper womanhood, or *zhenstvennost':* "In a culture that still demanded silence, obedience, and invisibility from its women, actresses became highly visible representatives of, and concrete points of reference for both the preservation of old, and the construction of new models of '*zhenstvennost'.*' "[22] The Russians' contrasting responses to two touring western stars—Sarah Bernhardt and Eleonora Duse—prefigured their moral judgment of native talent. The outrageous Bernhardt provoked consternation on account of her self-promotion and sexual depravity, whereas the angst-filled Duse earned rave reviews for her modesty, "devotion to her man," and "immense capacity for suffering."[23] Like Duse, a number of Russian actresses—Maria Ermolova, Polina Strepetova, and Vera Komissarzhevskaia—achieved an approved *zhenstvennost'* in spectators' eyes by excelling in the part of transcendent victim, the signal role of the melodramatic heroine. All three actresses won audience love through their projection of intense suffering and self-sacrifice in varying roles—Ermolova through historical figures, Strepetova through peasant and merchant women, and Komissarzhevskaia through ultrasensitive, educated ingenues.[24]

Polish actresses gained a similar, if not greater, public presence through the melodrama, because under the conditions of nineteenth-century partitioned Poland, when most expressions of nationalism were severely censored by the occupying empires, theatrical performance itself allowed actresses the coded role of public patriot, a role generally charged with high drama and tragic expectation. The legendary Polish actress Helena Modrzejewska (Modjeska) recalls an early infatuation with the melodramatic in her memoirs: her first assay at playwriting prescribed that the sweetheart of a man fatally wounded on a secret patriotic mission deliver "a desperate speech and a convulsive sob over the dead lover's body."[25] She subsequently commemorates the strong emotions aroused by "Polish historical plays," particularly a melodrama performed during the 1863 uprising when theaters were "rightly" kept open to give the rebels "a few moments' pleasure before they went to sacrifice their young lives for their country":

> The play was a Polish melodrama, with national costumes and songs. In the last act almost every actor in the play had to sing a "couplet" suited to the occasion, the words of which were pencilled in a hurry in the dressing-rooms before the play. . . . They were words of farewell and good wishes, or appeals full of patriotic meaning, spurring the young men to brave deeds. The youthful volunteers cheered at every verse; the actors sung, choking with tears, and there was such a bond of sympathy between the audience and the stage that were it not for the footlights, they would have all joined in one embrace.[26]

In the best case, the melodramatic heroine in partitioned Poland reasserted this crucial "bond of sympathy" and articulated the nation, conveying through character emotion what contemporary Krakow theater director Stanisław Kozmian distinguished as "the most human element, what most separates man from animal—love of one's country."[27] At the same time, the Polish heroine, like her Russian counterpart, could only exercise her patriotic power through proper behavior. Specifically, she had to abide by a socially approved gender identity that safeguarded against the "aberrant" effects of Poland's conspiratorial and insurrectionary nationalism. As exemplified in the historical figure of Emilia Plater, a gentry woman who joined the troops revolting against the tsarist occupiers in 1831, Polish women actively and visibly fomented political revolt for the nation's sake. Analyzing the "daughters of Plater" scripted for the Polish stage, Halina Filipowicz traces how these heroines are proofed against Plater's transgressive sexuality (her cross-dressing and combat experience) and diverted into the more "feminine" role models of teacher or philanthropist.[28] The 1893 melodrama *A Heroine of the Insurrection of 1863* illustrates this tempering process, motivating the Plater-like heroine to join the insurrection in order to escape a rapist, keeping her in female dress, and finally reinventing her "as a Positivist heroine who . . . translates heroic virtue into civic responsibility."[29] The heroine is granted the cultural spotlight on condition of her conventional femininity.

This mixed legacy of the melodramatic stage heroine was passed on to the female protagonists of *The Leper* and *Keys,* although its degree of sexual censorship greatly differed. In both stories melodramatic effects serve, on the one hand, to give the heroine symbolic depth and empathetic resonance and, on the other, to subject her sexuality to a discipline culminating in an inexorable and transcendent death penalty. Although she is hailed and loved as "life itself," Mania Eltsova in *Keys* enters life in her mother's abusive care and under the evil star of her mother's hereditary madness. These handicaps do not render Mania a permanent victim, but they underlie her periodically self-destructive behavior and rear up as obstacles against the progress of her romance, as when Nelidov decides to vet her family for "degeneracy" before he proposes. Melodrama mainly attends Mania's sexual exploits. Schooled by her short-lived mentor and first love, Prince Yan Sitsky, Mania struggles against, in the book's terms, an enslaving maternal femininity in order to pursue her desire, to express her sexuality with the freedom socially reserved for men. "If you kiss me in the morning, and in the evening your desire drives you into another's arms, heed your desire!" (34) Yan preaches, and Mania accordingly practices, giving herself freely to Steinbach, Nelidov, and the modernist poet-playwright Harold.

But sexual freedom does not come easily to Mania, and it is striking that her difficulties stem less from social censure—what we might expect in a rebel's story—than from her suffering soul. Each ending of a passionate affair, actual or apparent, results in dramatic depression. Even her first innocent infatuation with the painted image of an angel prompts ostentatious acts of self-destruction—self-starvation and exposure to the cold. Likewise, Mania's soul is "frozen over" when Steinbach absents himself too long after their first night of lovemaking. Her most "enlightened" romp with Harold, an affair she undertakes to stoke her creative fires, eventually subsides into scenes of a frozen, depleted Mania anticipating the end with the faithful Steinbach at her side, awaiting the night that "will once more avidly embrace me and suffocate me" (245). Her separations with Nelidov—the one man who elicits her maternal femininity and, not incidentally, fathers her child—drive her to suicide, an act attempted at the close of book 2 and repeated with terrible success at the novel's end.

These seemingly involuntary self-punishments counterbalance Mania's forthright displays of sexual desire. In spite of the novel's undeniable feminism, it appears that the heroine pays for each act of indulgence with an approximation of dying. One scholar of the melodrama asserts the general tendency of nineteenth-century bourgeois melodramatists to "make an example of the heroine," to enforce, on her body, the lessons of "fidelity and submission to the male."[30] In *Keys,* Mania's psyche, rather than her lovers, metes out the discipline, and her depression underscores the punitive, enervating aspects of a conventional femininity. In Mania's melodrama, the villainy has been relocated: the heroine suffers *from* womanhood.

Nonetheless, Mania's suffering, like that of a Ermolova or a Komissarzhevskaia, makes riveting theater. Her episodes of depression imprint the most profound and sympathetic portraits of the heroine, exposing her to cosmic forces and depicting her as victim in extremis, a moving spectacle of tormented life played out before the inevitable audience of adoring friends. Mania excels and revels in such chamber performances. Once she renounces Harold, she immediately summons Steinbach to be present at the dramatic aftermath. And once she truly decides to end her life, she typically pauses to sit down and pen her final soliloquy, again to Steinbach, in which she reiterates her position in the tragic spotlight—falling from the heights, standing at the threshold of death, buried in an exclusive park-shrine. Occupying center stage, she declaims her final testament to teach her daughter, build her theater, keep her memory:

> Death has swung open the prison gates for me and the breath of infinity is already blowing in my face, and my eyes have a premonition of eternal light. But I wish to shout to everyone who tomorrow will

> see the earth's sun, the sky high above, and the diamond drops of dew: Love life! Appreciate life! Bless it for both good and evil, both happiness and suffering, both day and night, and for the peace that awaits us—the tired—the peace that will never deceive us. (289)

Exit. Curtain. Epilogue.

Stefcia's story unfolds along much more traditional lines. The sexual turbulence she weathers with an initially rapacious and eventually ardent Michorowski does not much exceed that of the typical romance heroine's experience. There is even the obligatory near-seduction scene in the conservatory, where Michorowski draws Stefcia to him, nostrils flared and eyes "alight with a dark fire," and the heroine flutters away "like a bird" in the nick of time (v. 1, 360–61).

Yet Stefcia's virtue is never seriously threatened, and her conventional femininity never in question or in doubt. This heroine is far more shaken by the prospect of assuming her place in Poland's first family. What is important to Stefcia's "theatrics" is the endurance of her beauty, its constantly tested proof of her worthiness and purity. Lavishly detailed appearances are everything in this novel, for its class-conscious, fashion-conscious narrator thus passes judgment on the characters' value. A typical passage shows the heroine scoring "aristocratic" high marks: "The ladies and young people stared mainly at Stefcia, making various comments. The men scrutinized her beauty, and everyone had to admit that she was lovely, very refined, and utterly royal (*pałacowa*)" (v. 1, 221).

Untouched by sex, Stefcia does not undergo Mania's psycho-physiological metamorphoses. In the socially conservative terms of *The Leper,* Stefcia's victimization must come from the outside and her melodramatic triumph obtains in her unchanging image, which combines both fashionable refinement with heavenly virtue, the proper class with the proper religion. Just prior to her fatal attack, Stefcia is serving, characteristically, as fashion plate, unable to resist trying on her magnificent wedding dress and regarding her model-*cum*-angel reflection:

> For a long time she couldn't tear herself away from the mirror. The dress, elegantly, yet modestly designed, draped her with fashionable refinement. The veils enveloped her like white mist, like transparent and windblown clouds. The veil's delicate silken falls created a marvelous, but imperceptible background for her stylish head piled with shining golden hair and her subtly, artfully sculpted features, as if she were one

of the pearls in the morning star at dawn. She stood there—so young, so slender, emanating enchantment, as if she'd just flown down from the clouds, from the rosiness and delicate azure above. Her eyes shone with happiness. (v. 2, 249)

Then, in a sort of duel of true and false mirrors, Stefcia doffs her gown and confronts her "leprous" image in an anonymous poison-pen letter sent to prevent her marriage to Michorowski. Most anxious about her acceptability, Stefcia is instantly struck down by brain fever, literally maddened by social disharmony and deviant hatred. Yet throughout her well-documented suffering, she remains beautiful, inviolate, and appealing. Michorowski's first bedside glimpse of her diseased image is as aesthetically stunning as his visions of the healthy Stefcia: "Her lips were parted somewhat, very crimson, parched by fever, her burning breath came in short, uneven gasps. . . . Her hair, streaming out from under the compress, surrounded her head in a dark gold wreath. . . . The sight of the girl's bared forehead, smooth, pale pink, encircled by wet hair, moved Waldemar. With a feeling of despair, he leaned over and touched her temple with his lips" (v. 2, 260–61). Stefcia thus plays her deathbed scene in tight close-up, transfigured from "heavenly" fashion plate into a compelling icon of suffering, sacrificial beauty. She lies before her audience looking marvelous, occasionally racked by convulsions and whispering mysterious phrases and touching platitudes. Even after death, her lips remain parted and crimson, if now smiling, and her "long lashes cast shadows on the delicate pallor of her face" (v. 2, 272), although her countenance now seems to be at peace. Stefcia's static beauty and the reverence it elicits resonate with Catholic religiosity—the images of both martyred female saint and a perpetually Virgin Mary.[31]

Stefcia's deathbed performance seems designed to enact a religious function: to evoke universal love and idolization. Her death successfully achieves her novel-long quest to win both the approval and the hearts of the aristocracy. To this end, the narrative devotes inordinate attention to the grand parade of Stefcia's mourners. We are privy to the sincere grief, noble gestures, and stately attire of the various "royals" who make the pilgrimage to her funeral and graveside. We witness the capitulations of those who still hesitated to accept her in life, and the vanquishing of her petty-minded persecutors. Stefcia's mightiest opponent, her fiancé's grandmother, impresses all with her attendance as a kind of queen-mother in mourning: "The princess-grandmother entered this maidenly grotto as though she were a funereal banner, evoking a feeling of alarm. The light rustle of her satin intensified the impression of some implacable power" (v. 2, 280). As I have noted elsewhere, Michorowski ultimately and eternally effects Stefcia's inclusion in Poland's first families by hanging her portrait in his family gallery.[32] The truly beautiful, authenticated aristocrat Stefcia is fixed as an absolute, and Michorowski ensures that her icon is perpetually revered.

Both heroines therefore die "a beautiful death," as Mania was explicitly instructed to do by her philosopher-lover Yan. Death essentially enables their greatest star turn, rendering them charismatic power and audience approval.

## Melodrama and the Consumer

Even in the case of the experienced Mania, melodrama serves to ennoble and chasten the romance heroine, to depict the triumph of conviction over worldly compromise, of strong emotions and selfless suffering over blinkered domestic bliss. But a problematic femininity was not melodrama's only pathogen. Verbitskaia and Mniszek also put their heroines to death so as to spare them a problematic enfranchisement, to deflect their role models from a final, wealthy, complacent wifehood to a different kind of renunciation and purification. The melodramatic end effectively disowns the family happiness and creature comforts in place at the close of the western popular romance.

I have discussed how both novels ostentatiously display luxury items and experiences, a frequent reader lure used in the romance in particular and popular fiction in general. This display also schools the novice shopper-heroine in a high art of consumption. It is exceedingly important that Stefcia and Mania, two girls from rather undistinguished middle-gentry stock, learn convincingly, or, better yet, know somehow instinctively how to live like aristocrats. Stefcia impresses the snobbiest of "Waldy's" powerful set with her unerring grace and taste. Mania consistently behaves like a temperamental princess, and positively reveres the exquisite vestiges and gestures of the very rich and noble. Their consumer education is sponsored, respectively, by Michorowski and Steinbach, two highly experienced, indulgent aesthetes and activists. Wary of gold diggers, these rich men recognize true coin in their intendeds, and convey to them their own ambivalence about their enormous wealth. One of Steinbach's first conversations with Mania dwells on the unceasing moral burden of his millions. In good positivist fashion, Michorowski counters the stereotype of aristocratic bon vivant with his achievements as both industrialist and philanthropist. Neither man finds satisfaction in making money and doing business. In fact, it is significant that both heroes come to affluence through inheritance rather than successful entrepreneurship, and both prove to be conscientious, cultivated stewards rather than the robber barons famed and depicted elsewhere in this era.

The heroines accordingly make consumer educational tours with their patron lovers—Stefcia of Michorowski's exemplary estates, pet projects, and exhibits at a national trade fair, and Mania of Steinbach's showcase residences and the major cultural sites of Europe. The men's status and fortune, coupled with the women's sensibility and educability, already place the heroines safely beyond the pale of western-style bourgeoisification. They are preserved from materialist contamination in other ways as well. Stefcia's altruism is secured by her repeated affinity for nature. At the very outset, Mniszek establishes Stefcia's home in the park rather than the palace and cultivates throughout her character's identification with native flora, often against the foil of the imported or man-made. A definitive testimonial comes from Miss Rita, a kindly aristocrat who recognizes Stefcia's superiority to "us hothouse flowers": "She is a luxuriant bloom, full of life, warmed by the sun and not some artificial warmth, she is a charming flower with a delicate and refreshing scent, not like those potted plants stiffly bound to their stakes" (v. 1, 128). Michorowski, also appreciating her likeness, at first courts and then fetes Stefcia with flowers, showering her with blossoms in a much-recalled scene of erotic and funereal symbolism and transforming her room into a garden with his constant shipments (to which Stefcia's family adds their own wildflower bouquets).

To pursue Mniszek's own rambling motif, Stefcia's grace inheres in her naturalness. Her uneasiness, in turn, signals the presence of something ambiguous or downright evil, an alarm set off in response to Michorowski's lust or, especially, his worldly goods and family status symbols. Michorowski's grand estate intermittently oppresses her, for, unlike her foil the Countess Barska, Stefcia entertains no plans for its redecoration once she is married.[33] A visit to the family portrait gallery, with its array of haughty physiognomies, drives her to near hysteria. Presentation of the family jewels only prompts in her a cold foreboding, which, true to the laws of melodrama, does augur tragedy. It becomes very clear, as Stefcia suffers the greedy Barska's escalating slights, that this heroine is incapable of marrying for money or withstanding family disapproval.

Stefcia's dying and death absolutely finalize her embodied judgment. Her fall begins as she dares to costume herself as Michorowski's bride. Once she lies dying, no specialist, however expensive, can save her from the lack of unanimous love, the one thing for which she plaintively begs. Nor can her titled lover "preserve" her, as her family once presumed. Stefcia breathes her last on the glorious morning of her wedding day, as all living, thriving, blossoming, sweet-smelling nature wafts into her open window and a nightingale's song escorts her sunlit soul heavenward. The virginal heroine serenely fuses with a divinely inspired nature; it falls to the manly hero to endure violent physical suffering. Stefcia ultimately is refined into spirit, whereas Michorowski remains trapped, with his wealth and rank, in the tormented flesh.

Mania Eltsova's death also amounts to an act of purification, but not along so direct a trajectory. Mania is not "naturally" averse to man-made riches, and her "new womanhood" requires her attention, albeit grudging, to issues of earning a livelihood. Insofar as she is able, Mania aims for financial self-sufficiency as a caricaturist and a performing artist. In spite of her great love for Nelidov, she firmly rejects his proposal, realizing in a rare moment of lucidity that such a marriage would prohibit both her dreams and her autonomy. When she finally weds the wealthy Steinbach, she does so with her artistic reputation established, her fortune made, her appetites thoroughly indulged, and Steinbach a proven partner and manager rather than a patron.

Mania, the working woman and working *mother*, handily relies on a series of helpmates who unburden her of the dirty details of self-promotion, booking, budgeting, and domestic maintenance. Steinbach advances her the money for her studies and surreptitiously bankrolls her advertising. Her dance teacher, Iza Jimenez, who was forced to take care of her own business, helps with Mania's promotion and public relations. The faithful Frau Kessler, once Mania's teacher in boarding school, voluntarily undertakes the management of Mania's household and the care of Nina, her illegitimate child by Nelidov. Their labors keep inviolate Mania's self-declared identity as the charismatic, passionate, reckless Gypsy, a type incidentally invoked by Russian writers of the period who sought to distinguish their businessfolk from more calculating, soul-shriven western stereotypes.[34] In her self-perception and presentation, Mania cleaves to the social extremes of bohemian and princess valorized by her culture.

The gypsy-princess mix ensures Mania's nonmaterialist identity, constantly displacing extravagance with generosity, high custom with iconoclasm. A similar, if not so iterated, pattern obtains in Mania's habits of consumption. The erudite Steinbach manages to elaborate Mania's innate penchant for select goods and experiences into a form of cultural enlightenment and even spiritual uplift. He not only validates her characteristically modernist interest in material self-expression and the material arts, but he also refines her tourism into a communion with historic masterpieces and departed souls. Mania consumes goods, sights, and people in order to become enraptured, transported. Human beauty, captured in portraits, sculptures, or life, affords her a special point of reflection and embarkation. In a fascinating material-spiritual about-face, Mania first falls in love with Nelidov when she, still a schoolgirl, is spellbound by his likeness in a picture book of legendary portraits. Her first encounter with Nelidov in person, therefore, seems a déjà vu. In short, Mania's consumption illustrates the materialist underpinning of the modernist, and particularly the symbolist, spiritual adventure: money really buys her access to beauty and a mysterious beyond.

The credibility and morality of Mania's quest, however, depend on its successful completion. Repeated once too often, her sure leap from material stimulus to spiritual rapture could become routine and disaffect readers as a self-deluding addiction. By the end of *Keys,* there is a sense that Mania has exhausted all the spiritual satisfactions that money, fame, and talent can provide, and that in casting about for a new cause she toys with the panacea of worker theaters, the inevitable wedding of her art to politics. But this rather lackluster denouement—particularly in the post-1905 climate of political disillusionment—is not to be. I submit that Mania's giant step backward after Nelidov is not only more psychologically compelling, but also a necessary act of renunciation, a final purifying leap into the Beyond. Gazing on Nelidov's beautiful *dead* face, which now "emanate[s] tranquillity and peace," Mania understands that her greatest material enticement is dead as well, that she neither could nor would consume anything more: "Here is my wedding night, about which I always dreamed when I was tired from a whole day's struggle and work. What did I struggle for? What was I aiming for? Of all that I gained, what do I need right now? Peace. Peace and silence" (287). For the umpteenth time in the novel, a beautiful face summons Mania into the hereafter, and this time she pursues it to the point of no return, renouncing delectation for transfiguration. Thus, her indubitable regression to an enslaving femininity also can be said to constitute a redemption of her high living, an escape from a potentially damning materialism.

Why do these women die? I contend that the concluding tragedies of *Keys* and *The Leper* point up crises of gender and class identity in the readers they presume to reflect and succeed in engaging. As beneficiaries of new opportunities and public roles for women, Verbitskaia and Mniszek were aware of the charismatic, if ambiguous, power of the melodramatic heroine, and they created distinctive variants in their own protagonists. In Mania and Stefcia they valorized the importance, both ethical and aesthetic, of women's suffering and sacrifice, but they differed in their evaluation of "proper" feminine behavior. Stefcia's death asserts the divinity of that behavior; Mania's suicide expresses its deadliness. Sensing an audience of socially aspiring readers, Verbitskaia and Mniszek themselves aimed to write "seriously," but also contemplated and advertised the pleasures of material success and social advancement through the features of the popular romance. Yet the two novels ultimately renounce those pleasures and wheel out the equally formulaic, popular genre of the melodrama to repel the romance's juggernaut. The "moral occult" that Brooks locates in the secular melodrama works in both stories as a drastic, dramatic correction of the romance's charming materialism. Addressed to readers striving for economic *and* cultural betterment, these novels thus leave unresolved the painful tension between the two. *Keys* and *The Leper* strongly imply that their heroines had to die in order to remain heroines—and, further, that sympathetic rich heroines in their flawed sociopolitical contexts could only be tragic. In the final analysis, then, both the manner and the cause of death in these novels contribute to the heroine's star power. It would seem that the unhappy ends of the poor little rich girls Stefcia Rudecka and Mania

Eltsova were dictated by their symbolically burdened sexuality, theatrical appeal, and *spiritual* upward mobility.

### Notes

1 Helena Mniszek, *Trędowata,* vols. 1 and 2 (Krakow: Wydawnictwo Literackie, 1972), 271. All quotations are from this edition and subsequent citations appear parenthetically in the text; translations are mine.

2 Anastasia Verbitskaia, *The Keys to Happiness,* edited, abridged, and translated by Beth Holmgren and Helena Goscilo (Bloomington: Indiana University Press, 1999), 289–90. Subsequent citations appear parenthetically in the text.

3 See my "The Birth of the Middlebrow? Russian and Polish Romances," in *Rewriting Capitalism: Literature and the Market in Late Tsarist Russia and the Kingdom of Poland* (Pittsburgh: University of Pittsburgh Press, 1998), 93–114.

4 For summary accounts of the popular romance, see Tania Modleski, *Loving with a Vengeance: Mass-Produced Fantasies for Women* (Hamden, Conn.: Archon Books, 1982); Margaret Ann Jensen, *Love's Sweet Return: The Harlequin Story* (Bowling Green, Ohio: Bowling Green State University Popular Press, 1984); and Janice A. Radway, *Reading the Romance: Women, Patriarchy, and Popular Literature* (Chapel Hill: University of North Carolina Press, 1984).

5 Until Poland was ceded independence in 1918, Mniszek's part of Poland and the bulk of Polish publishing were under the jurisdiction of occupying tsarist authorities.

6 For ample discussion of these changes, see, for example, the articles in Harley D. Balzer, ed., *Russia's Missing Middle Class: The Professions in Russian History* (Armonk, N.Y.: M. E. Sharpe, 1996); Edith W. Clowes, Samuel D. Kassow, and James L. West, eds., *Between Tsar and People: Educated Society and the Quest for Public Identity in Late Imperial Russia* (Princeton: Princeton University Press, 1991); and Stephen P. Frank and Mark D. Steinberg, eds., *Cultures in Flux: Lower-Class Values, Practices, and Resistance in Late Imperial Russia* (Princeton: Princeton University Press, 1994). See also Jeffrey Brooks, *When Russia Learned to Read: Literacy and Popular Literature, 1861–1917* (Princeton: Princeton University Press, 1985); Laura Engelstein, *The Keys to Happiness: Sex and the Search for Modernity in Fin-de-Siècle Russia* (Ithaca: Cornell University Press, 1992); and Louise McReynolds, *The News under Russia's Old Regime: The Development of a Mass-Circulation Press* (Princeton: Princeton University Press, 1991). On the Polish scene, see Janusz Dunin, *Papierowy*

*bandyta. Ksi,a:zka kramarska i brukowa w Polsce* (Łodz, 1974); Zenon Kmiecik et al., *Prasa Polska w latach 1864–1918* (Warsaw: PAN-IBL, 1976); Jacek Kolbuszewski, *Od Pigalle po kresy: Krajobrazy literatury popularnej* (Wrocław: Wydawnictwo Uniwersytetu Wrocławskiego, 1994); Ryszard Kołodziejczyk, *Miasto, mieszczaństwo, burżuazja w Polsce w XIX w.* (Warsaw: PWN, 1979); Janina Kulczycka-Saloni, *Życie literackie Warszawy w latach 1864–1892* (Warsaw: Panstwowy Instytut Wydawniczy, 1970); and Robert E. Blobaum, *Rewolucja: Russian Poland, 1904–1907* (Ithaca: Cornell University Press, 1995).

7 Holmgren, *Rewriting Capitalism,* 95–98.

8 For an overview of Verbitskaia's extremely variable highbrow reception, see Louise McReynolds, "Reading the Russian Romance: What Did *The Keys to Happiness* Unlock?" *Journal of Popular Culture* 31, no. 4 (April 1998): 95–108.

9 See, of course, Laura Engelstein's pioneering analysis of this period in *The Keys to Happiness,* especially 215–53.

10 In his biographical-critical study, *Mniszkowna* (London: Unicorn, 1993), Tomasz Kalita reports on Mniszek's own account of her meeting with Prus (19–23). Apparently Prus's good opinion of the work persuaded Mniszek's father to finance her publishing debut.

11 See Henryk Markiewicz's excellent study of the movement and its literary reflections in *Literatura pozytywizmu* (Warsaw: IBL-PWN, 1986).

12 See Radway, *Reading the Romance;* and Modleski, *Loving with a Vengeance.*

13 Holmgren, *Rewriting Capitalism,* 100.

14 I elaborate this argument of women's fiction as a consumer guide in "Gendering the Icon: Marketing Women Writers in Fin de Siècle Russia," in *Russia, Women, Culture,* ed. Helena Goscilo and Beth Holmgren (Bloomington: Indiana University Press, 1996).

15 Christine Gledhill, "The Melodramatic Field: An Investigation," in *Home Is Where the Heart Is: Studies in Melodrama and the Woman's Film,* ed. Christine Gledhill (London: British Film Institute, 1987), 30.

16 Peter Brooks, *The Melodramatic Imagination: Balzac, Henry James, Melodrama and the Mode of Excess* (New Haven: Yale University Press, 1979).

17 Remarking on the Russian scene, Catherine Schuler observes: "Russian actresses were more constrained than most by their association in the minds of the public with prostitution" (Schuler, *Women in Russian Theatre: The Actress in the Silver Age* [London: Routledge, 1996], 51).

18 I've borrowed this term from Aleksandr Amfiteatrov, who hailed the influence of actress Mariia Ermolova as "a great moral disinfectant" (cited in Schuler, *Women in Russian Theatre,* 86).

19 Liubov Nikulina-Kositskaia, "Notes," trans. Mary F. Zirin, in *Russia Through Women's Eyes,* ed. Toby W. Clyman and Judith Vowles (New Haven: Yale University Press, 1996), 125.

20 Anastasia Verbitskaia, "To My Reader," trans. Judith Vowles, in *Russia Through Women's Eyes,* 339.

21 Ibid., 366.

22 Schuler, *Women in Russian Theatre,* 11.

23 Ibid., 13–15.

24 Ibid., 84–85, 95, 160.

25 Helena Modjeska, *Memories and Impressions of Helena Modjeska: An Autobiography* (New York: Macmillan, 1910), 46.

26 Ibid., 94.

27 Quoted in Tadeusz Sivert, ed., *Teatr polski od 1863 r. do schyłku XIX wieku* (Warsaw: Państwowe Wydawnictwo Naukowe, 1982), 234.

28 Halina Filipowicz, "The Daughters of Emilia Plater," in *Engendering Slavic Literatures,* ed. Pamela Chester and Sibelan Forrester (Bloomington: Indiana University Press, 1996), 34–58.

29 Ibid., 49–50.

30 Leon Metayer, "What the Heroine Taught, 1830–1870," in *Melodrama: The Cultural Emergence of a Genre,* ed. Michael Hays and Anastasia Nikolopoulou (New York: St. Martin's Press, 1996), 235–44.

31 In *The Cult of the Virgin Mary: Psychological Origins* (Princeton: Princeton University Press, 1986), Michael P. Carroll notes that "Mary's *in partu* virginity and her perpetual virginity are more closely associated with Roman Catholicism alone, and are generally rejected by Protestants" (6).

32 Holmgren, *Rewriting Capitalism,* 113.

33 See Mniszek, *Trędowata,* vol. 1, 365, 394.

34 See Holmgren, *Rewriting Capitalism,* 35–36, 197–98.

*Otto Boele*

# Melodrama as Counterliterature?

## Count Amori's Response to Three Scandalous Novels

At the turn of the twentieth century, the commercial publishing industry in Russia experienced an unprecedented boom. Increasing literacy rates, technological improvements in printing, and the abolition of prepublication censorship in 1905 contributed to a rapid growth in the quantity and variety of printed material.[1] One of the immediate consequences of the mass production of cheap popular fiction was the marginalization of "serious" literature, which, for the previous fifty years or so, had functioned largely as a vehicle for the expression of social and political criticism. The growing number of nonintellectuals among Russia's readers introduced an altogether more consumer-oriented attitude toward literature, which directly affected the traditional didactic role of the writer. Although the intelligentsia continued to view their work as a mission of enlightenment and social service, many a newcomer on the literary scene saw literature simply as a way to make a living. In a recent article, Abram Reitblat has drawn attention to a frequently recurring plot in late-nineteenth-century literature featuring an unsuccessful "serious" author whose financial hardship forces him either to withdraw from literature and choose a new career or to give up his integrity and sell himself to the commercial press. The "novel of literary bankruptcy," as Reitblat calls it, not only reflects the growing role of commerce in the literary trade, but, above all, it expresses the anxieties of a traditionally select group, the literary intelligentsia, which became increasingly aware of its declining moral prestige.[2]

Although the commercialization of the publishing industry did alter the social standing of the profession, it would be wrong to assume that it made the author's role as a teacher and critic of social evils completely obsolete. The enlightening and potentially subversive function of literature still appealed to (neo)realist writers, such as Maxsim Gorky and Alexander Kuprin, as well as to liberal and left-wing critics in general. More important, however, is that although the intelligentsia now only had a small share in the entire literary production, some of its traditional paradigms were appropriated in the "lower" regions of Russian literature, notably in boulevard fiction. Anastasia Verbitskaia, for example, whose commercial success was symptomatic of the changing literary culture in fin de siècle Russia, took her social obligations as a writer very seriously. Although her novels catered to the needs of a predominantly nonintellectual audience, they were intended to offer more than mere entertainment. As Beth Holmgren argues in her essay in this volume, Verbitskaia's bestseller *The Keys to Happiness* did not only promote a feminist message of professional fulfilllment and sexual freedom, but with its Nietzschean overtones it also laid claim to a modernist orientation.

The nation's increased literacy rates thus affected the course of Russian literature in several ways. As the nonintellectual reader became a more important factor in the literary business, the market share of "serious" literature—highbrow realism, not to mention modernist poetry—dropped dramatically. Yet because increasing numbers of people were becoming equipped to get at least a smattering of "high" culture, middlebrow literature could successfully absorb certain themes from the cultural establishment. Although the advent of modernism entailed the emergence of a new elitist culture, the old cultural hierarchy with its clear divide between the illiterate mass and the intelligentsia gradually disintegrated.

For the purpose of this essay it is important to bear in mind that by the beginning of the twentieth century the traditional call for social engagement and "tendentiousness"—a term that I will tentatively define as the demand for "significant" issues and truthful social descriptions—had a considerable impact on boulevard fiction. The indignation aroused by Mikhail Artsybashev's pseudopornographic novel *Sanin* (1907) shows, as I will demonstrate, that it was written and read in keeping with the tradition of the nineteenth-century "tendentious" novel. Although

Artsybashev and Verbitskaia have always been associated with the vulgarization of high culture, they themselves did not make light of the social and moral responsibilities that were traditionally ascribed to the literary profession.

In the pages following I will examine three works by Count Amori, a man whose literary career seems to epitomize the two tendencies outlined above: the commercialization of the literary text and the increased "tendentiousness" of boulevard fiction. Although it is highly improbable that Count Amori was driven by anything other than the pursuit of money, he posed nonetheless as a "serious" author who had a moral duty toward the public. As he put it himself: "An author's social responsibility is something very serious. One cannot get away with propagating absurd ideas, even if their very absurdity is not always clear to the masses. A great percentage of the readers, the younger ones in particular, is ready to accept blindly the lectures of some literary characters, while the author is morally accountable for the sad result."[3] Even if we doubt the sincerity of these clumsily formulated concerns—and I think we have every reason to do so—the fact that a purely commercial writer could adopt such a pose is highly significant. At the beginning of the twentieth century even pulp fiction could articulate a certain awareness of the national tradition of socially involved literature.

## "I Have Developed My Idea": Taking a Moral Stand against Contemporary Literature

Between 1912 and 1914 Russian literature witnessed a peculiar case of plagiarism. Three works that had caused a stir because of their explicit treatment of sexual issues, Anastasia Verbitskaia's bestseller *The Keys to Happiness,* Alexander Kuprin's grimly realist work *The Pit,* and Mikhail Artsybashev's scandalous novel *Sanin,* were all supplied with hastily and poorly written "sequels."[4]

The author of these sequels, using the pseudonym of Count Amori, was by no means an uneducated man. Under his real name, Ippolit Rapgof, he enjoyed a considerable reputation as a music teacher and critic. He had even coheaded one of St. Petersburg's most prestigious piano courses in the 1880s. Following a disagreement with his brother and business associate in 1888, he embarked on a new career, the course of

Count Amori, pseudonym of Ippolit Rapgof. From *Russkie pisateli 1800–1917: Biografischeskii slovar,* vol. 2 (Moscow: Nauchnoe izdatel'stvo, 1992), 13.

which would be determined mainly by a number of early-twentieth-century technological novelties. Count Amori successfully promoted the gramophone in Russia, worked as an interviewer for the boulevard daily *Peterburgskii listok,* and eventually produced more than twenty scenarios for Russia's budding film industry.[5]

Count Amori's remarkable ability to exploit anything new strongly suggests that his literary career also was sparked by the prospect of making a fast ruble. The bulk of his work appeared during the last decade of the tsarist regime when Russia enjoyed the luxury of an almost free press, and the climate for literary entrepreneurship was more favorable than it had ever been before. A closer look at Amori's work adds to the suspicion that his literary interest was purely commercial. Not unlike the tabloids for which he once worked, Count Amori's writings betray a clear predilection for the scandalous and the sensational, particularly for the alleged moral decline of the educated youth. His rambling and incoherent style, the inconsistent portrayal of his characters, the editions of ten thousand copies or more, and finally the low price of his novels (from five kopecks to a ruble or more), are further indications that he was aiming at an audience of only rudimentary education.[6]

All of this makes it tempting to regard Count Amori's sequels as the ultimate example of his unlimited resourcefulness. And, indeed, the idea that he was a charlatan who merely cashed in on the scandalous success of other authors is commonly accepted.[7] The question arises, however, why Count Amori insisted on writing "sequels" or "alternative endings," and why he added to each of them an introduction or an afterword in which he explicitly attacked the author of the original. This would suggest that these works were not just simple rip-offs by a scribbler who has jumped on the bandwagon, as with partial rewritings or "counterliterature," that is, literary texts that are provoked by and take issue with some single controversial work.[8] As Count Amori states in the preface to *The Finale* (his ending of Kuprin's novel *The Pit*): "I have developed *my* idea, *my* answer to the question put forward by the author and I feel the need to share *my* opinion with the Russian reader."[9]

Count Amori was certainly not the only one to engage in a polemic with authors such as Artsybashev and Verbitskaia by producing alternative endings to their novels. In the course of this essay I will show other examples of counterliterature (plays, fictional diaries) in which the authors tried to debunk what they perceived as the pernicious message of the original. Yet what makes Count Amori's case so intriguing is that he was addressing a different audience than were the authors of the originals. Although there may have been some overlap (especially with Verbitskaia's readers), and the readership of Artsybashev and Kuprin was by no means a socially homogeneous group, a brief look at the originals and their sequels is enough to reveal that their intended readers cannot possibly have enjoyed the same level of education.[10] One can even speculate that Count Amori's audience was not familiar with the original novels, or that, if some of his readers were, they had read them because of the spectacular rumors surrounding them, *not* so much because their social standing obliged them to keep track of the latest in Russian literature.

Count Amori, then, did something quite remarkable. He polemicized with three popular novelists who wrote for a mainly intellectual audience (Verbitskaia excepted) about topics such as the crisis of the revolutionary movement, the woman question, free love, and prostitution. The characters who debated these issues were also mostly intellectuals, or at least representatives of the educated classes: students, teachers, artists, and doctors. Their "shocking" topics notwithstanding, *Sanin* and *The Pit* (again, *The Keys to Happiness* may be somewhat of an exception) thus conformed to the old paradigm in that they were intended for the intelligentsia and were largely *about* the intelligentsia. Count Amori, however, appropriated that discourse for an audience that could hardly have been expected to have attended a university. Whereas he preserved the social setting of the original, the social background of his readers must have been largely different.

This shift from one audience to another entailed a number of consequences that strike me as extremely significant. First, Count Amori's decision to write about "highbrow" themes for semieducated readers had a direct bearing on the choice of genre. By juxtaposing his sequels to the original novels we can trace how a work of Russian realism, with its emphasis on "objectivity" and social criticism, is transformed into a piece of melodrama, which values heightened emotionalism and poetic justice. I will argue that the sequels do not just take a moral stand against the perceived message of the original works, but that they are governed by a completely different "moral logic" that is typical of the melodramatic world view.

The second consequence is that the social discrepancy between the reader and the environment depicted in the sequels directly affected the rhetoric of the narrative. If the original novels were about "us" (the intelligentsia reading about itself), then Count Amori's sequels were explicitly about "them" (the intelligentsia as read by nonintellectuals). Admittedly, this is also the case with Anastasia Verbitskaia's work; *The Keys to Happiness* is set in the contemporary avant-garde movement to which its intended readers had no access. Yet the difference is that Verbitskaia depicted that milieu with gusto, that is, as something remote but desirable, whereas Count Amori described it in a negative, almost xenophobic manner, urging his readers *not* to aspire to the world that they saw portrayed.

In order to place Amori's work in the proper context, let me first discuss the original novels and establish why they were considered so controversial.

### Finishing the Unfinished: The Sinner Repents

At face value it seems obvious why Count Amori decided to exploit the novels in question. Although only *Sanin* had been confiscated on charges of pornography, *The Pit* and *The Keys to Happiness* had also caused quite a sensation. Leo Tolstoy, typically, but also the well-known critic Kornei Chukovsky, conjectured that in writing *The Pit* Kuprin, while pretending to expose the horrors of state-licensed prostitution, had actually derived sexual pleasure from describing particular scenes.[11] Therefore, by selecting infamous sexually charged texts, Count Amori undoubtedly hoped to have ensured himself of a large audience.

Commercial considerations aside, however, there was also a certain kind of logic to Count Amori's creations in that the original novels were either uncompleted, or at least perceived as such by the readers. This was particularly evident in the case of Kuprin who, as was generally known, had great difficulty in finishing *The Pit.* The first installment, published in 1909, ended with the student Likhonin boldly conceiving the idea of saving and educating the prostitute Liuba. Yet the second and the third installments, which showed how this plan ended in failure, appeared nearly five years later (1914–1915). By that time Count Amori had already published his own ending, *The Finale,* for which he had brazenly used Kuprin's statements in the press about the possible denouement of his novel.[12]

Verbitskaia was too prolific an author to suffer from writer's block and keep her readers waiting as long as did Kuprin, but the length of *Keys* and the time span in which it appeared (1908–1913), may well have evoked a sense of "endlessness" in the eyes of those critics who were skeptical of her success (notably again Chukovsky). Whatever the case may be, Verbitskaia's novel was still uncompleted when Count Amori published his conspicuously misogynous ending, *The Conquered,* in 1912.

*Sanin* stands apart from the other two novels in that it had long been completed when Count Amori finally decided to have his say. Serialized in the course of 1907 in the journal *Sovremennyi mir* (The contemporary world), *Sanin* provoked a heated discussion about the future of the revolutionary movement and, in particular, about the sexual morality of the educated youth. Yet the storm subsided somewhat after 1909 and eventually died away completely. The mere fact that Count Amori's sequel was published as late as 1913 already suggests that it was not intended as a serious contribution to the debate on the "moral decline" of the intelligentsia. We know for a fact that Alexander Blok had read *Sanin* and was fascinated by it, but it is very unlikely that nearly seven years later he was interested in *The Return of Sanin.*[13]

Nonetheless, there also seemed to be something "uncompleted" about Artsybashev's *Sanin.* Its open ending, featuring the hero Vladimir Sanin secretly leaving his hometown and jumping off a train, was felt to be highly unsatisfactory, as the "immoral" behavior he had displayed throughout the novel thus remained unpunished. Apart from having triggered two suicides, Sanin had forced the attractive teacher Zinaida Karsavina to have sex with him and he had even repeatedly cast a lustful gaze at his own sister. On top of this bad behavior, Artsybashev had given Sanin ample opportunity to elaborate his ideas on unlimited sexual freedom in seemingly persuasive fashion. It seemed impossible *not* to conclude that the author condoned his hero's conduct and had presented him, a *former* revolutionary, as a role model for the educated youth.[14]

Artsybashev's apparent reluctance to have his hero brought to justice provoked a number of sequels and other forms of counterliterature in which the immorality or inconsistency of Sanin's ideas is finally "exposed." Instead of his usual display of eloquence, we now see him fumbling for words; he jumps off of a train again, but this time he breaks his neck.[15] The extremely productive novelist Alexander Amfiteatrov published a fictional letter by Sanin in which he had him point out a number of "inaccuracies" in the way he and his sister Lida were portrayed and attacked Artsybashev for his notoriously poor writing style.[16] There exist more texts, often anonymous, in which the hero revolts against his author, or in which some Sanin-like character suffers the consequences of a life based on free love.

Obviously, then, there was nothing original about Count Amori's undertaking in itself. Yet whereas most critics speculated on what *could* have happened to Sanin and his philosophy had he been surrounded by slightly less mediocre characters, Count Amori was eager to show what *should* have happened to him in order to satisfy the reader's sense of justice. In other words, instead of suggesting alternative, more realistic plot lines that would reduce Sanin's promethean stature (and simultaneously undercut the premises of his teachings), Count Amori set out to describe the *only* outcome he deemed acceptable from a moral point of view.

This moralistic intent is clearly expressed in the introduction to *The Return of Sanin,* in which the author argued that Artsybashev actually tried to bring about some moral catharsis, but did not quite succeed because of a certain duality in his psyche. On the one hand, Count Amori posits, Artsybashev is a "doctrinarian" (*doktriner*) who, like so many of his contemporaries, is obsessed with sexual issues. He is also, however, a "talented author" whose descriptions of nature are a "delight to every reader."[17] If Sanin's pernicious ideas reflect Artsybashev the "doctrinarian," then the story's peculiar open ending is an ethical correction of those ideas dictated by the author's artistic talent. The reason that Sanin suddenly leaves his hometown is not because he is "bored" with his family and the revolutionaries (although he believes that himself), but because he can no longer face the consequences of his hideous deeds: "During his short stay in his parental house, after a sustained period of absence, Sanin has created such a mess, has ruined so many lives, that having no desire to face the consequences, of course, he flees. There is a lot of truth in this. Sanin turns out to have a conscience after all. He becomes aware of his guilt, although he boasts of putting evil on the pedestal of the ideal."[18] Count Amori suggests here that Sanin cannot persevere in his ruthless hedonism, and he is destined to begin to change toward the end of the novel. Amori goes on to imply that the artist in Artsybashev would have developed this idea if his other half, the doctrinarian, had not prevented him from doing so. Torn between these two poles in him, Artsybashev could only allude to Sanin's spiritual crisis by having him abruptly leave his hometown, and thereby end the story.

Most critics viewed *Sanin* as somehow unfinished, first because of its open ending, and second because it did not tell the "whole" story. What if Sanin had gotten the worst in his scuffle with his sister's lover, the officer Zarudin? What if he had faced more eloquent opponents when defending his "right" to pursue sensual pleasure? Count Amori went even further than these critics and ignored the criterion of verisimilitude, arguing instead that Artsybashev was on the right track but "had not finished his idea" (*ne zakonchil svoei mysli*); hence his bold assertion that his sequel merely "followed the path already outlined by the author."[19]

At this point it is useful to take a closer look at the plot of the sequels, notably that of *The Return of Sanin.* I have chosen to keep the focus mainly on this text because its story is relatively straightforward—at least in comparison with the other two sequels—and can therefore be fruitfully juxtaposed to the original. Later in the discussion I will examine *The Finale* and *The Conquered,* but here scrutiny of *The Return of Sanin* can help us to grasp the moral intent behind Count Amori's writings specifically on the level of the action. Let me start by recalling two of the most controversial elements in Artsybashev's novel from which

Count Amori departs: first, Sanin's fight with the officer Zarudin, who because he is knocked down feels so humiliated that he shoots himself; and second, the overtly incestuous overtones in Sanin's relationship with his sister Lida.

In the beginning of *The Return of Sanin,* the hero still appears to be the self-assured athlete described in the original work. He finds a job at the estate of an aristocratic family where his strength soon attracts the attention of the local girls and, in particular, of Marusia, the daughter of the house. Sanin seduces her, and when she becomes pregnant he flees to Moscow, leaving her behind in despair. Later he will read in the newspaper that his victim has committed suicide.

In Moscow, Sanin is arrested on suspicion of revolutionary activities and sentenced to five years of forced labor in Siberia. To this point Sanin has been able to suppress a nagging feeling of guilt caused by Marusia's suicide, but in exile, with his health rapidly deteriorating, he begins to feel remorse over his terrible crimes. He also comes to understand that his hostility toward Zarudin did not spring from the laudable wish to protect his sister, but from the fact that he was in love with her himself (Sanin dreams about Zarudin being *him*). This becomes clear when Lida arrives in Siberia and starts taking care of her brother. The two are not only "inseparable," but their "relationship displays a tenderness which is rarely seen between siblings." In addition, the narrator stresses that in the eyes of the local population they are a "handsome couple" and their intimacy engenders the "wildest rumors."[20] Although Amori does not give any suggestive descriptions of an incestuous relationship, he goes further than Artsybashev who only hinted at the possibility of incest between Sanin and his sister.

Sanin's happiness with his sister is short-lived, however. Tormented by remorse over her relationship with her brother, Lida retires to a monastery determined to do penance. She confesses her sins in a letter to her mother, and this action produces a dramatic boomerang effect. The mother dies on learning the horrible truth about her children, and the news about her death subsequently kills Lida. So in addition to the two suicides in the original, Sanin is also responsible for the deaths of Marusia and his own mother and sister.

At the end of the story Sanin faces a bitter truth. Glancing through Lida's diary he learns that although she did indulge her carnal passions with him, she never really loved her brother. In her heart she always stayed true to Zarudin. Thus, posthumously rejected as the lover of his own sister, and deprived of any support from family or friends, Sanin has reached the end of his tether. The climax of the scene features Zarudin's ghost appearing to Sanin, who, nearly driven to insanity, prepares to hang himself. At the very last moment, however, the ghost of his mother intervenes, reaching out as if to stop him. Sanin falls on his knees, embraces the Christian faith, and happily returns to the Ukraine.

I have relayed the plot of *The Return of Sanin* in some detail because it shows the basic pattern underlying each of the sequels: haunted by their crimes and sins, the characters in question increasingly feel the need for some form of moral redemption. Although initially they try to expunge the past from their memory, they eventually face the choice either to repent and be spiritually reborn or to persist in their devious ways and pay the price for doing so. Obviously, this plot structure is exploited in full in *The Return of Sanin* because of the Superman-like status of the hero and the outspokenness of his ideas. In *The Finale,* the sequel to *The Pit,* the evildoer turns out to be the police officer Kerbesh, a peripheral character in the original who is rumored to have killed his wife. But although it may vary in significance and in outcome, in each sequel the story of the repenting sinner shines through. Even if he or she is not redeemed, the reader is to find solace in the idea that somehow justice is done and that Good has triumphed over Evil.

### The Melodramatization of the "Tendentious" Novel

Anyone remotely familiar with the reputation of *Sanin* will agree that Count Amori's sequel is far from convincing as a form of counterliterature. We understand that there is some clumsy poetic justice in having Sanin repent and turn into a pious Christian, but the story is often too chaotic to discredit successfully the hero's infamous ideology. Interrupted by completely irrelevant conversations and endless digressions on such topics as the degeneration of the European race or the glory of Russia, *The Return of Sanin* often seems to forget its own claim to be a sequel to an existing novel. Its haphazard character abundantly testifies to the haste with which it must have been written and confirms the purely commerical nature of Count Amori's work.

Yet there is another reason why Count Amori did not, or rather, *could* not, fulfill the expectations aroused in his introduction, a reason far more significant than his desire to extract a profit from other people's work (although the one reason is intertwined with the other). Although claiming to respond to what are essentially "tendentious" novels grounded in the tradition of social and didactic realism, the sequels are certainly not tendentious themselves (at least not in that specific sense). In my view they should be read as melodramatic *adaptations,* because of their specific moral logic and because they seek to entertain, rather than to instruct. At this point a few words on the tendentious novel are necessary to understand how Count Amori appropriated certain highbrow themes for an audience that stood outside the tradition of the intelligentsia.

Formulated by Peter Tkachev in 1873, "tendentiousness" involves the notion that a work of literature must render reality in an objective, almost scientifically exact, manner and, paradoxically, also give voice to the author's own views on that reality. In addition, it should deal with socially important issues and show significant—that is, socially representative—characters. Elaborating on the so-called real criticism of Nikolai Chernyshevsky and Nikolai Dobroliubov, Tkachev believed that the main task of literature was to "explain" contemporary society and, by doing so, function as an agent for social change.[21]

This conception of literature was still dominant among the traditional intelligentsia, of which Kuprin, Artsybashev, and perhaps Verbitskaia considered themselves to be part. *Sanin* and *The Pit* not only dealt with "significant" issues such as prostitution and the crisis of the revolutionary movement, they clearly fulfilled the aesthetic of realism by striving toward truthful social descriptions. *Keys* differed from the other two novels in that it already gravitated toward melodrama with its preference for emotional outbursts and luxurious settings. But, as I argued at the beginning, these elements in her work did not prevent Verbitskaia from taking seriously her social role as a writer. Thus, no matter where we situate the original novels in Russia's literary hierarchy, they all share a conspicuously premodernist belief in the enlightening and didactic function of literature.

The commonly accepted practice to read realist writings as chronicles of contemporary life may help us to understand why *Sanin* created such a scandal. Most critics were distressed precisely because they believed that the novel signaled an alarming tendency in society, and that its hero presented a portrait of the new intellectual who had turned away from the revolution after its failure in 1905. Blessed with an impressive physique and exuding self-confidence, Vladimir Sanin reminded the critics of that other great "New Man" and iconoclast, Evgeny Bazarov, who once had scoffed at the ideals of *his* father's generation, the idealists of the 1840s. Sanin, however, seemed to propagate an even more radical nihilism than Turgenev's protagonist, as he blatantly refused to place himself in the service of the people and expected nothing more from life than the fulfillment of his own "natural desires."[22]

From a diachronic perspective, Sanin could be linked to a whole group of literary misfits, each of whom was believed to mark a specific stage in the ongoing conflict between society and the individual (that is, the westernized intellectual). Sanin not only descended from Bazarov, but, by implication, also from Rudin, the idealist of the 1840s, and the romantic heroes Pechorin and Chatskii. Thus, each historical period produced its own "hero of our time," with Sanin only the latest version of an essentially invariable type.[23]

In his introduction to *The Return of Sanin,* Count Amori did not hesitate to repeat this argument, including the standard listing of Sanin's precursors, and he concluded by saying that "unfortunately every intellectual is a bit like Sanin, and that is a fact."[24] Evidently Count Amori also read Artsybashev's novel as a tendentious work. Yet in an attempt to define Sanin's specific features, he singled out two shortcomings that appear to be of a generally human, rather than social-historical, nature: "unlimited self-conceit" (*bezgranichnoe samomnenie*) and "injustice" (*nespravedlivost'*). Not only did Sanin "think that he was much smarter than everybody else," throughout the novel he applies double standards. He granted himself the privilege of seducing women whenever he pleased, but denied Zarudin the same right to take advantage of his sister. "Hypocrisy," Count Amori diagnosed, "is a fundamental characteristic of contemporary people."[25]

In spite of the references to the modern intellectual and other "heroes of our time," Count Amori emphatically ignored the category of "tendentiousness." Sanin's ideas on free love are not presented as part of a coherent (albeit immoral) worldview, typical of a particular social group in a particular historical situation, but as devices, tricks, and ad hoc strategies with which he seeks to fulfill his own petty desires. Whereas Artsybashev portrayed his hero as the bearer of a "new" morality, Count Amori transforms him into a villain whose entire raison d'être consists in violating all norms, but without revolting against society as such. In spite of Count Amori's assurances to the contrary, Sanin has lost his social typicality, representing nobody but himself.

This is also true of Likhonin, the main character in Kuprin's novel *The Pit,* who in the original work is clearly defined as a representative of the intelligentsia. He not only debates with his fellow students the evils of prostitution, he decides to save a prostitute, Liuba. In doing this he follows the pattern that was expected of a radical intellectual: to marry a fallen woman and to emancipate her through education and decent work.[26] With so many attempts in real life having ended in failure ever since the model for it was introduced by Chernyshevsky in his most celebrated novel, *What Is to Be Done?* (1862), the reader must have been anticipating that Likhonin was not going to succeed. And indeed in the second installment, the social gap between him, an intellectual, and Liuba, an illiterate and slow-witted woman, turns out to be too great. Likhonin loses his patience, finds a cheap excuse to leave Liuba, and thus forces her to resume her old work.

In Count Amori's sequel, on the other hand, Likhonin's social identity is virtually annulled. Still a student, he is surprisingly well-off, taking Liuba to expensive restaurants and buying her fancy clothes. Although his attempts to teach her to read are as unsuccessful as they are in Kuprin's version—a specific detail that seems to lend weight to Kuprin's accusations of plagiarism—the reason that he breaks with Liuba has no bearing on their respective backgrounds. As long as he is able to treat her like a sister and can resist sleeping with her—the ultimate proof that he respects her as a comrade and does not desire her as a woman—his commitment does not really diminish. Yet when he ends up in her bed after all, he is ashamed to admit that he wanted this (and only this!) all along: "Why look for excuses? I wanted her; in every fibre of my being I longed to possess her. And, of course, she gave herself to me."[27]

The differences between *The Pit* and *The Finale* are obvious. In the original Likhonin fails because, like so many before him, he cannot live up to the ideals that he is expected to uphold as a member of the intelligentsia. In other words, the model that inspires him has its origins in a specific ideology of a specific social group. In the sequel the driving force behind Likhonin's plan is his sexual urge, not his adherence to a set of class-bound ideals. Technically speaking Likhonin, just like Sanin, is an intellectual, as the narrator does not fail to point out on several occasions, but, on closer inspection, his actions are dictated by human impulses not confined to one or another class.

This lack of social typicality in the sequels is characteristic of a number of genres in popular fiction, notably the picaresque novel and its modern form, the boulevard novel. Viewed in even more general terms, one can say that it is a definite feature of all melodramatic literature, ranging from modern soap operas to Dostoyevsky's novels.[28] Characters appearing in melodramas do have some social identity, of course (after all, Sanin and Likhonin are explicitly said to belong to the Russian intelligentsia), but the dramatic situations in which they find themselves have a universal significance that goes beyond class distinctions. Critics immediately connected Sanin's hedonistic philosophy of life with his social background, pointing out that he was an intellectual and a former revolutionary. Count Amori repeated this argument in his introduction, as we have seen. Yet Sanin's actions in the sequel are not shown to be rooted in any class-bound ideology, but are governed by pure selfishness.

Sanin's overt villany in the sequel is perhaps the clearest indication that Count Amori is consistently melodramatizing the subject matter of Artsybashev's novel. In keeping with the demand for "poetic justice" typical of melodramatic fiction, *The Return of Sanin* refracts the questions raised in the original through a narrowly moralistic prism.[29] Apart from promoting a straightforward ethical message, it thus presents a highly personalized vision of evil located in the hero rather than in society.[30] Typically, Sanin's "friendly smile" (*laskovaia ulybka*)—his hallmark in the original—has suddenly acquired an unmistakably diabolic character. Observations such as "his smile had something Mephisto-like" and "a nasty smile disfigured his face," clearly establish him as purely evil.[31] Therefore, instead of debunking Sanin's ideology, as the authors of other countertexts attempted to do, Count Amori does away with Sanin himself by having him spiritually reborn in Siberia.

Poetic justice, then, is of vital importance in Count Amori's sequels, especially in *The Return of Sanin*. The evildoer is either punished or repents the sins he or she committed in the original novel. Yet the demand for justice is more than the need for a happy ending, a simple "all's well that ends well." As Peter Brooks has shown, melodramatic morality has a distinctively metaphysical dimension.[32] Ethics is felt not to be a matter of convention or rational decision making (a morality based on a "social contract"), but a sphere of absolute and eternal truths, the "moral occult," which must impose itself on each human being at a certain point in time.[33] This is particularly evident in melodrama's predilection for dreams and similar states of being, a preference that it shares, of course, with the gothic novel.[34] Besides adding to the suspense required to enthrall the reader, nightmares and visitations from beyond function as the ultimate medium through which the moral occult reveals itself. Asleep or delirious, the villain is confronted with his terrible past, which he normally is able to suppress.

Dreams and terrifying visions play a significant role in all of Count Amori's sequels, but in *The Return to Sanin* they are absolutely crucial. Not only do they reveal the "genuine," immoral nature of Sanin's actions, both to himself and to the reader, they also help Lida to return to the straight and narrow after she has committed incest with her brother. Her decision to leave Sanin and to do penance in a monastery immediately follows a dream in which she sees her late father reproachfully pointing to a church and in which she herself appears as a nun. Sanin's nightmares, as we have seen, center mostly on Zarudin, for whose death—in Count Amori's vision—he is directly responsible. In addition to enhancing his sense of guilt, Sanin's dreams about Zarudin also reveal that in many respects the two men are one of a kind. When he approaches Zarudin's coffin and glances over the rim, Sanin discovers *himself* lying in state, while Lida stands by in tears.[35]

Although the dreams set in motion a process of moral purification, it is not until the dead start to visit Sanin that his spiritual resurrection actually takes place. The preposterous horror scene featuring the ghosts of Zarudin and Sanin's mother fighting for his soul marks the final crisis from which Sanin eventually emerges as a new man. In this connection it is interesting to note that *The Return of Sanin* follows the same mythic pattern that stands out in far more distinguished novels such as Dostoyevsky's *Crime and Punishment* or Tolstoy's *Resurrection*. In *The Return of Sanin* the hero's moral regeneration also occurs in Siberia, which appears as the functional equivalent of a temporary death.[36]

All in all, Count Amori's sequels voice an optimism that is typical of melodramatic literature (with the exception of *The Conquered* in which the heroine loses her mind). Sanin repents and becomes a new man. Lida atones for her sins in a manner so convincing that she wins the hearts of all the nuns in the monastery and leaves a great void behind her when she dies. Still more reassuring is Liuba's fate. Although Likhonin experiences a certain "satiety" after having sex with her—which is only natural, Count Amori explains, if a man does not *really* love a woman,[37]—he helps her to set up her own business, a cafeteria, and eventually passes her on to a millionaire (to the complete satisfation of all parties involved). At the same time, the inveterate scoundrels do not escape their well-deserved punishment. Kerbesh, for example, the corrupt police officer in *The Pit,* is finally convicted for the murder of his wife. Thus, the overall impression is one of justice and moral satisfaction.

### Melodrama and the Tabloids: Bashing the Intelligentsia

In the previous two sections I argue that Count Amori turned tendentious novels into relatively simple tales of sin and retribution. This was particularly clear in *The Return of Sanin,* in which the hero is transformed into an almost archetypal rogue, all of whose actions are motivated by his very evilness. In the other sequels, too, the characters appear to be propelled by universal passions rather than by the feelings and ideals that have a bearing on their social identity.

In view of this lack of social typicality it is all the more striking that Count Amori stubbornly kept reminding his readers that most of his characters did actually belong to the intelligentsia. Although they perform very basic, timeless roles, frequently there are explicit and generalizing statements that seek to reinforce their representational significance. A comment such as "every intellectual is a bit like Sanin," for example, clearly suggests that the sequels did not purport to tell everybody's story. On the contrary, although they were intended for nonintellectual readers, they were specifically *about* the intelligentsia. Count Amori's undertaking, I am suggesting here, did not only involve a generic shift from the "sophisticated" tendentious novel to the "not-sophisticated" form of melodrama, it also affected the rhetoric of the story by introducing a particular social antagonism that is absent in the original. Count Amori certainly did not promise his readers "more pornography" (and if there is any in *Sanin,* there is absolutely none in the sequel), but he offered them the possibility of freely indulging their moral outrage and feeling good about it because it was directed at a different social class.

In playing on the moral indignation of his readers, Count Amori resorted to a specific kind of voyeurism that one would normally associate with the tabloids and their willful disrespect for the private. As Joan Neuberger has argued about Russia's thriving boulevard press at the turn of the century: "The boulevard newspapers' reporting of scandalous crimes, outrageous behavior, and the private lives of public figures supplied engrossing reading but also offered readers unforgettable examples of improper behavior, defined the parameters of the acceptable, and reassured readers of their own superiority for never sinking so low."[38] In this way the tabloids performed a double function in that they offered entertainment that at the same time was reassuring and morally uplifting.

This particular combination of voyeurism and indignation is also operative in Count Amori's work. As various scholars have pointed out, the sensationalist discourse of the tabloids incorporated many themes and conventions of melodramatic literature.[39] Just like melodrama proper, tabloid sensationalism deals with basic emotions such as love, hate, jealousy, and greed, and prefers to show them in all their dramatic nakedness.

The similarities between Count Amori's work and the tabloids are not merely typological, however. Count Amori directly borrowed his topic from the contemporary boulevard press: the alleged degeneracy of the intelligentsia and, in particular, of the educated youth. Browsing the widely read daily *Novoe vremia* of 1908, for example, or the local newspapers of provincial towns such as Minsk and Poltava, we can see how one year after the publication of *Sanin* fiction and reality had begun to merge. In spring of that year it was rumored that a nationwide network of secret organizations had emerged in which the educated youth satisfied their "natural desires" by indulging in group sex.[40] Although there is no mention of collective sex in the novel, some sources maintained that these so-called Free Love Leagues were founded by enthusiastic *Sanin* readers who sometimes started their orgies by reading Artsybashev and other "pornographic" authors.

The rapidly expanding popular press played a crucial role in the dissemination of these rumors. Because sexual topics could be treated more openly after the relaxation of the censorship laws in 1905, the press eagerly supplied the public with juicy stories on loose behavior while at the same time condemning that conduct in the strongest possible terms.

Indirectly it also warned the reader against the Free Love Leagues by relaying the personal tragedies that occurred in their midst. League members reportedly wound up pregnant or contracted syphilis, and were left with no choice but to commit suicide. Thus, by taking a moral stand the boulevard press constructed a compelling narrative about young lives being ruined and respectable families falling apart.[41]

Indicative of the hysteria created by these reports is the profusion of plays and other literary texts that repeated that very narrative. Between 1908 and 1912 at least eight plays called *The Free Love League* were submitted to the censor, some of which seem to express a genuine anxiety over the nation's moral decline while others are clearly intended as classical "comedies of errors."[42] Not for the first time in Russian history did the boundaries between reality and fiction become completely blurred. How, then, did Count Amori's sequels fit into all this?

The extraordinary literary output described here shows that toward the end of the decade a potentially melodramatic discourse had emerged that oscillated between fiction and "reality" (as described by the tabloids). That discourse revolved around the supposed immorality of the intelligentsia and their younger colleagues, the educated youth, who allegedly devoted their time to drinking and reading racy fiction. The main difference between the fictional texts and the popular press, however, was the perspective they employed. Whereas the texts tried somehow to understand the devious ways of the educated youth and to familiarize the reader with them (whether that be in a serious and engaging way, or in the lighthearted style of a comedy), the tabloids were conspicuously voyeuristic and eager to accentuate the monstrosity of the practices on which they reported. It is precisely this voyeuristic perspective that Count Amori adopted from the boulevard press, and it is that which sets his work apart from most other contemporary texts that were provoked by the rumors about the intelligentsia's depravity.

In order to understand how this voyeurism functioned in the sequels, we turn to Verbitskaia's bestseller *The Keys to Happiness,* which seems to have irritated Count Amori even more than did *Sanin* or *The Pit.* Set partly in the dazzling world of the St. Petersburg bohemia, *Keys* was more or less intended as a portrait of the "New Woman," a female counterpart to *Sanin.* Just like Artsybashev's hero (whose ideas are even discussed in the novel) the rebellious Mania Eltsova claims the right to pursue the satisfaction of her sexual needs without committing herself to one partner for life. A gifted and innovative dancer, she is also professionally successful, thereby further challenging the traditional paradigm of femininity.

Laura Engelstein has pointed out that few critics acknowledged the emancipatory qualitites of *Keys,* but instead focused on its aesthetic flaws.[43] Kornei Chukovsky, judging from the vantage point of serious literature, especially had nothing but contempt for Verbitskaia's "vulgar" writings, which he saw as a threat to "high" culture. Count Amori, however, aligning himself with the other end of the social spectrum, vigorously attacked the feminist tendencies in Verbitskaia's novel. This in itself is hardly surprising, of course, but the social implications of the attacks are worth noting:

> Certain men and women writers have set out to destroy, or at least, weaken age-old principles, without creating a new morality. They seek to free women from some non-existing "chains of slavery," propagate sexual freedom and recommend women and young ladies to pursue their happiness ignoring existing norms of decency. Referring to the corrupt morals of the men of our intelligentsia, certain men and women writers recommend a similar line of action for the fair sex. Leaving aside that this would lead to debauchery, a deterioration of morals, we cannot close our eyes to the future of our posterity. Under those circumstances sacred values like mother, father, brother, and sister will perish in the Lethe.[44]

The "delusion" of women's liberation, Count Amori is saying, is just another expression of upper-class sexual depravity. It is nothing more than a license for indecent behavior of which, alas, the male part of the intelligentsia had already proven capable. Women's emancipation is not so much an unwholesome idea in itself, but is indicative of a larger and even more disturbing phenomenon: the sexually deranged mentality prevalent among the highest circles, especially the intelligentsia.

Ironically, perhaps, although both Chukovsky and Count Amori viewed Verbitskaia's novels as symptomatic of some social Other, they approached her work from opposite ends of the cultural hierarchy and therefore defined the social Other differently. Chukovsky believed that Verbitskaia appealed to hairdressers and shopkeepers, while in Count Amori's vision her work embodied the value system of the contemporary intellectual.

Вышелъ въ свѣтъ
и продается во всѣхъ книжныхъ магазинахъ
НОВЫЙ СЕНСАЦІОННЫЙ РОМАНЪ
ГРАФА АМОРИ
РАБЫ СТРАСТИ.
90% всей интеллигенціи—рабы страсти. Массовое проникновеніе идеаловъ Санина и Вербицкой, въ семейный строй, знаменательно. Не описанію вертеповъ и „Ямъ“ посвященъ настоящій романъ, а всей вакханаліи, разнузданныхъ нравовъ, прикрываемой внѣшнею благопристойностью.
Цѣна 1 руб.
Складъ изданія: Спб., Вас. Остр., 2ая линія, 3
Товарищество „УЛЕЙ“.

Advertisement for *Slaves of Passion* by Count Amori (1913). The text reads, in part: "Ninety percent of the entire intelligentsia consists of slaves of passion. The massive penetration of Sanin's and Verbitskaia's ideals into family life is a telling sign. The novel is dedicated to the description not of hangouts and 'pits' but of all the bacchanalia and moral dissolution that is veiled by outward decency."

Despite his hostility toward Verbitskaia as a member of the "degenerate" intelligentsia, Count Amori may well have been targeting the same readers as she did. *The Conquered* certainly surpasses *The Keys to Happiness* when it comes to stock phrases, trite characterizations, and other cheap effects, but we may safely assume that most of Count Amori's readers were equipped to handle Verbitskaia as well. The difference, as I stated earlier, resides in the fact that although Verbitskaia tried to bewilder her readers by evoking a world of luxuriously decorated drawing-rooms and journeys abroad, thus giving them a vicarious experience of "high" culture, Count Amori clearly sought to alienate his audience from it. He consciously foregrounded those phenomena that he expected to be beyond his readers. Let me illustrate this point with a few examples from *The Conquered.*

One of the highlights of this sequel describes the heroine attending a soiree to hear a certain Mr. Crook (*Kruk*), speak on "relativism, . . . the latest in English philosophy." As if anticipating that his reader is unfamiliar with the practice of attending lectures on philosophical topics, Count Amori explains: "Now there was a trend of theosophy and philosophy, of lectures and papers, of speeches and debates."[45] This very enumeration, as well as the oddly euphonic pattern supporting it, encourages the reader to lump together different forms of intellectual discourse, as if they come down to one and the same thing. In other words, the reader is urged to decode this list of unfamiliar terms and to lay bare their "true," "meaningless" content.

There are other indices that define this exclusively intellectual environment as frivolous, if not outright immoral. Some of the attendants find fault with Mr. Crook—*nomes est omen?*— for denying the existence of any eternal ethical laws, yet their alternatives are equally suspect: one of Mania's lovers, the decadent poet Harold, reacts with a verbose and hollow appeal for "aestheticism," while the Christian view on "relativism" is unconvincingly expressed by a Catholic priest (by definition an untrustworthy figure for orthodox readers). Thus, among the crème de la crème of Russian society, the true faith is represented only in its corrupted form by the "heretic" Catholic church.

Like the tabloids, Count Amori tended to link the supposedly loose mores of the intelligentsia with political radicalism and "decadent" literature. Instead of regarding them as independent phenomena, he viewed them as being part of an overarching paradigm of moral corruption. A brief look at Harold's biography shows that this paradigm could also acquire distinctly anti-Semitic overtones. Having introduced Harold as a Jew and a phony, Count Amori immediately establishes him as a radical and a hypocrite: "At the zenith of the liberation movement he appeared at meetings, spoke about freedom, and at night, at the expense of the rich Count Koranovskii, he drank champagne with prostitutes [*s kokotkami*], whom he especially liked to tease. . . . Later he tried to join the modernist movement, successfully wrote on civil themes, gained a foothold in red circles and became a trendy writer."[46] This ludicrously overdefined image contains all the elements that occur in the tabloids' reporting of immoral and scandalous behavior during the years 1907–1914: political activism, "modernist" literature, unlimited sexual freedom, a strong inclination toward hedonism, and sometimes the suggestion of a Jewish conspiracy. Characteristically, all these tendencies are not arranged in a chronological-causal order. They are simply listed as random expressions of a more fundamental phenomenon: the degeneracy of the upper class. The liberal and radical critics writing for the sophisticated "thick" journals, by contrast, were convinced that the petty pursuit of personal happiness that they saw embodied in modernist writings had *replaced* the former ideals of social service and altruism. To Count Amori, modernist literature, political radicalism, and sexual depravity were mutually interchangeable.

Anti-Semitism stands out even more conspicuously in *The Finale,* which catered to the popular belief that Jews played a crucial role in prostitution in the capacity of traffickers.[47] Chapter 8 of the sequel tells the story of Zosia, a beautiful girl who is a symbol of innocence and moral purity. Unscrupulously sold by her father to "some Jewish woman" she lives for some time with another "Jewish woman" in Kiev, who eventually hands her over to Madame Therese, or Rivka Shmuil'son, as she is really called.[48] Having passed through all the stages of this exclusively Jewish network, Zosia is finally "prepared" by her employer to enter the world of commercial sex. For her first night she is plied with alcohol and then introduced to a group of seemingly respectable guests, including a writer from St. Petersburg, a few officers, a journalist, and a well-known aristocrat from Kiev—Baron Fon der Goffen.[49] When Zosia prematurely comes out of her alcoholic stupor and panics, the guests suddenly pretend to be appalled at the cruel methods of the house. Although they are regular visitors of brothels and understand that this is common practice, they make a great fuss about the whole incident and thus persist in their hypocritical indignation.

Xenophobia and high melodrama are also blended in the story of Zhenia, a somewhat older prostitute with an independent and cynical mind. We learn how she is seduced by an officer as a young girl, takes revenge by flirting with his best friend (thereby forcing him to fight a fatal duel), and subsequently starts working as a shopgirl for a rich merchant. Trying to make ends meet, Zhenia wavers between the merchant, who offers her financial security in exchange for her love, and a handsome Georgian, whose "glowing, southern eyes" and "wild manliness" fill her with passion. After a long inner struggle she decides to follow her heart and take off with the Georgian, who then turns out to be a notorious trafficker, supplying innumerable brothels with "live stock" (*zhivoi tovar'*). Affirming traditional notions of "oriental treachery," the Georgian immediately delivers Zhenia to Anna Markovna (the madam in *The Pit*) and thereby seals her fate.[50]

These examples make abundantly clear that the world in Count Amori's sequels is a dangerous one. Jews and Caucasians cater to the sexual appetites of a depraved and hypocritical elite, while the lower, exclusively Russian, strata of society fall prey to their despicable practices. By using a voyeuristic perspective similar to that of the boulevard press, Count Amori exploited the social and national animosity of his readers, reassuring them of their own moral and religious superiority.

Count Amori's endeavors as an author coincided approximately with the last decade of the imperial period when the publishing industry was rapidly expanding. Viewed from a literary-historical perspective his career seems to exemplify all that is incompatible with the traditional image of the nineteenth-century writer: an outspoken commercial interest instead of political criticism, and a consumer-oriented attitude toward literature instead of the obligatory service to the people. Yet although profit became an increasingly important factor, even pulp fiction of the type produced by Count Amori could evoke the venerated image of the writer as a socially responsible figure. The fact that a scribbler such as Count Amori compared Artsybashev's hero to other "superfluous people" in Russian literature shows that the commercialization of literature also entailed the possibility of upgrading cheap popular fiction by introducing themes traditionally deemed "significant."

The interrevolutionary period was, of course, also a time of political and social uncertainty, a time in which seemingly self-evident moral values were debated and reevaluated. The success of novels such as *Sanin* and *The Keys to Happiness,* which purported to introduce a new sexual ethic, was perceived as a telling sign of the times. Not the ideas themselves, which had already been expressed in one way or another by Dostoyevsky, Nietzsche, or Max Stirner, but the fact that they seemed to appeal to large groups of people was, in the eyes of many contemporary observers, their most unsettling aspect. What makes Count Amori's work even more timely than its commercial character is the fact that it expressed these widely felt anxieties through the distinctly moralistic mode of melodrama. With its straightforward conception of good and evil, melodrama presented itself as an appropriate genre for refurnishing the amoral literary universe of the original novels with the "traditional imperatives of truth and ethics."[51] Count Amori's eagerness to reformulate certain moral issues of fin de siècle Russia as clear-cut moral contradictions is, perhaps, the most significant expression of the ethical and ideological uncertainty that characterizes a society in transition.

## Notes

Research for this essay was made possible by fellowships from the Netherlands Organization for Scientific Research and the Royal Netherlands Academy of Arts and Sciences.

1 Jeffrey Brooks, *When Russia Learned to Read: Literacy and Popular Literature, 1861–1917* (Princeton: Princeton University Press, 1985), xiii–xxii, 12–18, 59–62. The censorship reform of 1905 is discussed by Louise McReynolds in her book *The News under Russia's Old Regime: The Development of a Mass-Circulation Press* (Princeton: Princeton University Press, 1991), 218–22.

2 A. I. Reitblat, "Roman literaturnogo krakha," *Novoe literaturnoe obozrenie* 25 (1997): 6.

3 Graf Amori, "Posleslovie," *Pobezhdennye* (St. Petersburg: N. I. Kholmushin, 1912), 223.

4 Graf [Count] Amori [Ippolit Rapgof], *Pobezhdennye: Okonchanie romana "Kliuchi schast'ia" A. Verbitskoi,* 4th ed. (St. Petersburg: N. I. Kholmushin, 1914); *Final: Roman iz sovremennoi zhizni. Okonchanie proizvedeniia "Iama" A.I. Kuprina,* 3rd ed. (St. Petersburg, 1914); and *Vozvrashchenie Sanina* (St. Petersburg: Izd. Knizhnoi torgovi, 1913). For reasons of convenience, I have used a more recent edition of *Vozvazshchenie Sanina,* Biblioteka noveishei literatury, vol. 103, knigoizdatel'stvo "Gramatu Draugs" (Riga: Granatu Draugs, 1931).

5 Rapgof's full name was Ippolit Pavlovich Rapgof (1860–1918[?]). For an account of his life, see E. T. Iaborova, "Graf Amori," in *Russkie pisateli 1800–1917: Biograficheskii slovar',* vol. 2 (Moscow, 1992), 12–13. Information on Count Amori's activities after the Revolution is scarce and contradictory. Jay Leyda and Richard Stites maintain that he adapted remarkably well to the new situation, playing a prominent role in the early soviet film industry. Iaborova, on the other hand, conjectures that in 1918 Count Amori was one of the cofounders of an anarchist state in Rostov-na-Donu, which lasted only one day. He was reportedly shot immediately after the seizure of the city. See Jay Leyda, *Kino: A History of the Russian and Soviet Film* (1960; Princeton: Princeton University Press, 1983), 163; and Richard Stites, *Russian Popular Culture: Entertainment and Society since 1900* (Cambridge: Cambridge University Press, 1992), 27–28.

6 According to Jeffrey Brooks, Count Amori was able to sell "tens of thousands" of copies of his ending to *Keys. The Finale,* the ending to Kuprin's novel *The Pit,* sold seventeen thousand copies in three editions. Some of his original installment novels were published in editions of fifty thousand copies (Brooks, *When Russia Learned to Read,* 154, 161). Unfortunately, I do not have any exact figures on the print runs for *The Return of Sanin,* but the fact that it was republished in Latvia as late as 1931 suggests that its commercial potential had not yet been exhausted. One can therefore safely assume that the prerevolutionary editions of *The Return* at least approximated that of the other sequels.

7 Brooks, *When Russia Learned to Read,* 154; Leyda, *Kino,* 163.

8 The concept of "counterliterature" was introduced by Peter Ulf Møller, *Postlude to the Kreutzer Sonata: Tolstoj and the Debate on Sexual Morality in Russian Literature in the 1890s* (Leiden: Brill, 1988), 163.

9 Amori, *Final,* 4.

10 For a discussion of *The Keys to Happiness* and its readership, see Laura Engelstein, *The Keys to Happiness: Sex and the Search for Modernity in Fin-de-Siècle Russia* (Ithaca: Cornell University Press, 1992), 396–420. See also the introduction to the English translation of Anastasia Verbitskaia's *Keys to Happiness,* edited, abridged, and translated by Beth Holmgren and Helena Goscilo (Bloomington: Indiana University Press, 1999).

11 A. I. Kuprin, *Sobranie sochinenii v 6-i tomakh,* vol. 5 (Moscow, 1958), 750 (commentary).

12 Part 1, on which Count Amori based his sequel, was published in the almanac *Zemlia* in 1909 (vol. 3). Part 2 appeared in 1914 with the final chapters being published only in 1915 (vols. 15–16, 1914–1915).

13 A. A. Blok, "Literaturnye itogi 1907 goda," in *Sobranie sochinenii v 8-i tomakh,* vol. 5 (Moskva-Leningrad: Gos. izd. khud. lit., 1962), 228.

14 Both the year of publication (1907) and Sanin's former involvement in the revolutionary movement were viewed as telling indications. See, for example, Ia. Danilin, *"Sanin" v svete russkoi kritiki* (predislovie), (Moscow, 1908), 8; P. M. Pil'skii, "Reaktsiia zamuzhem," in *Problema pola, polovye avtory i polovoi geroi* (St. Petersburg: n.p., 1909), 112.

15 See, for example, "Iziatyi Sanin," *Kievskie vesti* 199, (1908): 3. In this lighthearted sequel, Sanin does not break his neck but is arrested by the police (an allusion to the confiscation of Artsybashev's novel after it had appeared as a separate edition). The newspaper report contains references to other sequels, which do have a fatal ending.

16 A. V. Amfiteatrov, "Protest V. P. Sanin," in *Protiv techeniia* (St. Petersburg: n.p., 1908), 67–69.

17 Amori, *Vozvrashchenie Sanina,* 10.

18 Ibid., 11.

19 Ibid., 16–17.

20 Ibid., 156.

21 P. I. Tkachev, "Tendentioznyi roman," in *Izbrannye literaturnokriticheskie stat'i* (Moscow-Leningrad: Zemlia i fabrika, 1927).

22 A number of critics pointed out the similarities between Sanin and Bazarov. See, for example, Semion Frank, "Etika nigilizma," in *Sochineniia* (Moscow: Molodaia guardiia, 1990), 77; V. V. Vorovskii, "Bazarov i Sanin: Dva nigilizma," in *Estetika, literatura, iskusstvo* (Moscow: Iskusstvo, 1975).

23 Count Amori explicitly labeled Sanin a "hero of our time" and ranked him with Chatskii, Onegin, and Pechorin (see *Vozvrashchenie Sanina,* 6). See also E. A. Koltonovskaia, "Nasledniki Sanina," in *Kriticheskie etiudy* (St. Petersburg: n.p., 1912), 70.

24 Amori, *Vozvrashchenie Sanina,* 13.

25 Ibid., 9.

26 For a discussion of this model, see Irina Paperno, *Chernyshevsky and the Age of Realism: A Study in the Semiotics of Behavior* (Stanford: Stanford University Press, 1988).

27 Amori, *Final,* 87.

28 This lack of social specificity in the boulevard novel and in Dostoyevsky's work was first pointed out by Mikhail Bakhtin in *Problemy tvorchestva Dostoevskogo* (Moscow: Sovetskaia Rossiia, 1979), 119–20.

29 My discussion of the specifically melodramatic qualities of Count Amori's work relies on the following: Peter Brooks, *The Melodramatic Imagination: Balzac, Henry James, Melodrama, and the Mode of Excess* (New Haven: Yale University Press, 1976), 15–22; Marvin Carlson, *Theories of the Theatre: A Historical and Critical Survey from the Greeks to the Present* (Ithaca: Cornell University Press, 1984), 214; and John Franceschina, ed., *Sisters of Gore: Seven Gothic Melodramas by British Women, 1790–1843* (New York: Garland, 1997), 1–13. See also the introduction to this volume by Louise McReynolds and Joan Neuberger, especially their discussion of the concept of poetic justice.

30 Brooks, *The Melodramatic Imagination,* 16.

31 Amori, *Vozvrashchenie Sanina,* 82, 136.

32 Brooks, *The Melodramatic Imagination,* 202.

33 For a discussion of Brooks's concept of the moral occult, see the introduction to this volume.

34 Brooks, *The Melodramatic Imagination,* 20.

35 Amori, *Vozvrashchenie Sanina,* 176.

36 On the significance of this pattern, see Iurii Lotman's article on "plot-

space" in the nineteenth-century Russian novel: "Proza Turgeneva i siuzhetnoe prostranstvo russkogo romana XIX stoletia," *Slavica* 18 (December 1986): 16.

37 Amori, *Final,* 88.

38 Joan Neuberger, *Hooliganism: Crime, Culture, and Power in St. Petersburg, 1900–1914* (Berkeley: University of California Press, 1993), 18.

39 See, for example, Judith Walkowitz's article "Jack the Ripper and the Myth of Male Violence," *Feminist Studies* 8, no. 3 (fall 1982): 546.

40 For a general impression of what was probably a hoax, see A. Peshekhonov, "Na ocherednye temy: 'Saninstsy' i 'Sanin,'" *Russkoe bogatstvo* 5 (1908): 113–17.

41 "The lives of many female free love practioners end tragically; they commit suicide because they have become pregnant, or sometimes because they have become completely insane. At least that is what people say, and it is impossible not to believe it" (G. Ozerov, "Liga svobodnoi liubvi," *Minskoe slovo,* May 2, 1908, 2).

42 To name only a few: Anatolii Sergeev, *Liga svobodnoi liubvi* (komedia V 4-kh deistviiakh), 1908; Aleksandr Zabelin, *Liga svobodnoi liubvi* (p'esa v chetyrekh aktakh), 1909; S. A. Funkendorf, *Liga svobodnoi liubvi* (p'esa v trekh aktakh), 1910. Texts are available at the St. Petersburg Library of Theatrical Art.

43 Engelstein, *The Keys to Happiness,* 404.

44 Amori, *Pobezhdennye,* 221.

45 Ibid., 139.

46 Ibid., 42–43.

47 See also Engelstein, *The Keys to Happiness,* 300.

48 Amori, *Final,* 65–66.

49 Ibid., 72.

50 Ibid., 144–46.

51 Brooks, *The Melodramatic Imagination,* 15.

*Louise McReynolds*

# Home Was Never Where the Heart Was

## Domestic Dystopias in Russia's Silent Movie Melodramas

Hearth and home traditionally have supplied one of the primary sites for melodramatic narratives. The nature of the melodramatic family, however, changes continually with the social structures that engender it. In the first productions of melodrama, which originated in revolutionary France, siblings were separated and parents forced to conceal their identities. As the bourgeois order emerged from the Enlightenment, a different basis for melodramatic tension arose. The problems of personal identity were subordinated to those of social stability. The family setting, as society's bedrock, formed a backdrop appropriate to the essentials of the genre: it re-created a microcosm of the patriarchal status quo, and it placed the female, the arbiter of moral values in the bourgeois world, at the center of the action.[1] As Peter Brooks argues, melodrama "foregrounds, through familial relations, what the social order forbids and represses."[2]

Moreover, by the late nineteenth century dramatic situations obtaining from the domestic economy directly implicated melodrama's principal audience at the time, women.[3] Melodrama traffics in secrets, threats, and repression, and when these undercurrents endanger the heroine, who was presumed to be more vulnerable to external forces than a man would be, evil would seem easier to identify. The public world is by its very nature corrupt, so when the degradation spills over into the idealized moral haven of the private home, the need to restore order appears all the more pressing.

Melodramatic domesticity produced a unique paradigm for prerevolutionary Russian history. The focus on the family shifts attention to an overlooked substratum in historiography—namely, the depth of the roots of bourgeois values evident in the structure of familial relations.[4] Given that the Bolshevik regime expended such energy trying to eradicate an idealized version of this powerful social structure, it is imperative to uncover the fault lines of the prerevolutionary family, which melodrama rendered as a microcosm of the audience's larger world.[5]

The family structure in imperial Russia, as in most societies, began with the patriarch, with the tsar as the metaphorical head of the household.[6] In 1905, the nation protested against this paternal authority, and the revolution of that year challenged Tsar Nicholas's claim to projecting himself as the paterfamilias of the nation. This challenge to the supreme authority figure resulted from the wholesale changes that society had undergone during the rapid industrialization of the 1890s, and it came from all levels of the social structure, dislodging centuries-old impediments to individual freedoms. The combined forces of urbanization, professionalization, and commercialization had helped to reconfigure social roles and public spaces. A sexual insurrection induced wives to demand physical satisfaction in conjugal relations, and men found their status on the streets under attack by the growing number of women entering the public sphere as everything from aspiring professionals to consumers.[7] A genuinely popular commercial culture emerged in these conditions, much of which struggled to free its consumers from the stranglehold of tradition.[8] This culture decoded political change and reconfigured it in representations that could be readily absorbed. Melodrama emerged as one of the most successful commercialized genres, accessible through industrialization's newest gift to the masses: the motion picture.

The heyday of Russia's silent movie melodramas, 1913–1917, was also the period when the Great War was dragging the autocratic empire into the modern world and forcing a reassessment of social and political hierarchies. Gender structured one of those hierarchies, and the female, the indispensable anchor for the family who was necessarily taking on new duties, provided the core of the early film audience in a situation where millions of men were at the front.[9] Movies figured heavily in the construction of the "New Woman," who emerged to take up the new roles being assigned to her in Russia. To give them their distinctively Russian spin, these films should be thought of as *domostroi* dramas, in reference to the sixteenth-century manual for maintaining order in the household. Deeply conservative, the *Domostroi* invested the patriarch with immense power, and although many of its sentiments held sway into the twentieth century, modernity had rendered it as anachronistic as it had the principle of autocracy. The tension between the old ways and the new, and the patriarch's desperate grasp to maintain his authority, was played out in the celluloid melodramas, where the movie heroine emerged as an ambiguous role model for women trapped in custom but often as insecure as they were ambitious about setting themselves free of it.

By manipulating familiar cultural categories, Russia's silver-screen melodramas encouraged their audiences to reflect on social and political change. The movies problematized real choices by exaggerating them, thus allowing for identification but also providing the safety of distance. As Tania Modleski has argued, melodrama is especially important to women who have been silenced by their patriarchal environment because it provides "an outlet for the repressed feminine voice."[10] This outlet, however, is always contingent, always temporary. Even when the heroine manages to escape a specific set of circumstances, she still finds herself enmeshed in the oppressive structure that gave rise to her precarious situation in the first place.[11] Melodrama's unique cultural authority derives from the way in which it exposes the stress points in those structures for all to see.

This essay analyzes four of Russia's silent movie melodramas, each based in the domestic economy, in order to re-create the central problematics associated with the family as a basic unit of social stability at the end of the old regime. Representative of the literally hundreds of melodramas shown at the time, these four films were selected specifically because of their broader connections to popular culture: one was based on a novel by the most influential female novelist of the era, two were directed by the dominant figure in movie melodramas, and the fourth was based on a factual event. Offering rare glimpses into the world of bourgeois Russia, these movies presented one aspect of how commercial culture portrayed the social and political unraveling of the period through the perspective of family relations. To the extent that melodrama works to expose the contradictions of the ideology that underlies the dominant culture, these movies illustrate the dissension developing between competing concepts of public obligations and private desires.[12]

## The Freudian Family

Sigmund Freud casts his shadow over all discussion of melodrama because, as Brooks has pointed out, the genre is deeply implicated in much of Freud's own thought.[13] Although Freud himself exercised little direct influence on psychiatry in prerevolutionary Russia, many of his ideas were precipitated by the same cultural and intellectual controversies that beset all of Europe at the turn of the century.[14] Lynn Hunt has ably demonstrated the value of applying Freud's ideas outside of his specific time frame by reading aspects of the French Revolution through a Freudian lens; as she points out, criticism of his conclusions "[does] not vitiate the importance of the questions raised by Freud or of the general metaphorical structure that he outlined."[15]

Family relations are as central to Freudianism as to melodrama, a further indication of how psychoanalysis and popular culture feed off many of the same issues.[16] Freud's most famous idea, the Oedipus complex, enjoyed cultural resonance long before Freud rearticulated Greek tragedy to explain the psyche of modern societies. The key significance of his oedipalization of social organizations is that what Freud identified as a transition from childhood into adulthood could also be understood as a strategy for maintaining a male-based sociopolitical hierarchy. Inspired by the Enlightenment's search for a unified individual self, Freud wanted to account for the split nature of the human mind between its conscious and unconscious dimensions.[17] This preoccupation placed his research at the heart of another major philosophical issue of the nineteenth century, the separation between the public and the private spheres. Because Freud read Oedipus subjectively as well as symbolically, he allowed the individual to stand in for society at large. By formulating pseudoscientific explanations for irrational behavior, Freud also gave a patina of respectability to the gothic mysticism that had influenced the origins of melodrama. Most important, he made sexuality, so critical to the construction of individualism, equally crucial to social transformation.

To paraphrase Brooks's argument, like melodrama Freud used family relations to foreground the issues that the larger society has repressed in its subconscious because they are too potentially devastating to acknowledge directly. Freud's emphasis on the sexual nature of these issues placed his ideas at the nucleus of popular culture at the turn of the twentieth century. The centrality of family, the significance of repressed emotions, and the applicability of these ideas at both the micro level of the individual and macro level of society made for a natural alliance between psychoanalysis and melodrama, especially through the medium of the cinema, which imparts meaning through subconscious spectatorship. Ideas later identified with Freud found multiple reflections throughout Russia's cinematic *domostroi* dramas—in their plots, their aesthetics, and their subtextual intimations of the danger that lurks when instincts better left suppressed find release.

Thus the discourse of domesticity converged with that of psychotic repression in early-twentieth-century Russia, and their intersection became personalized in melodramatic conflict on the silver screen.[18] The movies analyzed in this essay are divided according to the sex of the head of the household: two look at domestic circumstances dominated by mothers, the other two by fathers. Notably, all of the children in the films are daughters; this family structure differs meaningfully from equivalent western domestic melodramas, where sons predominate.[19] The centrality of daughters rather than sons presents a crucial distinction between Russia and the West because it raises the issue of what happens when women try to assert themselves. In Freudian theory, the mother serves as a function of her child's life, a conduit to maturity who must sacrifice her *self* in order for her child to become an individual.[20] When the child is male, the mother's success is measured by whether or not her son accepts the symbolic law of the father, which is depicted by the way that the son establishes his independence from her and then takes on responsibility for her.[21]

The mother must also bring her daughter into adulthood; for the female child, however, this means entering the same secondary status that her mother occupies. Moreover, according to the formulaic dictates of oedipalization, the mother and daughter must find themselves placed in competition for the attentions of the same men. Thus resentment and rivalry color mother-daughter relations. Their relationship has a distinct cultural advantage, however, because of the insights it offers into generational conflicts emerging at the turn of the century.

The father-daughter relationship is fraught with even greater personal risk because of the undercurrent of incest that threatens domestic harmony. As John Forrester points out: "Incest, we should remember, is that psychoanalytic theme par excellence."[22] Ironically, the daughter is almost forced into this forbidden relationship because, according to Freud, she is obligated to both imitate and compete with her mother. Incestuous themes recur frequently in melodramas, in particular because this exceptional violation of natural law was one that could never be either fully articulated or completely reconciled. The daughter, objectified by her father's desire, would have no grounds on which to compete for power, as she would with her mother. Social identity falls into turmoil when bloodlines become suspect, and the paterfamilias cannot be trusted in his own home. In Russia, where into the twentieth century the tsar still dominated as metaphorical head of the political family, allegories of incest were especially suggestive of social friction.[23]

Tsar Nicholas, with his wife and five children, also found himself trapped in the modern discourse of family. Even without the late-twentieth-century vocabulary to describe the dysfunctional household, the contradictions between obligations to the public and desires felt in private emanated from the Winter Palace.[24] Life in the palace on the Neva River fulfilled the requirements of melodrama, brimming with the excesses performed by the hysterical tsarevna and the palpable evil represented by the Siberian mystic Rasputin. An ineffectual father, an heir with tainted blood, and four virginal daughters rounded out this family.

The last act of the Romanov melodrama, however, which left the family dead at the hands of revolutionaries, had the ambiguous advantage of offering a uniquely Russian denouement. Using the Romanovs to symbolize both *a* family and *the* family of prerevolutionary melodrama, their outcome had already been anticipated by the silent movies based on domestic dilemmas. Unlike Russia's movie producers, however, who had the option of filming an alternative ending for the export version of their films, the Romanovs found themselves trapped in what Russians considered an "inevitable" resolution.[25] In the western melodramatic tradition, evil was identified, eradicated, and the status quo restored—hence the predictably happy ending. That the Romanov family ended in a tragedy reminiscent of the era's melodramas underscores the utility of the genre as a category of political as well as social analysis.

## The Self-Sacrificing Mother

The first two films discussed in this essay, *Vavochka* and *For Happiness,* address the mother-daughter melodramatic narrative. In her study of the origins and development of the function of the maternal in American movie melodramas, E. Ann Kaplan identifies a Master Mother Narrative that explains formulaic repetitions within a recognizable plot.[26] Originating in Jean-Jacques Rousseau's articulation of the place of the virtuous mother in the private sphere of post-Enlightenment society, this narrative situates motherhood within the political ideology of the modern industrial world.[27] The archetypal mother in the maternal melodrama has no husband and only a single child to raise. The absence of a husband puts the mother in the falsely "natural" position of repressing her sexuality in order to devote her emotional attentions to the child. Kaplan demonstrates convincingly that despite the ostensible support it lends to the patriarchal order, when woven as a thread through the popular culture fashioned by and/or for a female audience, the Master Mother Narrative works just as effectively to register misgivings about the "natural" subordination of women.

Russia's best-read female writer of the fin de siècle, Anastasia Verbitskaia (1861–1928) used melodrama effectively as a medium of social critique. Author of the novel (of the same name) on which *Vavochka* was based, Verbitskaia despised what she saw as the forced domestication of women, and she wrote often on the perils that this created for both individuality and society.[28] *Vavochka,* her first novel, appeared in 1898 as a serial in the middlebrow journal *Zhizn'* (Life).[29] Featuring female characters in the Freudian vein, the book tells the story of a mother who sacrifices her own sexuality for her pathologically self-centered daughter. Significantly, the reviewers read the novel as a commentary on the egotism of the new generation, concentrating on their financial rather than their emotional greed.[30] Rushed into production immediately after the smashing success of the film version of Verbitskaia's most infamous blockbuster, *The Keys to Happiness,* the movie *Vavochka* focused on the sexual subtext that poisoned the relationship between mother and daughter and denied happiness to both.[31] Although *Vavochka* did not attract the quantity of fans that *Keys* did, the movie's value lies in its contribution to Russia's maternal melodramas.[32]

In *Vavochka* the widowed mother, Alexandra Iasneva, who is a music teacher, has maintained a close relationship with a local doctor, Tikhmenev, for ten years, while her daughter Vavochka is away at boarding school.[33] Iasneva will not marry him, however, until her daughter no longer needs her. After graduation, the postpubescent Vavochka returns home. Initially indifferent to Tikhmenev, who treats her as a daughter, Vavochka is persuaded by one of her girlfriends to make a game of stealing the doctor from her mother. Tikhmenev falls victim to her calculated flirtations, which arouse in him "something that he fears to awaken." Iasneva remains ignorant of their relationship, which as yet has only been consummated in the knowing looks the two exchange. Tikhmenev gives Vavochka a diamond ring for her birthday, but the narcissistic girl is blinded by the sparkle and indifferent to what else such a gift might suggest.

The story's climax is precipitated by one of Vavochka's companions, someone considerably more observant than her mother. The jealous doctor has gone to watch Vavochka interacting with her youthful friends; during one of their games, a boy in the crowd, Mal'tsev, kisses Vavochka on the lips. Mal'tsev watches the doctor pale in stunned reaction, and deduces the situation immediately. The next day, after Iasneva has left on a trip to Moscow, Mal'tsev comes by and persuades Vavochka to walk with him to a friend's house. When she sits down on the road to remove her painful shoes, "not losing a second, Mal'tsev throws down his coat, nestles up to her, and begins kissing her feet with greedy lips." He then rapes her.[34] Deprived of her virginity, Vavochka loses any shade of the innocence she might have claimed in her flirtation with Tikhmenev.

Three days pass. Iasneva returns unexpectedly, and from the kitchen door she watches her daughter and Tikhmenev in an evidently intimate conversation. Vavochka has changed; her wild laughter betrays signs of hysteria.[35] When Iasneva makes her presence known to them, Tikhmenev is mortified and Vavochka almost frenzied. Clearly, the doctor has come to his senses and realized the true and sordid nature of his desire for Vavochka, and how this has affected one of his dearest friendships. He falls at Iasneva's feet, begging her forgiveness, a move that only intensifies Vavochka's resentment. Actions and on-screen emotions over the course of the next few days of the story indicate that Iasneva wants to make peace with her old friend, who is trying to end his relationship with her daughter. The now hysterical Vavochka, however, cannot accept either his rejection or her mother's friendship with him. Tikhmenev therefore leaves town.

After an indeterminate amount of time passes, Iasneva writes Tikhmenev that Vavochka has a fiancé, a wealthy local man. This is followed by a telegram informing him that Vavochka has fallen ill. He returns to help Iasneva, whose maternal instincts cause her to insist that he marry her daughter, as that is the only way to calm Vavochka. The faces of those at the wedding suggest that they are attending a funeral instead. Shortly after the ceremony, Iasneva collapses on her divan, resigned to a fate that can satisfy none of the three principal characters, but can only postpone her daughter's impending breakdown. She has not navigated Vavochka's entry into emotional maturity, but rather left her mired in the narcissism and hysteria that resulted from their competition over the doctor. Vavochka was raped because she was vulnerable, because her mother was not taking proper care. As a result, Vavochka transformed the wish to humiliate her mother into an obsession with the object of her mother's desire. Consumed by something that could never truly be hers, she preferred to bring down the house rather than relinquish her self-indulgent desires.

The theme of a mother sacrificing her sexuality in order to placate a selfish daughter was played out again in the 1917 film *For Happiness.*[36] Directed by the reigning king of movie melodramas Evgeny Bauer, and starring popular actress Lydia Koreneva, this cinematic version of the oedipal triangle embroidered the relationships with glamour and lush settings. Yet it still could not come up with a resolution to satisfy any of the three characters involved. The daughter, Lee, although spared a rape, nevertheless collapses in hysterical blindness as the only recourse to the untenable situation.

The plotlines of the two movies follow the same formulaic path, although Lee is a tamer version of Vavochka and she does not succeed in her bid for her mother's suitor. Zoia Verenskaia, a wealthy widow, has carried on clandestinely for ten years with Gzhatskii, a lawyer. She refuses to commit to him out of concern for Lee's devotion to her dead father. The widow and the lawyer behave decorously in Lee's presence, sneaking off to his office for their trysts. Frustrated, he tries to persuade Verenskaia that Lee can handle the truth. Verenskaia dares not chance this because her daughter suffers from an undisclosed illness

Verenskaia begs Gzhatskii to wait in Evgeny Bauer's *For Happiness* (A. Khanzhonkov and Co., 1917).

that threatens blindness. Medical clues suggest that she suffers from a form of hysteria: anxiety aggravates her condition, which can be treated by rest at the seashore. Verenskaia begs Gzhatskii to hold out just a bit longer because Lee has reached the age when she should soon marry. This scenario, in which Lee will transfer her emotions for her father to her prospective husband, plays manifestly on the oedipalization of women, with its concomitant consequences of the hysteria that results from compulsory sexual repression.

While the adults are mulling over Lee's fate, the audience has become aware that Lee has already found the perfect object in Gzhatskii, her father surrogate, who figures in her fantasies as a potential lover. But even if the teenage Lee remained unaware of the depth of his relationship with her mother, her ignorance was in part self-delusional, as Gzhatskii often reminded her that he thought of her as a daughter. Lee's excited reactions to his fatherly attentions have betrayed her desire to the audience. When the family doctor counsels Verenskaia to take her to the Crimea for Lee's health, and Lee balks at the trip, viewers know that she dreads separation from Gzhatskii. Finally persuaded to go, in the Crimea she meets Enrico, a young artist (played by future soviet experimentalist director Lev Kuleshov, who also worked on the sets for this movie). Enrico's amorous attention prompts Verenskaia to assume that her daughter has now "decided her future." She hastily writes this good

The shock has triggered what her mother feared most, hysterical blindness; a scene from Evgeny Bauer's *For Happiness* (A. Khanzhonkov and Co., 1917).

news to Gzhatskii, still in Moscow but too distracted to mind his business properly. Ecstatic at what this might mean, he rushes to the Crimea. Out for a stroll, however, he and Verenskaia overhear Lee tell Enrico that she cannot return his love because her heart belongs to Gzhatskii. In a finely crafted scene that moves the daughter-crossed lovers back and forth between bright sunlight and dark shadows, Verenskaia forces Gzhatskii to leave once again because she cannot bring herself to destroy Lee's illusions.

Unlike Tikhmenev in *Vavochka,* Gzhatskii never evidences any romantic interest in his companion's daughter. Like Iasneva, however, Verenskaia puts her daughter's desires above her own. Preparing the way for a visit from Lee, she goes to Gzhatskii's office and begs him to marry the girl. When Lee arrives, Gzhatskii finally tells her the truth, that he is in love with her mother. Lee staggers from the room, crumpling against a statue in the hall. The shock has triggered what her mother feared most, hysterical blindness. The movie's closing shot shows both women staring off into space, one blind physically, the other metaphorically. The situation cannot be reconciled to anyone's satisfaction, much less to his or her pleasure.

The inability of these two Russian mothers to bring their daughters into responsible adulthood had chilling implications for late imperial society.[37] If modern women are such poor mothers, and girls cannot cope with their sexualities, and men are ineffectual, what could the future hold? The mother-daughter relationship functions along two intersecting levels, gender and generation, and these cinematic relationships evidence none of the balance sought in the childcare manuals that structured the mother's social role.[38] As representatives of youths entering adulthood, Vavochka and Lee betoken a frightening egoism, an absorption with the self so consuming that it blinds, literally in Lee's case, the girls to the fundamental rules of social organization.[39] The mothers obstruct the transition to adulthood by infantilizing their daughters, unwilling to articulate what they know to be true: that their daughters are their explicit sexual rivals. That the young girls turn to weak father figures rather than to men their own age, and that their sexuality turns them into destroyers rather than procreators, is equally disturbing.

## The Predatory Father

Vavochka and Lee essentially undergo a rite of passage into adulthood, which makes their sexual designs on their prospective stepfathers normal within the Freudian script of family relations. Their mothers must be held accountable for their daughters' respective inabilities to attain maturity, to join society as grown-ups answerable for their actions. When fathers prey on their daughters, however, a different set of problems rise to the social surface. This reverse oedipalization, which turns the good father bad and makes *him* rather than the child the agent in the sexual relationship, upends not only the family's social base, but also the autocratic political structure that relies on faith in a righteous father figure.

In 1913, coinciding roughly with the publication of Freud's *Totem and Taboo,* Evgeny Bauer directed a film version of the ultimate taboo, *The Father's Forbidden* [*prestupnaia*] *Passion.* Filmed at the Drankov Studio, which deserved its reputation for specializing in sensational movies, the screenplay was written by the prolific scenarist B. V. Chaikovskii. The movie starred popular actress N. A. Chernova, whose next film would also be with Bauer, *Twilight of a Woman's Soul,* one of his first melodramas for the more reputable Khanzhonkov Studio where he made his career. Although the celluloid version of *The Father's Forbidden Passion* itself has not survived, the libretto recreates both the plot and the melodramatic atmosphere characteristic of Bauer's films.[40]

*The Father's Forbidden Passion* begins with the widower Baron von Al'bert bringing his daughter Louisa home from boarding school after her graduation. Although the setting appears to be in Germany, the film was advertised as "a vivid portrayal of the inadequacies [*nedostatki*] of our society," not an indictment of Russia's longtime cultural adversary for its moral turpitude. Like Vavochka and Lee, Louisa stands at a particular crossroads in maturity, between youth and adulthood. Moreover, the changes that modernity is introducing into the lives of these young women has left them in an ambiguous place. They enjoy more opportunities than women of their mothers' generation, who likely would have had less schooling and been married off at this age. Louisa, a child when she last lived in the same house as her father, has now reached the age where she can replace her deceased mother. The emotions she evokes in him turn from paternal affection into sexual passion. The nature of his changing attentions ignites a similar sensation in her, feelings that "gradually begin to take on tangible form."

Declaring their love, the baron and Louisa plan a tryst in her bedroom. As they embrace, the ghost of the wife/mother appears before them, crying out that they stop. This apparition bears a distinctive Bauer touch; he often used such special effects as phantoms and dream sequences to bring his characters' unconscious to life on the screen. Louisa, sobered by the close call, now develops a guilty conscience for the sin she almost committed, and her guilt drives her to join a convent. The baron, still infatuated, begs her to come away with him. When she refuses, he goes insane. This denouement forces the daughter from public life and strips the father of the ability to function in it because he has lost his powers of reason.

Baron von Al'bert falls as far as a father can go. His forbidden passion, writ large against the backdrop of mounting social and political tensions that immediately preceded the Great War, intimates the collapse of the family, the indispensable foundation of society. As Freud had argued in *Totem and Taboo,* incest is ultimately more about the policing of social borders than it is about sex, a point subtly reinforced by the context in which the film appeared. *The Father's Forbidden Passions* may well have exceeded the boundaries that even the sensation-hungry audiences were willing to accept,[41] but a second movie released in 1913, the comparatively low-budget *The Merchant Bashkirov's Daughter,* also raised the issue of how a father's control over his daughter's body resulted in a sexual violation of it.[42] Instead of crossing explicit boundaries, this film used social metaphors to tell the story of a predatory father. Making the transgression less direct might have lessened the shock to filmgoers, but it would not have watered down the message of a daughter's vulnerability.

Produced by a small provincial company, the movie was reputedly based on an actual local scandal. Subtitled *Drama on the Volga,* the story draws on the works of playwright Alexander Ostrovsky for clichés of the brutality of life among Russia's unenlightened merchantry. In this quintessential *domostroi* drama, the merchant Bashkirov runs his family according to the rules of the sixteenth century rather than those of the twentieth. The director relied on costume to demarcate simply and vividly the characters' perspectives: the bearded merchant, his hair parted in traditional style down the middle, wears the long blouse and overcoat that had exemplified his estate for generations. His wife and daughter also wear the braids and long, heavy dresses typical of the modesty demanded by the father, whereas the young shop steward who loves his daughter wears short hair and more modern clothes. Their clothing renders Christian names superfluous, and no one is identified by name, emphasizing the extent to which this film was self-consciously working through images of social estate.

One day the merchant brings home another man in traditional merchant dress, and as the horrified wife stands listening behind the table, her husband bargains away their daughter. In a figurative juxtaposition of personal expression, the daughter kisses the man she wishes to marry on the lips, while her father kisses the man whom he has selected to be her husband on both cheeks and then the mouth, according to ritual. The mother's support for her daughter reveals her own unhappiness with life à la *domostroi,* an important indication that dissatisfaction with the old ways was not simply generational. When the hapless steward comes to visit his beloved, the mother helps her daughter to hide him from the father, who is busy with more negotiations. In an unfortunate move, the women bury the suitor under the heavy quilts on the daughter's bed, and when the coast clears and they attempt to retrieve him, they find his suffocated body. The stricken women enlist the peasant who does odd jobs around the house to help them out of their predica-

The peasant overpowers the daughter in *The Merchant Bashkirov's Daughter* (G. Libkin's Volga Co., 1913).

ment. They pay him to dump the corpse in the Volga River, making it appear as though the clerk drowned and thereby erase any connection with them.

Although the peasant does as he is told, he is not the serf of the bygone era. No longer a mere backdrop to the actions of the social estates superior to his, the peasant handyman now acts on his own desires. Aware that the pretty daughter is indebted to him, he returns for more money and then attempts sexual blackmail. She fends him off, but only temporarily. To buy his silence, she goes to his hut and tries to appeal to his mercy. He has none, and he rapes her. The film shows the two of them struggling, the peasant finally overpowering the daughter. In a rapid cut the scene shifts to the peasant entering a rundown tavern. Seated with a bottle, he finds the white handkerchief he had grabbed from his stricken victim, evidence of his conquest (and ironically reminiscent of *Othello*), and he gives it to a boy to return to her. The daughter then goes to the tavern where, feigning submissiveness, she pretends to drink and pours vodka for the rapist and his friends until they pass out in a dead drunk. In order to assure that they will not awaken from their stupor she sets the tavern ablaze and bolts the outside doors. Exacting revenge against the handyman, however, does not mean liberation from her father. The peasant represented the evil associated with the life her father forced her to live, so the fire eradicated only the symbol rather than the evil itself.

The final scene shows the daughter reduced to hysterics, watching the flames from her room.

In Russian melodrama, when evil is a feminine characteristic, it destroys by wanting what it cannot have; it is a consuming force. As a masculine attribute, evil is singularly violent. More important, however, is the absence of a countervailing goodness, no heroes or heroines to set matters right. Men cannot protect the women entrusted to their guardianship by a legal system that denies women rights independent of their fathers or husbands.[43] In a remarkable departure from western melodramatic formulas, Russia's prerevolutionary movie heroines have to fend for themselves, even within the family and against their social inferiors. The millions of Russian males engaged along the western battlefront at the time when these movies were playing to full houses could not find much symbolic support for their actions, perhaps because their own defensive lines were crumbling under superior German forces. However, even when the male characters enjoyed an abundance of women on the homefront, as in *Vavochka* and *For Happiness,* neither Tikhmenev nor Gzhatskii ended up with the woman of his choice.

The image of Russian manhood suffered badly in these movies. Notably, the melodramas were not counterbalanced by movies starring heroic soldiers during the war years.[44] Educated professional males, represented by the lawyer Gzhatskii and the doctor Tikhmenev, were theoretically the best positioned to lead Russia into the twentieth century. Not even they, however, could establish a stable family. One of the most loathsome of the new men appeared in one of the last of these melodramas, *Little Ellie.* Released in 1918 and starring Ivan Mozzhukhin, one of prerevolutionary Russia's most popular actors, the film focuses on the town mayor, the pinnacle of power and respectability.[45] Pursuing one woman, he accidentally kills her younger sister in an alcohol-induced attempted rape. His crime undetected, he subsequently marries her sister. In fine Freudian fashion, he is haunted throughout the rest of the film by hallucinations from his repressed unconscious, and ultimately he shoots himself.

The weakness of the bourgeois male parallels uneasily the brutality characterizing his brothers from the lower classes. The melodramatic depiction of the peasantry on the silver screen found no traces of the bygone idealization of the potential nobility of the savage. *The Daughter-in-Law's Lover,* a product of the Khanzhonkov Studio in 1912 and also starring Mozzhukhin, featured a peasant taking his daughter-in-law by force, resulting in her suicide. In Bauer's *Twilight of a Woman's Soul* the peasant's urban confederate, the worker, rapes a woman who is bringing him charity. This victim, like the merchant Bashkirov's daughter, avenges herself by murdering the worker in his postcoital stupor.

Because the trope of rape appears sufficiently often in Russian melodramas, it is necessary to consider the larger cultural implications of this violation. Not only did Verbitskaia have Vavochka raped, but she made it crucial to character and narrative development in *The Keys to Happiness,* where the heroine ultimately commits suicide because she cannot relinquish her sexual desire for the man who raped her. To return to Modleski's point that melodrama gives voice to the repressed female, these melodramatic rape sequences in stories by and/or for women might be construed as a form of rape fantasy. Molly Haskell has argued that when women fantasize about rape they do so not out of sexual desire, but as one means of coping with the anxiety and fear stimulated by the pervasive violence in their societies.[46] Russia, wracked by revolution, strikes, and world war, was an especially violent place, particularly for the masses of women who found themselves too often at the end of a misogynist stick.[47]

A late-twentieth-century viewing of the films might interpret these women as empowering themselves when they exact revenge.[48] The question therefore arises about whether or not the vengeful Russian heroines are asserting agency, taking back their lives.[49] By resorting to violence the women underscore how powerless the Russian male had become, but in their vengeance they do not appropriate the power that the men failed to obtain after the 1905 revolution. To keep these films in context, the retaliatory females personify the precarious restoration of the tsarist government in 1907.[50] However much their actions mocked the impotence of the males, they themselves did not assert an alternative authority.[51]

## Russian Melodrama's "Unhappy" Ending

Cultural and social concerns loom large in the way that a society resolves its fictional conflicts. In early-twentieth-century Russia, when traditional social and political relationships were struggling to retain their hierarchical integrity against the leveling forces of industrialization, the way in which the movies presented these issues for popular consumption can provide key insights into how changes were being assimilated. The endings to Russian movies of the period, which did not resolve conflicts by restoring order, reveal a radical departure from western notions of the importance of reconstituting the family. On this score, the Russian melodramas anticipated later critical arguments that melodrama is fundamentally a disruptive genre, one that addresses the concerns of those excluded from circles of political power.[52]

When in its final reel a movie restores order, that ending is deemed "happy" within the formula validated by western movie melodramas. This genre equated virtue triumphant with the restoration to power of a trustworthy male figure over a vulnerable female. Two contemporaneous examples of western domestic melodramas that are recognized as classics of the genre, D. W. Griffith's *Way Down East* (1920) and Abel Gance's *Torture of Silence* (1917), also feature mothers who transgress social boundaries. These mothers are initially punished by losing their children, only to have the love of an honest man restore their integrity, allowing them to reenter the family.[53] In the West, Kaplan's Master Mother Narrative continues to hold sway as an important melodramatic device for achieving the subordination of woman as mother. In the two classic American melodramas starring the mother who sacrifices all for her daughter, *Stella Dallas* (1925, 1937, 1990) and *Mildred Pierce* (1945), both mothers concede their own inadequacies and return power to the fathers in the end.

Russian melodramas, which did not restore order, accordingly had "unhappy" endings. An American movie critic in 1918 commented on the "tragic note" sounded at the end of Russian films, and worried about how they would be received by "our public." According to a Muscovite reviewer, though, Russian audiences "stubbornly refuse to accept" that "all's well that end's well," asserting "that we need tragic endings."[54] The commercial market went so far as to dictate the production of an alternative ending for some films designated for export. The meanings of this distinctively Russian style, however, must be explored beyond the clichés of the melancholy Slavic soul. Soviet film historian S. S. Ginzburg laid the blame for Russia's cynical resolutions to cinematic conflicts at the door of the decadent bourgeoisie, who could offer only a "philosophy of despair, a hopeless outlook on life, the contraposition of passion to reason, belief in the reign of dark, latent desires over the human will."[55] This reasoning, ostensibly buttressed by the political failure of the bourgeoisie, has long enjoyed currency.[56] It should be remembered, however, that Ginzburg was writing from the perspective of the bright socialist future just beyond the horizon, when the soviet movies about social problems had acquired Hollywoodesque resolutions by restoring the Party Line.

It would be more fruitful to recoin the concepts of "happy" and "unhappy" as "conservative" and "ambiguous." Laura Mulvey has pointed out that the value of melodrama as a cultural indicator is in how it "symptomizes the history of its own time."[57] The most conspicuous social malaise that can be diagnosed from the symptoms viewed in the *domostroi* drama is confusion about traditional structures. The matriarch is not competent to run the family because of her inability to suppress her maternal instincts and recognize that the new situations require her to shoulder a greater disciplinary role. If the self-sacrificing mother was incapable of running the modern household, however, the predatory father exercised an even more bogus authority. Whereas the daughter enjoyed a kind of social equity with her mother, as the object of her father's desires she enjoyed no independent identity: Louisa was forced to retreat from the public world, and the merchant's daughter resorted to murder to avenge herself on her father. Incest soured the family romance, causing the group to implode and thereby bring down the structures that had failed to sustain it. The Russian audience watches in vain for a credible father figure; the authority figures in these movies invited greater disgust than confidence.[58] Not even decent men could achieve their ambitions for a stable household.

Russia's silent-screen melodramas materialized as cultural artifacts from specific discourses at a given historical moment. Leaving incipient bolshevism out of the picture and Lenin and Stalin nowhere in the frame, these movies identify issues of class, politics, and gender in new tropes, new to both the age that defined them and the subsequent historiography that has described the era in a predominantly political vocabulary. The movies provide visual clues that betray just how precarious prerevolutionary society was for the family—its most basic point of social and political organization. Hunt has emphasized the role of the family in melodrama's efforts to reinscribe morality after the collapse of traditional values, but the family in these films offers no sanctuary for its members.[59] The dominant imagery of 1917 is one of revolutionary explosion, but the movie melodramas offer the alternative vision of implosion.

Russia's *domostroi* dramas projected onto the silver screen cultural images of precisely the situation that the tsarist government had tried to prevent from being fully articulated: just how unsustainable the autocracy had become in the twentieth century. Portraying as they do the anxieties of a society battling the demons of modernization, these movies do not offer much prospect for the kind of stability necessary to forestall the collapse of basic social institutions, as happened in 1917 at the height of popularity of the genre. After all, not one of them gave the audiences much to hope for, not even in the world of make-believe.

## Notes

The International Research and Exchanges Board and the Kennan Institute provided funding that allowed me to conduct research for this essay. I am also grateful to Linda Engelberg of the University of Hawai'i for tracking down the movies. Margot Henriksen and Joan Neuberger bounced ideas around with me, helped me to sharpen my cultural readings, and made invaluable comments on the first draft.

1 Thomas Elsaesser, "Tales of Sound and Fury: Observations on the Family Melodrama," in *Home Is Where the Heart Is: Studies in Melodrama and the Woman's Film,* ed. Christine Gledhill (London: British Film Institute, 1987), 34–69.
2 The words belong to E. Ann Kaplan, "Mothering, Feminism, and Representation: The Maternal Melodrama and the Woman's Film 1910–40," in Gledhill, ed., *Home Is Where the Heart Is,* 117.
3 Judith Walkowitz, *City of Dreadful Delight* (Chicago: University of Chicago Press, 1992), 87–88. Walkowitz argues that melodramatic anxieties reflected the instability of the culture of the market and that "the home, as a haven in a heartless world [was] a trope that tended to women's larger social connections and resources beyond the home" (169).
4 Although much work remains to be done on the family in Russia, Jessica Tovrov, in *The Russian Noble Family: Structure and Change* (New York: Garland Press, 1987), shows how the nobility was moving toward more "bourgeois" concepts of emotionalism in family relationships.
5 See Wendy Goldman, *Women, the State, and Revolution: Soviet Family Policy and Social Life, 1917–1936* (Cambridge: Cambridge University

Press, 1993), especially chapters 1 and 5; Diane Koenker, "Men against Women on the Shop Floor in Early Soviet Russia: Gender and Class in the Socialist Workplace," *American Historical Review* 100, no. 5 (1995): 1438–64; and Anne E. Gorsuch, " 'A Woman Is Not a Man': The Culture of Gender and Generation in Soviet Russia, 1921–1928," *Slavic Review* 55, no. 3 (fall 1996): 636–60.

6 The tsar as paterfamilia of both royal family and nation dates from the reign of Nicholas I (1825–1855). As Richard Wortman writes: "The association between domestic morality and autocratic government outlived Nicholas's reign and remained intrinsic to the image of Russian autocracy for the duration of the empire. To violate the principle of autocracy became tantamount to a biblical sin against the father, while violation of family morality would throw into doubt the foundations of autocratic rule" (Wortman, *Scenarios of Power: Myth and Ceremony in Russian Monarchy,* vol. 1 [Princeton: Princeton University Press, 1995], 335).

7 Western ideas of female satisfaction were being translated and circulated in Russia, even before 1905 and much more after the revolution. See Karl Fongel'zen, *Gigiena medovogo mesiatsa* (Minsk: Vl. Zal'tsshtein, 1896); and A. Debe, G. Klenke, Paolo Mantegatsa, and S. Smails, *Kak vyiti zamuzh i byt' schastlivoi v supruzheskoi zhizni* (Moscow: A. A. Levinson, 1909).

8 Jeffrey Brooks, *When Russia Learned to Read: Literacy and Popular Literature, 1861–1917* (Princeton: Princeton University Press, 1985).

9 See, for example, Miriam Hansen, *Babel and Babylon: Spectatorship in American Silent Cinema* (Cambridge, Mass: Harvard University Press, 1991), especially chapter 2; and L. A. Handel, *Hollywood Looks at Its Audience* (Urbana: University of Illinois Press, 1950). Although these studies focus on the American cinema, the principles also hold true for other societies.

10 Tania Modleski, "Time and Desire in the Women's Film," *Cinema Journal* 23, no. 3 (spring 1984): 21.

11 Laura Mulvey, in "Notes on Sirk and Melodrama," in Gledhill, ed., *Home Is Where the Heart Is,* 75–79, focuses on the contradictions of the Hollywoodesque reconstruction of the status quo.

12 See, for example, Jacky Bratton, "The Contending Discourses of Melodrama," in Jacky Bratton, Jim Cook, and Christine Gledhill, eds., *Melodrama: Stage, Picture, Screen* (London: British Film Institute, 1994), 38–49.

13 Brooks, *The Melodramatic Imagination,* 201.

14 See, for example, Roger Shattuck, *Fin-de-Siècle Paris: The Banquet Years* (New York: Vintage Books, 1968); Carl Schorske, *Fin-de-Siècle Vienna:*

*Politics and Culture* (New York: Knopf, 1980); and Laura Engelstein, *The Keys to Happiness: Sex and the Search for Modernity in Fin-de-Siècle Russia* (Ithaca: Cornell University Press, 1992).

15 Lynn Hunt, *The Family Romance of the French Revolution* (Berkeley: University of California Press, 1992), 9.

16 Geoffrey Nowell-Smith discusses the link between Freud's concept of *Familienroman* and incest in the context of melodrama. As he points out, the term is "variously translatable as 'romance' and 'novel,'" the latter of which addresses the ways that people can write themselves into narrations (Nowell-Smith, "A Note on 'Family Romance,'" *Screen* 18, no. 2 [1977]: 119).

17 Terry Eagleton, *Literary Theory: An Introduction* (Minneapolis: University of Minnesota Press, 1983), 156–57.

18 The journal *Vospitanie i obuchenie,* published from 1866 until the Bolshevik revolution, functioned as a quasipolitical forum that integrated questions of family, especially child rearing, into the larger sociopolitical structure. Although the journal itself was anything but melodramatic, it nonetheless illustrates how questions raised in *domostroi* dramas were also being debated by the educated professionals.

19 Kaplan, "Mothering, Feminism, and Representation," 117.

20 Ibid., 116–20.

21 Ibid., 120–23.

22 John Forrester, *Truth Games, Lies, Money, and Psychoanalysis,* quoted in Graham Little, "Couched in Freud," *Australian Review of Books* 3, no. 4 (July 1998): 5.

23 Lynn Hunt, in her discussion of the origins of melodrama in late-eighteenth-century France, notes the importance of incest as a theme because of the confusion about paternity after the murder of the king-father (Hunt, *The Family Romance,* 181–91).

24 Richard Wortman, "The Russian Empress as Mother," in *The Family in Imperial Russia: New Lines of Historical Research,* ed. David Ransel (Urbana: University of Illinois Press, 1978), 72–74.

25 Yuri Tsivian, "Some Preparatory Remarks on Russian Cinema," in *Silent Witnesses: Russian Films 1908–1919,* ed. Paolo Cherchi Usai, Lorenzo Codelli, Carlo Monanaro, and David Robinson, with Yuri Tsivian (London: British Film Institute, 1989), 24–26.

26 Kaplan, "Mothering, Feminism, and Representation."

27 As Ann Daly points out: "There have always been mothers, but motherhood was invented" (quoted in Marianne Hirsch, *The Mother/Daughter Plot: Narrative, Psychoanalysis, Feminism* [Bloomington: Indiana University Press, 1989], 14).

28 See the newspaper article by Verbitskaia in her archive, published in 1891 in *Smolenskii vestnik* (RGALI f. 1042, op. 1, d. 37, 1).

29 The novel was published commercially by A. A. Levenson in 1901.

30 See, for example, the review by Mordvin in *Novoe vremia,* no. 8908, December 13, 1900. The reviewer in *Sever,* no. 17, April 20, 1901, went so far as to suggest that *Vavochka* would be better appreciated had it appeared in France.

31 *Vavochka* also borrowed many personalities from the production crew for *Keys:* director V. Gardin and cinematographer A. Levitskii worked on both *Keys* and *Vavochka,* and character actress E. Uvarova played the role of mother in both. See V. E. Vishnevskii, *Khudozhestvennye fil'my dorevoliutsionnoi Rossii* (Moscow: Goskinoizdat, 1945), 29, 37.

32 Jay Leyda, *Kino: A History of the Russian and Soviet Film* (1960; Princeton: Princeton University Press, 1983), 63.

33 The libretto for *Vavochka* was published in *Zhivoi ekran,* nos. 5–6 (Rostov-na-donu, 1914).

34 In the novel, Mal'tsev is a sexual predator who seduces many of the female characters.

35 In the 334-page novel, Verbitskaia specifically discusses hysteria and other mental afflictions.

36 *Za schastie,* dir. Evgeny Bauer, A. Khanzhonkov and Co., 1917.

37 In contrast, in a real-life American version of the mother versus the wanton daughter, Mrs. Kelly had her daughter Eugenia arrested in a successful attempt to bring her to her senses and return home. See Lewis Erenberg's *Steppin' Out: New York Nightlife and the Transformation of American Culture, 1890–1930* (Chicago: University of Chicago Press, 1981), 77–85.

38 These movies contest the effectiveness of the advice offered in such "ladies home" journals as *Vospitanie i obuchenie.*

39 Although the Russian authors did not invoke Freud, he wrote at length about the way in which mother/daughter relations produce hysteria when the daughter cannot detach herself successfully. Quoted in Hirsch, *The Mother/Daughter Plot,* 99.

40 The libretto was reprinted in *Peterburgskie kinemoteatry,* no. 98, January 1914.

41 However, a movie titled *The Great Sin,* released in 1917 from an obscure studio, was also evocatively subtitled *A Father's Forbidden Passion.* V. E. Vishnevskii, *Khudozhestvennye fil'my dorevoliutsionnoi Rossii* (Moscow: Goskinoizdat, 1945), 83.

42 *Doch' kuptsa Bashkirova,* dir. Nikolai Larin, G. Libken's Volga Co., 1913.

43 William Wagner, *Marriage, Property, and Law in Late Imperial Russia* (Oxford: Clarendon Press, 1994).

44 In his *Patriotic Culture in Russia during World War I* (Ithaca: Cornell University Press, 1995), Hubertus Jahn notes that the vast majority of films produced during the war were "civilian," which he also considers "escapist" (154). He does not, however, observe how truly few movies featured heroic soldiers.

45 *Malyutka Elli*, dir. Iakov Protozanov, prod. I Ermol'ev, Ermol'ev Studio, 1918.

46 Molly Haskell, "The 2,000-Year-Old Misunderstanding: 'Rape Fantasy,'" *Ms.* 5 (November 1976): 84–98.

47 Misogyny was a prominent feature in the often violent popular culture. See, for example, Catriona Kelly, "'Better Halves?' Representations of Women in Russian Urban Popular Culture," in *Women and Society in Russia and the Soviet Union,* ed. Linda Edmondson (New York: Cambridge University Press, 1992), 5–31.

48 Female students in particular cheer in my classes when the merchant's daughter sets fire to the bar.

49 See, for example, Sharon Willis, "Hardware and Hardbodies, What Do Women Want? A Reading of *Thelma and Louise,*" in *Film Theory Goes to the Movies,* ed. Jim Collins, Hilary Radner, and Ava Preacher Collins (New York: Routledge, 1993), 120–28.

50 Engelstein, in *The Keys to Happiness,* chapter 7, "End of Innocence and Loss of Control," also discusses the violence and impotence that followed 1905.

51 As Laura Mulvey points out, when the woman is the central protagonist and is "unable to achieve a stable sexual identity," she finds her Freudian self "torn between the deep blue sea of passive femininity and the devil of regressive masculinity" (Mulvey, "Afterthoughts on 'Visual Pleasure and Narrative Cinema' inspired by *Duel in the Sun,*" in *Psychoanalysis and Cinema* ed. E. Ann Kaplan [New York: Routledge, 1990], 25).

52 Studies by and about Douglas Sirk pioneered in viewing melodrama as disruptive. See Barbara Klinger, *Melodrama and Meaning: History, Culture, and the Films of Douglas Sirk* (Bloomington: Indiana University Press, 1994); and David Rodowick, "Madness, Authority, and Ideology: The Domestic Melodrama of the 1950s," in Gledhill, ed., *Home Is Where the Heart Is,* for discussions of the ways in which melodrama disrupts the ideologies that work to contain it.

53 Christine Viviani, "Who Is without Sin? The Maternal Melodrama in American Film, 1930–39," in Gledhill, ed., *Home Is Where the Heart Is,* 83–99. Although this article deals specifically with later films, the western maternal formula dates from the silent era.

54 Tsivian, "Some Preparatory Remarks on Russian Cinema," 24–26.

55 S. S. Ginzburg, *Kinematografiia dorevoliutsionnoi Rossii* (Moscow: Izkusstvo, 1963), 380.

56 For similar contemporary perspectives, see Richard Stites's review of the British Film Institute video series in his essay "Dusky Images of Tsarist Russia: Prerevolutionary Cinema," *Russian Review* 53, no. 2 (April 1994): 285–95.

57 Laura Mulvey, " 'It Will Be a Magnificent Obsession': The Melodrama's Role in the Development of Contemporary Film Theory," in Bratton, Cook, and Gledhill, eds., *Melodrama,* 122.

58 Anne Friedberg emphasizes the connection between cinematic identification and patriarchy: "Identification is a process which commands the subject be displaced by an *other;* it is a procedure which refuses and recuperates the separation between self and other, and in this way replicates the very structure of patriarchy" (Friedberg, "A Denial of Difference: Theories of Cinematic Identification," in Kaplan, ed., *Psychoanalysis and Cinema,* 36).

59 Hunt, *The Family Romance,* 188.

*Julie A. Cassiday*

# Alcohol Is Our Enemy!

## Soviet Temperance Melodramas of the 1920s

Historians of the Soviet Union's revolutionary theater ordinarily focus their attention on the playwrights and directors who forged entirely new types of drama and techniques of staging and who consequently have exerted a lasting influence in both Russia and the West.[1] Yet at the same time that such luminaries as Vladimir Mayakovsky, Evgeny Vakhtangov, Vsevolod Meyerhold, and Sergei Eisenstein utterly transformed previous conceptions of the theater and film, a significant number of dramatists, directors, and cultural authorities turned to one of the western theater's more conventional forms, melodrama, as the dramatic genre best suited to the new country's revolutionary stage and screen. Melodrama's roots in the French Revolution, which Bolsheviks consciously strove to imitate in the years immediately after 1917, suggested that melodramatic plays and films would satisfy the perceived needs of the country's previously disenfranchised working classes.[2] In addition, the genre's use of Manichaean oppositions, its privileging of social conflict over psychic drama, and the accelerated consciousness-raising of its characters all recommended melodrama as an appropriate form for revolutionary art. Understandably, cultural authorities such as first Commissar of Enlightenment Anatoly Lunacharsky and Maxsim Gorky found the persuasive moral message of melodrama highly attractive, and they ardently advocated the genre's inclusion in revolutionary culture after 1917. Although the ideological slant and political benefit of much avant-garde drama in the 1920s was ambiguous at best, what cultural authorities perceived as melodrama's long, democratic history suggested that it would deliver politically attuned messages of direct relevance to the lives of soviet workers and peasants.

Unlike Meyerhold's experiments in constructivism and Eisenstein's pioneering use of montage, melodrama had already proven its appeal before 1917 to the same audience that a large percentage of early soviet propaganda had as its target. The ability of melodrama not only to attract a mass audience but also to elicit tears—that is, to produce a visible token of spectators' intense emotional engagement—provided proof positive of the genre's affective and persuasive impact.[3] In addition, melodrama's cast of stock characters (the noble hero, the hidden villain, the innocent and vulnerable heroine, et cetera) caught in the struggle between good and evil provided an accurate aesthetic model for Russia's Marxist revolution, even though it was at odds with marxism itself.[4] Melodrama's underlying principle of *enantiodromia,* commonly called poetic justice, fortuitously overlapped with the Marxist historical dialectic, providing a popular teleology for the Bolshevik revolution, in which the evil capitalists got their just deserts and relinquished power to the innocent and long-suffering proletariat.[5] As a master trope for the Bolshevik revolution and a genre with proven mass appeal, melodrama seemed eminently appropriate for teaching revolution to the new audience in the country's theaters and movie houses.

In spite of these promising qualities, melodrama did not take root in the world of avant-garde theater and cinema during the 1920s. Many dramatists and directors had no desire to heed the call to return to what they considered a hopelessly cliché-ridden and outmoded form of drama, and those who attempted to renovate and revolutionize the genre had little lasting success with melodrama as an experiment in soviet avant-garde entertainment. True to its democratic heritage, melodrama proved to be most successful on amateur stages and in popular movie houses during the 1920s, especially in the numerous courtroom dramas staged and filmed at the time. This legal propaganda borrowed liberally from the melodramatic mode to instruct the soviet populace on a variety of issues as diverse as slacking on the job, venereal disease, and alcoholism. Much early soviet legal propaganda served simply to promulgate the country's new laws and statutes—for example, in newspaper reports of prominent trials or in documentary newsreels depicting the enemies of the soviet people. However, the most ideologically weighted instances of legal propaganda from the 1920s combined melodrama with courtroom drama, placing imaginary criminals before a fictional court that tried them for breaches of the country's new civil and criminal codes. In theatrical mock trials, called *agitsudy,* and in their filmed counterparts, melodrama intensified the social conflict represented in fictional litigation, pointed the way to the mock court's final verdict, and generated exemplary lessons in bolshevism that propagandists hoped would be readily consumed by proletarian and peasant spectators.[6]

The suitability of the melodramatic mode for early soviet legal propaganda can be seen in a number of anti-alcohol *agitsudy* that appeared on stages and screens during the 1920s. The temperance play had already proven itself an especially sensational, popular, and didactic variation on traditional melodramatic themes during the nineteenth century.[7] Soviet adaptations of the temperance melodrama omitted the highly spectacular scenes of delirium tremens that drew spectators to theaters in England and America; nonetheless, the anti-alcohol *agitsud* culminated, much like its western counterpart, in a direct appeal to the audience to take a pledge of sobriety.[8] In addition to replicating the call to immediate reform, soviet temperance melodramas copied the character of the dipsomaniac victim/villain, whom western drama had canonized as the temperance play's hero.[9] Unlike other stock melodramatic heroes, the drunkard combined innocence and villainy in a single person, conflating moral positions that were usually polarized in separate good and evil characters. Although the drunkard was himself a victim of temptation or liquor, he spent most of the temperance melodrama victimizing others, and he ended his despicable career only with a violent conversion from dissipation to abstinence that provided the perfect model for conversion to bolshevism. Two courtroom dramas from the 1920s—*The Trial of Stepan Korolev,* a 1924 *agitsud* by Boris Sigal, and *Saba,* a 1929 film by Mikhail Chiaureli—illustrate the uses of the temperance melodrama in early soviet propaganda and the didactic power of literalizing poetic justice on the soviet stage and screen.

## Lunacharsky's Call to Melodrama

Although Anatoly Lunacharsky sounded the call "Back to Ostrovsky!" much louder and with far greater results in professional theaters of the 1920s, the Soviet Union's first commissar of enlightenment believed in the utility of melodrama for the revolutionary stage just as passionately as in that of the Russian theater's classical repertoire.[10] Lunacharsky's advocacy of revitalized melodrama assumed a general affinity of the genre with revolution, and he had espoused melodrama as the means of creating a genuinely popular theater with socialist inclinations long before bolshevism became the country's dominant ideology.[11] Lunacharsky's belief in melodrama's serviceability for social and political goals drew directly on the French socialist Romain Rolland's highly influential book *The People's Theater* (1903), an entire chapter of which provided a manifesto of melodrama as the genre most suited for revitalizing the theater at the turn of the century.[12] Rolland's expansive yet critical definition of melodrama as a theatrical genre motivated Lunacharsky to adopt his position and to encourage a renaissance of melodrama on the Russian revolutionary stage.

As part of his declaration of the need to return theater to the masses, Rolland rewrites the history of melodrama and retraces the genre's aesthetic lineage. Rather than describe melodrama's genesis in the plays of Pixérécourt on the French stage at the end of the eighteenth century, Rolland looks back from modern-day, popular playhouses to the amphitheaters of ancient Greece. Reacting against the snobbery of theater critics in his own day, Rolland turns accusations of melodrama in the plays of Aeschylus, Sophocles, and Shakespeare on their head, and claims that the alleged shortfallings of these great western dramatists were, in fact, the surest sign of their genius. Careful to contrast the cheap melodrama of the boulevards with *Oresteia, Oedipus Rex,* and *Macbeth,* Rolland asserts that the greatest playwrights, regardless of time and place, have all incorporated melodrama in their tragedies as well as in their comedies.[13] As he describes this intersection of tragedy and melodrama, Rolland in effect re-creates both genres as a single, hybrid theatrical form: the lofty language and finely crafted dramatic action of Sophocles or Shakespeare come together with the social relevancy and emotional affect of Pixérécourt. In essence, Rolland's vision of revitalized melodrama places the western theater's rich history of tragedy in the modern, revolutionary context of melodrama.[14]

After granting the popular theater of his day this distinguished heritage, Rolland lists the four most important qualities for a successful melodrama: varied emotions, "true realism," a simple moral, and getting one's money's worth.[15] All of these terms describe actual melodramatic productions of Rolland's day, which indeed combined laughter with tears, depicted realistic scenarios, delivered a simple, moral message, and were compelled to give their audiences something for their money. Yet Rolland follows this list with a call to apply these rules with artistic integrity, urging playwrights to purify an admittedly popular genre, to raise it from lowbrow to highbrow tastes, and to infuse it with a noble, moral aim. The fact that large popular audiences already watched and enjoyed "the simple emotions, the simple pleasures" of melodrama on a regular basis encouraged Rolland to refine the genre for his vision of a people's theater.[16] Rather than invent some new and untried type of dramatic spectacle that would bridge the gap between popular and intellectual audiences, Rolland prefers to nominate a melodramatic reading of tragedy as the reincarnation of ancient Greek drama for the theater of the future.

Lunacharsky unabashedly expresses his debt to Rolland's vision in postrevolutionary calls for melodrama on the soviet stage.[17] Lunacharsky copies Rolland's somewhat fanciful family tree, which traces the connection between melodrama and Attic tragedy, as well as the assertion that the genre had the greatest appeal, and hence the most utility, for the mass audience.[18] Like Rolland, Lunacharsky coupled the need to entertain the popular spectator with the desire to teach a simple, yet noble, moral message, and he elaborated his own set of defining characteristics essential to melodrama. Lunacharsky's list, highly similar to Rolland's, culminated in "the ability to stimulate undivided and total emotional reactions of compassion and indignation; the connection of action with simple and hence majestic, ethical tenets, with simple and clear ideas."[19] Lunacharsky even duplicates Rolland's recommendation that the melodramatic playwright learn from his audience before he composes plays intended to teach the masses.[20] In fact, Lunacharsky's only substantive alteration of Rolland's plan is the rather predictable addition of a proletarian worldview as the foundation of melodrama on the revolutionary stage, an addition that promised to create the propaganda messages needed in the 1920s.[21] Lunacharsky's decision to adopt Rolland's view of melodrama shows the first commissar of enlightenment's unusually practical and synthetic view of dramatic art after 1917. Many directors in the theater conducted radical experiments that tossed old dramatic genres and techniques off the steamship of theatrical modernity; yet Lunacharsky understood the need to renew prerevolutionary melodrama—as it appeared both in popular, fairground *balagany* and on the stage of Russia's nineteenth-century professional theater—if revolutionary art ever hoped to reach its intended audience.[22]

Echoing Lunacharsky's ideas, Gorky also declared the need "to return to a clarity of emotion, even to a primitiveness . . . [of the] 'grand' emotions, on which the greatest experts of the human soul—the Greek tragedians, Shakespeare, Schiller, Goethe, and so on—constructed their dramas."[23] A handful of prominent members of the Soviet Union's theatrical avant-garde responded to these appeals for melodrama in the first half of the decade. In 1920, theater critic Pavel Markov wrote that melodrama was the genre most capable of realizing and synthesizing the leftist theatrical experiments of the previous decade and of putting them to revolutionary work.[24] Meyerhold, the director responsible for much of the Left theater, declared in a lecture devoted to his production of *Teacher Bubus* (1925) that melodrama, in its purest form, indeed constituted a revival of ancient Greek drama.[25] On the other end of the artistic spectrum, the director Alexander Tairov applied melodrama's poetic justice, in which good is promptly rewarded and evil inexorably punished, to his production of *Rosita* (1925).[26] In spite of this enthusiasm, the professional theater never brought about what Lunacharsky and Gorky had hoped would be a rebirth of melodrama on the soviet stage. A number of directors staged revivals of nineteenth-century French melodramas; a handful of new soviet melodramas also appeared; but the two Moscow theaters that devoted their entire repertoire to the genre, the Free Theater and the Romanesque Theater, both collapsed after only a single season.[27] A 1919 playwriting contest, which Lunacharsky and Gorky cosponsored to encourage the composition of revolutionary melodramas, presaged the genre's failure on the Soviet Union's professional stage: not one of the forty-one submissions merited a first prize, and the only entry that was widely produced, Alexander Vermishev's *Red Truth,* failed to meet the jury's definition of melodrama.[28]

In great contrast, popular soviet cinema heeded the call to melodrama and implemented Lunacharsky and Gorky's recommendations in films that hoped to diminish soviet viewers' adoration of western stars such as Mary Pickford, Harry Piel, and Harold Lloyd. Although Lunacharsky initially sounded the call to melodrama expressly for the stage, by the mid-1920s he had shifted his attention to the screen, which he believed was better suited than the theater to melodrama and mass propaganda: "Our films must be just as attractive and just as entertaining as bourgeois films. The melodramatic form is the best form for cinema in the appropriate treatment, of course, because in this respect cinema is 'in all its facets' considerably richer than the theater."[29] Adapting the bourgeois genre of cinematic melodrama to soviet purposes would allow cinema to function "as an instrument of intelligent propaganda and as a purveyor of intelligent entertainment and also as a source of revenue."[30]

Ambitious as this formula sounds, Lunacharsky himself proved the ability of film melodrama at least to entertain and to turn a considerable profit by coauthoring the screenplay of the decade's largest domestic box-office hit, a distinctly unsoviet melodrama titled *The Bear's Wedding* (directed by Konstantine Eggert in 1925). Rather than producing a script with a simple soviet moral, Lunacharsky rewrote Prosper Mérimée's tale of vampirism and perversion. *The Bear's Wedding* revolves around the marriage of an innocent girl to a sinister count, who ravages his young bride on their wedding night when he is transformed into a predatory demon during a supernatural seizure.[31] In *The Bear's Wedding* and other melodramatic screenplays, Lunacharsky proved the popularity and viability of melodrama for cinema, "the most important of the arts."[32] However, this lurid movie, whose flimsy political message clearly had been tacked on at the last moment, failed to meet the high standards that Lunacharsky himself had set for the genre and supported critics such as Adrian Piotrovskii, who saw melodrama as inherently bourgeois and individualistic, and hence unsuited for soviet film.[33]

Both Piotrovskii's hatred of and Lunacharsky's attraction to melodrama on film undoubtedly arose from the country's already established tradition of cinematic melodrama, which constituted the most popular genre of domestic and imported films in Russian movie houses before 1917.[34] As critics pointed out, Lunacharsky's screenplay for *The Bear's Wedding* had much in common with prerevolutionary blockbusters that, like the Russian stage melodramas of the previous century, emphasized protagonists' internal emotional states and archtragic "Russian endings."[35] However, not all postrevolutionary melodramas on film followed the model of their prerevolutionary predecessors; instead, many film directors looking to educate as well as to entertain after 1917 focused on social conflict and fast-paced action, and contrived only happy endings, for which Hollywood melodramas were known.[36] Although the Hollywood model of movie making was brought into soviet films with serious reservations about Americanization, the convergence of soviet cinema with Hollywood melodrama promised to create propaganda with tremendous audience appeal, undeniable emotional impact, and clear revolutionary values. Revitalized and revolutionized melodrama on film would perform the minor miracle of simultaneously fulfilling a popular audience's demands for lively entertainment and the soviet state's mandate for suitable content on the country's movie screens.

### The Trial of Stepan Korolev

Immediately after the revolution, revitalizing and revolutionizing melodrama in the new country's cinema proved to be virtually impossible. Soviet film production during the 1920s limped along under the crippling effects of a severe shortage of film stock and camera equipment, a dearth of suitable screenplays, and fierce competition with foreign, especially American, movies.[37] In great contrast, the number of amateur theatrical clubs was so great during the decade that, to quote Viktor Shklovsky, "nobody knows what to do with the dramatic circles; they are multiplying like bacteria."[38] During the early 1920s, amateur theater provided the artistic medium of the soviet masses, heeding Lunacharsky's call to infuse dramatic art with the spirit of melodrama in small theatrical genres such as the *agitsud*.[39] The need to depict conflict between polar opposites of good and evil, to infuse mock trial testimony with clear moral purpose, and to elicit strong emotions as a means of persuading viewers rendered melodrama the most appropriate mode for the *agitsud,* even if the rigid structural confines of theatrical mock trials prevented them from being stage melodramas in their purest form. The literalization of melodrama's poetic justice in the *agitsud* provided an effective and affective theatrical form that propagandists working in all areas of soviet life could fill with appropriate content, thereby making mock trials a widespread and popular type of theatrical agitation.[40]

As a relatively modest genre of amateur theater, the *agitsud* did not pretend to artistic immortality but rather used the poetic justice of melodrama to teach peasant and proletarian audiences bolshevism's answers to the burning questions of the day. These questions included the agricultural campaign, the crusade for atheism, the battle against illiteracy, and the fight to improve public health, to which the genre's most prolific author, Doctor Boris Sigal, dedicated some thirteen *agitsudy.* As typical examples of theatrical mock trials, Sigal's plays put their action "strictly in the framework of an actual court," so that "the production creates an impression on the audience not of a dramatization or a play, but of a real-life trial."[41] Realistic courtroom furnishings and procedures helped to create this illusion, including signed oaths by defendants and witnesses and threats of prosecution for perjury from the mock court's judge. As proponents of revolutionary theater unanimously recommended, audience participation played an important role in the *agitsud,* which usually began with the election of two to three audience members as people's assessors, who sat on stage throughout the play and helped to determine the sentence at the end of the mock trial.[42]

If such realistic touches were not enough to grab spectators' attention, authors of *agitsudy* such as Sigal recommended that amateur theatrical clubs use written scripts only as a general canvas, which they were supposed to splash liberally with their own local color.[43] Yet beneath the painstaking reproduction of contemporary courtroom ritual and the multipronged effort to engage spectators in the action on stage lay the archetypal, melodramatic conflict between hidden villains and their helpless victims, who would be rewarded or punished as was fit in the verdict announced at the end of the play. Although the audience could easily label victim and enemy at the mock trial's start, the denouement of the average *agitsud* consisted of the defendant's own recognition of a crime he had repeatedly denied—that is, of his confession and repentance before a court and theater composed of his peers. The defendant's melodramatic unmasking and his tearful statement of contrition were intended to move the audience itself to tears and to encourage spectators to reproduce the hidden enemy's self-criticism, or *samokritika,* so that they, like the defendant, could be rehabilitated and reintegrated into soviet society at the play's end.[44]

Sigal's 1924 *The Trial of Stepan Korolev (as a Result of Drunkenness)* illustrates how the *agitsud*'s rigid courtroom realism functioned much as a traditional temperance melodrama.[45] The testimony that constitutes the play's dialogue is regrettably marked by what one Glavrepertkom (Main Repertory Committee) censor calls "dryness, heaviness, and verbosity . . . defects [from which] all the numerous sanitary *agitki* [short agitational plays] of the present author suffer."[46] Notwithstanding Sigal's uninspired use of courtroom procedure and legalese at the expense of character development, *The Trial of Stepan Korolev* draws a clear line between the friends and the enemies of soviet life during its very first moments. The action described in the play's dry, heavy, and verbose dialogue portrays the many newspaper reports of drunken violence from the era, and it is the typical stuff of melodrama, as the mock court's opening indictment of the defendant Korolev shows: "The citizen of Leningrad, Stepan Korolev, 34 years of age, is handed over to the court under accusations of systematic drunkenness, theft of factory goods and materials, battering his wife and children, assault with a knife, and attempted murder of a policeman."[47] As various witnesses take the stand, the story behind these crimes comes to light: the once industrious and upstanding Korolev succumbed to the pressure of an alcoholic friend and began to drink in the establishment of a local bootlegger. In spite of his awareness that such a slippery path could only lead downward, Korolev became addicted to drink, began stealing from the factory where he worked, was fired from his job, sold his wife's clothes and children's school books to finance his drinking bouts, and ended up consoling himself by beating his family, cavorting with a woman of loose virtue, and lashing out in violent attacks against local law enforcers. Like the typical drunkard of earlier temperance plays, Korolev is not only the victim of temptation, alcohol, and bootleggers but also the perpetrator of multiple crimes against his family and society.

In keeping with the earlier paradigm of temperance melodramas, Korolev's family sustains the most damage from his bouts of dipsomania. His beleaguered wife has been reduced to providing for her family by washing and ironing the clothes of others, an activity dangerously close to destitution in actual life and to prostitution in the popular imagination. Korolev's bruised and battered son was compelled to buy back in secret his school books at the local bazaar in order to continue his studies. The improbability of Korolev's accelerating spiral downward, which began with a single night of drunken fun but ends in a broken home, unemployment, murderous violence, and dangerously weak health, points to the melodramatic modeling of the defendant's crime. Such undermotivated chains of events in which, in the words of Steve Neale, "there is an *excess* of effect over cause," characterize melodrama and contribute to the teleology of its poetic justice.[48] In the case of Stepan Korolev, the accumulation of crimes proves to the audience, beyond any shadow of a doubt, that not the defendant but, more important, "alcohol is our old enemy." Much as in earlier temperance melodramas, the bootlegger Pavlenko, who embodies all the temptations and evils of alcohol, turns out to be the true villain in Sigal's play. Although this "spider that drinks in the worker's body and sucks his blood" can never find a place in the soviet way of life, Korolev's combined victim/villain status allows for his eventual rehabilitation.[49]

In spite of the lifeless dialogue of witnesses and almost ten pages of testimony by an expert on the effects—medical, social, and hereditary—of alcohol, Sigal's *The Trial of Stepan Korolev* was meant to move its spectators to compassion and indignation, as Lunacharsky had recommended in his description of melodrama. The anger-provoking facts of Korolev's crimes were relieved by the copious tears shed on stage by the defendant's elderly neighbor and his wife, and by himself in his final confession. Sigal's careful placement of not only tearful but also tear-jerking testimony throughout the play suggests a gradual buildup toward the spectator's own tears: the old woman next door is the third to testify at the trial; Korolev's wife takes the stand immediately before the last witness, the medical expert; and Korolev's own lachrymose final statement falls at the play's end. In his last burst of weeping, the poetic justice demanded by the narrative of Korolev's many crimes meets actual justice in the court as the defendant accepts his guilt: "Now I see that I hurt my wife and children, and yes, they had reason to reproach me. I am guilty before them. Forgive me, citizen judges, and I won't do this anymore. I see that this leads a person to misfortune, I want to become a person again, I ask you to have mercy on me. . . . So many miseries because of me. Let me make up for my guilt, acquit me (he cries). I will do everything so I won't give in anymore."[50] In the coda to his teary confession, Korolev is reunited with his wife, who weeps once again when she hears that the court's sentence of three years of hard labor has been suspended because of her husband's proletarian background and sincere promise to abstain. By the end of Sigal's play, the repeated weeping of characters on the stage has found its reflection in the compassionate sentence of the mock court, which benevolently grants Korolev the opportunity to be reunited with his family as well as with his fellow proletarians. By recognizing the villain within himself, Korolev validates his status as a victim of the bottle and merits the mercy the court shows him in its final sentence.

Authors such as Sigal hoped that the ultimate rendering of poetic justice in the *agitsud* would be the application of the melodramatic modeling of friends and enemies to the spectator's life. By identifying with the court's judge, the people's assessors, and the accused Korolev, the spectator would discover his own potential to be both victim and villain and was encouraged to give up alcohol before he found himself in Korolev's shoes. Although some seventy years later Sigal's drama seems stilted and contrived, the mass proletarian audience for which he wrote *The Trial of Stepan Korolev* had little exposure to professional theater and could have plausibly mistaken an *agitsud*'s counterfeit court for true coin, as in fact an editor for *Pravda* actually did in a review of a 1921 production of *Trial of a Prostitute*.[51] The editor's oversight gave *Trial of a Prostitute* the serious reception that theatrical propagandists such as Sigal felt the *agitsud* deserved and showed the similarity of mock trials to the real criminal cases that newspapers and magazines of the day covered as part of their standard reporting. The almost pedantic adherence to realistic courtroom detail in the *agitsud* most probably encouraged the *Pravda* editor to mistake this mock trial for the transcript of an actual trial, which figured as an important genre of popular literature even before 1917. The educational impact of the theatrical mock trial arose from this ability to blur the distinction between fiction and reality, as well as from its audience appeal and legibility, its stark contrasts used to create a moral message, and its strong, persuasive emotions, all of which Lunacharsky had described in his call to revolutionary melodrama.

## Saba

For all their merits, melodramatic and otherwise, fictional courts in the theater proved to be limited in their impact, and the *agitsud* began to disappear from amateur stages in the second half of the 1920s. The increasingly detailed directions in the genre's instructional literature—not simply for stimulating but also for directing and even scripting audience participation—betrayed a growing distrust in the spontaneous creativity of the peasant and proletarian masses as the decade progressed. Participation in the *agitsud* had been premised on a seemingly simple and predictable act of mimesis: proletarian and peasant viewers watched the poetic justice of revolution on the stage and reproduced it in their own lives once they left the theater. However, such participation presented a myriad of problems, such as inappropriate or poorly timed interference in the play's action or, even worse, a complete absence of any type of audience involvement. Putting mock trials on the country's movie screens offered a practical solution to this troubling problem because audience participation in film required little more than the spectator's presence in the movie house. According to the emerging theories of montage in the 1920s, viewer participation resulted from the creative juxtaposition of images on film, which spectators were compelled to interpret by making new, hitherto unthinkable connections between edited images. This process caused a fundamental restructuring of the viewer's consciousness and united individual spectators in a collective creative act. Whether one preferred Lev Kuleshov's experiments in visual continuity or Eisenstein's colliding images, revolutionary cinema promised to carry out what the revolutionary theater had ultimately failed to do by the end of the decade—that is, to resurrect the collective dramatic action of ancient Greek tragedy.[52] As a small part of this ambitious cultural project, courtroom dramas on film continued to teach the same lessons as the *agitsud* but expanded the melodramatic mode utilized on the stage into full-blown melodrama on the movie screen.

Mikhail Chiaureli's 1929 silent film *Saba: A Melodrama in Six Parts* provides a good illustration of how adaptation to film fundamentally altered the intended message and the anticipated reception of an *agitsud* such as Sigal's *The Trial of Stepan Korolev.*[53] Sigal placed the action of his play in Leningrad in approximately 1924, while Chiaureli's film is set in Tbilisi at the very end of the decade; nonetheless, these two tales of the dangers of drink bear a striking resemblance because of their shared origin in the temperance melodrama. The most obvious difference between the two works is *Saba*'s greater narrative breadth: in contrast to the *agitsud,* which took place entirely within the confines of a contemporary courtroom, only the last of *Saba*'s eight reels depicts "The Show Trial of the Former Trolley Conductor Saba Dzhaliadshvili." The preceding seven reels show Saba's crimes in all their despicable and colorful detail, which viewers of the film could see in great contrast to the mere narration of Korolev's crimes in Sigal's play. The moviegoers themselves witness Saba's slide into alcohol abuse, wife battering, child neglect, unemployment, theft, drunken brawls, and homelessness, which only ends when Saba nearly kills his son in a drunken trolley-driving accident. In addition to the chain of Saba's many misdeeds, the viewer sees the appalling consequences of intemperance in the lives of his wife and their son, rather than simply hearing about them at the trial. Like Korolev's wife in the earlier *agitsud,* Saba's wife must make her living washing clothes, and his young son cannot participate in Young Pioneer activities at school because the dissolute father has given him a black eye and destroyed his model plane, making him the target of the other Pioneers' ridicule. Saba's wife and son vividly bear the marks of his misdeeds, which the movie viewers actually see as they anticipate the poetic justice that will punish Saba and reward his beleaguered family. As a filmed temperance melodrama, *Saba* replaced the spoken testimony of defendants and witnesses in the *agitsud* with compelling images of crime and its personal, familial, and social consequences.

By the time Saba comes to trial, the audience in the movie theater was intended to have already reached the same conclusion that it did while watching Sigal's play: "Alcohol is our class enemy." Nonetheless, the testimony of Saba himself and that of the leader of his son's Pioneer circle are interspersed with flashbacks that repeat Saba's crimes and reinforce the inescapable connection between them and the trial in progress. The flashbacks of his own debauchery and cruelty to his family prompt Saba to recognize his victim/villain status and to beg the court to judge his actions: "It's true, I was the undoing of my own son. . . . Judge me." Yet these flashbacks do not function exclusively on an individual level to activate Saba's long-dormant conscience; in addition, they remind the spectator at the trial and in the movie house of the rips in the social fabric of Saba's home and at his workplace. The broad, social implications of Saba's crime become clear in the intertitles and clips from documentary films that support the testimony of expert witnesses. Much like officials and experts in a typical *agitsud,* the court's president states: "We are not judging only [Saba]. The old way of life, with its drinking binges and debauchery, is at the defendant's dock." At this point in the film, grotesque images of several men disfigured by the effects of chronic alcohol abuse (most probably taken from medical films of the time) appear, proving the judge's contention and warning Saba, the trial's spectators, and the film's audience of the fate that awaits those who drink to excess. Although the trial constitutes only a fraction of the film's plot, the use of images from earlier in the narrative and from outside of *Saba*'s fictional world give this scene greater visual persuasion than its theatrical counterpart, connecting the fictional trial on film to the world of its viewers and urging the desired response of moviegoers who might have missed *Saba*'s didactic message in earlier episodes of the film.

Filmed legal propaganda such as *Saba* translated much of the spoken drama of the *agitsud* into forceful, melodramatic images. Yet for all their visual persuasion, fictional trials on film struggled to compensate for the loss of orality that came with moving the *agitsud* to the silent screen. The need to communicate the precise details of crime and the legal technicalities of its consequences meant that directors often used an unusually large number of intertitles to guarantee that spectators would correctly understand the film's action. In particular, trial scenes such as Saba's relied on frequent and sometimes lengthy intertitles to gloss the film's images. Although the oral component was lost when soviet temperance trials came to the movies, a strong verbal component, which had been a distinguishing feature of prerevolutionary Russian films, remained to complement and reinforce the visual construction of the battle between good and evil.[54]

As Saba's compliant confession shows, defendants in filmed mock trials unmasked their enemy status with just as much regret and just as many tears as they did in theatrical *agitsudy.* But unlike its theatrical predecessor, the fictional trial on film could actually depict reintegration into society, something that lay beyond the narrative confines of the *agitsud.* The collective nature of Saba's crimes dictated that the social networks that sustained damage, namely his family and his coworkers, be the ones to determine his punishment and decide if they can invite him back with open arms. Like Stepan Korolev, Saba's initial fall from sobriety took place when he buckled under the pressures of his alcoholic, working-class peers and spent his entire paycheck on drink. Correspondingly, the collective that pressured him into crime must discipline not only Saba, but also itself, before he can be welcomed back. After Saba's confession and the harsh words of the prosecution, the collective of workers from which Saba was expelled states: "He alone shouldn't be judged . . . but our entire collective." First, they point their collective finger at the true villains in the film, those who sell alcohol to innocent men such as Saba. After demanding that bars in working-class neighborhoods, such as the one where Saba met his downfall, be closed; they then ask for leniency in Saba's sentencing. After these requests, Saba's wife and son take the witness stand, where they weep and beg to be reunited with the head of their family. Interestingly enough,

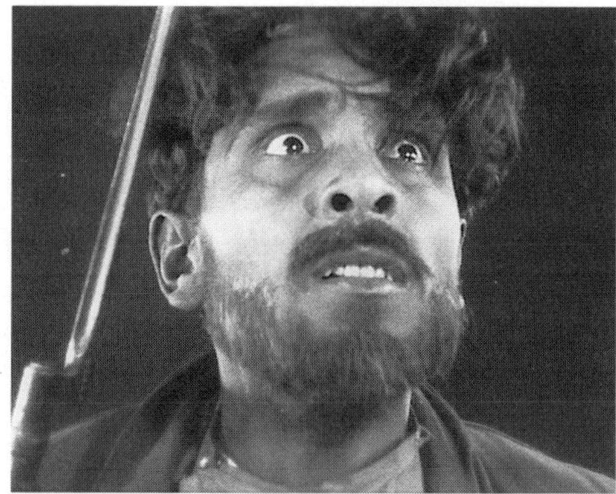

Saba looks on anxiously during his trial in Mikhail Chiaureli's *Saba* (1929).

Saba's wife and son arrive at his trial in Mikhail Chiaureli's *Saba* (1929).

after these two pleas for clemency, no official sentence is ever read by the court's president or appears in intertitles at the end of the trial scene. In spite of the number and gravity of Saba's crimes, the film ends on a happy note, with the title character cured of his alcoholic tendencies, reunited with his wife and son, and working once again as a trolley conductor. Moviegoers could actually see the rehabilitation of the defendant, which was only discussed as the future outcome of sentencing

A close-up of Saba's wife and son at his trial in Mikhail Chiaureli's *Saba* (1929).

Saba's family reunited after his trial in Mikhail Chiaureli's *Saba* (1929).

during the closing moments of *The Trial of Stepan Korolev.* Fictional trials on film reproduced the theatrical mock trial's formula for conversion to bolshevism, but placed new emphasis on the final moment of reintegration into the socialist community.

In addition, a new character appeared in mock trials on film, one whose composition and position were so similar to those of the film's actual viewing public that it promised to stimulate spectators' indignation and compassion, as every good melodrama should. This new character was none other than the trial's audience, which constituted the collective reaction to and judgment of the testimony of the trial, much like a melodramatic revision of an ancient Greek tragic chorus. In *Saba,* the audience in the courtroom is comprised of a mixed crowd of men, women, and children, who attentively follow the testimony of Saba's case and react with tremendous emotion and heartfelt compassion. After Saba's wife and son plead for his release, the camera pans across the audience and shows that several of its members have been moved to tears by their own empathic reaction to the weeping of the wife and son. Although the viewers outside of the film could not hear the words that accompanied these tears, the visual signs of feeling in the viewers inside the film were intended to trigger an identical display of emotion in their real-life counterparts. This correspondence between the audience inside and that outside of the film continues as *Saba* comes to its end: the actual moviegoers were meant to experience the same joy that they saw on the faces of the happy crowd who left the courtroom for the streets, as a mock funeral of alcohol made its way through Tbilisi. In addition, documentary shots of young members of the local Komsomol and trade union, to whom Saba's now cheerful son lectured on the evils of drink, reinforced the tie between the audience of Saba's trial and the spectator in the movie house. The unpredictable participation of those who watched *agitsudy* had been replaced by the entirely scripted response of the audience in the film, which not only cues the audience outside the film as to its own reaction but also provides a good approximation of the response that organizers of theatrical mock trials had hoped *agitsudy* would elicit.

The movement from stage to screen changed the nature of soviet courtroom drama in the *agitsud,* expanding its melodramatic modeling and allowing it to reach and affect a significantly larger audience, even as it coincided with the theatrical genre's demise. By turning the rigidly realistic theatrical mock trial into a cinematic temperance melodrama with a legal setting, both the entertainment value and educational impact of soviet courtroom drama were significantly increased. The soviet state's greater control over cinema as an art form, the ability to reproduce mechanically and to distribute such films throughout the entire country, and the elimination of active spectator participation in the theater in favor of passive spectator reception in the movie house, all made film the preferred medium for courtroom drama by the end of the decade. When Lunacharsky sounded the call to revolutionize melodrama, he probably did not have a film as tendentious as *Saba* in mind, because he hoped "wherever possible [to] avoid tendentious films—that is, large-scale films in which a didactic theme is unraveled rather obviously."[55] Nonetheless, in the very year in which Stalin relieved Lunacharsky of his post as commissar of enlightenment, dogmatic film propaganda such as *Saba* realized the formula for melodrama that Lunacharsky first described ten years before.

The two temperance trials examined above show that melodrama presented a host of advantages as a revolutionary genre, which amateur theater and popular cinema realized during the 1920s. Lunacharsky addressed his initial call to melodrama to the country's revolutionary stage, where a renovation of the genre indeed took place in the form of melodramatic *agitki* and the *agitsud.* Later in the decade, soviet film heeded Lunacharsky's call by taking the form of American cinematic melodrama and filling it with appropriate soviet content. Russia's prerevolutionary tradition of melodrama foiled attempts to transfer the genre into the avant-garde theater and cinema and limited its appeal to the same mass audience that had always enjoyed melodrama in *balagany* and on the nineteenth-century stage. Nonetheless, the fundamental compatibility of melodrama with the Marxist message of revolution meant that the revised form and content of the genre made a profound impact on the country's popular imagination, as well as on its official artistic policy by the end of the decade.

In particular, the combined victim/villain status exemplified by the reformed drunkard offered an effective means for figuring the internal enemies of socialism during the 1920s. Although it was necessary to condemn ruthlessly the criminal acts committed by the alcoholic, his victimization at the hands of bootleggers and tavern owners mitigated his culpability and allowed for his rehabilitation. Although reintegration into the family and society required a confession of guilt and contrition, the drunkard ultimately bore no responsibility for succumbing to the temptation that had been placed in his path. Similarly, the unconscious worker or peasant found himself under the influence of the old way of life, inadvertently sabotaging the construction of socialism until the error of his ways was finally shown to him. Unenlightened citizens might commit villainous acts that hindered soviet power, but they nonetheless did so as a result of their victimization by an oppressive regime. By confessing their past transgressions and swearing to reform, the unconscious worker or peasant could join the new society, much like the reformed drunkards Korolev and Saba.

Internal enemies of the soviet state were figured as victim/villains throughout the 1920s and 1930s. Although an increasing number of external enemies—that is, the political equivalents of bootleggers and tavern owners entirely hostile to soviet power—were found lurking in soviet society, unwitting enemies of the construction of socialism still existed and continued to be offered the chance of rehabilitation on the stage and screen during the Stalin era. Plays such as *Fear* (1931) and films such as *The Party Card* (1936) persisted in the melodramatic depiction of the country's internal enemies, including their sensational unmasking before a jury of peers. In fact, the institution of socialist realism as the country's sole mode of artistic expression in 1932 canonized the melodramatic mode in all forms of soviet art. The word *melodrama* regained its negative connotations of a bourgeois art form and contrived bathos, and the especially lachrymose quality of earlier movies and plays fell into disfavor during the 1930s. Nonetheless, melodrama lived on in theater and film, as the overwhelming preponderance of effect over cause continued to determine the forms that poetic justice could take in works such as *Fear* and *The Party Card.* On the other side of the footlights and the movie screen, this melodramatic modeling of friend and foe extended into the Soviet Union's actual courtrooms, where the real-life justice administered in show trials such as the 1928 Shakhty Affair set a melodramatic stage for Stalin's Great Terror.

## Notes

1 For examples, see Konstantin Rudnitsky, *Russian and Soviet Theatre: Tradition and the Avant-Garde,* ed. Lesley Milne, trans. Roxane Permar

(London: Thames and Hudson, 1988); James von Geldern, *Bolshevik Festivals, 1917–1920* (Berkeley: University of California Press, 1993); and Robert Leach, *Revolutionary Theatre* (London: Routledge, 1994).

2 For a description of melodrama's genesis in revolutionary France and its subsequent history on the popular stages of France, England, and the United States, see Frank Rahill, *The World of Melodrama* (University Park: Pennsylvania State University Press, 1967).

3 For a discussion of the importance of emotional affect as manifest in tears for the reception of cinematic melodrama, see Steve Neale, "Melodrama and Tears," *Screen* 27, no. 6 (November–December 1986): 6–22.

4 Wylie Sypher, "Aesthetic of Revolution: The Marxist Melodrama," in *Tragedy: Vision and Form,* 2nd ed., ed. Robert W. Corrigan (New York: Harper and Row, 1981), 216–24.

5 For a brief discussion of *enantiodromia* within melodrama, see Robertson Davies, *The Mirror of Nature: The Alexander Lectures, 1982* (Toronto: University of Toronto Press, 1983), 26–27.

6 Courtroom scenes were a recurrent feature of melodrama on the French, English, and American stages, as Rahill notes (*The World of Melodrama* 53–60). In addition, Linda Williams connects melodrama to courtroom dramas in her conclusion to a reevaluation of melodrama as a genre of Hollywood film. She writes: "Audiences of melodrama are positioned like juries of common law trials. Guilt or innocence is determined by orchestrated recognitions of truth that are inextricably tied to how audiences, who are essentially juries of peers, feel toward the accused" (Williams, "Melodrama Revisited," in *Refiguring American Film Genres: History and Theory,* ed. Nick Browne [Berkeley: University of California Press, 1998], 81).

7 For brief descriptions of the temperance play as a genre of melodrama, see Rahill, *The World of Melodrama,* 240–46; Michael R. Booth, "The Drunkard's Progress: Nineteenth-Century Temperance Drama," *Dalhousie Review* 44, no. 2 (summer 1964): 205–12; Michael R. Booth, ed., "Introduction," in *Hiss the Villain: Six English and American Melodramas* (New York: Benjamin Blom, 1964), 28–29; and Jeffery D. Mason, "*The Drunkard* (1844) and the Temperance Movement," in his *Melodrama and the Myth of America* (Bloomington: Indiana University Press, 1993), 61–87.

8 Mason describes the religious nature of temperance melodramas in nineteenth-century America and their similarity to revival meetings of the same era ("*The Drunkard,*" 65–66, 77). For a good example of such an appeal to the audience, see the closing song of *Ten Nights in a Bar-Room,* which ends with the comic reformed drunkard's question:

Who'll jine my cause? Will you?—or you?
You will?—'nuff sed; we'll put her through.
I'll raise my standard—spread it bold and high:
Down with rummies—'root, hog, or die!

William W. Pratt, *Ten Nights in a Bar-Room,* as quoted in Booth, *Hiss the Villain,* 202.

9 The complex blend of victimization and responsibility that characterizes the drunkard in American melodrama is described by Mason in *The Drunkard,* 72–73.

10 Sheila Fitzpatrick, *The Commissariat of Enlightenment: Soviet Organization of Education and the Arts Under Lunacharsky, October 1917–1921* (Cambridge, Eng.: Cambridge University Press, 1970), 153. For discussions of Anatolii Lunacharskii's call "Back to Ostrovskii!," see Leach, *Revolutionary Theatre,* 142–50; and Rudnitsky, *Russian and Soviet Theatre,* 116–19.

11 In his contribution to the influential collection of essays on the new theater, *Teatr: Kniga o novom teatre,* Lunacharsky had already mentioned melodrama as the most desirable genre (A. Lunacharskii, "Sotsializm i iskusstvo," in *Teatr: Kniga o novom teatre: Sbornik statei* [St. Petersburg: Shipovnik, 1908], 34). He also discussed the utility of melodrama for the mass spectator in "Voskresshaia melodrama," *Teatr i iskusstvo,* no. 18 (May 3, 1915): 304–6. In addition, Lunacharsky wrote in 1922 that "for already twenty years, I have pointed out, in speeches and the press, the enormous significance of melodrama" (A. V. Lunacharskii, "Pravel'nyi put'," in *Sobranie sochinenii,* vol. 3 [Moskva: Khudozhestvennaia Literatura, 1964], 112). Maxsim Gorky also advocated melodrama for a revitalized theater as early as 1914, see K. D. Muratova, "M. Gor'kii i sovetskii teatr," in *Iz istorii russkikh literaturnykh otnoshenii, XVIII–XX vekov* (Moskva-Leningrad: Izd. Akademii nauk SSSR, 1959), 292. All translations are mine unless otherwise noted.

12 Romain Rolland, "Quelques genres de théâtre populaire: Le mélodrame," in *Le Théâtre du Peuple: Essai d'Esthetique d'un Théâtre Nouveau* (Paris: Albin Michel, Éditeur, 1913), 130–36. For the Russian translation, see Romen Rollan, "Melodrama," in *Narodnyi teatr,* trans. I. Gol'denberg (St. Petersburg: Znanie, 1910), 94–99. Muratova provides a résumé of Rolland's influence in the revolutionary melodrama debate ("M. Gor'kii i sovetskii teatr," 288–89). For a brief assessment of Rolland's impact on Russia's revolutionary theater, see Evg. A. Znosko-Borovskii, *Russkii teatr nachala XX veka* (Praga: Plamia, 1925), 411.

13 Rollan, "Melodrama," 98.

14 Linda Williams discusses the merger of tragedy and melodrama in American culture, which has resulted in the fact that "Americans read Greek tragedy melodramatically" ("Melodrama Revisited," 53–54).

15 Rollan, "Melodrama," 97–98.

16 Ibid., 95.

17 A. Lunacharskii, "Kakaia nam nuzhna melodrama?" in *Sobranie sochinenii,* vol. 2, 212; and "Pravel'nyi put'," 112. The former article originally appeared in 1919 in the journal *Zhizn' iskusstva* as part of a five-article series on the viability of melodrama on the revolutionary stage (Muratova, "M. Gor'kii i sovetskii teatr," 292).

18 Lunacharsky asserted in his 1918 article "Voskresshaia melodrama," that "the tragedies of Shakespeare are the essence of melodrama" (305).

19 Lunacharskii, "Kakaia nam nuzhna melodrama," 213.

20 Ibid., 213–15.

21 Lunacharskii, "Pravel'nyi put'," 113–14.

22 von Geldern, *Bolshevik Festivals,* 110.

23 M. Gor'kii, "O geroicheskom teatre," in *Arkhiv A. M. Gor'kogo,* vol. 3 (Moskva: Gos. Izd. Khudozhestvennoi Literatury, 1951), 221.

24 P. A. Markov, " 'Dve sirotki': Vol'nyi teatr," in *O teatre,* vol. 3 (Moskva: Iskusstvo, 1976), 7–8.

25 V. E. Meierkhol'd, " 'Uchitel' Bubus' i problema spektaklia na muzyke (Doklad, prochitannyi 1 ianvaria 1925 g.)," in *Stat'i, pis'ma, rechi, besedy,* vol. 2 (Moskva: Izd. "Iskusstvo," 1968), 76.

26 Alisa Koonen, *Stranitsy zhizni* (Moskva: Iskusstvo, 1985), 304. For a discussion of Tairov's unique approach to melodrama as a revolutionary theatrical genre, see Rudnitsky, *Russian and Soviet Theatre,* 55–57.

27 For a chronology of the melodrama debate and productions of melodramas in soviet theater of the 1920s, see Daniel Gerould and Julia Przybos, "Melodrama in the Soviet Theater 1917–1920: An Annotated Chronology," in *Melodrama,* ed. Daniel Gerould (New York: New York Literary Forum, 1980), 75–92.

28 Robert Russell, *Russian Drama of the Revolutionary Period* (Basingstoke, Hampshire: Macmillan Press, 1988), 34–36. See also Muratova, "M. Gor'kii i sovetskii teatr," 298–300; and Gerould and Przybos, "Melodrama in the Soviet Theater," 79. For a reprint of the newspaper advertisement soliciting contributions to this play-writing competition and the article announcing the decision of the jury, see N. S. Pliatskovskaia, ed., "Dramaturgicheskie konkursy," in *Russkii sovetskii teatr, 1917–1921,* ed. A. Z. Iufit (Leningrad: Iskusstvo, 1968), 359–60.

29 Anatolii Lunacharskii, "Revolutionary Ideology and Cinema—Theses,"

in *The Film Factory: Russian and Soviet Cinema in Documents,* ed. and trans. Richard Taylor and Ian Christie (Cambridge, Mass.: Harvard University Press, 1988), 109. For the original Russian version of Lunacharskii's theses, see A. V. Lunacharskii, "Revoliutsionnaia ideologiia i kino: Tezisy," in *Lunacharskii o kino: Stat'i, vyskazyvaniia, stsenarii, dokumenty* (Moskva: Iskusstvo, 1965), 35–39.

30 Lunacharskii, "Revolutionary Ideology and Cinema," 110.

31 *Medvezh'ia svadba,* dir. K. Eggert and V. Gardin, Mezhrabpom-Rus', 1925, with K. Eggert, V. Malinovskaia, and N. Rozenel' in leading roles. Denise Youngblood describes the plot of *The Bear's Wedding* in her *Movies for the Masses: Popular Cinema and Soviet Society in the 1920s* (Cambridge: Cambridge University Press, 1992), 84–86. The screenplay for this movie was published as A. Lunacharskii, *Medvezh'ia svad'ba: Melodrama na siuzhet Merime v 9 kartinakh* (Moskva: Gos. Izd., 1924).

32 Lenin allegedly made this legendary statement in conversation with Lunacharskii (Anatoli Lunacharskii, "Conversation with Lenin. I. Of All the Arts . . . ," in Taylor and Christie, ed., *The Film Factory,* 56–57). See also A. M. Gak, ed., *Samoe vazhnoe iz vsekh iskusstv: Lenin o kino* (Moskva: Iskusstvo, 1973), 164; and G. Boltianskii, *Lenin i kino* (Moskva-Leningrad: Gos. Izd., 1925), 19.

33 Adrian Piotrovskii, "Melodrama ili tragediia?" in *Teatr, kino, zhizn'* (Leningrad: Izd. "Iskusstvo," 1969), 63–65; and "Kudozhesvennye techeniia v sovetskom kino," also in *Teatr, kino, zhizn',* 234–40.

34 Youngblood, *Movies for the Masses,* 72–73.

35 For a discussion of the reception of *The Bear's Wedding,* see Youngblood, *Movies for the Masses,* 85. For a discussion of the stylistic peculiarities of prerevolutionary Russian cinema, see Yuri Tsivian, "Some Preparatory Remarks on Russian Cinema," in his *Silent Witnesses: Russian Films, 1908–1919* (London: British Film Institute and Edizioni Biblioteca dell'Immagine, 1989), 24–43. For detailed treatment of the reception of early Russian films, see Tsivian's *Early Cinema in Russia and its Cultural Reception* (London: Routledge, 1994); and Louise McReynolds's article in this volume.

36 Mary Ann Doane, "Melodrama, Temporality, Recognition: American and Russian Silent Cinema," *East-West Film Journal* 4, no. 2 (June 1990): 69–89.

37 Youngblood, *Movies for the Masses,* 13–28. For histories of the early soviet film industry and the development of cinema in the Soviet Union, see Jay Leyda, *Kino: A History of the Russian and Soviet Film* (1960; Princeton: Princeton University Press, 1983); Richard Taylor, *The Politics of*

*the Soviet Cinema, 1917–1929* (Cambridge, Eng.: Cambridge University Press, 1979); and Denise J. Youngblood, *Soviet Cinema in the Silent Era, 1918–1935* (Ann Arbor, Mich.: UMI Research Press, 1985).

38 Viktor Shklovskii, *Khod konia: Sbornik statei* (Mosvka/Berlin: Knigoizd, Gelikon, 1923), 59.

39 For information on the emergence and development of amateur theater in early soviet culture, see Lynn Mally, "The Problem of the Amateur: Defining *Samodeitel'nyi teatr,*" unpublished essay cited by permission of the author.

40 For broader studies of the *agitsud* as a genre of propaganda theater, see Julie A. Cassiday, *The Enemy on Trial: Early Soviet Courts on Stage and Screen* (DeKalb: Northern Illinois University Press, 2000), chapter 3; and Elizabeth A. Wood, "Performing Justice: Agitation Trials in Revolutionary Russia," unpublished manuscript cited by permission of the author.

41 B. Sigal, *Sud nad Stepanom Korolevym. (Posledstviia p'ianstva). Instsenirovka suda v 2-kh aktakh* (Moskva: Zhizn' i znanie, 1924, 1926), 3; and *Sud nad p'ianitsei* (Leningrad: Leningradskaia pravda, 1929), 5.

42 Sigal, *Sud nad Stepanom Korolevym,* 3; *Sud nad p'ianitsei,* 6.

43 Sigal, *Sud nad Stepanom Korolevym,* 3; *Sud nad p'ianitsei,* 4.

44 Lunacharsky also pointed to tears as an infallible indicator of audience involvement in melodrama ("Voskresshaia melodrama," 305–6).

45 At least four of Sigal's agitsudy treat the problem of alcohol abuse. I have chosen to focus on *Sud nad Stepanom Korolevym* because of its striking similarity to the film *Saba,* which is discussed below. Sigal's other mock trials on this topic include *Sud nad p'ianitsei Ivanom Nikiforovym* (Samara: Izd. "Seiatel' pravdy," 1925), which is addressed to the peasant milieu; *Sud nad Ivanom Lobachevym po obvineniiu v p'ianstve i khuliganstve* (Leningrad: Rabochee Izd. "Priboi," 1926), which focuses on young workers and on members of the Komsomol; and *Sud nad p'ianitsei,* which constitutes a reworking of *Sud nad Stepan Korolovym,* at the behest of Glavrepertkom, to delete *samogon* (home brew) and add bootlegging for the 1929 audience.

46 Rossisskii gos. arkhiv literatury i isskustva (RGALI, f. 656, op. 1, d. 2636). "Otzyv no. 1203" of *Sud nad Ivanom Lobachevym.*

47 Sigal, *Sud nad Stepanom Korolevym,* 13.

48 Neale, "Melodrama and Tears," 6–7.

49 Sigal, *Sud nad Stepanom Korolevym,* 4.

50 Ibid., 56.

51 Given the playwright's use of speaking names for his dramatis personae in the mock trial of a prostitute, the *Pravda* editor's mistake is quite remarkable. For the text of this production, see A. I. Akkerman, *Sud nad prosti-*

*tutkoi: Delo gr. Zaborovoi po obvineniiu ee v zaniatii prostitutsiei i zarazhenii sifilisom kr-ts Krest'ianova* (Moskva-Petrograd: Gos. Izd., 1922). For *Pravda*'s original article and its retraction, see "Vorova s prostitutsiei," *Pravda,* no. 179, 14 August 1921, 4; and "Popravka," *Pravda,* no. 183, 19 August 1921, 2. For another example of a mock trial that was received as a real trial, see the report of "Sud nad sifilitkom," in *Rabochii zritel',* no. 19, 14–21 September 1924, 17. Walter Duranty also reported that a mock trial held in 1929 of twelve textile workers received the same press coverage as a real trial (*Duranty Reports Russia,* ed. Gustavus Tuckerman Jr. [New York: Viking, 1934], 364).

52 Ia. Brukson, *Tvorchesvo kino* (Leningrad: Kolos, 1926), 33–35; S. Krolov, *Kino vmesto vodki* (Moskva-Leningrad: Moskovskii rabochii, 1928), 30–31; Pavel Poluianov, *Gibel' teatra i torzhestvo kino.* [*Pamflet.*] (N. Novgorod: Tip. Nizhpoligraf, 1925), 35, 42; A. Toporkov, "Kinematograf i mif," in *Kinematograf: Sbornik statei* (Moskva: Gos. Izd., 1919), 48, 52.

53 *Saba: Melodrama v 6 chastiakh,* dir. Mikhail Chiaureli, Goskinprom Gruzii, 1929, with S. Dzhaliashvili, V. Andzhaparidze, L. Dzhanuashvili, and E. Chavchavadze in leading roles.

54 Tsivian, "Some Preparatory Remarks," 34–38.

55 Lunacharskii, "Revolutionary Ideology and Cinema," 109.

*Lars T. Lih*

# Melodrama and the Myth of the Soviet Union

In 1935, the soviet literary critic Abram Gurvich confidently predicted that socialist reality would give rise to a new dramatic genre:

> The old world created a magnificent genre of its own—tragedy—and can justly take pride. . . . It is the highest monument of pre-socialist culture. Nothing was as successful for that culture as a dramatic form which portrayed the path of man to ruin. . . .
>
> In full correspondence to the new conditions of our reality, there arises a completely new motif that is directly opposed to the old tragedy. Here despair, decline, catastrophe appears as the starting point, and then these are gradually overcome and bring the hero to self-affirmation, to a natural and free existence. Man travels toward life. There we have death, here we have birth.[1]

Gurvich called for a genre that would start with an acknowledgment of the trouble and strife in the world but move toward a ringing affirmation of harmony. But as it happens, the "old world" had produced just such a genre in the previous century: melodrama. Can the outlook and procedures of nineteenth-century melodrama and its subgenres help us understand the kind of political mythic narrative that Gurvitch wanted to see reflected on the stage? I believe the answer is yes: melodramatic elements lie at the very heart of the constitutive myths of the prewar Soviet Union.

By paying close attention to these melodramatic elements, important shifts in soviet political myths can be mapped. In this essay, I will use two subgenres of nineteenth-century melodrama to analyze one such shift that occurred during the 1930s. Early in the decade, party-minded playwrights produced a type of drama that I call political temperance drama. The label is taken from the temperance drama developed in the mid-nineteenth century by antialcohol activists in the United States. Political temperance drama portrays a struggle for the loyalty of the "waverer"—the peasant, the intellectual, the backward worker—caught between revolution and counterrevolution. As the 1930s wore on, political temperance drama faded: the official myth was now that the waverers had all been convinced. One paradoxical consequence of this assertion was a somber melodrama whose dynamics are very similar to the classical melodrama of Guilbert de Pixérécourt and his contemporaries at the beginning of the nineteenth century.

The narrative behind this new political myth can be traced directly to Stalin. Instead of the waverer, the spotlight was now placed on the slanderous villain that Stalin labeled the *dvurushnik* (usually translated "double-dealer"). Soviet society was convulsed by an imposed melodrama whose climactic scene in the Moscow show trials was meant to definitively rip the mask off the dvurushnik. The relative confidence of political temperance drama was replaced by the barely controlled hysteria of Stalin's version of classical melodrama.

### The Struggle for Recognition: Two Types of Melodrama

A bit of rapid-fire dialogue from Pixérécourt's *The Man with Three Faces* (1801) gives us the archetypal situation of classical melodrama: protest against a villain's slander. Vivaldi, a Venetian nobleman, has been successfully framed by the villainous Count Orsano. Rosemonde, who is secretly married to Vivaldi, defends him as she talks with her father, the Doge of Venice, who regards Vivaldi as a justly condemned traitor:

DOGE: So, the decree that condemns him . . .
ROSEMONDE: Is unjust.
DOGE: His crime . . .
ROSEMONDE: Imaginary.
DOGE: The proofs . . .
ROSEMONDE: Assumed.
DOGE: His accuser . . .
ROSEMONDE: A monster who sought revenge for my scorn by per-

> secuting the most ardent soul and the most zealous servant of the republic.[2]

This excerpt illustrates the basic conflict that defines classical melodrama. It involves three basic forces: the villain, the slandered victim and her or his defenders, and the recognizer—that is, the basically good person who is tempted to believe the villain. The suspense of the plot derives from this question: will the recognizer see through the villain's mask of virtue and restore the victim's rightful place in the community?

The technical term in French theater for the villain of melodrama is *traître.*[3] The term is useful because it shows that the villain's slanders are not only aimed at the victim but also are an attack on a virtuous community. By slandering a member in good standing of this community, the *traître* is also seducing the community into committing an injustice. In *The Man with Three Faces,* the *traître*'s threat to the community is made explicit: the slanderous Count Orsano is also preparing a coup d'état against the Doge. The *traître* is not motivated by any competing ideal or alternate conception of virtue. He represents the anticommunity, whose mission it is to destroy virtue by smearing it with "infamy" (a key concept in classical melodrama). Thus the *traître* is not a self-righteous hypocrite who believes his own accusation: rather, he is always perfectly lucid about his own evil motives.

The force that resists the *traître* is composed of the victim and her or his defenders. The vindication of the victim's virtue requires the active initiative of those who understand the vital importance of uncovering the truth and who are able to perceive it when it is still clouded by false appearances. As in later Bolshevik conceptions of political leadership, moral leadership in the melodrama consists principally of dispersing false consciousness.

Although the recognizer—the Doge in our example—is often a minor character, he nevertheless has the pivotal function of deciding the outcome of the battle between those who wish to maintain the virtuous community and those who wish to destroy it. In order to fulfill this function, the recognizer must be fundamentally upright but also vulnerable to being taken in by false appearances. The recognizer thus represents the community. The climax of classical melodrama is the community's moment of recognition of the truth about both the victim and the *traître.* The virtuous community is then reconstituted by casting out—purging—the *traître.*

Although the recognizer has a pivotal function in classical melodrama, he remains a secondary character: the main spotlight is on the clash between slanderous villain and wronged victim. In contrast, temperance drama puts the recognizer front and center while the *traître* and the victim recede to the sidelines. The *traître* and victim now act as the two opposing poles of attraction who fight for influence through and within the recognizer: the seductive villain who represents the dissolute anti-community of Prince Alcohol versus the weeping wife who represents the virtuous community of home and hearth. The suspense of temperance drama comes from this question: will the drunkard recognize the virtuous community as his true home or will he be seduced by the anti-community of the saloon and its disreputable denizens?

The key assumption of temperance drama is that the drunkard cannot stand still. He can travel in either direction but he must keep moving along the one-dimensional "road to ruin" until he either ends up at complete ruin or makes the return journey to complete salvation. The drunkard is not really making choices based on his own individual psychology; rather he is the site of a struggle between virtue and vice—the prize for which they contend. He is thus trapped within a force-field that will not allow him to stay in one spot for any length of time or to strike out in another direction altogether, or even to think of his life as something other than a road either to ruin or salvation. The temperance drama ends either by showing "the fallen saved" in the bosom of his family or by showing the drunkard "a bloated corpse . . . in a lonely room."[4]

Each of these two types of melodrama flirts with a hysteria in which unknown but deeply frightening forces are out of control. In classical melodrama, the potential hysteria comes from anxiety about masks—the double fear of being slandered and of being misled. Masks allow single individuals to do immense damage to the community. In temperance drama, the fear of other people's weaknesses and an exaggerated view of their eagerness to be seduced leads easily to hysteria and moral panic: take a single drink and you may end up a corpse on the floor! In both cases, hysteria resolves itself into a view of the community under siege from hidden enemies within.

Soviet marxism is sometimes said to have described the world in terms of vast impersonal forces. Vast, yes; impersonal, no. Prerevolutionary Russian radicals debated the moving forces (*dvizhushchie sily*) of the coming revolution: these forces interacted and struggled as the dramatis personae (*deistvuiushchie litsa*) of an epic world-historical drama. As heirs to prewar social democracy, the Bolsheviks saw the main characters of this drama as classes struggling to impose their vision on society as a whole. A key theme in the plot of this doctrinal myth is leadership: the party's ability to lead the proletariat and the proletariat's ability to lead other classes.

In a speech in 1933 on the tasks of soviet drama, the Bolshevik commissar of enlightenment, Anatoly Lunacharsky, summed up one aspect of the Bolshevik myth of leadership in a pithy aphorism: "*Proletariat—velikii klass-vospitatel.*" A *vospitatel* is a teacher in a very broad sense. The noun *vospitanie* is usually translated as "upbringing," and it signifies a blend of education, transformational leadership, behavior modification, and "reforging." I shall translate it as "education." Lunacharsky's dictum thus means: "The proletariat's greatness is that it is a class that educates." The proletariat's educational efforts are directed toward the "waverer" (*kolebliushchiisia*), a key term in Bolshevik doctrine: "[The proletariat] educates the poor peasants and middle peasants, it educates the rural proletariat that is so close to it, it educates its own backward strata, it re-educates its own self, it educates the intelligentsia—which requires a great deal of education, right up to the most learned academic."[5]

The battle for the soul of the waverer is the central theme of three classics of soviet theater from the early 1930s that fit my category of political temperance drama: *Optimistic Tragedy* by Vsevolod Vishnevsky, *Bread* by Vladimir Kirshon, and *Fear* by Alexander Afinogenov.[6] These plays were the product of a short-lived window of opportunity for serious dramatization of soviet political myth. During the first decade after the revolution, committed Bolshevik playwrights were so absorbed by the titanic struggle of the civil war that they gave scant attention to the problems of postrevolutionary society. After this period they were no longer able to discuss real issues even for the purpose of assimilating

The commissar is alone but represents the party and the sailors are united but have yet to recognize the party; in *Optimistic Tragedy* (1933). From Konstantin Rudnitsky, *Russian and Soviet Theater 1905–1932* (New York: Harry N. Abrams, 1988), 286.

them into myth: serious and honest myth making became tawdry and evasive myth making.

As in nineteenth-century temperance drama, these plays portray the struggle between virtuous community and anti-community. On one side stands "models of socialist consciousness [whose] example will help in the socialist rebirth of those who have not yet freed themselves from the weight of the old slavish feelings, ideas and habits." On the other side stand those who embody the pull of the old slavish feelings.[7]

Waverers can only join the virtuous community by disciplining anarchic self-assertion and recognizing the virtuous community as an expression of their true individuality. This is the moral of Vishnevsky's *Optimistic Tragedy* (1932), a moral expressed even better by the rejected title *Out of Chaos.*[8] The central conflict in *Optimistic Tragedy* is over the self-identity of a band of anarchist sailors during the civil war: are they a self-governing "detachment" or will they accept the discipline of a "regiment" integrated into a larger whole? Representing the waverers who will decide the outcome of the struggle are Aleksei, an anarchist sailor, and Behring, a former tsarist naval officer. They are caught in a force-field set up by two opposed and mutually repellent poles: the sailor's anarchist chief, the *vozhak,* and the female commissar sent by the party. Vishnevsky's plot may remind today's readers of movies in which a gutsy female teacher civilizes a classroom of unruly hoods.

The anarchist *vozhak,* for all his influence over his fellow sailors, is ultimately only a parody *vozhd* (a Russian word meaning "inspiring leader" that was regularly applied to Stalin in particular). When the commissar comes on board, he says, "don't worry, we'll educate [*vospitat*] her," but of course, he fails miserably.[9] Although in the past the *vozhak* has earned his revolutionary credentials, he has degenerated and reveals his nihilist sentiments in a semi-aside to his henchman, after giving the sailor Aleksei a Judas kiss: "Don't trust either him or her [the commissar]. (Wipes his lips with distaste and spits.) I've kissed a reptile. [His henchman asks: 'who should I trust? Only you?'] Not me either. We're all lying cattle. Everybody has been poisoned. We must cut at the root: the old life still lives on in each of us."[10]

The self-contradiction underlying the *vozhak*'s anti-community is grasped by Aleksei in his moment of insightful recognition: "You are a denier of power [*vlast*] who has seized power!"[11]

The party's outraged innocence is presented in standard melodramatic fashion by means of an attempted gang rape of the female commissar (the *vozhak* thinks that this is an effective means of education). The *commissar*'s first act of leadership and countereducation is to shoot down her attacker. The attempted rape shows the horrors that result when virtue is not accorded proper status: the horror is not that a *woman* is being raped but that a *party representative* is being raped. As the commissar says: "Well, who else wants to try out a commissar's body?"[12]

Political temperance drama typically reveals both confidence and a potential for hysteria. Vishnevsky shows confidence when he allows Aleksei and Behrens to voice genuine doubts about accepting Bolshevik discipline. The hysteria potential can be glimpsed in the final act of the play. The anarchist threat lives on—in devious cloaked form—even after the virtuous community has been established by the condemnation and execution of the *vozhak*. The *vozhak*'s henchman Gravel-Voice (*Siplyi*) is a physical embodiment of the degenerating anticommunity: syphilis is destroying his body just as alcohol destroys the bodies of its votaries. The community foolishly allows him to stay on after the *vozhak*'s execution, and he literally stabs them in the back; his murder of a sentry leads to the destruction of the whole community, including the commissar. This is a parable of the dangers created by masked enemies posing as loyal members of the virtuous community.

In the literary polemics that pepper the first version of this play, Vishnevsky made clear his preference for a melodramatic approach. This helps account for his decision to give the roles of slandered victim and defender to a single female character. A melodrama victim was typically an unprotected woman who revealed the vulnerability of the community as well as its ultimate power to protect its own. In the same way, the commissar dramatically reveals the power of the party that acts through her. She opposes Aleksei's male anarchism with the female schoolmarmism of the party. At the same time, she represents the party's secret feeling of self-pity as a slandered and misunderstood force for good. The dark unruly masses may try to rape the party, so it has to shoot back. But that is only to get their attention, and soon the party's innate virtue will be recognized by all.

Vishnevsky pictured the civil war as a struggle for the loyalty of waverers. In *Bread* (1930), Vladimir Kirshon does the same for collectivization. Although an emergency grain collection is the explicit issue, the play's subtext is the mass collectivization drive that was underway in

The attentive peasant villagers in the play represent the audience as both learn to distinguish between true and false leaders, in *Bread* (1931). From Konstantin Rudnitsky, *Russian and Soviet Theater 1905–1932* (New York: Harry N. Abrams, 1988), 273.

1929–1930. Kirshon had earlier served his apprenticeship writing political melodramas of a lurid type—for example, relating the adventures of a daring group of Komsomol youths foiling the efforts of a gang of White Guard saboteurs. By 1930, he had become one of the pioneers of political temperance drama.[13]

*Bread* has two intertwined plots. In one, the waverer is the peasant village as a whole, forced to choose between the two contending poles of the kulaks and the party. In the other, the waverer is a party leader who shows signs of incipient deviation and degeneration. The two plots drive each other: the degeneration of the party leader reveals itself in political mistakes that almost tip the balance in the village toward the kulaks. The most vivid character in the village story is the kulak leader Kvasov. I cite one of his speeches at length to show just how forcefully political temperance drama could allow its negative characters to speak:

> We have gathered here, dear guests, in secret. In our own home village we must hide our heads from everybody. We must behave as if we were in the house of a stranger where we don't belong. Yet who are we? We are the foundation. The belly of Mother Russia is filled with our bread. It is we who clothe Moscow, we who provide shoes for her, we who feed her. But who orders us about? Ragged tramps, beggars,

drunkards. Those in Moscow are hardly worried about that. Russia for them is just a field for experiments. They want to raise a special brand of European herb on it. On that field we are the poisonous weeds—the broom-rape, the wild grass. They've begun to weed us out. By the roots they are weeding us out. They're mowing us down with a scythe. The hour has come when we must either lie down under the scythe or shout so that all Russia can hear us: "You're wrong, you Moscow agronomists! We're not weeds—we're oaks!"[14]

This is explosive material: an accurate portrayal of a countermyth that in the long run has proved to be more durable than the Bolshevik myth itself. Today this speech would be applauded rather than hissed. To undercut the power of this countermyth, Kirshon uses devices from nineteenth-century melodrama to portray his villain. Kvasov relies on slander and defamation of the virtuous community of the builders of socialism. He claims that the workers are living high on the hog while the peasants starve. On a more personal level, he lies to his own daughter after she begins to recognize the superior virtues of the party representatives: he tells her that the party people sneered at her. As the play draws to a climax, Kvasov uses vodka to incite a crowd of supporters who trample through the village, and he is so carried away with the struggle that he gives orders to burn down a hut even though his own son is inside.

*Bread* shows how the party's relations with the peasants could be structured as a melodrama: the party battles for the allegiance of the waverers, supremely confident that that proper leadership will be able to dispel the slander of the kulaks. The village plot thus shows relative confidence. The party plot shows more potential for the hysteria that results when any member of the virtuous community is seen as a potential masked enemy. Here the waverer is Raevsky, a party official who has taken the first steps down the primrose path toward deviation and opposition. Raevsky is not ill-intentioned, but his capacity for self-deception and his self-dramatizing nature come close to inciting a peasant rebellion. As the play ends, it is still unclear whether "self-criticism" will be able to halt him on his road to ruin.[15] Like any waverer, Raevsky will keep moving until he ends up at one of the two communities that are struggling in and through him. If he continues in the direction of the anti-community, he could very well turn into a masked *dvurushnik* with an enormous potential for stabbing the party in the back.

Alexander Afinogenov's *Fear* (1931) looks at waverers among the intellectuals. It allows its main character, Professor Borodin, to stand up and express the slanderous thought that soviet reality is based entirely on fear. Borodin's indictment is so powerful that during the perestroika era Afinogenov was portrayed, quite unconvincingly, as a daring subversive critic of Stalinism—even though *Fear* was hailed immediately after its first production in 1931 as one of the outstanding successes of the new socialist theater.[16]

According to the categories of the time, *Fear* is a "psychological drama" that deals with the inner conflicts of individuals. Yet Professor Borodin is less of an individual than he is the site of a struggle between contending forces. He dominates the play not because of his powerful personality but because he is the central waverer and, as such, the most visible expression of the play of forces. The plot is set in motion by Professor Borodin's distrust of the new standards of social promotion: his daughter doesn't win a sculpture contest, his student is not chosen to go abroad, he himself is forced to take on a young proletarian woman as an assistant, and so forth. Feeling that virtue and status are growing apart from each other, he begins to gather material that will allow him to chronicle all the resentment felt by the losers under the system. He expresses their indictment in a great public speech of accusation.

But Borodin is not a slanderous villain like Kvasov: he is a waverer who still can be won over. The process starts with a counterspeech by Klara, an older woman who is a party member of long standing. When Borodin is taken away to State Political Administration (GPU) offices, he begins to recognize the true nature not only of Klara but of the people who had tried to make use of his speech for antisoviet purposes. These demoralized members of the anti-community betray each other as well as Professor Borodin. Borodin ends his wavering when he admits after his release that he had lost sight of the big picture: "I joyously greeted every manifestation of fear and I failed to notice fearlessness. I welcomed the madness of Kimbaev, and I overlooked the growth of his reason."[17]

As usual, the predominant note of confidence is accompanied by more unsettling images. The plot depends on the assumption that a band of conspirators and dupes could take over a scientific institute and use it for antisoviet purposes. Incipient hysteria can be heard in the suspicious remarks of Borodin's proletarian assistant: "On the surface it seems to be all right. . . . But then—then all of this material accumulated by us—the professor takes with him into his private study, where he locks himself in and works on it all by himself. We scientific workers are in the position of slaves who deliver the raw material to some mysterious factory. But we want to know now what is being manufactured in that factory—whether it's boots or wax candles, or poison gas."[18]

Like the other political temperance plays, *Fear* makes use of tried-and-true melodramatic devices. One such device is the angel-child, whose function is both to see through the veils that we adults put over things and to lead us on to our better selves. Nineteenth-century angel-children such as Eva in *Uncle Tom's Cabin* or Joe Morgan's daughter in *Ten Nights in a Bar-Room* receive their special grace because they are close to death and to heaven. Afinogenov's angel-child is named Natasha. Although she is hardly mentioned in critical accounts of *Fear,* Natasha is actually quite important to the mechanics of the plot. Her special grace comes not from her closeness to death but from her connection to the future. In contrast to the villain who sings naughty Maurice Chevalier songs, Natasha sings pure and innocent Young Pioneer songs. She also lisps such sentiments as these: "Papa, which is the greater menace—a Left deviation or a Right deviation? I think that the greatest menace are the *dvurushniki.*" Or this: "Seryozhka was expelled from our [Young Pioneer] detachment. . . . Our detachment leader [*vozhatyi*] said that if Seryozhka could deceive the detachment, he could deceive the working class. . . . And do you know who the most important leader [*vozhatyi*] is? You don't? Well, I know: it's the Party."[19]

Thus out of the mouth of the angel-child comes the prevailing sentiment of the play: a horror of deception and masks. When Natasha eavesdrops and discovers her father has been covering up his bourgeois origins, she is devastated. Her horrified reaction signals his moral doom: "Papa! Where have you gone? You have deceived the working class. You have deceived the leader [*vozhatyi*]." In contrast, Natasha seeks out the good characters and leads them into the virtuous community. In the play's final scene, she completes the rebirth of the chastened and lonely Professor Borodin, who begins to see life anew and to murmur, "Ah, to be fourteen years old again!"[20]

For these playwrights, melodrama was not just a way of popularizing a political outlook, it *was* a political outlook. They resorted to melodramatic devices not through clumsy inexperience but because these devices were tried-and-true ways of getting across the underlying doctrinal myth about the struggle to enlist the waverer into the virtuous community. The waverers—the anarchist sailors in *Optimistic Tragedy*, the peasants in *Bread*, the intellectuals in *Fear*—must learn to accept the discipline needed to carry out the tasks of the virtuous community. They must learn that the anti-community promises only an ultimately demoralizing false freedom. Each of these plays flirts with hysteria in ways that foreshadow the coming obsession with masked *traîtres* within the virtuous community. But the dominant note remains one of confidence. If the virtuous community can overcome the doubts and hesitations of its own members, it can then exert the kind of leadership that will put the waverer in touch with his deeper and better self. The story ends with the waverer's triumphant recognition of and acceptance by the builders of socialism.

### Stalin's Melodrama: "The *Dvurushnik* Unmasked"

In the mid-1930s, Stalin claimed that the virtuous community had triumphed in real life because the foundations of socialism had been laid in the Soviet Union and the waverers had all been won over. Unfortunately, the curtain did not go down at this point. Pushed front and center was a new figure who was very much like the slanderous *traître* of classical melodrama: the *dvurushnik*.

A soviet dictionary defines *dvurushnik* as "someone who, under the mask of loyalty to someone or something, acts in the interest of the enemy." The Stalinist textbook of party history, the *Short Course*, elaborates: "Political *dvurushniks* are an unprincipled gang of political careerists who, having long ago lost the confidence of the people, strive to insinuate themselves once more into their confidence by deception, by chameleon-like changes of color, by fraud, by any means, only that they might retain the title of political figures."[21] In other words, the *dvurushnik* is "the man with two faces."

The *dvurushnik* was the chief villain and driving force of a vast melodramatic narrative in which the Moscow show trials were only a single if climactic episode. A case can be made for regarding Stalin himself as the author of this narrative, because it is presented with peculiar intensity in his speeches as well as in authoritative pronouncements such as the *Short Course*. Stalin's justification for the trials and the purges of 1936–1938 is usually described as a theoretical argument about "the intensification of the class struggle in proportion to the advance toward socialism."[22] Stalin did come close to advancing a theoretical argument of this kind in 1928–1930, on the eve of a genuine intensification of what Bolsheviks called the class struggle. But as we shall see, the *dvurushnik* narrative was actually based on quite a different premise: the triumph of the virtuous community and the resulting proliferation of masks. This reading is supported by Stalin's own pronouncements during the period covered by the *dvurushnik* narrative—1932 to 1938—as the following paraphrase shows (the passages in quotation marks are taken from his speeches and authoritative party pronouncements).[23]

By 1933, Stalin claimed, the main struggle to establish socialism in the Soviet Union was over, and the power of the opposing classes—*kulak,* hostile specialists, nepmen—had been broken in open battle. Their social roots had been destroyed and only shattered remnants remained. The great majority of the population supported the new socialist institutions such as the collective farms and nationalized industry. The time of major sacrifices and strained tempos was drawing to a close and the task was now to make the new institutions work. But this new situation certainly did not mean that the class struggle had ceased, and Stalin warned:

> Thrown out of their groove, and scattered over the whole face of the USSR, these "former people" [members of the prerevolutionary elites] have wormed their way into our plants and factories, into our government offices and trading organizations, into our railway and water transport enterprises, and principally into our collective and state farms. They have crept into these places and taken cover there, donning the mask of "workers" and "peasants," and some of them have even managed to worm their way into the party. . . . There is no filth or slander that these former people will not throw on the soviet power and use to mobilize backward elements.[24]

These masked internal enemies were *dvurushniks.* The officers for this army of malicious malcontents are provided by the former party oppositionists who claim to have returned to the fold. The logic of struggle brings together a heterogeneous gang united only by hatred of soviet socialism. Not only do the Right and Left oppositions—the Bukharinites and the Trotskyites—join forces, this combined bloc then links up with the security police of the fascist powers.

Stalin considered it vital to recognize the difference between the *dvurushnik* and the class enemy of yore. Don't expect the kulak to flaunt his villainy and look like the caricature on a propaganda poster. Don't expect the new wrecker specialists to be like Professor Borodin or the defendants in the Shakhty trial of 1928. Although Borodin and his ilk were openly alien figures, they were comparatively honorable opponents whose class hostility was at least grounded in a well-developed worldview. Don't expect the two-faced former oppositionists to openly proclaim their views as former wreckers did. We face a new situation and a new type of danger: the class enemy now has a party card. The aim of the *dvurushnik*'s wrecking activities is not only to cause direct damage, but even more fundamentally to throw filth on (*napakostit*) soviet reality. Slow down soviet economic growth, lower living standards, and cause popular discontent, bog the system down in an endless stream of minicrises—the *dvurushnik* will do anything to slander socialism, to make it look bad and reduce its innate attractive powers. If the new system doesn't work as it should, despite the immense advantages of socialism, the sabotage perpetrated by masked *dvurushniks* is the main reason.

The *dvurushniks* are only a handful of degenerates. Their power for evil comes from the trust placed in them by myopic patriots who are too engrossed in their own narrow sphere. The job of the true party leader is to reveal what's really going on and to unmask the *dvurushnik*. These true leaders can be at the top: the Central Committee has often given signals about the ubiquity of the two-faced wrecker. Or true leaders can arise among the "little people"—for example, Comrade Nikolaenko, a Ukrainian woman who denounced corruption in high places and was expelled from the party for her pains. In either case, the true leader exposes those who try to throw filth on socialism: "An essential quality of any bolshevik under present circumstances is the ability to recognize an enemy of the people, no matter how well masked."[25] It must be admitted, Stalin would concede, that even the top leadership was late in understanding the full extent of the danger of the *dvurushnik* with a party card. The murder of Comrade Kirov in 1934 was a wake-up call. Each of the three major trials during 1936 to 1938 revealed a more widely flung conspiracy than the last. Partly because of the looming danger of war, the time was ripe in 1937 for a massive purification campaign.[26] But unfortunately, this mass campaign itself offered an opportunity to throw filth on the system. Careerist party officials used a mask of supervigilance in order to protect themselves. Even more insidious was a new type of *dvurushnik:* "Many of our party organizations and the leaders still to this day haven't learned to see through and expose the artfully masked enemy who attempts with cries of vigilance to mask his own enemy status . . . and who uses repressive measures to cut down our bolshevik cadres and to sow insecurity and excessive suspicion in our ranks."[27] Worst of all, *dvurushniks* infiltrated the NKVD, the organization dedicated to exposing *dvurushniks.* There they "consciously distorted soviet laws, committed forgeries, falsified investigative materials, investigated and arrested people on flimsy foundations or no foundations at all, created 'cases' against innocent people for purposes of provocation, and using all these measures in order to hide and save from destruction their colleagues in this criminal anti-soviet activity."[28] The danger represented by the *dvurushnik* will not be overcome until the slandered party loyalist is reinstated and the real *dvurushniks* exposed and eliminated.

Stalin's *dvurushnik* narrative marks a shift from political temperance drama to classical melodrama where the central figure is no longer the waverer/recognizer but the *traître* who is falsely trusted and almost succeeds in wrecking the virtuous community. The recognizer function is reassigned to the community at large: it must move from myopia (*blizorukost'*) to vigilance (*bditelnost'*). Suspense now revolves around this question: will the *dvurushnik* be unmasked before the community suffers mortal damage?

The key link between the political myths of the mid-1930s and classical melodrama is anxiety about masks: the fear of being slandered and the fear of relying on *traîtres.* This passage from a Pixérécourt play reads like one of Stalin's speeches about the *dvurushnik:* "Indeed, the more his life has been free from reproach—the more confidence and respect people have accorded him—the more he is guilty. . . . You, Eloi, whom people have received with compassion, who has met with the most generous hospitality, whose good behavior and uprightness are attested by all—you had nothing but the mask of virtue and this misleading exterior hid the perverse soul of a villain [*cette enveloppe trompeuse cachait l'âme perverse d'un scélérat*]."[29]

A host of reasons—the Bolshevik underground experience, the devastating social chaos of the revolutionary years, the repressions and denunciations of the Stalin era, the imposed hypocrisy of the new centralized economic system—ensured that anxiety about masks would be a powerful presence in soviet culture. The specific melodramatic form given to this anxiety, however, was due in large part a result of Stalin's insistence that the waverers had all been won over and the virtuous community already established. In the old days of the political temperance drama, the waverer had helped to make opposition understandable and even acceptable. The waverer's doubts could be explained by relatively objective social markers: there did in fact exist anarchists, peasants, and intellectuals with views roughly similar to the ones ascribed to them. Because the waverer had comprehensible doubts, his ultimate conversion was also comprehensible—in fact, dispelling the waverer's doubts was a central test of the party's leadership abilities. But now that the virtuous community had been established, doubts were no longer legitimate or comprehensible. Opposition could only be explained by unreasoning hatred or by orders from powers outside the community. The doubter realized that the virtuous community would reject him if he explained his real outlook, and so he had to wear a mask. His slanders thus no longer took the form of open speech but rather of covert wrecking. He could not be won over—he had to be rooted out. The doubter had changed from a waverer to a *dvurushnik.*

The anxieties accompanying life in a society of mobile strangers, intensified by revolutionary suspicions and the incomprehensible workings of the new system, helped to create a frightening, unstable world of masked *traîtres* who were nowhere and everywhere. The only way to preserve one's sanity in a world of masks was to rely on the top party leadership who (in the words of an Afinogenov character) could lead us "by ripping off masks from many highly-educated leaders who had unlimited possibilities and yet bankrupted themselves."[30] But Stalin proved unable or unwilling to contain the vertiginous logic of his narrative. "The *dvurushnik* unmasked" represented melodrama gone mad.

## "Millions Will Shudder": The Show Trial as Melodrama

One of the devices used by melodrama to escape vertigo and to allay the anxiety it itself provokes is the climactic courtroom scene. Here all masks are torn off as virtue and villainy are officially accorded the status they deserve. The virtuous community, reassured that its honor has been protected, purifies itself by the condemnation and expulsion of the *traître.*

The courtroom as a forum for the recognition of slandered virtue was a direct link between melodrama and socialism. Heroic courtroom defenses bulked large in the stories—both fictional and historical—that prewar social democracy told about itself. One of social democracy's founding myths was Ferdinand Lassalle's defense in his trial for treason in 1848. Trotsky was much taken with Lassalle; in 1905 he published an analysis and translation of Lassalle's defense speech. A year later Trotsky got his own chance to star as a revolutionary hero in a courtroom drama. Russian revolutionaries had their own tradition of heroic courtroom defenses. In the famous case of Vera Zasulich, a Russian jury in 1878 had acquitted a woman who had openly tried to assassinate a tsarist official. Gorky amalgamated international and local traditions for his novel *Mother* (1908)—the prototype of socialist realism—in which one of the climactic scenes is a trial of dedicated revolutionaries.

Political temperance drama usually included scenes that functioned very much like courtroom scenes: public meetings that affirmed the victory of virtue over slander. In 1932, Kirshon went further and wrote a full-fledged courtroom drama called *The Trial.* Kirshon's play was set in Germany, and this location points to a serious problem. The pathos of the trial in the social democratic narrative depended entirely on the defendant's heroic defiance of the powers that be. As in many other areas, the Bolsheviks faced a dilemma when they themselves became the power in the land: how can a political trial retain its pathos when the good guys are not the defendants but the prosecutors? The first attempt at an elaborate show trial—the 1922 trial of leaders of the Socialist Revolutionary Party—was a relative failure for just this reason: the Bolsheviks used all the resources at their command to impose the proper meaning on the trial but their massive campaign only increased the pathos of the lonely defendants.[31] Indeed, the 1938 Moscow trial itself is often seen by western and postsoviet observers as a heroic courtroom defense in which the heroic *dvurushnik* Bukharin manages to condemn the Stalinist regime even while pretending to plead guilty.

The basic solution to the dilemma of putting on a convincing show trial while in power was outlined by Stalin in a 1930 letter to Molotov about the possibility of bringing some "wreckers" to trial: "By the way, how about Messrs. Defendants admitting their mistakes and disgracing themselves politically, while simultaneously acknowledging the strength of the soviet government and the correctness of the method of collectivization?" If the defendants would cooperate by demonstratively unmasking themselves, then a state-sponsored show trial could reap the advantages of a traditional melodramatic courtroom scene.[32]

The show trials of the Stalin era were based on this logic. This is particularly true of "the trial of the Right-Trotskyite bloc" in March 1938—the third in the series of Moscow show trials and the only one that took place during the purification campaign of 1937–1938.[33] In many ways, the trial was meant to be the climactic episode of the whole *dvurushnik* narrative. The official indictment and the summary speech by state prosecutor Vyshinsky offer a revealing look at the bloc and its crimes:

> The bloc of Rights and Trotskyites was formed at the behest of foreign masters: the *razvedka* of various hostile powers plus Trotsky. Deprived of any prospect of support from within the Soviet Union, the bloc rested its hopes on foreign aggression and covert wrecking. In order to get help from outside, the bloc agreed to restore capitalism and to dismember the Soviet Union. Domestic wrecking took various forms. Uprisings were fomented: this category of wrecking can be further subdivided into kulak uprisings and uprisings in the national republics. Another major form of wrecking tried to foul up the soviet economic system in order to create popular dissatisfaction. Finally, the bloc in its desperation resorted to the murder of staunch Stalin loyalists such as Kirov and Gorky.
>
> Twenty-one members of the bloc were brought to trial in March 1938. At the top of the list were the two leaders of the right opposition, Bukharin and Rykov, who fomented uprisings, approved political murders and gave general direction. Next came prominent Trotskyites such as Konstantin Rakovsky. The Trotskyites were part of a larger group of spies—paid agents of foreign *razvedka* services. Indeed, NKVD investigators revealed that the spying activities of Trotsky and his associates started in the early 1920s—even earlier than formerly realized. In general, the Trotskyites were more ruthless and aggressive than the Rights.
>
> The rest of the bloc were mostly small fry: some wreckers from the economic commissariats, a group of three provocateurs from tsarist days, and the people directly involved in political murder. The murderers were all people whose betrayal of trust was especially heinous: doctors, Gorky's personal secretary, and the former head of the NKVD,

Genrikh Yagoda, the man who should have been protecting the soviet system. Eighteen of the defendants were sentenced to be shot; the sentence was carried out immediately. The remaining three (including Rakovsky) received long prison sentences.

The trial of the Right-Trotskyite bloc was the continuation and climax of the previous political trials. While building on earlier revelations, this trial portrayed an even vaster and more comprehensive conspiracy. The bloc included SRs, Mensheviks, bourgeois nationalists and provocateurs from the tsarist secret police as well as Rights and Trotskyites sensu stricto. "Implicated in this 'case' are the remnants of *all* anti-soviet forces, groups and organizations, and at least, as has been exactly established by the trial, four foreign intelligence services—the Japanese, German, Polish and British."[34] The trial threw a searching light into the past: "It is just these crimes that explain the real course of developments, the real logic of the events and the struggle that brought two worlds face to face, two blocs."[35]

The foregoing summary of the indictment shows how the trial fit into the larger melodramatic story of the clash between the bloc of soviet patriots versus the bloc of *traîtres,* the virtuous community versus the anticommunity. In order to examine the dramatic structure of the trial itself, we shall look at how it was packaged and presented on the pages of *Pravda.*[36] The newspaper's characterization of the forces in conflict fit neatly into the framework of classical melodrama: recognizers, victims and their defenders, and *traîtres.*

The recognizer was the trial's audience, an audience hardly confined to those physically present in the courtroom—it included all of soviet society and progressive humanity: "Hundreds of millions of workers, peasants and honest intellectuals throughout the world will shudder from indignation and loathing, when they learn of the monstrous conspiracy" (February 28). *Pravda* used many devices to ensure that the audience was an active character in the drama of the trial. The extended audience from around the country made its presence felt by means of resolutions that demanded the death sentence, expressed gratitude to Ezhov, and promised vigilance. As the title of one resolution put it: "The entire people steps forth as accuser" (March 4). These resolutions filled at least half a page of *Pravda* each day.

Just as frequent were photographs showing the audience in its many forms—in the courtroom itself, in factories hearing newspaper reports,

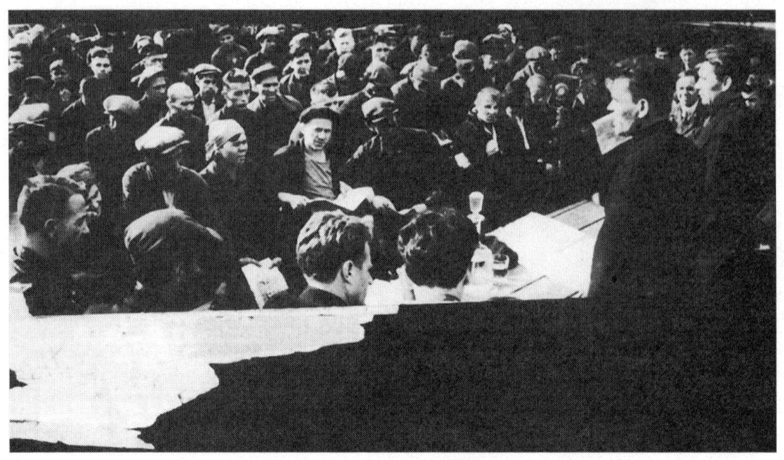

Propaganda photomontage for the show trial of August 1936. From Isaac Deutscher and David Kin, *The Great Purges* (Oxford: Basil Blackwell), 94.

and in barracks listening to comrades who had seen the real thing. The audience in all these shots looks at the speaker with attentive and unsmiling concentration. The climax of this series of photographs showed Vyshinsky giving his final summation: in a large photo spread at the top of the first page, we see Vyshinsky on the left facing a panoramic shot of the courtroom audience on the right (March 12).

*Pravda* also had a regular section titled "From the Courtroom," which sometimes was written by journalists and sometimes by ordinary citizens. These audience reports often bring out, rather than obscure, the trial's resemblance to melodrama. A journalist reports that some of the defendants have an eerily familiar quality: if you take away their decent soviet suits and picture them dressed in appropriate clothing —say, stereotypical dark glasses and overcoats—you would recognize them as tsarist secret police (March 4). A worker commented, perhaps a bit naïvely, about the same defendants: "I had earlier seen such types only at the movies, on the screen, and now I had to look at them in real life. Disgusting" (March 6).

As the dimensions of the vast conspiracy become apparent, the audience understands that it had too easily believed slanders against soviet power. The lesson is driven home with disarming forthrightness in an article on cooperatives: "Now that the masks have been ripped off the fascist degenerates sitting on the bench of the accused, each collective farm worker, each worker, man and woman, sees who is to blame for the unsatisfactory work of the rural cooperatives and who withheld from the toilers such items as sugar, salt, tobacco—all of which exist in abundance in our country" (March 6).

No wonder the audience reacts in appropriate "hiss the villain" style. One journalist sitting in the hall reported that he wanted to jump up and grab the accused by the throats (March 3). Another observer shuddered to think: what if their wicked plans had succeeded (March 4)? A journalist pinches himself in order to realize that some of the grotesque scenes are not fantasy but the "monstrous truth of class power"—a truth that would be too horrible to contemplate except for the "happy and irrevocable fact" that the people and its vigilant *razvedka* won out in the end (March 9). At the end, the audience arises in just indignation and demands purification: "Outside the walls of the *Dom Soiuzov* (House of unions), where the trial took place, a storm of popular anger raged. Rallies of many thousands and meetings demanded one thing: annihilate the cursed vermin" (March 16).[37]

The exciting trial that the recognizer/audience is watching is presented to the *Pravda* reader each day in the form of long excerpts from the official transcript. These excerpts read exactly like a play script: the prosecutor and the accused exchange their lines, with occasional dramatic interventions from the judges or from other defendants. In a manner entirely consonant with the norms of melodrama, *Pravda* surrounds the dialogue with commentary that leaves no ambiguity about who is slandered victim and who is faithless *traître*.

The main victim is the virtuous community, defined as "socialism, the bolshevik party and the soviet people who are building socialist society" (February 28). The most visible vindicator is state prosecutor Vyshinsky, who "rips off the masks" with "annihilating force" (March 12). In the background but constantly mentioned are Ezhov and the "valiant soviet *razvedka*" who stand "keen-eyed [*zorko*]" in defense of the soviet people (February 28). Ezhov is victim as well as vindicator: we learn that the villains were so afraid of the "iron hand of the one sent by the Stalinist Central Committee" that they tried to kill him as well. Ezhov gallantly fought back at risk to his life and damage to his health (March 14).

Stalin himself had a very low profile in the coverage of the trial; he is mentioned only in passing as one of the intended victims back in 1918, along with Lenin and Sverdlov. Although Stalin had very few speaking lines, he was a ubiquitous part of the environment in his adjectival form. The continual use of *stalinskii* has an effect that is difficult to reproduce in English with its different rules about turning names into adjectives. Locutions such as *Stalinskii narkom* (Ezhov, people's commissar of internal affairs), *Stalinskii Tsentralnyi Komitet, Stalinskaia Konstitutsiia, stalinskoe zadanie* ("Stalin assignment"), and others make Stalin less an individual character and more of a ground of being for the virtuous community. As such, he is the number-one victim of the assault against the community.

The villain of the piece was, of course, the Right-Trotskyite bloc. The twenty-one defendants were presented as a heterogeneous group united by only one thing: the *traître*'s urge to "slander" the virtuous community. Wearing masks followed from this basic motivation: "The more their real face was uncovered before the whole people, the stronger their hatred toward the party of bolsheviks. Wearing masks, playing the *dvurushnik,* using the most underhanded methods, the Trotskyites and Bukharinites turned into naked bandits, fascist murderers from ambushes, spies, saboteurs" (February 28).

All enemies of Soviet power belonged together because principled political opposition was impossible: "They were spies *because* they were Rights and Trotskyites. The two categories are inextricably intertwined: one goes right into the other" (March 5). The grandiose clash between good and evil portrayed by the show trials required an equally grandiose motivation, and so *Pravda* emphasizes "savage and inhuman hatred" rather than petty calculation (March 2). But the result is that the villain's motivations are disconnected from any objective basis.

Julia Przybos points out that in many ways the true victim of classical melodrama is the *traître.* It is he who is sacrificed, expelled from the community without compassion or remorse, so that the others can affirm their virtuous solidarity.[38] The *traître* as sacrificial victim certainly fits the Moscow show trials. Strident calls for execution sound like a drumbeat throughout *Pravda*'s coverage. The accused must die in order to protect the purity of the virtuous community: they cannot expect to live among "honest folk" on the "holy soviet land" that has no place for "contemptible vermin."[39] The demand for purification gives rise to a strong filth versus purity imagery in the rhetoric of the trial: "A foul-smelling heap of human garbage" contaminates a land "illumined by the sun of the Stalin Constitution."[40] The trial reaches its grand climax in Vyshinsky's call for a rite of purification in which Stalin himself acts as high priest:

> Time will pass. The graves of the hateful traitors will grow over with weeds and thistle, they will be covered with the eternal contempt of honest soviet citizens, of the entire soviet people. But over us, over our happy country, our sun will shine with its luminous rays as bright and as joyous as before. Over the road cleared of the last scum [*nechist*] and filth of the past, we, our people, with our beloved *vozhd* and teacher, the great Stalin, at our head, will march as before onwards and onwards, towards Communism![41]

As poet Sergei Vasilev put it in an apostrophe to the accused: the nightingales will sing sweeter when you are dead (March 11).

For the most part, the *traître*/defendants dutifully played their role as self-accusers who now recognized the virtue of the community as well as their own evil nature. The only challenge resulted from the efforts of Krestinsky and Bukharin to depart from script. Although Krestinsky's direct denial of his pretrial testimony was dealt with quickly, Bukharin's extraordinary defense became a major topic for *Pravda.* The following discussion is not an effort to discover what Bukharin was really up to but simply to examine the character of Bukharin as portrayed by *Pravda.*

From the beginning Bukharin was presented as the *dvurushnik* par excellence. This epithet was applied to him and not to the other chief criminals such as Trotsky, who, as head of the gang, disdained masks. The other labels attached to Bukharin—Jesuit, lawyer, sly, fox-like, two-faced, cry-baby—all strengthened his basic characterization as a *dvurushnik.* Because many of these epithets had been used much earlier by Stalin and his circle to describe Bukharin in private, it is even possible that Bukharin was the real-life original from which Stalin drew many features of his narrative's protagonist.[42]

When the dimensions of Bukharin's countertrial became evident, the *Pravda* commentators used this basic characterization as a way of keeping the story on track: see how the ultimate *dvurushnik* denies his guilt right up to the last minute. But it is clear that they (or more likely their boss) were infuriated by Bukharin's defense. As seen through the prism of their refutation, Bukharin's case was that he was a "theoretician" who accepted only *political* responsibility rather than *criminal* responsibility for sabotage and assassinations. *Pravda* granted that the purely political responsibility that Bukharin did accept was heavy enough, and it stated that his "verbal poison of restorationist, bourgeois, kulak, fascist mini-ideas, formulas and slogans" was as dangerous as a terrorist bullet (March 7). But *Pravda* was also insistent that Bukharin should accept material responsibility for actual crimes—so insistent that it brought out rather than obscured Bukharin's denial of criminal responsibility.

It is likely that the full meaning of this duel must be sought in the long-standing and highly intense personal relations between Stalin and Bukharin. For our purposes, we should note that Bukharin's resistance was partly a struggle against the genre of classical melodrama that Stalin wished to impose on him. Bukharin portrayed himself as someone like Raevsky, the erring party leader in Kirshon's *Bread* who was a wavering doubter whose leadership mistakes pushed other waverers into the camp of crime. The angry insistence of Vyshinsky and the *Pravda* commentators that Bukharin was an out-and-out criminal was an attempt to keep Stalin's classical melodrama from turning into outmoded political temperance drama.

Stalin longed for "clarity" in the state's messages to society; he detested a confusing diversity of voices (what he called *raznogolositsa*). Yet having a centralized propaganda apparatus would no more guarantee the abolition of the anarchy of meanings than having a centralized economic apparatus guarantee the abolition of the anarchy of the market.[43] To use metaphor, Stalin was like the producer of a large studio production. The main story idea behind the show trial was his, the ultimate control was his, and yet his artistic intentions were constantly disrupted by the wide variety of people employed, the temperament of the actors in the major roles, the varying talents of the actual scriptwriters, the technical means of representation, and the imperatives of marketing—not to mention contradictions and incoherence in the original story idea.[44] The result was "The Trial of the Right-Trotskyite Bloc," an effective if lurid climactic scene for "The *Dvurushnik* Unmasked." And yet even in this highly scripted production we can see a clash of meanings that was impossible to overcome.

## Epilogue

I have argued that melodrama is not just a way of popularizing a political outlook: it *is* a political outlook. The political temperance dramas by soviet playwrights are not simply dramatizations of political doctrine, they are accurate expressions of the same narrative myths that energized political doctrine. In many ways they are a more adequate expression than the attempts by party theorists to put the myth in abstract propositional form. Similarly, the heart of Stalin's rationale for the campaign of terror was not a theoretical proposition about "intensification of the class struggle" but a highly charged narrative about a threatened virtuous community.

What unites these expressions of doctrinal myth is an insistence that the true community is constituted and maintained through a struggle for the recognition of virtue. But this common melodramatic outlook should not obscure real changes in soviet doctrinal myth. The switch from the relatively optimistic focus on the political waverer to the vertiginous world of the *dvurushnik* narrative was a deep-seated one. It is ironic that Stalin's repressive narrative was built around the assumption that the virtuous community of socialism had already been established. It is tragic that he was able to force an entire society to act out his melodramatic fear of masks and two-faced wreckers.

It is fitting to end this study with a story of individual citizens who had to cope as best they could with soviet political melodrama. In 1937, two of the creators of political temperance drama, Kirshon and Afinogenov, were caught up in Stalin's *dvurushnik* narrative. Both were viciously attacked in an open meeting as minions of the deceased *dvurushnik* Averbakh (a prominent literary theorist and official of earlier years). Averbakh was sneeringly referred to as a literary *vozhd* who ruled by "the Trotskyite-style methods of disintegration and disunion." Kirshon evidently didn't realize he was trapped in a real-life melodrama—he tried to defend himself and eventually perished.[45]

Afinogenov quickly cast himself as an innocent who realizes he is on the path to ruin. "Afinogenov spoke of how the demoralizing atmosphere, both creative and everyday, that prevailed at RAPP [the writers' organization headed by Averbakh] drew him away from life, from the party, from honest and sincere people—how he descended into the filth of Averbakh's world, arrived at catastrophe, slid down into a bog in his own literary creation." He had "lost the qualities of an honest bolshevik and soviet playwright," but now he wanted to reform.

One observer, Nikolai Panov, noted bitterly that "during Afinogenov's speech it was sickening to observe how, behind the melodramatic gestures of a 'proper gentleman,' stood a self-satisfied philistine." Nevertheless, Afinogenov's invocation of a vulgar kind of political temperance drama allowed him to survive. He realized more quickly than most that life was being forced to imitate bad art.[46]

## Notes

1 A. Gurvich, *V poiskakh geroia* (Moscow: Iskusstvo, 1938), 348.

2 Guilbert de Pixérécourt, *Théâtre choisi,* 4 vols. (1841–1843; Geneva: Slatkine Reprints, 1971), vol. 1, 199–200. Space constraints force me to give only a general acknowledgment of my debt to the many insightful observers who have written about melodrama from Pixérécourt's day to ours.

3 I will keep *traître* in French to mark it as technical term and to distinguish it from "traitor."

4 William W. Pratt, *Ten Nights in a Bar-Room* (1858) in Michael Booth, ed., *Hiss the Villain: Six English and American Melodramas* (New York: Benjamin Blom, 1964), 199; W. H. Smith's *The Drunkard, or, The Fallen Saved* can be found Richard Moody, ed., *Dramas from the American Theatre 1762–1909* (Cleveland, Ohio: World Publishing, 1966).

5 Anatolii Lunacharskii, *Sovetskie dramaturgi o svoem tvorchestve* (Moscow: Iskusstvo, 1967), 28.

6 For a discussion of actual temperance plays during the soviet period, see Julie Cassiday's essay in this volume.

7 Lunacharskii, *Sovetskie dramaturgi,* 40.

8 *Optimistic Tragedy* was written in 1932 and published in 1933; it was then heavily revised for the Moscow production in late 1933. The revised version was published in 1934 and is now the canonical text. My analysis is based for the most part on the original version as published in 1933, because the contours of the underlying myth show up even more starkly than in the standard version. *Optimisticheskaia tragediia,* 1st ed. (Moscow, 1933).

9 Ibid., 22.

10 Ibid., 53–54.

11 Ibid., 22.

12 "Nu, Kto eshche khochet poprobovat' komissarskogo tela?" in *Optimisticheskaia tragediia,* 15.

13 On Kirshon's early career, see L. Tamashin, *Vladimir Kirshon: Ocherk tvorchestva* (Moscow: Sovetskii pisatel', 1965). For *Bread,* see Kirshon, *Khleb* (Moscow, 1933); Kirshon, *Izbrannoe* (Moscow, 1958); Eugene

Lyons, *Six Soviet Plays* (Boston: Houghton Mifflin, 1934); and A. Gurvich, *Tri dramaturgi* (Moscow, 1936).

14 Kirshon, *Khleb,* 72; Lyons, *Six Soviet Plays,* 290.

15 *Bread* is a narrative version of Stalin's March 1930 article "Dizzy with Success" (*Golovokruzhenie ot uspekhov*) calling for a halt in the excesses of the collectivization campaign—or, rather, *Bread* reveals the underlying melodramatic structure of Stalin's intervention.

16 *Strakh* in Aleksandr Afinogenov, *Izbrannoe,* 2 vols. (Moscow: Iskusstvo, 1977), 243; Lyons, *Six Soviet Plays,* 468–69.

17 Kimbaev is a young Kazakh whose "thirst for knowledge and intellectual zeal skirt the edge of the ludicrous" (Harold Segel, *Twentieth-Century Russian Drama: From Gorky to the Present,* updated edition [Baltimore: Johns Hopkins University Press, 1993], 242).

18 Afinogenov, *Izbrannoe,* 216; Lyons, *Six Soviet Plays,* 432. Compare Vyshinsky in the Moscow show trial of 1938: "Who else [but a high official like Chernov] could set up factories specially for the preparation of infections serums? He alone. And he did it. He has himself told us here that 25,000 horses were destroyed at his behest" (*Report of Court Proceedings in the Case of the Anti-Soviet "Bloc of Rights and Trotskyites"* [Moscow, 1938], 674).

19 Afinogenov, *Izbrannoe,* 197, 213; Lyons, *Six Soviet Plays,* 409, 428.

20 Afinogenov, *Izbrannoe,* 215; Lyons, *Six Soviet Plays,* 431.

21 S. I. Ozhegov, *Slovar' russkogo iazyka* (Moscow: Sovetskaia entsiklopediia, 1970), 149; *History of the Communist Party of the Soviet Union (Bolsheviks): Short Course* (New York: International Publishers, 1939), 291.

22 For example, Oleg Khlevniuk, *Mekhanismy politicheskoi vlasti v 1930-e gody* (Moscow: ROSSPEN, 1996), 194, from which this particular formulation is taken.

23 References in the text are taken from Stalin, *Sochineniia,* 13 vols. (Moscow, 1946–1952) as well as the additional three volumes in this series edited by Robert H. McNeal (Stanford: Stanford University Press, 1967).

24 Stalin, *Sochineniia,* vol. 13, 207, 212.

25 Stalin, *Sochineniia,* vol. 14, 192.

26 "Purification" (*ochishchenie*) was the official label given to the events of 1937–1938 that we usually call the Great Purge or the Great Terror. For examples of its use, see *Pravda,* 1 January 1938 (looking back over the achievements of 1937); and Stalin, *Sochineniia* (vol. 14, 368–69), speech to the eighteenth party congress in March 1939.

27 Central Committee resolution of January 1938, as printed in Richard Kosolapov, *Slovo tovarishchu Stalinu* (Moscow, 1995), 148–49 (everything after "expose" is underlined in the original).

28 Government resolution of November 1938, as printed in Kosolapov, *Slovo tovarishchu Stalinu,* 157. For further entry into the vertiginous world of Stalin, read Ezhov's tearful apology in November 1938 for allowing spies to infiltrate the NKVD in O. Khlevniuk et al., eds, *Stalinskoe Politbiuro v 30-e gody* (Moscow, 1995), 168–71.

29 Pixérécourt, *Théâtre choisi,* vol. 3, 171; compare especially Stalin's concluding remarks to the Plenum of February–March 1937 (*Sochineniia,* vol. 14, 225–47), in which he argues that successful economic performance may only be part of a wrecker's artful mask.

30 A. Karaganov, *Zhizn' dramaturga* (Moscow, 1964), 305–6.

31 Marc Jansen, *A Show Trial under Lenin: The Trial of the Socialist Revolutionaries, Moscow, 1922* (The Hague: M. Nijhoff, 1982).

32 L. T. Lih, O. V. Naumov, O. V. Khlevniuk, eds., *Stalin's Letters to Molotov* (New Haven: Yale University Press, 1995), 210–11.

33 For the full transcript of the trial, see *Report of Court Proceedings.* For extended analyses, see Stephen F. Cohen, *Bukharin and the Bolshevik Revolution* (New York: Vintage, 1971); and Robert Tucker's introduction to Tucker and Cohen, eds., *The Great Purge Trial* (New York: Grosset and Dunlap, 1965).

34 *Report of Court Proceedings,* 629; emphasis added.

35 Ibid., 633.

36 All citations come from *Pravda* for February and March 1938; the date of a particular citation is given in the text.

37 *Pravda* was so eager for audience reaction that although the death sentence was announced at four o'clock in the morning, reporters still went out immediately to ask night-shift workers for their reaction (March 13).

38 Julia Przybos, *L'entreprise mélodramatique* (Paris: Corti, 1987).

39 *Pravda,* February 28 and March 1, 1938. "Vermin" is *gady:* an extremely emotive word that also has connotations of feces, reptiles, and repulsive people.

40 *Report of Court Proceedings,* 631; *Pravda,* March 13, 1938.

41 *Pravda,* March 12, 1938; *Report of Court Proceedings,* 697. In Russian folk belief, *nechist'* was the unclean one, the devil. See my comment on an earlier use by Stalin of this term in *Stalin's Letters to Molotov,* 50.

42 According to *Pravda*'s pretrial introduction of the main villains, Trotsky is a Judas, Rykov is a "malicious enemy of the party and people," and Bukharin is a "base Jesuit and contemptible *dvurushnik*" (March 1).

43 Stalin, speech of October 1, 1938, to propagandists about the recently published *Short Course,* in *Istoricheskii arkhiv,* no. 5 (1994): 27. The multiplicity of meanings is intensified by the other stories jostling together with the trial on the pages of *Pravda:* the heroic Arctic expedition of

Ivan Papanin, the Nazi takeover of Austria, efforts to improve economic performance, and the inadequate attempts by local party bodies to implement the Central Committee resolution of January 1938 that called for rehabilitation of people slandered during the purification campaign.

44 Robert Tucker comments: "In addition to acting by remote control as the [1936] trial's chief producer, Stalin took a hand in creating the script. In doing so he applied to serious political business a dramaturgical bent that was rooted in his self-dramatizing nature" (Tucker, *Stalin in Power: The Revolution from Above, 1928–1941* [New York: Norton, 1990], 316–17).

45 All citations from this meeting come from *Literaturnaia Gazeta,* May 1, 1937.

46 Jochen Hellbeck, "Writing the Self in the Time of Terror: Alexander Afinogenov's Diary of 1937," in *Self and Story in Russian History,* ed. Laura Engelstein and Stephanie Sandler (Ithaca: Cornell University Press, 2000), 69–93.

*Alexander Prokhorov*

# Soviet Family Melodrama of the 1940s and 1950s

## From *Wait for Me* to *The Cranes Are Flying*

> If the notion of the family is conceived of flexibly, the family can be said to represent melodrama's true subject, making the family melodrama a genre, where all other films are only to a greater or lesser degree melodramatic. — Robert Lang, *American Film Melodrama*[1]

> How one can suddenly come to terms with Veronika's betrayal, have sympathy, and forgive after the virtuous moralism of Simonov's "Wait for Me" and Stolper's film adaptation of the poem, after so many years of complicity with screen commandments? — Irina Shilova, . . . *i moe kino*[2]

Family melodrama emerged as an important cinematic genre during the Great Patriotic War (1941–1945) and became the preeminent cinematic form during Khrushchev's Thaw.[3] The genre provided less monumental visions of the two major tropes of soviet culture: that of the family, to represent the society, and that of war, to represent the society's mode of existence. Katerina Clark in her work on the soviet novel demonstrates the centrality of the war and the family tropes for Stalinist culture.[4] The war trope casts the relations between nature and soviet civilization as a confrontation with the elemental forces of nature. Capitalist "them" are conceived as part of the elements. The militaristic resolution of the conflict between capitalist "them" and soviet "us" becomes part of the war on nature. In addition, the soviet novel and soviet film established the vertical bond between the positive hero and the party as the core of the "big family," which represents the basic social structure.

Although early post-Stalinist films and novels never questioned the centrality of war and family tropes, their narratives attempted to redefine the meaning of these tropes by reducing the scale of the family unit, thereby making war an internal experience of a small family and a personal experience of the family's members. Most important, war as internal crisis became an indispensable part of the soviet family. The immediate family as the organizing principle of the composition of the characters complicated the possibility of using violence to resolve the opposition of "us" versus "them," an opposition so central to Stalinist culture. As Thomas Schatz notes regarding the family in Hollywood melodrama, "unlike the genres of order, the melodrama's social conflicts and contradictions could not be resolved by violently eliminating one of the opposing forces."[5] In soviet culture during the war and Khrushchev's Thaw, family melodrama also became the main genre to reenact the crisis and reconstitute the nuclear family. In the films *Wait for Me* (1943) and *The Cranes Are Flying* (1957), each of the female protagonists becomes the narrative center of both the crisis and its resolution.[6] *The Cranes Are Flying,* however, marked a departure from Stalinist cultural values. Most important, the narrative structure of *Cranes,* mise-en-scène, and camera use consciously polemicize with the melodramatic conventions of Stalinist family melodrama, and of *Wait For Me* in particular.

Even though soviet critics typically denied that soviet directors made melodramas, the genre of family melodrama became especially popular in Russia during World War II.[7] Its popularity may be explained by the predominantly female film audience and the shifts in iconography of soviet culture after the outbreak of the Great Patriotic War, which specifically redefined the war and family tropes. Before the Nazi invasion of Russia, the primary instantiation of both the war and the family tropes was the Russian Civil War—the epic war of the "big family" 's origins. World War II became the second major instantiation of the war trope in soviet culture. For contemporaries, this war became the personal drama of separation, of extreme violence and emotions, and, most important, the moral polarization of characters, objects, and events into "us" and "the enemies."

During the Thaw period, the war and the family tropes underwent the most radical redefinition in film melodrama, where the family became the site of internal conflict triggered by the war. In melodramas such as *The House I Live In* (1956) and *The Cranes Are Flying,* war stopped being culture's modus vivendi, resolving all ideological crises and contradictions. Instead it became the victimizer of a vulnerable protagonist. In these films, the family as the model for social organization ceases to be an omnipotent institution that protects the protagonist. On the contrary, the family is either absent or turns into a site of conflict, even the site of the protagonist's victimization. In the final analysis, the major function of Thaw-era homefront melodrama becomes pathos evoked by the loss of the fundamental elements of the cultural landscape: the big family as the cradle of communal security and the war as the way to expand the space of the family.

The reconstitution and preservation of the nuclear family, which replaces the big family touted under Stalinism, becomes the prime goal of family melodrama of the Thaw period. The cinematic genre of a family melodrama developed a visual language to reimagine the tropes of war and family. The main focus of this essay is the elaboration of these tropes in Stalinist and Thaw-era family melodrama. The two case studies for my discussion are Aleksandr Stolper's *Wait for Me* and Mikhail Kalatozov's *The Cranes Are Flying.* The dictum "wait for me" in these melodramas is the sine qua non for the integrity of the family and the successful resolution of the confrontation between "us" and "them."

*Wait for Me* begins with a farewell party at the apartment of a pilot, Ermolov, who is scheduled to be sent on a mission. His friend Vainshtein, a journalist, takes a farewell picture of Ermolov, Ermolov's wife Liza, and their friends. Before leaving, Ermolov takes the key from the apartment with him as a promise of his eventual return. Later, Ermolov's plane is shot down and he is lost in action, but Liza believes in Ermolov's survival even when everyone else has lost hope. Meanwhile Liza's friend, whose husband is also missing in action, stops waiting for him. Eventually, the husband of Liza's friend is wounded and dies in the hospital. Ermolov, on the other hand, returns home at film's end and opens the door with the key that he has carried all this time in his pocket.

On the narrative level, the Thaw-era *The Cranes Are Flying* is a remake of *Wait for Me.* In *The Cranes Are Flying,* the character Boris redefines the role of the male protagonist, and Boris's fiancée Veronika rewrites

The key to Liza's door in Alexandr Stolper's *Wait for Me* (TsOKS, 1943).

the function of the female lead. After the outbreak of the war, Boris volunteers to fight the Nazis. Veronika loses all contact with her fiancé and soon loses her family when her apartment is destroyed by German bombs. She starts living with the family of Boris, where Boris's cousin Mark rapes her and convinces her to marry him. Visually, the film links the night of Veronika's fall with the day of Boris's death. Veronika is unhappy in her marriage with Mark and tries to commit suicide, but she is redeemed when she chooses to save the life of a homeless boy instead of jumping under a train. As Neia Zorkaia notes, the major difference between *Cranes* and its narrative predecessor, *Wait for Me,* is the latter's absence of judgment on the fallen protagonist.[8]

### War-Era Melodrama: Blueprints for the Fighting Family and the Faithful Female

War-era melodrama favors a direct appeal to the viewers' emotions in representing the hardships of war. To evoke a pathetic response, melodrama often employs as one of its main devices a sadistic treatment of the protagonist.[9] Accordingly, war as a threat to the stability of the family (national and/or nuclear) and to the powerless members of the community (above all, women and children), is a recurring motif in melodrama. During the Great Patriotic War, Stalinist culture used family melodrama to naturalize the images of war as the ultimate resolution of the ideological conflict between the family of "us," on the one hand, and "them" as the antifamily, on the other. In Stalinist melodrama, the preservation of the nuclear family signifies the survival of the soviet big family.

Stalinist melodrama also identifies gender roles within the war-time family, in particular the woman's role of wife or girlfriend waiting faithfully for her man—usually an officer and, often, a pilot, whose military feats and victorious return home the film depicts. The seeming death of the hero is usually a red herring: despite rumors and even eyewitnesses, the protagonist inevitably survives by the end of the film. Eventually, he comes back home, his survival guaranteed by his wife's faithfulness and her belief in him. The husband's return, often placed at the end of the film, mirrors success at the front line.

*Wait for Me* is one of the best-known film melodramas of the war era.[10] Its female protagonist, Liza, guards the home front, while her husband, the pilot Ermolov, fights the Nazis. The cause-effect relationship between the narrative sequences is never disrupted. The narrative's predictability is confirmed by the omniscience of the female protagonist: even when Ermolov's buddies have lost faith in his survival, Liza never ceases to believe that he is alive.

As the guard of the home front and keeper of the family, Liza is central to the narrative. This important role was entrusted to the famous actress Valentina Serova, who was the major star of Stalinist cinema, one of Stalin's favorites, and the widow of a famous test pilot.[11] The similarity between Liza's role at the home front and Ermolov's role as the defender of the nation at the military front is shown by cross-cutting sequences in which Liza talks about Ermolov's survival and Ermolov fights the Nazis. The war trope is enacted twice in the film: first, between faithful Liza and the weak of faith; and, second, between Ermolov and the Nazis.

During this era of grand ideological pronouncements, one of Liza's distinctive features is her verbal strength, the key element of women's film narrative.[12] The family guarded by Liza extends beyond the nuclear family, incorporating the pilots who serve with Ermolov. The opening shot of the film introduces this family-military unit. This shot also visually establishes the melodramatic tone of the film: at the husband's farewell party Liza is in black, while her foil, an unfaithful wife of her husband's friend, wears a white blouse. Ermolov's friends constantly come to Liza to regain their faith in his survival, while Liza visits the air base, searching on military maps for the places where Ermolov could have landed. The blurring of the border between the family and the military unit locates the female protagonist in the middle of a family structure that makes no distinction between nuclear and national family. Russia is one big family fighting the external enemy.

The director domesticates the national through his use of interior sets and the stability of symbolic objects—two features that are characteristic of his mise-en-scène. The major symbolic object in the film is the key to Liza's apartment and, metonymically, also to her invisible chastity belt. After Ermolov's plane is shot down, the key, which Liza gives to Ermolov before his departure, is shown to the viewer to confirm that the symbol of fidelity has not been lost. The concluding episode opens with a shot of somebody inserting the key into the keyhole of Liza's apartment door. Fortunately, it is Ermolov who has returned home. The key is never lost, nor do the wrong hands touch it. Through closeness of space the interior sets of the mise-en-scène confirm the security of the community.[13] Liza's apartment is the citadel of faith and fidelity. In addition, Liza is prominently present at air base headquarters, whereby the film underscores the strategic importance of Liza's waiting as part and parcel of the war effort.

*Wait for Me* also introduces the stairwell leading to the protagonist's apartment as the recurring element of war melodrama's setting. Stairs establish the vertical axis of the film's space, essential to the melodramatic quest for the moral occult that Peter Brooks deems essential to melodrama.[14] In *Wait for Me,* stairs lead the characters upward toward the entrance to Liza's apartment, elevating them to her superior moral plateau. During the Thaw, especially in *Cranes,* stairs and the stairwell become primary transitional space in the film, with deep metaphorical and metaphysical significance.

The secure internal spaces associated with Liza are mirrored in the internal spaces associated with Ermolov. After he is shot down and joins the partisans, the viewers mostly see Ermolov inside a safe and clean dugout. This parallel space assures the viewer that he is as safe at the front line as Liza is safe and secure on the home front. Moreover, his fidelity reflects hers, for he resists the blandishments of a secondary female character who flirts with him, never succumbing to the dangers of promiscuous sex. The parallel plotline shows the consequences of infidelity: Liza's friend is unfaithful to her husband and this is, according to the film's symbolism, the major cause of his eventual death.

The closed, secure spaces are illuminated by the whiteness of the female protagonist's face. A distinctive feature of the film's visual style is the constant focus on the protagonist's brightly highlighted face and her blonde hair. The close-ups of Liza's face emphasize her fidelity and perseverance, just as the brightness of Liza's face also echoes the iconic images illuminated by the divine light, the main function of which is to preserve spirituality in the face of war's trials.

*Wait for Me* amply demonstrates the main features of war-era family melodrama: the family's stability and completeness as the prime goal of the narrative, the female protagonist as the guard of the home front, and a dual enactment of the war trope. During the Great Patriotic War, the front is everywhere: up front and back home.

If *Wait for Me* reestablished war family melodrama as an important film genre in soviet culture, then Ivan Pyrev's film *At 6 P.M. after the War* is probably the most popular war-era rendition of the "wait for me" narrative, a soviet classic that still appeals to many Russians of the older generation. The story features a female protagonist, Varia, who waits for her beloved, Vasily. Varia loses Vasily in the chaos of the war; Vasily, in turn, loses a leg. The lovers locate each other, however, and meet at Red Square at 6 P.M. after the war. The concluding scene of Pyrev's film provides a visual quotation for the opening of Kalatozov's film *The Cranes Are Flying.* However, in *Cranes* the clock on the Kremlin tower chimes four times: at 4 A.M. on 22 June 1941, the Nazis invaded the Soviet Union. By means of inversion, *Cranes* implicitly signals its main goal to reconfigure the conventions of Stalinist melodrama through a new instantiation of the war and the family tropes.

## Reconfiguring the War and the Family Tropes in Thaw-Era Homefront Melodrama

*The Cranes Are Flying* underscores the dominant narrative of home-front melodrama during the Thaw: the reconstitution of the nuclear family around the trauma of irrecoverable loss generated by war. Unlike the melodramas of the era that primarily focus on the reconstitution of the troubled family, *Cranes* shifts the focus to the war experience of the most powerless and sinful member of the community: the unfaithful woman.[15]

In Thaw-era home-front melodrama, war's significance as the cause of loss and instability becomes an ambiguous signifier because the victimizer is usually not an external enemy but a sadistic "us." Kalatozov's melodrama reconfigured the war trope inherited from Stalinism, transforming the ideological confrontation between "us" and "them" into a conflict between the female protagonist and the war equated with familial "us." War victimizes the disempowered, orphaned, and fallen Veronika. Her individual feminine experience becomes the locus of Thaw-era values.

Films of the Thaw period emphasized the visualization of the protagonist's sufferings. The resurrection of visual expressivity in post-Stalinist film made camera work critical for Thaw-era filmmaking, and Kalatozov owes much of the success of *Cranes* to his cameraman Sergei Urusevsky.[16] My discussion of *Cranes* concentrates on the elements of its structure that contributed to post-Stalinist reimagining of both the war and the family tropes: the protagonist's characterization through the uses of mise-en-scène and camera, the personalized temporality of war, and the family structure.

*Cranes* not only problematizes the conventions of Stalinist melodrama, but also defines the protagonist, Veronika, against the background of ideal Stalinist womanhood, as envisioned by views during the Thaw. Veronika's foil, Boris's older sister Irina, incarnates this ideal: she is articulate, reason-driven, sexually repressed, and dressed in a military uniform. Kalatozov, however, presents Irina's model of femininity as unfit for the Thaw's envisioned new deal. The military uniform, a low masculine voice, and military body language are presented as a gender mismatch. Irina's father even complains that in being a successful surgeon his daughter made only one mistake—she was born a female. The primacy of reason at the expense of emotionality is presented by the filmmakers as Irina's deficiency of sensitivity. Moreover, Irina's repressed sexuality is channeled into sadistic energy, used to torment the victim-protagonist of the film.

### Visual Style and Expressive Mise-en-Scène

The expressive mise-en-scène of *The Cranes Are Flying* makes visible the protagonist's inner suffering, which supports Mary Ann Doane's argument that the distinctive feature in the structure of the melodramatic character is "the externalization of internal emotions and their embodiment within the mise-en-scène."[17] In characteristic family melodrama fashion, Veronika's body is especially important, because she, unlike the Stalinist ideal female, has a weak command of language.[18] Tania Modleski notes that "many of the classic film melodramas from the 30s through the 50s are peopled by . . . women possessed by an overwhelming desire to express themselves . . . but continually confronting the difficulty, if not the impossibility to realize the desire."[19] This observation accurately describes the dilemmas confronting Veronika, who cannot give form to her sufferings through language and painfully searches for alternative channels of self-expression. At the beginning of the film, Veronika either asks questions or speaks in incomplete sentences. The best example of her inarticulateness is a song about cranes, which Veronika sings at the beginning of the film.

> The long-billed cranes
> Are flying overhead,
> Gray ones, white ones,
> Ships in the skies.[20]

In this fragment, the narrative or facts fade into irrelevance, as the value of mood and emotion replaces them.

Veronika lacks the paternal source of discourse available to Stalinist women. All the males who could potentially empower her with their ideologically impeccable logos disappear from the narrative. Veronika loses her biological father and her fiancé in the first months of the war. The discourses offered by the other two male characters, Mark and Fedor, are corrupt. Mark is unfaithful and constantly lies to Veronika. When Fedor Ivanovich pronounces his diatribe against unfaithful women, he adopts the official discourse and pushes Veronika toward a suicide attempt—after his speech Veronika decides to jump off the bridge under a train.[21]

Being inept at verbal language, Veronika retreats to the language of emotional bodily gesture, which the film promotes to the status of natural language.[22] Body language provides the most efficient way to convey the inner self. Tellingly, at the beginning of the film Veronika and Boris agree on the time of their next date by using fingers instead of words: more precisely, Boris speaks while Veronika uses her hands.

Other characters who share the protagonist's sincerity also favor emotional gesture over corrupt, reason-driven speech. When Fedor, for example, tries to explain why his son has to go to war he cannot find the appropriate words, and he starts crying and drinks a shot of alcohol. When Boris's friend Volodia jokes about the likelihood of Veronika's being unfaithful to him, Boris also abandons words and uses his fists as a means of communication. When Volodia realizes that he mistakenly has told Veronika about Boris's death, speech fails him, and instead he kisses her wet hand covered with soap.

Although Veronika's bodily gestures create a sincere discourse beyond the corrupt word, Veronika's body also becomes a major site of war trauma, conveyed through two major elements of mise-en-scène: lighting and the color of her clothing. Veronika's clothes create a polarized realm of white and black. The two colors signal the protagonist's fall and resurrection as parts of the hyperbolized melodramatic world, where, according to Peter Brooks, every dress change "has little to do with the surface realities of a situation, and much more to do with the inner drama in which consciousness must purge itself and assume the burden of moral sainthood."[23] Veronika's black-and-white clothes serve as the ultimate surface signifier exteriorizing her inner conflict.

Kalatozov's second mode of inscribing visual trauma on Veronika's body is through his use of lighting. In *Wait for Me* the bright light on Liza's face and blonde hair underscores her fidelity and perseverance amid the darkness of war, whereas the onset of war in *Cranes* covers the face of the protagonist in shadows. The shadows emphasize her vulnerability and anticipate the brutality of war. Once the war begins, the bright high-key lighting disappears from the film.

During Boris and Veronika's last meeting, shadows envelop them and only their eyes are highlighted by bright patches. The ominous potential of shadow receives full realization in the rape scene, when the flashes of bomb explosions cast grotesque shadows on the protagonist's body. The rape experience is visualized as patches of black on Veronika's face, in a conflation of national and bodily invasion. The thinner and lighter shadows in the second part of the film signal Veronika's gradual recovery from the rape of war. The concluding scene, however, represents but does not resolve the contradiction between personal loss and common victory. The high-key, bright light shining over the celebratory crowd contrasts with the darkness of Veronika's eyes and hair.

To represent the protagonist's emotional state, Kalatozov employs Vsevolod Pudovkin's notion of "plastic material," that is, "those forms and movements that shall most clearly and vividly express in the images the whole content of the idea."[24] In *Cranes* such plastic material carries extraordinary emotional weight. For example, the stuffed squirrel that Boris gives to Veronika, whose nickname is "Squirrel," materializes the characters' emotional state (love, grief) or implies the generation of intense emotions (signaling betrayal, resurrection). Passed on to Veronika as Boris's birthday gift to her, the squirrel transforms into a symbol of their love after his departure. After Mark rapes and then marries Veronika, he steals the squirrel and presents it as a birthday gift to his mistress, thereby transforming the squirrel into an antithetical symbol, that of betrayal. When the stuffed squirrel is returned to Veronika and she belatedly reads the birthday card from Boris hidden inside it, the stuffed toy (an extremely antimonumental object) comes to symbolize the promise of Veronika's resurrection.

A distinctive feature of Thaw-era melodrama's setting, and that of *Cranes* in particular, is the subordination of space to the temporality of lateness, separation, and loss. *Cranes* is radically different in this respect from Stalinist works that favor spatial metaphors of war. In *Wait for Me,* Liza searches for her husband on a map in a room where numerous portraits depict Stalin with maps and battle plans. By contrast, Thaw-era homefront melodrama allows time "out of joint" to dominate the space of the film. War becomes a time of personal tragedy instead of an epic space for a monumental battle.

Temporality dominates space, starting from the initial frame showing the film's title, which appears against the background of the clock on the main Kremlin tower. Clock sounds and images constantly remind the viewer about war as a time of loss. The clock chime of the radio foreshadows the announcement of war. When viewers hear the radio signal, they see Boris's empty chair at the family table. The family clock ticks deafeningly when Veronika opens the door into the abyss of her apartment, which has been destroyed by a bomb.

If time signifies the personal tragedy of war, then Veronika's recovery from the trauma is conveyed through the images of the protagonist transgressing the spatial borders that separate her from other people. To represent visually the protagonist's ordeal, Kalatozov favors two types of spatial composition within the film's shots: a space marked by dividing and separating lines and borders, and a space dominated by the protagonist's motion across them. The divided space appears more often

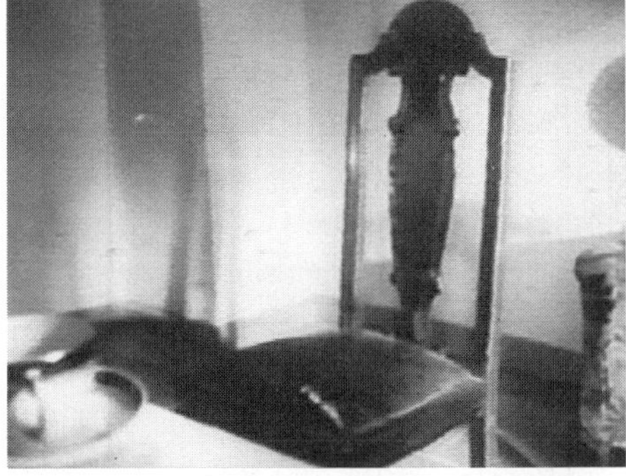

Boris's empty chairs and below, the steel fence separates Veronika from Boris. Both from Mikhail Kalatozov's *The Cranes Are Flying* (Mosfilm, 1957).

in the first part of the film until Veronika's suicide attempt (note, for example, the farewell scene shots, where the prison-like bars of the steel fence separate Boris and Veronika).

The film contrasts such divided frames and claustrophobic rooms with transitional spaces, in which the protagonist experiences radical transformations. Mikhail Bakhtin has argued that "on the threshold . . . the only time possible is crisis time, in which a moment is equal to years."[25] The crisis/threshold chronotope precisely characterizes the emotional intensity of Veronika's existence in the transitional spaces. Her arrival in such a space indicates her extreme emotional state and the drastic change in her life. Among various types of such spaces, two are of decisive importance for the construction of the protagonist and her relationship to the war: bridges and staircases.

A bridge serves as the space of psychological/spiritual transition to Veronika's resurrection and reconciliation with the losses of war. Veronika comes to the bridge to save the life of an orphan and thereby saves her own soul. At film's end, Veronika crosses the bridge in an attempt to come to terms with her loss. Likewise, the three stair sequences provide transitional spaces in which characters experience the unavoidability of war suffering en route to their eventual salvation. The stairs spatially symbolize the death-shadowed time of war as the inversion of life's temporality. Consequently, the living characters move counterclockwise—that is, against the time of war—while the dead characters move clockwise, in tune with the temporality of death. Significantly, both Boris and Veronika favor an ascending motion, associated with a reconstitution of their "moral sainthood."[26] Stairs belong to the vertical axis of Thaw-era melodrama, linking the earthly and heavenly worlds.

The camera's primary function in *Cranes,* like that of the mise-en-scène, is to create the melodramatic protagonist. If mise-en-scène employs the protagonist's excessive bodily gestures to represent the sincerity and uniqueness of her emotions, then the camera employs close-ups for the same end. Close-up shots focus mainly on Veronika. They foreground and validate the sufferings of the most disempowered and marginalized member of the film's social and family hierarchy—a raped orphan. Moreover, to obliterate the significance of the background, cinematographer Urusevsky often used short-focused lenses and blurs the background of his close-ups.[27]

The camera emphasizes the intensity of Veronika's emotions by tilting her face in the frame, disrupting the tonal homogeneity of the image with shadows and placing an obstacle between the protagonist's face and the viewer's gaze. An upside-down close-up indicates the destruction of peace-time norms and hierarchies. Urusevsky presents through a carnivalesque close-up the ultimate trauma of the protagonist as Mark rapes her.

The close-ups conveying emotional excess also serve an important narrative function. They break the linear flow of the narrative and usually frame sequences designed to evoke pathos. For example, the sequence of Veronika's rape and Boris's death opens with a close-up of Veronika's face and ends with a close-up of Boris in the throes of death. His dead eyes acquire a glass-like quality, echoing the image of broken glass on the floor of the room where Veronika was raped. Serving as a framing device of the sequences dominated by extreme feelings, close-ups emphasize emotional intensity as the distinctive trait of the protagonist.

To convey the intensity of the protagonist's emotions, Urusevsky also

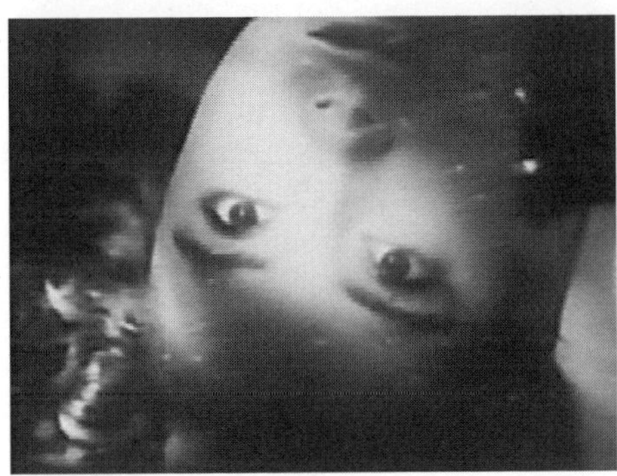

Blurred background and below, upside-down close-up. Both from Mikhail Kalatozov's *The Cranes Are Flying* (Mosfilm, 1957).

employs extremely long tracking or panning shots.[28] For example, he structures the concluding scene, in which Veronika runs to see Boris's friend Stepan, from whom she learns about her beloved's death, as a combination of radically extended tracking shots of Veronika. The temporal excessiveness of the tracking shots underscores Veronika's passionate hope, while the abrupt cut to a close-up of her and Stepan visually captures her despair when she learns about Boris's death. To impede the narrative flow and to intensify the emotional excess of the episode, the filmmakers also use real time in their long tracking shots, the effect of which, is described hereby critic Vitaly Troianovskii: "The extralong tracking shot filmed in real time goes on and on. And you suddenly feel choked up from your proximity to another's soul."[29] If the close-ups emphasize the authenticity of suffering, then the length of the takes underscores the scope of individual trauma.

Finally, the third important camera device is the use of unconventional angles, extremely high and low, to represent the protagonist's psychological state. In the introductory part of the film, high-angle crane shots suggest the scale of the lovers' happiness through the openness and expanse of space. Shifts to low-angled shots focusing on the couple foreground the significance of their togetherness. With the beginning of the war, the high-angled shots gradually disappear and the closed form conveys the claustrophobic nature of Veronika's space. She lives in the attic, where the camera's eye is always confronted with objects blocking the view, thereby creating an aura of entrapment.

High-angled shots reappear only at the very end of the film, which closes with a crane shot of the protagonist. These shots return Veronika to the peaceful life established at the beginning of the film. The camera here serves as a deus ex machina that tries to bring the film to a happy closure and to symbolize Veronika's coming to terms with her tragedy. Moreover, the concluding high-angled shot—where the camera becomes a sort of eye in the sky—and the reappearance of the paternal figure (Fedor) emphasize the restoration, if only partial, of the patriarchal order that presumably will protect Veronika in the future. The protagonist's emotional state, however, hardly coincides with the camera's attempts to regain the space of innocence. In the words of Linda Williams, *Cranes* "begins, and wants to end, in a space of innocence."[30] But Veronika never lets the old space of innocence be unambiguously restored.

## The Rhetoric of "Too Late"

Mary Ann Doane points out that "the 'moving effect' " of melodrama "is tied to a form of mistiming, a bad timing, or a disphasure."[31] Soviet home-front melodrama of the 1950s in general, and *The Cranes Are Flying* in particular, redefined the nature of soviet time by foregrounding the temporality of the protagonist's losses and her powerlessness in the face of time's irreversibility. The melodramatic mistiming was a departure from the temporality of Stalinist culture, which favored a teleological vision of great historical time: the inevitable progression of history toward the triumph of communism. Existing in such a temporality, the characters were supposed to create features of the future in the present, by, for example, overfulfilling production plans and thus being several months or years ahead of schedule.

*Cranes* also shifted the direction of soviet temporality; instead of overcoming the future, the film's protagonist seeks reconciliation with her past. Thaw-era melodrama shifts the focus from official state time to personal, individual time; more precisely, the film dramatizes the conflict between personal and state time. *Cranes* opens with a tilted shot of the frame of the clock on the Kremlin tower. This is the first visual clue to the film's concern with personal time. The narrative confirms the discrepancy between state time and the characters' personal time: at 4 A.M. on June 22, the Kremlin clock simultaneously chimes the end of Boris and Veronika's date and the beginning of war.

State time and the lovers' personal time are out of emotional tune throughout the film. Two events—the beginning of the war and the hard-won victory at its end—delineate state time. Boris and Veronika miss the official announcement of the outbreak of war because of their long rendezvous. They are also emotionally displaced vis-à-vis the moment of victory because Boris is killed and Veronika's irrecoverable loss prevents her from joining the general festivities.

Boris and Veronika are not only out of sync with state time, but also are never able to synchronize their personal times. The only moment when the lovers' personal clocks tick together is during the last morning of peace. With the outbreak of war, the rhetoric of "too late" takes over the characters' personal time. The traumatic separation of the two lovers starts with Veronika's lateness, first to the farewell party, then to the site of the recruits' departure, and culminates in the scene of Boris's death, where the last thing that Boris sees is himself arriving late to his wedding to Veronika.

The alternative to this temporality of belatedness and loss is the temporality of new beginnings, which derives much of its symbolism from the Christian notion of resurrection. Although it does not suspend the notion of loss and lateness, this temporality provides hope for rebirth. The rebirth chronotope occurs at the center of the narrative four times in scenes of extreme emotional intensity. The first two such scenes consist of miraculous coincidences—a distinct feature of melodramatic narrative. When Veronika chooses to save the life of an orphan instead of committing suicide, the saved boy's name, improbably, turns out to be Boris. Similarly, when Veronika is betrayed by Mark she finds a note from her dead fiancé, its message articulated by his "posthumous" voiceover, wishing her a happy birthday. Boris's greetings fall not on Veronika's actual birthday, but close to Christmas Day—the moment of Veronika's spiritual rebirth.

The two miracles in *Cranes* are followed by two naturalized metaphors of rebirth. First, spring returns to the town where Veronika is staying during the war. Second, at the very end of the film, the cranes—birds that abandon Russia in winter—return to postwar Moscow.

By defining its dominant temporality as the personal time of the protagonist's loss and rediscovery of hope, *Cranes* rejects the Stalinist overcoming of the present so as to project it into the future. Veronika's personal time reasserts, in Brooks's words, "the need for some version of the Sacred and offers further proof of the irremediable loss of the Sacred in its traditional, categorical unifying form."[32] Thaw-era home-front melodrama conceived of the resacralization of time as a personal reconciliation with the losses of the war.

In addition to destabilizing the structure of the nuclear family, *Cranes* complicates the family's hierarchy by contradictions in the construction of the father's masculinity. The major contradiction arises from the juxtaposition of the official paternity discourse of the state and the discourse of the small family's paternal authority, Fedor. Official paternity is represented most often through acoustic devices, especially radio announcements. Of the two central radio messages in the film, the first announces the outbreak of war (thereby linking the official discourse with war), and the second assures listeners that nothing special has happened at the front—right after the episode where Boris falls victim to enemy fire. The incompatibility between the tragedy of Boris's death and the tone of the official news lays open the contradiction between the personal experience of war and the perception offered by the radio, the mouthpiece of the state. Similarly, Stepan's official speech at the end of the film contrasts with Veronika's silent mourning. Stepan's offscreen, upbeat voice is at diametric odds with the close-ups of Veronika's wordless anguish.

Fedor, in contrast to state paternity, avoids and even ironizes the style of official speeches, as he does at the farewell dinner before Boris's departure. His paternal discourse mirrors Veronika's melodramatic sincerity, as he stumbles through his toast and resorts to tears. The closing scene shows Fedor as silent as Veronika, connecting him emotionally with her trauma of war and contrasting with the conventionality of Stepan's loud public speech.

Such a splintering of paternity affects the meaning of both the war and the family tropes. *Cranes* identifies the "big family" of "us" with the war forces that brutalize the individual. State paternity is part and parcel of the murderous "us," as opposed to the paternity of the small family. Home-front melodrama does not resolve the conflict between state paternity implicated in war and small-family paternity attempting to intercede on behalf of the victimized protagonist. It represents the conflict and suspends judgment.[33] The small family with a melodramatic emotional father provided one of the first proto-private spaces as an alternative to the totalitarian national family of the Stalinist era. This space, like the protagonist, celebrates its virtue through its vulnerability and suffering.

## Thaw-Era Culture Re/Views *The Cranes Are Flying*

If in retrospect evoked pathos seemed to be the hallmark of the entire post-Stalinist period, the immediate critical responses to *The Cranes Are Flying* castigated the film precisely for its melodramatic stance.[34] Two aspects of the film's structure were the hardest both to articulate and to accept: the reconfiguration of the war and the family tropes and the emotional excess of the protagonist that periodically disrupted the linear narrative and distorted the realistic mise-en-scène. The discussion of the film in Russia's principal film journal, *The Art of Cinema,* captures the critics' struggle with the film's style.[35]

Kalatozov's *Cranes* not only stirred passionate debate among the critics, but also influenced the style of many Russian film directors of the late 1950s and the 1960s. The most significant and immediate directorial response was Grigorii Chukhrai's *Clear Sky* (1961), a remake, simultaneously, of *The Cranes Are Flying* and of Stolper's *Wait for Me.* Chukhrai focused on the sufferings of his female protagonist, Sasha, at the home front and tried to follow Kalatozov's reading of the war trope as the confrontation of a powerless individual with forces hostile to her, especially to her emotional world.

Chukhrai, however, politicized his film by making melodramatic conventions serve an overt anti-Stalinist message. As a result, *Clear Sky* eschewed *Cranes*'s ambiguity while reviving many aspects of Stalinist binarism. The female protagonist Sasha becomes morally flawless and impervious to the advances of anybody but her beloved. Moreover, the reconstitution of Sasha's family is completely dependent on the state's divine intervention. The major threat for her family comes from the state, which unjustly persecutes Sasha's husband, a military pilot and a POW during the war. In contrast to the destabilization of the nuclear family at the end of *Cranes,* the nuclear family in *Clear Sky* regains stability and merges with the "big family" when authorities rehabilitate Sasha's husband and even award him the decoration of Star of the Hero of the Soviet Union.

Numerous Stalin-era visual metaphors resurface in Chukhrai's film. Among them, two metaphors are especially important for soviet culture in general and for the discussion of home-front melodrama in particular: a clear sky and an airplane. A clear, sunny sky was central to Stalinist landscapes, symbolizing the absence of obstacles en route to the radiant future. The airplane was the vehicle of modernity effecting the triumphant journey to communism. Chukhrai, in his anti-Stalinist melodrama, unwittingly reestablished the metaphors of Stalinism that are associated with the Stalinist big family and the victorious war of "us" against the elemental forces of "them." In contrast to Chukhrai, Kalatozov deliberately abandoned the man-made "steel bird" in favor of the cranes as a "natural" metaphor, although he had used airplanes symbolically before the Thaw.[36]

By reviving the features of Stalinist aesthetics, Chukhrai's film demonstrates that an overt political message destroys the potential of Thaw-era melodrama for stylistic ambiguity. The war trope in *Clear Sky* instantiates again the conflict between "us" (now anti-Stalinists) and "them" (now "the heirs of Stalin"). The film's family representation revived the Stalinist menage à trois of the state, a husband, and a female who never falters in her fidelity to both state and husband.

### Masochistic Pleasures of the Thaw Period

The centrality to Thaw-era culture of narratives focusing on the family and its war experience underscores the fact that the family and the war tropes underwent a change of status, from the fundamental tropes of the culture to the loci of culture's crisis. Thaw culture started abandoning such Stalinist values as monumentalism, a teleological vision of history, the primacy of spatiality over temporality, and an emphasis on the unambiguous significance of culture's narratives and tropes. In Stalin's time the "big family" was the only possible community for soviet "us." The militaristic conflict between "us" and the elemental forces of "them" was predestined to be resolved in favor of "us."

The Communist Party allowed the producers of Thaw-era culture to negotiate the meaning of the war and the family tropes within the limits of socialist realism. The reduction of scale and even the shift from the primacy of space to the primacy of temporality—specifically, the melodramatic temporality of loss—did not violate the boundaries of the permissible in Thaw-era culture. Within these limits of the permissible, soviet writers and filmmakers replaced the single model of the "big family" and the "Final War" on the elements with variants of the war and the family tropes. Whereas during this era literature was drastically restricted by the method of socialist realism, the less logocentric medium of film provided more radical departures from Stalinist instantiations of the family and the war tropes. Thaw-era culture made family melodrama its key cinematic genre. It was an ideal visual narrative form for redefining the major tropes of Stalinist culture and for articulating the new values: antimonumentalism, the cult of the small family, and the individual, whose personal experience is as valid as the communal experience.

The development of family melodrama after the 1940s and its centrality in soviet culture of the 1950s coincided with what Vera Dunham calls the rise of the soviet middle class, a state-financed intellectual and bureaucratic stratum with a standard of life above the survival minimum provided for workers and collective farmers—the "ruling classes" of the USSR, according to the fantasy of soviet propaganda.[37] The values and fears of this middle stratum found expression in the style of 1950s melodramas. Two fears in particular nurtured the style of these texts: fear of the state, which constantly interfered with the privacy of the nuclear family, and fear of ideological purges, which threatened the integrity of individual identity.

Ironically, Geoffrey Nowell-Smith's definition of 1950s Hollywood melodrama, although not applicable to the production circumstances of soviet film industry, adequately describes the role of melodrama as social praxis in early post-Stalinist culture: "The importance of melodrama . . .

lies precisely in its ideological failure. Because it cannot accommodate its problems, either in the real present or in an ideal future, but lays them open in their shameless contradictoriness, it opens space which most Hollywood forms have studiously closed off."[38] Soviet family melodrama of the 1950s turned the Stalinist war trope inward by representing the sadistic treatment by the domestic "us" of the weakest and most vulnerable among the "us." In turn, the family trope ceased functioning as the locus of social and ideological security and became the site of loss and victimization. Most important, such films as *The Cranes Are Flying* present the reconfigured war trope as an irresoluble conflict within the family of "us," the open wound of a personal trauma that cannot heal.

After *Cranes*'s domestic success viewers waited for a sequel about Veronika. Although it was never made, even twenty-five years later actress Tatiana Samoilova was asked how she would envision the fate of her protagonist if such a sequel were made. Her answer is revealing: "She would simply be passed on from one man to another."[39] The reenactment of abuse as part of the communal treatment of the individual would not stop with the end of war's hardships.

## Notes

1 Robert Lang, *American Film Melodrama: Griffith, Vidor, Minelli* (Princeton: Princeton University Press, 1989), 49.

2 Elena Shilova, . . . *i moe kino* (Moscow: NII Kinoiskusstva/Kinovedcheskie zapiski), 55.

3 Peter Brooks contends that film has not just used melodrama but that melodrama is the dominant mode of cinematic representation (Brooks, "The Melodramatic Imagination," in *Imitations of Life: A Reader on Film and Television Melodrama,* ed. Marcia Landy [Detroit: Wayne State University Press, 1991], 53). Such critics as Thomas Schatz or Thomas Elsaesser, however, note that based on visual style and narrative and thematic conventions, one can distinguish a genre of Hollywood family melodrama. See Thomas Elsaesser, "Tales of Sound and Fury: Observations on the Family Melodrama," in Landy, ed., *Imitations of Life,* 68–91; and Thomas Schatz, *Hollywood Genres* (New York: Random House, 1981), 226–28.

4 Katerina Clark, *The Soviet Novel* (Chicago: University of Chicago Press, 1981).

5 Schatz, *Hollywood Genres,* 228.

6 *Wait for Me,* dir. Aleksandr Stolper, TsOKS, Alma-Ata, 1943; *The Cranes Are Flying,* dir. Mikhail Kalatozov, Mosfilm, 1957.

7 Elena Shilova, "Melodrama," in *Kinoslovar'* (Moscow: Sovetskaia Entsiklopediia, 1986), 264. On prerevolutionary Russian melodrama, see Neia Zorkaia, *Na rubezhe stoletii: U ostokov iskusstva v Rossii 1900–1910 godov* (Moscow: Nauka, 1976). On Hollywood and French film melodrama, see Ianina Markulan, *Kinomelodrama, fil'm uzhasov: Kino i burzhuaznaia massovaia kul'tura* (Leningrad: Iskusstvo, 1978). Maia Turovskaia was among the few who wrote on the role of melodrama in contemporary soviet culture, see her "Pochemu zritel' khodit," in *Zhanry kino* (Moscow: Iskusstvo, 1979), 138–74. See also Nina Dymshits, *Sovetskaia kinomelodrama vchera i segodnia* (Moscow: Znanie, 1987).

8 Neia Zorkaia, *The Illustrated History of Soviet Cinema* (London: Hippocrene Books, 1989), 212.

9 Mary Ann Doane, "The Moving Image: Pathos and the Maternal," in Landy, ed. *Imitations of Life,* 283–306.

10 My analysis of *Wait for Me* relies on Andrea Walsh's discussion of women's film in her *Women's Film and Female Experience: 1940–1950* (New York: Praeger, 1984), 23–48.

11 Vitalii Vul'f, *Zvezdy trudnoi sud'by* (Moscow: Znanie, 1997), 64.

12 Walsh, *Women's Film,* 27.

13 Walsh points out that the interior settings of women's film can also be explained in economic terms, because films could be shot more cheaply in sets on the studio's lot (*Women's Film,* 27). The interior setting is also a departure from the open public space associated with Stalinist positive heroes in the films of the 1930s.

14 Brooks, "The Melodramatic Imagination," 53.

15 The most representative family melodramas of the Thaw period are *Big Family* (Kheifits 1953), *The Unfinished Story* (Ermler 1955), *The House I Live In* (Kulidzhanov and Segel 1957), *Ekaterina Voronina* (Anninskii 1957), and *My Beloved* (Kheifits 1958).

16 In Russian film histories, as well as in the works favoring an auteur approach in general, the director is usually mentioned as the main author of the film. The only exceptions are 1920s avant-garde film and Thaw-era cinema. Two famous cameramen of the Thaw period are Sergei Urusevskii, who worked with Kalatozov, and Vadim Iusov, who collaborated with Andrei Tarkovskii.

Sergei Urusevskii's contribution to soviet cinema is usually discussed within the context of reviving the tradition of the 1920s avant-garde film. See Iurii Bogomolov, *Mikhail Kalatozov: Stranitsy tvorcheskoi biografii* (Moscow: Iskusstvo, 1989), 157–61; Antonin Liehm and Mira Liehm, *The*

*Most Important Art: Soviet and Eastern European Film after 1945* (Berkeley: University of California Press, 1977), 199–200; and Maiia Merkel', *Ugol zreniia: Dialog s Urusevskim* (Moscow: Iskusstvo, 1980), 32.

Intelligentsia of the Thaw period also associated avant-garde film with black-and-white film stock, and late Stalinist film with excessive use of color. This was the other reason that many Thaw-era family melodramas avoided color and used avant-garde film techniques to convey melodramatic excess.

17 Doane, "The Moving Image," 285.

18 Marcia Landy and Amy Villarejo point out that a "mute quality" is one of the major characteristics of melodrama: "The verbal language is inadequate to the affect that melodrama seeks to communicate" (Landy and Villarejo, *Queen Christina* [London: British Film Institute, 1995], 27).

19 Tania Modleski, "Time and Desire in the Women's Film," in *Film Theory and Criticism,* ed. Gerald Mast, Marshall Cohen, and Leo Brandy (New York: Oxford University Press, 1992), 537.

20 Viktor Rozov, "Alive Forever," in *Contemporary Russian Drama* (New York: Pegasus, 1968), 24.

21 As Richard Stites notes, it was a literary reference that "no Russian could miss" (Stites, *Russian Popular Culture: Entertainment and Society since 1900* [Cambridge: Cambridge University Press, 1992], 141).

22 Discussing the reactions of Diderot and Rousseau to the Enlightenment crisis, Brooks notes: "Gesture appears in the *Essai* to be a kind of prelanguage, giving a direct presentation of things prior to the alienation from presence set off by the passage into articulated language" (Brooks, "The Melodramatic Imagination," 66).

23 Brooks, "The Melodramatic Imagination," 53.

24 Vsevolod Pudovkin, *Film Technique and Film Acting* (New York: Grove Press, 1949), 55.

25 Mikhail Bakhtin, *Problems of Dostoevskii's Poetics* (Minneapolis: University of Minnesota Press, 1984), 169–70.

26 Brooks, "The Melodramatic Imagination," 53.

27 Several critics identify short-focused optics as a distinctive feature of the film's style. See Leonid Kosmatov, "Sovershenstvuia khudozhestvennuiu formu," *Iskusstvo kino* 12 (1957): 26; Neia Zorkaia, *The Illustrated History of Soviet Cinema,* 212; and Bordwell and Thompson, *Film Art: An Introduction* (New York: McGraw-Hill, 1997), 216.

28 Russian works on Urusevskii's art call these long takes *superpanorama,* no matter whether they are pans or tracking shots. See Maiia Merkel', *Ugol zreniia;* and Vitalii Troianovskii, "*Letiat zhuravli* tret' veka spustia," *Kinovedcheskie zapiski* 17 (1993): 54.

29 Troianovskii, "*Letiat zhuravli* tret' veka spustia," 54.

30 Linda Williams, "Melodrama Revised," in *Refiguring American Film Genres,* ed. Nick Browne (Berkeley: University of California Press, 1998), 65.

31 Doane, "The Moving Image," 300.

32 Brooks, "The Melodramatic Imagination," 61.

33 Zorkaia, *The Illustrated History of Soviet Cinema,* 212.

34 The major reaction to the film, according to contemporaries, was one of tears, extreme emotional excess, and an inability to express verbally the overwhelming experience. See Lev Anninskii, *Shestidesiatniki i my* (Moscow: SK SSSR/Kinotsentr, 1991), 8–9, 33; Sergei Iutkevich, "Kann 1958," *Iskusstvo kino* 10 (1958): 144; Viktor Rozov, *Puteshestvie v raznye storony* (Moscow: Sovetskii pisatel', 1987), 379; and Tatiana Samoilova, "Eto bylo moe," *Kinovedcheskie zapiski* 17 (1993): 40. In short, critical reception mirrored melodramatic screen reality.

35 N. Gorchakov, "Blizkie nam liudi," *Iskusstvo kino* 12 (1957): 18–23; Rostislav Iurenev, "Vernost'," *Iskusstvo kino* 12 (1957): 5–14; Kosmatov, "Sovershenstvuia khudozhestvennuiu formu," 23–26; and Maiia Turovskaia, "Da i net," *Iskusstvo kino* 12 (1957): 14–18.

36 See Kalatozov's Stalin-era films *Courage* (1939) and *Chkalov* (1941).

37 Vera Dunham, *In Stalin's Time: Middle-Class Values in Soviet Fiction* (New York: Cambridge University Press, 1976).

38 Geoffrey Nowell-Smith, "Minelli and Melodrama," in *Home Is Where the Heart Is,* ed. Christine Gledhill (London: British Film Institute, 1987).

39 Samoilova, "Eto bylo moe," 43.

*Susan Costanzo*

# Conventional Melodrama, Innovative Theater, and a Melodramatic Society

## Pavel Kohout's *Such a Love* at the Moscow University Student Theater

In preparation for a recent trip to Moscow, I asked a colleague for the phone number of Olga, his close friend and a successful journalist who wrote on cultural issues for a popular Moscow newspaper.[1] Handing me the slip of paper with her number, he advised: "Just tell her that we're having an affair. She'll love that. You know how Russians are about that sort of thing." I nodded. We had both encountered Russians who romanticized the ongoing suffering of lovers involved in a hopeless liaison.

That fondness for the stuff of melodrama remains prominent in recent Russian cultural activity. A glance at the Moscow weekly *Leisure* reveals that the genre of melodrama encompasses an entire category of contemporary films. As other essays in this volume demonstrate, Russian popular culture has long embraced formulaic films devoid of political content. In the Khrushchev era, for instance, melodramatic depictions of World War II in film, including themes related to sexual betrayal, were enormously popular.[2] Harlequin romances offer a more recent indulgence as one of the newly acquired freedoms under glasnost.

But Russian melodrama has not been confined to popular culture; it includes serious dramatic works that would not automatically be associated with this supposedly lowbrow form. For Moscow theater audiences in the late 1950s, the depiction of a love triangle launched a directorial career and reconfirmed the tangible contributions of amateur theatrics to the Moscow professional cultural sphere. Rolan Bykov, an actor who was trying to break into directing, staged Pavel Kohout's play

*Such a Love* at the Moscow State University (MGU) student theater in 1958. The plot recreates the events leading to the death of Lida Matisova, a university student who is having an affair with a married faculty member, Petr Petrus. When the university's personnel department learns of the affair, Petrus must choose between Lida and his career. He abandons her, and she subsequently dies. On the surface, the story conforms to conventional melodrama, but analysis of the production reveals a multifaceted work with both eye-rolling banalities and clever subversions.

Bykov's interpretation demonstrates the persistence of melodrama in Russian and soviet high culture and its ability to shape prevailing assumptions about theater in the late 1950s. The MGU version of *Such a Love* also illuminates the genre's versatility. As issues related to private life reemerged in the Khrushchev era, melodrama's focus on personal relationships provided a particularly apt vehicle to address those issues. On a thematic level, the play examines the tensions between individuals' choices in private life and the ongoing public right to influence those choices. The conflict is not resolved unambiguously, and the drama simultaneously encourages and punishes both the adherence to integrity and the submission to social pressures. Melodrama's structure, which in broad terms resembles soviet socialist realism, typically concludes optimistically, but Kohout and Bykov undermined that convention with an unorthodox staging of this relatively orthodox story. *Such a Love* provided Muscovites with one of the first nonrealist productions since the 1930s.[3] By combining innovation and conformity, performances were tolerated by censors and appealed to Moscow's theatergoing public.

Kohout's play does not immediately suggest itself as an example of "Russian" melodrama, but Bykov's production and its reception demonstrate that the author's ethnic origins alone do not limit a work's inclusion. Kohout is, in fact, a Czech writer. *Such a Love* was first performed in Czechoslovakia in October 1957 and was published in the Soviet Union in July 1958, soon after it opened at MGU and several other soviet theaters, including the Stanislavsky Theater in Moscow, Leningrad's Gorky Drama Theater (often referred to by the acronym BDT), and an unnamed theater in Ukraine.[4] The play was an immediate hit in all of these venues.[5] Bykov's production was considered the best of them, according to one critic in *Literaturnaia gazeta* in 1959. In 1962, long after Bykov's production had closed, another critic recalled: "*Such a Love* was not just accepted by demanding Moscow spectators: it was a sensation [*sobytie*] in the theatrical life of the capital. And the competition with the Stanislavsky Theater showed that an amateur collective, if it enters the struggle with a relatively familiar theme, has a good chance for victory." That critic also maintained that Kohout himself concluded that the MGU version was the best that he had seen. Recent interviews confirm its superiority in the cultural memory.[6] It was performed for more than a year to over one hundred sold-out audiences, an unusual longevity for an amateur troupe at that time. As a result of the critical acclaim, the play, in spite of its foreign origins, can be considered within the horizon of the Russian cultural landscape.[7]

The growing notoriety of the production's young, unorthodox director enhanced its popularity. Rolan Bykov participated in amateur troupes as a teen. Trained as an actor at the Boris Shchukin Theater school affiliated with the Vakhtangov Theater, he began his career at the Moscow Theater for Young Audiences (known by its acronym TIUZ) in 1951. In 1956 he codirected and performed in the production of Vadim Korostylev's *What the Wizards Told.* The production was considered bold for its time and, according to Bykov, one member of the theater's artistic council labeled it *Meyerholdshchina,* a derogatory reference to the nonrealist techniques of Vsevold Meyerhold, the brilliant stage director who perished during the purges.[8] Daring productions of this sort met with greater acceptance at children's theaters, where directors could use nonrealist stage devices and claim that they represented the fantasy world of children. Reputable directors, such as Anatoly Efros, began their careers in these so-called marginal professional theaters. Such an opportunity was not immediately open to Bykov because he lacked formal training as a director. In the aftermath of *Wizard*'s success, he was invited to direct a production for one of the amateur groups at Moscow University's Hertsen Street house of culture. Because of the controversy surrounding *Such a Love,* Bykov never succeeded in directing a second production with the troupe. Although not all of his activities were so problematic, he later performed in a number of provocative films, including Andrei Tarkovsky's *Andrei Rublev* and the long-banned *Komissar.* More recently, and until his death in 1998, he directed movies, the most noteworthy of which was *Scarecrow,* which was also cast predominantly with amateurs.[9]

Bykov's brief tenure at MGU returned the troupe to its earlier preeminence as a serious cultural force in Moscow. The student theater was established as the first public theater in Moscow in 1756, a year after the university's inception. In the nineteenth century the theater spawned the Maly and Bolshoi Theaters. The troupe has also straddled the divide between amateur and professional realms. In its early history, some drama students remained in the theater after graduation and worked as paid professional performers; in the twentieth century, venerable professionals including Olga Knipper-Chekhova and Ivan Moskvin, both performers at Konstantin Stanislavsky's legendary Moscow Art Theater, lent their skills to amateur productions.[10] In the years leading up to Bykov's arrival in 1957, the story goes, the theater found itself in the doldrums associated with postwar cultural conservatism, although as his production soon illustrated, several talented amateur performers remained committed to the troupe. After Bykov's departure, other aspiring directors, including Mark Zakharov and Roman Viktiuk, created their earliest hits in the student theater. According to Alexandr Sherel, who participated in another amateur group there at that time, the Hertsen Street house of culture, along with the journal *Iunost'* (Youth) and the Sovremennik Theater, served as a hub for cultural heterodoxy during the Thaw.[11]

Given MGU's reputation and the demands of socialist realist tenets of the day, a "lowbrow" melodrama does not seem an obvious choice for a production. Careful analysis, however, reveals melodrama's kinship to socialist realism, and the similarities help explain its ability to persist in a supposedly hostile aesthetic environment. Although melodrama typically lacked the explicit political content that was often required in Stalin-era socialist realism, it presented themes and issues that often corresponded to other, broader regime goals. Like the genre's moral occult, socialist realism depicted ethical assumptions in soviet society and, especially in its early incarnations, provided clear role models for emulation. In order for art to perform its ideological function, according to proponents of socialist realism, the work also had to be comprehensible to a relatively unsophisticated population. Here too melodrama fit the socialist realist requirement of *narodnost'*, or accessibility via plain language and unambiguous presentation. In order to ensure that simplicity, socialist realist art was didactic, an attribute equally evident in melodrama. In the first half of the nineteenth century, for instance, de Pongerville wrote that in melodrama "crime always appeared odious, and was always punished; sincerity triumphed, innocence was protected by an invincible hand: finally, people were not shown the world as it is, but rather as it should be," a chilling foreshadowing of soviet pronouncements in the 1930s.[12] Robert Heilman suggests that this motif of positive social change is achieved in plays and literature through society's, rather than an individual's, victory over an identified evil: "In melodrama, [good and evil] are a public matter though they may have private repercussions."[13] This public interference in private matters in real life is the very issue that dominates Kohout's work, and the formula offers a straightforward if ironic means to illustrate this tension. As a result of these resemblances, soviet literary paradigms could accommodate melodrama as long as the basic content and ideological stance adhered to the prevailing dogma of the time.

The Manichaean element of melodrama corresponded to very real Communist Party efforts, particularly in the Stalin era, to assume the existence of irreconcilable conflict and to polarize society in terms of enemies and supporters of the regime. This battle would necessarily occur in the public realm, and the private sphere, which was far less amenable to control, was relegated to a subordinate position in society. The state, in the supposed interest of society, had the right and responsibility to dictate private preferences. Individual moral lapses, as defined in opposition to prevailing Communist Party priorities, were assumed to be detrimental to a society that was undergoing rapid modernization and industrialization in the name of a future utopia. Literature typically toed the line. Although private life in literature did not entirely disappear, public goals predominated over personal needs. Fictional conflict focused on the glorification of soviet power and the building of its institutions, especially industry. Characters who did not recognize and conform to official priorities were labeled "evil" and duly punished in literary terms. The triumph of virtue, at least on the printed page, offered reassurance to a society that was convulsing from the effects of collectivization, industrialization, the purges in the 1930s, and the devastation of World War II.

Melodrama's focus on personal issues was more appropriate than ever in the era following Stalin's death in 1953, and Kohout's play was no exception. *Such a Love*'s themes shared similarities with other official literature of the Khrushchev era. Post-Stalin literature began to challenge earlier assumptions by calling for an expansion of and respect for the private sphere. Beginning in 1952, mainstream writers, such as Vera Panova, Vladimir Dudintsev, and Il'ia Ehrenburg, wrote that meaningful intimate relationships were a critical component in the future success of soviet society.[14] Kohout likewise focuses on the importance of individual feelings and personal morality sometimes at the expense of short-term collective goals and ethics, and he spotlights professionals, rather than workers. *Such a Love,* however, presents a darker picture than its soviet counterparts; it questions whether emotionally based "true love" and integrity can exist in socialist society when private matters continue to face public scrutiny, and his critique holds society, rather than individuals, responsible for the problem. Although this message made the play more contentious at the time, melodramatic conventions provided some orthodox structural elements and the expectation for social change that mitigated against a potentially pessimistic, and, therefore, ideologically suspect undertone.

Issues concerning the role of private life in soviet society were not only a matter of intellectual and literary interest. The acceptance of the topic for literary representation corresponded to changing perceptions about personal issues, such as divorce, at that time. Scholars are just beginning to analyze society under Khrushchev, and Deborah Field has uncovered the discrepancies between official ideology regarding divorce and the realities that were confronted by the judges who presided in court. She notes that, from the official standpoint, the content of communist morality, which emphasized public duty over personal feelings, did not change under Khrushchev, but "greater importance [was] ascribed to it" because terror was no longer an option as a means of social control. "Teachers, social workers, local bureaucrats, and neighbors, as well as party, Komsomol, and trade union officials, were now authorized to monitor and intervene in individuals' private lives." In contrast to the official rhetoric, estranged spouses who were seeking divorces were indifferent to issues of social responsibility (except in cases where it buttressed their claims). They believed that their own needs and interests prevailed over public goals and, according to Field, judges typically agreed. As respect for private needs increased, official pronouncements that outsiders retained the right to interfere in the name of the social order lessened the tensions resulting from the changes.[15] Kohout aims his attack at this unwillingness to relinquish control over private matters.

*Such a Love* confronts the choice between a woman's private love for a married man and the pressures faced by both of them to renounce the affair in favor of his publicly sanctioned marriage. The plot depicts a hearing to determine responsibility for the death of Lida Matisova, an undergraduate student in a law department in Prague, who either committed suicide or died accidentally by falling under a train. In order to trace the events leading to her death, action fluctuates between this "trial" and flashbacks. An unnamed "Man in legal robes" is the "judge." He represents some higher moral authority but is unable to influence the course of events. One critic identified him as "man's conscience," while another suggested that he "is endowed with higher wisdom—the collective reason of our society—and is simultaneously a simple man," a nod to literary orthodoxy.[16] He does not seem to symbolize the Communist Party because his words are devoid of any ideological or political content. Instead, he embodies Peter Brooks's moral occult. The "Man" at first indicts four individuals: Matisova; her fiancé, Milan Stibor; her lover, Petr Petrus; and Petr's wife, Lida Petrusova. Each admits or denies various levels of responsibility for Matisova's death, although only Matisova accepts full responsibility. As is typical for melodramatic heroes and villains, their attitudes do not evolve over the course of the action. Although initially neutral toward the events, the "Man" grows increasingly sympathetic to Matisova's predicament and is ultimately merciless in his assessment of the other characters, who are each culpable in some way for her death.

Within this scenario, Lida represents a classic melodramatic victim. She is a female who lives simply as a student and, in Russian cultural terms, may as well be an orphan because her mother is dead. Her transgression is an affair with her married instructor Petr Petrus, whose name suggests a Czech everyman. Although this behavior alone is considered reprehensible, Lida compounds her dilemma by humiliating her fiancé, Milan Stibor, when she fails to appear for their wedding because she is with Petr. At the outset, the community of her peers, the university administration, and the "Man" conclude from an initial, superficial analysis of the events that she should be punished for her moral failing.

The Man in Legal Robes (Vsevolod Shestakov) confronts Lida Matisova (Iia Savviina) and Petr Petrus (Zinovii Filler) in *Such a Love.* Photo by V. Perel'man, in *Teatr.*

Along with the characters, the audience first sides with Milan and Petr, according to one reviewer of the production.[17]

At first glance Lida appears less than virtuous, but a closer look at the circumstances reveals otherwise. Her love for Petr began four years prior to the main events of the play, when he was an undergraduate and she was in high school in Brno. They broke up on her initiative when she concluded that she was hindering him from pursuing a successful career, and she left to study in Prague. Although they never communicated in the interim, her love endured, in spite of Milan. She tells the "Man," "Petr is my first and only love" (17). She justifies her acceptance of Milan's proposal in pragmatic terms for a twenty-three-year-old woman in a culture that expects women to marry: "He wanted to marry me, and I agreed because he is a good man and because I . . . because I had nothing against him" (18). When pressed on the depth of her love for Milan, she clarifies: "Of course, I did not love him like Petr;

really, I knew that I'd never love anyone that way. What was I supposed to do, go to a monastery? Did you in fact marry the person you loved most?" (18). Although she takes responsibility for leaving Petr after high school, Milan and the "Man" shift the blame to Petr for maintaining the separation (80). Lida is not even guilty of betraying Petrus's wife at the outset because he does not admit that he is married. His omission further confirms her innocence.

Her fidelity to Petr is sexual in addition to emotional. Milan pressures her to marry him in part because their relationship is platonic, and he is frustrated. As the "Man" prudishly points out to Lida: "It seems that you did not restrain [Milan's] feelings, but, on the contrary, encouraged them, and this led to the logical conclusion: the intention to formalize your relationship so that he could unimpeded, hmm . . . fulfill his conjugal functions—do you understand me?" (18). As a result of her constancy, Lida's sexual relationship with Petr, which began in high school and continues when they are reunited in Prague, does not represent a real betrayal of Milan. Within this melodramatic framework, Lida's affection represents love based on emotional attachment.

On another level, Kohout creates Lida's character as an embodiment of integrity. Lida is convinced of her innocence and angers official representatives of society by refusing to acknowledge any error and not submitting to social norms. She insists: "For me it's always important—to feel that I was right. However, I'm not obligated to answer to anyone" (18). Although she regrets hurting Milan, she never considers going back to him. This singleminded certainty marks her as a melodramatic heroine. Her unwavering belief is further established when she is given the opportunity to "rewrite" the events with the knowledge of Petr's marriage and his ultimate abandonment of her. At their first meeting after Petr arrives in Prague, Lida briefly resists his pleas for a rendezvous, but then relents:

PETR: . . . Will you come? At eight.
LIDA: I don't know.
PETR: Come.
LIDA: I'll come.
PETR: For sure?
LIDA: Maybe.
(She squeezes his hand and leaves. Petrus gazes at her for a minute as she goes and then leaves.) (52)

In the final scene after she's already "dead," the encounter is replayed at the insistence of the "Man" in spite of the obvious discomfort of the other characters. The stage directions indicate, "LIDA and PETR timidly recite the text, like amateurs at a rehearsal. Although the mechanical tone does not disappear for Petr, Lida becomes all the more agitated, natural and earnest with each word" (103–4). When Lida does not change the scene, the "Man" assumes that she misunderstood her "role": "There's no need for you to recite the text like a parrot. This is not an amateur play. You must now take a serious look at this fatal scene with your current eyes . . . (Suddenly he recalls that she is already not among the living)" (105).

The scene is repeated a third time, and, although the stage direction suggests that Lida is struggling to answer, it is not clear whether she doubts herself or feels defeated by the constant pressure to conform to social expectations of the other characters who hope that she will change the finale and absolve them of their guilt.

PETR: . . . Will you come? At eight. (He says this with fear.)
LIDA: I don't know. . . .
PETR: (barely audible) Come. . . .
(Pause. Everyone sitting on the benches leans forward.)
LIDA: I'll come.
(Commotion. Everyone gets up and screams at her.)
STIBOR: Lida!
MAIKA: Lida, come to your senses [*opomnis'*]!
MAN IN LEGAL ROBES: Matisova!
PETR: (with despair) For sure?
LIDA: For sure!

Her justification is predictable: she "helplessly raises her face to [the Man in legal robes]. 'I love him' " (106). Her conviction demonstrates not only her unwillingness to change, it also deflects attention from her more dubious stance that she would relive the experience while fully cognizant of Petr's wife. With this decision, Lida places her private morality of "true love" over the social morality of legally sanctioned marriage. With her death, Kohout avoids any judgment of her choice because he has created a conundrum for her: either she abandons her integrity, which compels her to privilege her private feelings over her public duties, or she has a morally problematic affair, because she can no longer claim ignorance. Spectators also never have to resolve this dilemma because her death renders moot their judgment. In Brooks's words, her choice is "a victory within the realm of the moral occult . . . predicated on the individual's 'sacrifice to the ideal.' "[18] Kohout's stance is clear: individuals have a right to private feelings, and they ought to remain true to those feelings.

The heroine's death does not automatically signal a tragedy. As Denise Youngblood points out, "lurid melodramas" were enormously popular in prerevolutionary Russia, and "romance was better thwarted, especially if ending in death—whether by murder, suicide or some other tragedy."[19] In Lida's case, Kohout suggests that her integrity makes her too pure to live in a banal world. She is also too virtuous to condemn her peers for their ordinary, albeit hypocritical, behavior. Throughout the play, she never confronts her detractors and antagonists; she merely resists yielding to them. In addition, this resolution is necessary to maintain the realistic basis of the play, which was still required for soviet drama (although a character who is dead before the action begins is a bit bizarre in socialist realist terms). Some kind of "happy end" may have also been less palatable to audiences grown weary of the contrived endings of earlier socialist realist literature.

Lida can be interpreted as a martyr, but her behavior is not completely valorized. Her death can also be understood as a punishment for her initiative and rebellion against social norms. Her ability to provide a model of virtue and idealism is narrowly circumscribed by a warning of the severe consequences. One can admire her courage without necessarily wanting to emulate her. Given the price to be paid for such nonconformity, it is possible to conclude that her stance is unattainable or superhuman, and a spectator can comfortably settle for empathy that requires neither changes in personal behavior nor other further action in society. Her punishment reflects the conservative underpinning of this melodrama that does not call for the overturning of the system, even though the play criticizes it.

Although the play raises the question of women's choices in society, it does not attempt to grapple with the issue and offer options for resolving these problems. There is no discussion among the characters about the limitations and expectations placed on women as women. Kohout's concern is not for Lida as a woman, but as an individual. Her character provides a self-sacrificing model of integrity and responsibility for women—and men—to follow. The play focuses on society's reluctance to address the complexities of human relationships, and Lida becomes a victim because other characters willingly bow to social expectations at the expense of their own integrity and emotional preferences.

Petr's abandonment of Lida makes him the obvious choice for the villain. He subordinates his feelings for her to his public duty, and he compromises his integrity in the process. His dishonesty both to his wife and to Matisova is compounded by his blasé assumption that society will exonerate him if he divorces for another woman. In essence, he has come to believe the oversimplified rhetoric in his lecture on family law: "In the sphere of our work medieval prejudices are still preserved. Family law! The law about the protection of the family—it sounds proud. But alas if it gets into the hands of dogmatists or dilettantes. They will start to worry only about the observance of form. But a contemporary marriage—it is a union of free people connected by feelings. . . . Love, and only love, ought to be henceforth and forever the basis, the point of departure and criterion of all human relationships!" (23–24). The lecture seems to privilege marriage based on emotional compatibility, but Petr's actual behavior reveals that reality is more complex. When he gives this lecture early in the play, his students applaud and accept him into the community. But he miscalculates and assumes that "progressive" socialist society has resolved the contradictions of extramarital love. When the affair later threatens his successful career, he decides not to ask his wife for a divorce, in spite of his promise to Matisova, and he again neglects to tell her the truth. When his wife finds out and volunteers to divorce, he still balks (69). Any remaining ambivalence ends when he is recommended to replace an ailing senior colleague, an unusual honor for someone of Petr's age and experience. But the opportunity is contingent on his renunciation of the affair (83). The polarity created by Lida's honesty and Petr's duplicity creates the necessary conflict for melodrama.

Petr's choice also reveals a second binary opposition in the play. In addition to the contrast of private feelings and public morality, Petr and Lida advocate different kinds of love: hers is based solely on emotional attachment, while his priority focuses less on passionate love and more on the practical elements of expedience and career opportunities. In a truly respected private sphere, individuals would be able to choose partners for whatever reasons suit them, but Kohout's play does not assume that the options are equally weighted in the 1950s. Petr's choice allows for external intervention, and his "successful" marriage entails a careful consideration of its public ramifications. Because Kohout wants to demonstrate the dangers inherent in such influences, the dramatic conflict between these two alternative privates is less important than questions of integrity and public intrusion. In Kohout's estimation, society, rather than individuals, discourages private priorities over public duties, and his play draws other characters into the realm of villainy in order to demonstrate this dynamic.

As other characters reveal their role in the events, the "Man" concludes that they too are complicit, and blame expands to include these antagonists who represent a microcosm of society. Each character initially fits some unflattering social stereotype. Petr's wife is a frigid, "masculine" career woman. In an inversion of traditional courtship, she is three years older than Petr, and she proposed marriage to him. When the "Man" asks if she loved him at the time of their engagement, she responds, "(after a pause). 'A sufficient degree' " (45). Petr explains his initial attraction to his wife: "I had just lost Lida [Matisova]. . . . And when a person burns himself, he instinctively pours cold water on the burn" (46–47). Other comments imply that if Petrusova had been a better wife, Petr would not have returned to Matisova. His rival and Lida's fiancé, Milan, claims to love Lida but only sees her in terms of what she provides for him. Addressing Milan, the "Man" wonders: "It seems to me that you took into account the feelings of Lida Matisova only to the degree that they corresponded to your own. If her gladness did not come from your gladness, if her fears were not your fears, you considered them more or less absurd" (76). If he had truly loved and accepted her for herself, she would have married him. Milan's mother is a clinging, busybody type who assumes that Lida is not good enough for her flawless son. Her unwillingness to accept her future daughter-in-law prompts her to meddle by informing both Petr's wife and the university law department about the affair. She initiates the public scandal that prevented a private, more successful resolution to the problem. The other characters also fit this pattern of types whose misguided intentions contribute to Lida's escalating crisis. As a result of their actions, their collective villainy contrasts with Lida's virtue.

Kohout attempts to create characters who reflect a greater degree of subtlety than a single defining characteristic, but ultimately he undermines his effort. As the "Man" elicits information from them, characters reveal their divided loyalties. Petr has some genuine affection for his wife, and she for him. Milan also loves Matisova for her own sake, not only his. Having faced enormous obstacles as a single parent, his mother wants him to marry someone who truly loves him. Although the characters demonstrate some development over the course of the play, Kohout overrides the complexities because the "Man's" judgment of them is unequivocal as he cross-examines each character and directly points out where they made incorrect choices. For the most part, he does not distinguish among varying degrees of guilt and thus nullifies their multifaceted characterizations. When the hearing is completed, he concludes from the evidence that their behavior was "antisocial" (*antiobshchestvennye*) (101). The only change from the initial charge is that he now includes all the characters, except Matisova (and an unnamed waiter who is little more than a bystander), in his evaluation. No one prevents Lida's death or acknowledges her virtue, and they refuse to shun Petrus, which is the typical fate of a melodramatic villain. The characters do not change their self-assessment of guilt at the end of the play.

In a conventional melodrama, the characters would be found guilty, but Kohout chooses not to oversimplify the resolution. Instead, the "Man" helplessly concedes that there are no laws to prosecute the characters, and he leaves. In response to his exit, Lida Petrusova asks in the final line of the play: "But who, then, will judge us?" (107). Although this ending seems to shift "the pronouncement of the final verdict . . . to the audience," as Marketa Goetz-Stankiewicz has argued, the "Man's" unwillingness to absolve them in light of his acquittal of Matisova suggests a shortcoming of justice rather than an ambiguity of the characters' complicity.[20] In terms of its relevance for the Khrushchev era, it is not clear whether Kohout is calling for better laws or is just pessimistic about the potential for a solution, but this outcome questions the ability of the legal system, or public institutions in general, to mediate the ambiguous ethical issues that characterize personal choices in private life.

The "Man's" dissatisfaction partially results from the characters' rejection of Matisova's superior virtue, the conventional outcome of melodrama and the seed for future social change. To varying degrees, they insist on their innocence and attempt to blame her for her own death, as best expressed by Lida Petrusova: "Why did she do it? What right did she have? She destroyed everything by doing it" (102). Only Milan attempts to take some responsibility, as he does at the play's opening, but he remains egocentric and does not acknowledge her transcendence: "I forgave her . . . I offered [to take her back]" (102). In terms of socialist realism and melodrama, these characters still conform to the two-dimensional portrayals that dominated the soviet literary landscape.

Communists are not exempted from this critique of a villainous society. The only identified communists in the play are Petr and Toshek, the head of the personnel department. Toshek attempts to persuade Lida to give up Petr rather than "complicate his life" (37). When she resists this pressure, he turns to Petr and justifies his meddling as a professional responsibility: "Your affairs are your affairs. Don't think that this is for my amusement, but I must look after [*berech'*] people when the government is spending money on their education" (39). When the "Man" confronts Toshek, he asserts: "Some look at this work as just a paycheck, but I have an old-fashioned view. I'm first of all a communist. What are you reproaching me for?" (84). He claims to have acted in order to save both Lida's education and Petr's career. But in the context of the play, his "old-fashioned" behavior embodies the medieval morality in Petr's lecture. In response to Toshek's rationalization, the "Man" excoriates him: "In your very activities the best intentions may have foul consequences. A personnel department worker may be rude or walk on his head [*khodit' na golove*]—that does not determine his qualifications. But he does not have the right to make superficial analyses . . . [and] to lose sight of what is important. . . . Both of you will have the sad opportunity to see [what you lost sight of] with your own eyes. . . . You as a person and you as a communist" (85). In Kohout's assessment, individual communists and their crude implementation of communist morality, with its preference for public duty and intervention, undermines individuals' opportunities to solve problems of private morality without such dire consequences.

This higher authority concludes that Toshek errs as a communist and that adherence to communism and an individual's humanity are separate, and the former does not automatically entail the latter.[21] Party membership does not presume an innate understanding of correct ethical choices. In short, the Communist Party no longer, if ever, holds an infallible moral authority, and the legal system does not necessarily have appropriate solutions for private social issues. In these circumstances, according to Kohout, individual communists have failed society and do not automatically provide a model for public emulation. Although this direct condemnation of a communist was as strong as any public criticism in the Soviet Union at the time, it is muted in the play because a hypocritical society, rather than the Communist Party and its ideology as a whole, is identified as the root of societal shortcomings. Although the party could be held responsible for these developments, critics did not voice this interpretation in the soviet press. Spectators, on the other hand, were free to draw this conclusion.

In spite of this pessimistic ending, a certain conventionality remained for Russian audiences. The "Man" reveals the ultimate purpose of the trial and the play itself near the end when Maika, Lida's inconstant friend, dismisses her death: "There are thousands of such cases!" He replies: "That's exactly why we are studying them in such detail" (102–3). In addition to the contradictory expectation of public examination of an issue that he earlier claimed to require private resolution, these words emphasize melodramatic recognition rather than a search for a permanent resolution to the issues that are raised in the play. In this respect, Kohout's play fits neatly into the Russian cultural tendency to assess blame rather than to offer solutions. Nancy Ries has recently analyzed this manifestation in her study of everyday conversations during perestroika. She finds antecedents in folklore with its emphasis on magical or miraculous solutions by "saviors."[22] As in the case of Russian litanies, as Ries calls them, no real answers appear in the play, and the effect is that Kohout's work functions as one long theatricalized lament. Underlying such an approach in literature and life lies the assumption that today's recognition is the same as future resolution, and no other efforts are necessary or, as Ries suggests, desirable. Blame replaces responsibility in this paradigm and in the play. Of all the characters who are accused in Matisova's death, only Lida herself is willing to be accountable for her actions and remains true to them throughout the play. But the play and the "Man" dismiss her responsibility, and she is reduced to a victim of society.

Although the guilt of the characters is unambiguous, the production at least asks the spectator to agree with the decision. In Kohout's trial, the audience performs a nominal role. In the far more destructive purge "trials" of the 1930s and in Khrushchev's subsequent denunciation of the excesses in 1956, changes in ideology and in the use of terror were dictated to the public. Its expected response to the revelations was likewise narrowly circumscribed. Khrushchev's remarks singled out certain individuals for rehabilitation, but others were not exonerated and remained in legal and moral limbo. Although individuals were encouraged to petition for the rehabilitation of family members, the public was not asked to weigh the evidence and determine the legitimacy of accusations against early communist leaders, such as Nikolai Bukharin or Lev Trotsky, who were not rehabilitated. Although there is no direct evidence to link the purge trials to the hearing in the play, the proximity of the production and the Khrushchev's Secret Speech of 1956 perhaps led some spectators to question the nature of trials, legality, and justice in recent soviet history.

The specter of the terror adds another dimension to the play's focus of accountability. In the same way that the characters do not condemn Petr, *Such a Love* can also be interpreted as a judgment against society for its complicity with respect to the purges. But within the cultural paradigm in which assessing blame ends the need for further discussion, the "guilty" verdict given by the audience suggests that Russian society has already settled these issues, as if the problems of the purges (and the play's characters) were solved when they were aired in Khrushchev's (and the play's) performance. This formula upheld the status quo because no changes or concrete mechanisms emerged to address past horrors or current social contradictions.

Given that the play ends on a pessimistic note as the "Man" admits his lack of legal authority, Kohout needed an alternative to make the play seem more upbeat. *Such a Love* retains its didactic function with its insistence that some valuable change is possible and indeed underway as a result of Lida's death. This optimism is evident on various levels in the production. The "Man," for instance, fulfills this function when he exonerates Lida from any responsibility for her own death. He commends her innocence and integrity, and so this higher authority holds some promise for future improvement. But his influence is limited because he remains an outsider who leaves the scene.

Kohout incorporated another means for creating a positive alternative that operated beyond the bounds of the main characters and the plot. Although the content of the play fit well enough into the evolving ideology in the Khrushchev era and into the conventions of melodrama, a critical component of its appeal involved repackaging the orthodox elements into a ground-breaking production. The originality involved more than the flashbacks, which had not been used in plays of high Stalin culture. This device alone would have been enough to create interest in *Such a Love,* but the play's other innovations were daring by the standards of the day. These techniques, some of which the author wrote into the script, simultaneously maintained melodramatic formulas while broadening their expression on a visual level. Through these devices Kohout creates additional societies, beyond the microcosm of the villainous dramatis personae, that ultimately validate the heroine's moral superiority and provide the basis for a more hopeful interpretation. An amorphous society is both complicit in Lida's death and ultimately embraces her moral superiority. This society, represented by a chorus in the production, has in Kohout's script a very small role as university students who listen to Petr's two lectures. The chorus itself did not represent a "reintroduction" in theater, but it rarely had been used since the 1930s.[23]

Although the use of the chorus was less than revolutionary, its ever-changing manifestations as a merciless barometer of public opinion offered a visual treat along with its metaphorical qualities. Bykov expanded the chorus's function in a novel way for soviet theater at that time. The script calls for twenty-eight scenes, but Bykov recalled that he staged fifty-six scenes by adding many *massovki,* crowd scenes often used in both professional and amateur performances in order to involve as many troupe members as possible.[24] But in *Such a Love* their function was not merely to observe the events and fill up space on stage. Although Bykov's recollection may be exaggerated, the constant shifting of locale would have been quite remarkable. These scenes are erased from the surviving record of the production except for those that were recounted in one review that described the *massovki* as the "materialization [*materializatsiia*] of public opinion." The chorus first appears as a group of students when Milan's mother reports the affair to Toshek: "With loud music of an orchestra a crowd of students pours out from a door on the right. Furiously and bitterly arguing, they—couple after couple—coil up like a spiral in the center of the stage. . . . Lida Matisova appears, and 'the spiral' untwists and disappears behind the door. They all go past Lida, displaying [their] condemnation of her." When Petr attempts to call his wife in order to ask for a divorce, Toshek, Milan, and the crowd, now representing students and faculty members, demand that Petr give up Matisova and not break up his family. As a result, he succumbs to the public pressure but lies to Matisova about it.[25] In these instances, the chorus provided an incarnation of the social demands that Petr and Lida face but that Kohout's script leaves unarticulated.

The scene of Lida's death illustrates the shift to recognition as this society participates in her demise but then glorifies her. The chorus depicts passengers on the fatal train as it leaves the station. As a unit, they wave and move toward the right side of the stage while Lida stands on a raised platform at the front stage left. Repeating earlier accusations of various characters to her, the chorus creates the sound and rhythm of train wheels. Lida screams, the light projected on her goes out, and, bathed in a red light, the chorus picks her up and en masse carries her offstage.[26] Her martyrdom is made complete in a later scene (included in Kohout's text) in which the chorus again portrays university students. Having learned of Lida's death, they disrupt Petr's lecture and refuse to allow him to spout platitudes about the primacy of love based on emotional attachment (99–100). This repeated role for the chorus neatly captures society's dual nature that is fundamental to melodrama: society is both the cause and the solution for ethical dilemmas. As a result, this positive metamorphosis suggests a conservative attitude toward change because it assumes that society can be transformed through individual sacrifice. The system itself is not challenged.

In addition to the chorus, Kohout and Bykov utilize an additional theatrical means to create another "society" that recognizes the victim's virtue and is expected to cast judgment on the events and the characters: the audience. *Such a Love* does not merely assume that spectators would fulfill this function in the conventional Stanislavsky manner of removed, empathetic observers, as already noted. The script utilizes several simple devices to include the hall as an extension of the action. Ignoring the socialist realist convention of an impenetrable separation between the stage and the hall, some characters, including the "Man" and Milan's mother, enter and exit the curtainless stage via the audience. The "Man" further undermines the assumed barrier of the fourth wall by stepping out of his persona and announcing the intermission (58). Bykov's direction strengthens the connection when characters, for instance Petr, who is particularly conscious of social approval, often glance furtively at the hall when discussing the public consequences of the affair.[27] In addition to serving this melodramatic function, the explicit incorporation of the audience represented another aspect of the production's freshness with the reintroduction of a device long absent from soviet theater. The technique further encouraged spectators to feel that the issues directly affected them, rather than just the characters. Theatergoers are supposedly left to decide which society, the chorus or the characters, will ultimately triumph. The device does not completely succeed because Kohout clearly reveals how he expects spectators to respond, although the audience always retains freedom of interpretation.

In addition to using stage techniques to produce the requisite optimism, Kohout's stage instructions added a twist to the melodramatic convention of an exotic setting. Although Prague remained exotic to Muscovites, most of whom were only beginning to travel abroad in the 1950s, Bykov followed Kohout's instructions in the script and did not rely on realistic props, which in any case would have appeared crude as stage design. Instead, he replaced the exotic setting with an "exotic" set by the standards of socialist realist theater of that time: one of the first nonrealist sets since the purges. In order to accommodate frequent scene shifts, the stage was bare except for a chair for the "Man," a bench, and a sofa. With these minimal decorations, the audience was expected to fill in the details of a particular locale: the trial room, Milan's living room, a train platform, Lida Petrusova's office, a tram stop. Although the set did not have the evocative or metaphorical qualities associated with the work of either Meyerhold or Aleksandr Tairov, who had also used nonrealist sets in the 1930s, its reliance on spectators' imaginations reestablished an alternative to orthodox stage design and provided another means to link the audience to the events on the stage.

The role of Kohout's play in the evolution of stage presentation and audience participation was especially relevant given the situation for Russian playwrights at that time. In the postwar era, dramatists were compelled to write plays that corresponded to the "no-conflict" theory. Its premise fatuously claimed that socialist society had advanced to such a degree that evil had been eliminated and, therefore, any conflict occurred between "good" and "better" elements within society. Some of the most abysmal plays in the soviet repertoire were written under these circumstances. Although dramatists gladly abandoned the no-conflict theory as early as 1952, their first innovations focused on content rather than style. Only the young Alexander Volodin introduced some stylistic innovations. His first play *The Factory Girl* in 1956 used the "lap-dissolve" technique of film that created seamless transitions between scenes.[28] Whether censorship dictated that plays still adhered to a traditional structures and techniques, or whether dramatists themselves were more concerned with raising previously taboo content issues, most writers were not yet creating plays that inherently necessitated a new approach to presentation. Although a director could choose to challenge conventional expectations regarding sets and structure in a realist play, Kohout's script demanded this innovation. As was the case in many arenas of reform throughout Russia's modern history, theater imported foreign texts as a means to hasten the process of change. But domestic playwrights were soon incorporating nonrealist devices in their writing. Volodin's 1959 play *Five Evenings* continued his earlier innovations, and by the early 1960s other Russian dramatists were moving toward increased theatricalization in their work.[29] These new plays did not end the interest in foreign drama but created more options for directors.

With the innovations embedded in the play, Bykov's production offered a new approach to theatrical presentation that is typically credited to Iury Liubimov. Liubimov, undoubtedly one of the most innovative and daring soviet directors in the Brezhnev era, began his string of controversial successes in 1963 with the production of Bertolt Brecht's *The Good Person of Sechuan,* which was first performed by his acting students at the Shchukin theater school. Although this production inaugurated his Taganka theater in 1964, Liubimov's unacknowledged debt to Bykov's earlier production is evident. Scholars including Alexander Gershkovich, Alma Law, and Birgit Beumers have characterized Liubimov's work as "synthetic," an approach to theater that utilizes all available sensory means to heighten the theatrical experience.[30] But Bykov's production was labeled as such by a *Teatr* critic in 1958: "[The MGU] theater is synthetic. . . . Music, dance, colors, [and] light must become the most important elements of the production."[31] In this instance, melodrama in *Such a Love* provided a familiar didactic function and structure that made palatable this new stylistic heterodoxy. As a result, the production was important not just as the most successful staging of Kohout's work in the Soviet Union, but it also created a prototype for post-Stalin theatrical techniques.

Efforts to expand stylistic diversity in the post-Stalin era for Bykov, Liubimov, and others point to a melodramatic tension in soviet society that polarized avant-garde theater and opponents of heterodoxy in the arts. This connection in *Such a Love* manifests itself through Kohout's attitude toward a society of spectacle. His text is replete with allusions to theater. In addition to several references to tragedy, characters comment that they feel as if their actions are occurring within some sort of performance. The "Man," for instance, warns Petr and Milan, when they confront each other about their feelings for Lida: "Don't make a scene—you're not in a theater!" (81). Petr later admits that he feels exactly that way when the chorus-students disrupt his lecture after Lida's death. He rebukes them: "What kind of people have the right to watch someone else's life as if it's a play?" (100). The frequent shifting of time and scene adds another unreal, theatricalized quality to the characters' experiences over the course of events. The entire trial becomes a form of theater for the characters as they try to perform persuasively so that the "Man" will find them innocent of any wrongdoing. Kohout uses these hints to bring attention to the roles that individuals are forced to play in society, and his work suggests that public life is inherently theatrical. This role-playing was especially apparent in the Soviet Union, where individuals were expected to adhere to official values, at least in public.[32] For the Moscow audience, Kohout's commentary on theatricality questioned the accepted roles that were publicly sanctioned but sometimes contrary to integrity and private concerns.

This discussion of the theatricalized aspects of public life in the play did not only occur on the level of individuals in the post-Stalin era. Bykov's production served on a broader level as a form of melodrama in which the student theater played the role of the hero/victim and the audience represented the community that was supposed to reject but later recognize the troupe's virtue. This intent partially belongs to Kohout. The play's opening remarks recall Brecht's approach to theater with its goal of direct confrontation with the audience: "In front of the eyes of the public we will attempt to reveal and contrast the fates of several people and will turn to the spectators themselves, calling on their experience and feelings so unambiguously and actively that in the end they will see themselves in the play. The success will be all the greater if the applause is less and the spectators are all the more offended [*obidiatsia*]" (3). (It is not clear if these statements were directly communicated to the audience during the performance.) By tolerating the repressive policies toward the arts pursued in the final years of Stalin's rule, soviet society was complicitous in the villainous effort to cast out cultural heterodoxy. Some playwrights and theaters, including Kohout and Bykov's student theater, saw themselves as victims in search of vindication from society for their adherence to integrity by raising pertinent issues and by utilizing innovative stage techniques.

This recognition of theatrical virtue, however, relied on a conventional framework of victims and villains that reinforced long-standing Russian cultural assumptions that slowed substantive change. Moscow University's production of *Such a Love* provided a familiar formula that contained enough orthodox socialist realism and familiar Russian cultural assumptions to appease censors and conservative Moscow University administrators, while the innovations intrigued Moscow's theatergoing public. Resonating with current social issues and recent historical nightmares, the production reveals that conflicts regarding personal ethics were contested in public alongside the growing acknowledgment in the Khrushchev era of the need for a distinction between public and private spheres. As theaters in the post-Stalin era began to reestablish their prerogative to provide a public and aesthetic forum for some issues of criticism and technical innovation, they presented their cause in terms of that same conflictual polarity of "us" and "them" within the play and within Russian society. That approach may have been so well received because Moscow society accepted that dichotomy to some extent as a "normal" aspect of Russian life, at least on a rhetorical level, even when the reality was more complex. Melodrama as an artistic form retained its relevance because it continued to provide meaning—but not resolution—to the contradictions of a theatricalized, melodramatic society.

## Notes

This essay is dedicated to the memory of Rolan Bykov. Funding for this research was provided by the American Council of Teachers of Russian.

1 Olga is not her real name.
2 Richard Stites, *Russian Popular Culture: Entertainment and Society since 1900* (Cambridge: Cambridge University Press, 1992), especially 141–42.
3 "Innovation" in the post-Stalin artistic context does not always mean that a particular technique or device had never been used in Russian theater. The onset of socialist realism in the 1930s severely curtailed the expres-

sion of certain topics and styles. As a result, many of these forms had to be "reinvented" as censorship relaxed somewhat after Stalin's death in 1953.

4 P. Kogout, *Takaia liubov',* perevod s cheshkogo N. Arosevoi i S. Shmeral' (Moscow: Otdel rasprostraneniia dramaticheskikh proizvedenii VUOAP, 1958). This version was the only official text in Moscow, and hereafter page numbers in parentheses in the text refer to this edition. For background on Kohout and the play in Czechoslovakia, see Paul I. Trensky, *Czech Drama since World War II* (White Plains, N.Y.: M. E. Sharpe, 1978), 152–55; Peter Hruby, *Fools and Heroes: The Changing Role of Communist Intellectuals in Czechoslovakia* (Oxford: Pergamon Press, 1980), 9–20; Marketa Goetz-Stankiewicz, "Ethics at the Crossroads: The Czech 'Dissident Writer' as Dramatic Character," *Modern Drama* 27 (March 1984): 112–23; Marketa Goetz-Stankiewicz, "Pavel Kohout: The Barometer of Czechoslovakia's Theatre," *Modern Drama* 20 (September 1977): 251–62; and Veronika Ambros, *Pavel Kohout und die Metamorphosen des sozialistischen Realismus* (New York: Peter Lang, 1993).

5 *Such a Love* first premiered in soviet theaters in February 1958 after the season was well underway, but by the end of the season it had been performed 413 times in twelve theaters. It is not clear whether those numbers include MGU performances because such statistics rarely incorporated amateur activities, although the production's immense popularity may have led to its incorporation. See "Repertuar teatrov v sezone 1957/58 goda," *Teatr* (March 1959): 136.

6 I. Shtok, "V sotyi raz," *Literaturnaia gazeta,* October 10, 1959; S. Prokof'eva, "Stan'te ego drugom!" *Iunost'* (June 1962): 103–4. The Stanislavsky Theater should not be confused with the Moscow Art Theater, founded by Konstantin Stanislavsky. In a biography of Bykov, M. G. L'vovskii writes that representatives of Czech theater also considered Bykov's version as the best (L'vovskii, *Chelovek, kotoromu veriat [kinematograf Rolana Bykova]* [Moscow: Soiuz kinematografistov SSSR, Vsesoiuznoe tvorchesko-proizvodstvennoe ob"edinenie "Kinotsentr," 1990], 30). Iurii Gorin, interview, Moscow, 11 October 1991. Gorin joined the MGU student theater in the years following Bykov's production. Vadim Golikov, interview, Leningrad, 18 July 1991. Golikov, who staged plays in several professional theaters and in the St. Petersburg (formerly Leningrad) university student theater, was in the late 1950s a directorial student of Georgii Tovstonogov, who produced the play at BDT. I conducted all of the interviews mentioned here, and the transcripts are in my possession.

7 I will discuss the play only in terms of its meanings for Russian and soviet

culture and will neither attempt to analyze its relevance for Czech audiences nor try to compare the official text or the Moscow production with analogous works outside the Soviet Union, although those differences are many and worthy of study.

8 Rolan Bykov, interview, Moscow, 23 September 1991. For a review of the TIUZ production, see M. Zlobina, "O tsvenykh snakh," *Teatr* (November 1957): 156–57.

9 In fall 1958, Bykov told a *Iunost'* reporter that the troupe was rehearsing a play by Mikhail Shatrov. Bykov also planned to produce a version of Il'ya Ilf and Evgenii Petrov's *The Twelve Chairs,* and playwright Nikolai Pogodin was writing a play for the company (L. Travkin, "Pervyi studencheskii," *Iunost'* [September 1958]: 115). None of the plays ever appeared at the theater. In late 1959 Bykov was offered a directing job in Leningrad. By then, university officials were making it very difficult for him to lead the student theater, and he accepted the Leningrad job. For the first public acknowledgment of his not completely voluntary departure, see A. Silin, "O teatre pokoleniia," *Klub i khudozhestvennaia samodeiatel'nost',* no. 15 (August 1980): 28. For additional biographical information on Bykov, see L'vovskii, *Chelovek.*

10 Iu. Ogul'nik, "Iz istorii studencheskogo teatra MGU," *Teatral'naia zhizn',* no. 14 (July 1988): 32–33. The university also sponsored amateur troupes in various academic departments and in the house of culture of the Lenin (now Sparrow) Hills campus.

11 Aleksandr Sherel', interview, Moscow, October 28, 1991. Other important cultural groups at the Hertsen Street location at that time included Our Home (*Nash dom*) amateur estrada theater and A. Kremer's amateur wind orchestra, which performed jazz and provided the music for *Such a Love.* Sherel' participated in Our Home. For further analysis of both Our Home and the MGU student theater, see my *The Emergence of Alternative Culture: Amateur Studio-Theaters in Moscow and Leningrad 1957–1984,* Ph.D. diss., Northwestern University, 1994, 34–64.

12 De Pongerville is quoted in Gabrielle Hyslop, "Pixérécourt and the French Melodrama Debate: Instructing Boulevard Theatre Audiences," in *Melodrama,* ed. James Redmond (London: Cambridge University Press, 1992), 65.

13 Robert B. Heilman, *The Iceman, the Arsonist, and the Troubled Agent: Tragedy and Melodrama on the Modern Stage* (Seattle: University of Washington Press, 1973), 23. For other discussions of the didactic qualities of Russian and soviet literature, see Katerina Clark, *The Soviet Novel: History as Ritual* (Chicago: University of Chicago Press, 1981); Evgeny

Dobrenko, *The Making of the State Reader: Social and Aesthetic Contexts of the Reception of Soviet Literature,* trans. Jesse M. Savage (Stanford: Stanford University Press, 1997); Rufus W. Mathewson Jr., *The Positive Hero in Russian Literature,* 2nd ed. (Stanford: Stanford University Press, 1975); and Régine Robin, *Socialist Realism: An Impossible Aesthetic,* trans. Catherine Porter (Stanford: Stanford University Press, 1992).

14 Vera Panova, *Vremena goda* (Moscow: "Sovetskii pisatel'," 1953); and Vladimir Dudintsev, "Ne khlebom edinym," *Novyi mir* (August–October 1956): 31–118, 37–118, 21–98; Il'ia Ehrenburg, *Ottepel'* (Moscow: "Sovetskii pisatel'," 1954).

15 Deborah A. Field, "Irreconcilable Differences: Divorce and Conflicting Conceptions of Private Life in the Khrushchev Era," *Russian Review* 57 (October 1998): 601, 603.

16 I. Borisova, "Pervyi studencheskii," *Molodaia gvardiia* (July 1958): 198; V. Grigor'ev, "Est' studencheskii teatr," *Teatr* (November 1958): 71.

17 Borisova, "Pervyi studencheskii," 199.

18 Peter Brooks, *The Melodramatic Imagination: Balzac, Henry James, Melodrama, and the Mode of Excess* (New Haven: Yale University Press, 1976), 6.

19 Denise J. Youngblood, *Movies for the Masses: Popular Cinema and Soviet Society in the 1920s* (Cambridge: Cambridge University Press, 1992), 2.

20 Goetz-Stankiewicz, "Pavel Kohout," 253.

21 Ehrenburg had already reached this conclusion in *The Thaw.* His condemnation of the factory director, a communist who ignores requirements to provide adequate housing for employees, is less direct.

22 Nancy Ries, *Russian Talk: Culture and Conversation during Perestroika* (Ithaca: Cornell University Press, 1997), see especially 161–88.

23 Aleksei Arbuzov had already used a chorus in the 1940s. See Alan Smith, *The Dramatic Works of Aleksej Arbuzov,* Ph.D. diss., Indiana University, 1981.

24 In Bykov's own estimation the approach partially led to its identification as the superior production of Kohout's play (Bykov, interview, September 23, 1991).

25 Grigor'ev, "Est' studencheskii teatr," 71–72.

26 Ibid., 73–74.

27 Ibid., 73.

28 For a survey of the period, see Harold B. Segel, *Twentieth-Century Russian Drama: From Gorky to the Present,* updated ed. (Baltimore: Johns Hopkins University Press, 1993), 329–59. See also Smith, *Aleksej Arbuzov;* Samuel G. Marinov, *The Dramaturgy of Aleksandr Volodin,* Ph.D.

dissertation, University of Kansas, 1993; and Tat'iana Lanina, *Aleksandr Volodin* (Moscow: "Sovetskii pisatel'," 1989).

29 Segel, *Twentieth-Century Russian Drama,* 361.

30 Aleksandr Gershkovich, *Teatr na Taganke (1964–1984)* (Moscow: "Soliaris," 1993); Alma Law, "The Trouble with Lyubimov," *American Theatre* 2 (April 1985): 4–11; and Birgit Beumers, *Yury Lyubimov: Thirty Years at the Taganka Theater (1964–1994)* (Toronto: Harwood Academic Press, 1997). Beumers characterizes Liubimov's approach as "poetic theater," and the synthetic aspects fall within this description. One of Bykov's leads, Alla Demidova, who played Lida Petrusova, joined Liubimov's original troupe.

31 Grigor'ev, "Est' studencheskii teatr," 75.

32 For an elegant portrayal of this dilemma, see Alexander Yashin, "Levers," in *The Year of Protest 1956,* ed. and trans. Hugh McLean and Walter N. Vickery (New York: Vintage Books, 1961), 193–209. The story originally appeared in *Literaturnaia Moskva II* in 1956. For a scholarly treatment of the issue, see Deborah A. Field, "Communist Morality and Meanings of Private Life in Post-Stalinist Russia, 1953–1964," Ph.D. diss., University of Michigan, 1996; and Vladimir Shlapentokh, *Public and Private Life of the Soviet People: Changing Values in Post-Stalin Russia* (New York: Oxford University Press, 1989).

*Joan Neuberger*

# Between Public and Private

## Revolution and Melodrama in Nikita Mikhalkov's *Slave of Love*

Melodrama flourishes in the borderlands between public and private life, precisely the terrain that soviet cultural authorities sought to police. When nineteenth-century melodrama uncovered the subconscious cracks in the pedestal under the cult of virtuous womanhood, it did so by shattering the wall that shielded the private from the public by exposing interior, domestic dramas to an external, public world of print, stage, and screen. Bolshevik valorization of the collective and political over the individual and moral made public culture solemn and domestic drama suspect. But the state's effort to restrict and supervise private life only forced it underground, which happens to be the ideal breeding ground for the "hysterical, neurotic, and paranoid" aspects of the melodramatic imagination.[1] As several essays in this volume have shown, melodrama's spotlight on the secrets of private life made Bolshevik cultural purists uncomfortable but made melodrama useful for Bolshevik cultural policy. Their goals may have differed—melodrama sought to expose the secret obsessions of the private and to celebrate emotional intensity, while Bolsheviks wanted to purify the private and eradicate its neuroses—but both involved penetrating the boundaries that divided the public from the private and the collective from the individual.[2]

Through the prism of melodrama, then, soviet culture appears to have had important similarities with its bourgeois predecessor. In both, the lines between public and private were problematic, which made it that much more imperative for cultural watchdogs to regulate the borders. As a result, Russians' thirst for melodrama and its continued presence in the soviet period meant that there was a considerable discrepancy between public ideals and private practice in the early decades of soviet social and political construction. After Stalin died and censorship relaxed, a marked resurgence in melodrama accompanied the official toleration of a wider sphere for private life. In all the arts, small domestic drama began to replace grand heroic epic, as Vera Dunham showed in her study of post-Stalinist literary socialist realism and as Alexander Prokhorov and Susan Costanzo have discussed in this volume.[3] By the 1970s, private life had become a common subject for fiction, theater, and film, although it was still fraught with the contradictions between ideological ideals and individual realities that marked all discourse about private life in soviet culture.

During the 1970s, the state's intrusion in private life considerably diminished, while the arena for public expression and the possibilities for private pleasure both expanded. Culture and everyday life were, of course, still constricted by political surveillance and economic controls, and censorship still operated: art exhibits were bull-dozed, directors were harassed, writers were exiled, human rights were violated. But in the late 1970s, it is worth remembering, one could see films that parodied Stakhanovism (*The Bonus*), collectivism (*The Garage*), and official morality (*The Red Berry Tree*); and Andrei Tarkovsky could make long existential movies such as *Andrei Rublev* and *Stalker* that would never have been funded in Hollywood. One needs only to read Tarkovsky's diaries from the period to understand the price that artists paid to work in these conditions and the fact that these films were "exceptions" to the general rule, but the exceptions add up to a culture that was lively and innovative, more so than that of many other countries at that or any other time.[4] Susan Costanzo has decribed elsewhere a play by Sławomir Mrozek produced in Moscow during this period, which features the image of a monkey in a cage, "leaping from the pole to the wirefencing and back again . . . in order to feel . . . the master of infinite spaces."[5] This image captures precisely the half-full/half-empty paradox of late-soviet, pre-glasnost culture: a monkey in a cage, to be sure, forced to amuse the spectators and zookeepers, but able to leap without fear of imprisonment, exile, torture, or death.

The greatest arena for monkey-jumping in the 1970s and 1980s involved the reclamation of private life from state surveillance. Conformity in modes of behavior, public expression, and individual identity became far less coercive, and the politicization of everyday life, the expectation that communal or political goals shaped individual desires, was muted and even ridiculed. Increasing numbers of people in Russia's major cities were moving out of communal apartments, gaining the basic prerequisite for private life: a cage of one's own.

For the successful artist, the renewal of private life offered a number of rewards, both intellectual and personal: access to foreign publications, films, and recordings; meetings with foreign colleagues; perhaps a car, a larger apartment; a dacha in Peredelkino or Komarovo; and international travel, which provided access to even more exotic treasures. But all this came with a price tag. Membership in the artistic unions required the willingness to avoid certain topics, to accept official "editing," to submit to prior censorship, to publically censure Solzhenitsyn and Sakharov. Publication required toadying to union administrators, mastering the arts of indirect speech, and sidestepping the complex issues that often made art worth producing. The 1970s generation was also sacked with the psychic baggage of survival, being just the first generation to come of age after the Stalinist terrors and the Second World War. Private life and personal comfort, the luxuries of relative peace and prosperity, and survival and success had to be paid for with an uneasy conscience. So it comes as no surprise that the topography of the individual conscience is the subject of some of the best work of the legal artists of the late-soviet period: Tarkovsky, Trifonov, Gherman, Liubimov (and Wajda and Kieslowski just across the border as well).

One of the more interesting (and much maligned) figures in this context is Nikita Mikhalkov. His early film *Slave of Love* (1976) is an extended meditation on the comparative virtues and costs of private and public life.[6] The plot of the movie follows the fate of a film crew desperately trying to finish shooting a commercial silent melodrama somewhere in the Crimea in 1918. The approaching revolutionary army threatens not only their film but their entire way of life, and ultimately their very lives, to put it melodramatically. Mikhalkov explores the artistic, political, and personal dilemmas they faced in trying, with some futility, to maintain a familiar world of private and professional pleasures while the encroaching revolution forced them to confront some unfamiliar but inescapable moral and political choices. As revolutionary and counterrevolutionary violence threaten to overrun the film set, a public culture of heroic, political commitment collides with an idyll of private, sensual pleasures. Predictably, soviet political morality emerges victorious, but it is a highly ambiguous victory, tainted by violence and personal sacrifice.

*Slave of Love* is a deeply ambivalent film. No single authorial voice entirely dominates in the conflict set up between private and public virtues. Both involve sacrifice, deception, and self-deception. There is no happy ending, and its sadness is neither cathartic nor consoling. This ambiguity makes *Slave of Love* a much more satisfying film than many of the movies Mikhalkov made subsequently. Ultimately Mikhalkov weighs in on the side of the personal over the political, or at least the need for a personal conscience to anchor the political, but the message is embedded in a film that also celebrates political awareness and commitment to the public good. At this point we cannot know for certain whether the film's particular balance between the political and the personal was imposed by censorship (or self-censorship) or was the full intention of the writers and director. In this essay I am concerned with the ways in which Mikhalkov constructed the contest between them, without trying to determine his intent.

*Slave of Love* has been dismissed by scholars and movie fans as a lightweight bit of "retro-chic" or romantic nostalgia for a lost bourgeois gentility.[7] But it is much more than that, just as it is more than self-indulgent play with a film genre or a simple parody of the world of prerevolutionary filmmaking. *Slave of Love* does offer a prerevolutionary bourgeois past affectionately visualized on lush, green lawns, but it is a world as troubled and ambiguous as the revolutionary alternatives that followed. Mikhalkov uses this historical setting to create resonant contemporary analogs with the 1970s, and (as is usual with historical films) *Slave of Love* has as much to say about the moral compromises of the present as it does about those of the past.

Mikhalkov sets *Slave of Love* in the world of early cinema melodrama not only for its ability to evoke the pleasures of an exotic lost world, but because the genre itself offers a model for exploring the shifting line between private and public in two different periods in Russian history. Like Douglas Sirk in the United States in the 1950s, Mikhalkov reinvented the genre to explore in new contexts the moral issues that melodrama had always raised. As the surface conformity of postwar Russian and American culture began to erode, melodrama offered a means of examining the tensions involved in maintaining the rigid public behaviors required (in different degrees of course) by Stalinist and postwar American codes of conformity.

In Russia, the reappearance of private life in public culture made melodrama a perfect tool for exploring the new tensions that artists faced in a world where official soviet values still dominated public discourse, but where lucrative, commercial success was once again a possibility. As Peter Brooks put it, melodrama provided a "principal mode for uncovering, demonstrating, and making operative the essential moral universe in a post-sacral era."[8] Mikhalkov's post-sacral era, post-Stalinism, is confronting issues different from those that appeared either in the aftermath of the French Revolution or with the collapse of Enlightenment rationalism at the end of the nineteenth century or in 1950s America. Mikhalkov uses melodrama and revolution as tropes to contrast two sets of morality that official ideology had relegated to opposite poles of the universe during the previous soviet period. He uses each to probe beneath the verities of virtue represented by the other. In *Slave of Love,* narrative, mise-en-scène, and art production combine to depict the morally ambiguous end of bourgeois life and commercial cinema as a mirror for the resurgence of commercial cinema and bourgeois pleasure in late-soviet, post-Stalin society. In both cases, a life of private pleasures and individual emotions came into conflict with public responsibilities and a heroic, collective, and utopian spirit. *Slave of Love* suggests that when either one is valorized at the expense of the other, something critical is lost and both the collective and the individual suffer as a result.

Mikhalkov has made a career of adapting Hollywood-style storytelling to Russian subjects, and *Slave of Love* shows his early skill at constructing a layered narrative with just enough to think about and enticing period detail to flesh out an entertaining story that is part romance, part historical drama, and part thriller. Although Russian critics have carped that this style is "un-Russian," Mikhalkov has always used his rich visual skills to evoke a vision of nature that personifies something quintessentially Russian. Whereas in later films Mikhalkov's lush landscapes become cloying and his symbolism forced, in *Slave of Love,* with a few exceptions, his celebration of natural beauty reinforces the film's central themes by providing a frame of reference that transcends both private pleasure and public responsibility. As background to the main drama, in which romantic attachment and revolutionary commitment struggle for the souls of the two main characters, the small world of the film set offers images of human ephemerality and physical permanence as counterpoint to one another. The fragrant grass and the birch trees, even the transitory pleasure of spring, outlast and overpower the human actors on this stage, if only in their nostalgic memories. Near the beginning of the film two characters, who must have spent their entire lives in cities, lament their exile not in missing the Moscow that they have left but rather the central Russian countryside, where they had gone only to shoot movies to represent Russia for their urban audiences.

If Mikhalkov's major characters are often larger than life and his humorous characters are often unkind caricatures, he also has a real talent for creating finely etched supporting roles that manage to convey a whole range of individual qualities and social subtleties in only a few frames. In *Slave of Love* Mikhalkov creates a fully believable, densely peopled world, whose minor characters convey the everyday pleasures of private life and bewildered disbelief at the threatened demise of their world. He does this in part through shot composition and his ironic use of close-ups and long shots to reverse some of the camera's conventional uses. Rather than revealing psychological penetration, the claustrophobic close-ups of hugely blown-up film posters depicting the silent film stars convey the surface emptiness of an individuality that is all ego and public persona. Psychologically revealing moments often come in middle or even long shots, placing faces amidst other people or bits of landscape. And Mikhalkov often uses long shots ironically to capture private moments lived outdoors, such as the director Kolyagin's endearingly futile attempt to jump up and catch a tree branch, or the family-like atmosphere among the crew as they wait with doomed delight on sun-drenched lawns.

The most compelling of all the structural devices used in *Slave of Love* is Mikhalkov's use of film within a film. This genre self-reflexivity is not used here to score postmodern points about representation but to show the power of the filmed image to move people and to shape their experience of the world in ways that lived experience cannot. Wrenching newsreel and entertaining melodrama are set up to contest one another for authenticity, but in the end it is the moving image itself that wins as the two narrative contestants—the personal and the political—collapse into one another. In the end the distinction between the real and the reel becomes impossible to make, although the consequences of the real are tragically clear.

*Slave of Love* is set somewhere in sunny Crimea where the Moscow film industry fled after the revolution. One of several film crews in the area is attempting to finish a new melodrama but is lacking a number of critical ingredients. They've run out of film stock, their leading man is stuck in Moscow, and the screenwriter is having trouble finding the words to finish the script. The set is awash in bourgeois idleness and *toska* (a Russian idiomatic word conveying melancholy, yearning, and nostalgia), which, it quickly becomes clear, have been forced on the crew by the revolutionary disruptions and their exile from Moscow. We meet our heroine Olga Voznesenskaia as she pines for her leading man and lover Ivan Maksakov. Maksakov is imminently expected but his delay is at first only slightly ominous. We meet the amiable film director Alexander Kolyagin and his nervous, money-minded producer Savva Iuzhakov in their enforced idleness, as they pine for the central Russia of their nostalgic memories and dream of plentiful film stock, high revenues, and the happy old days. The cinematographer, Viktor Pototsky, pines for Olga. She is not only the star of this film, but the biggest star of all Russian cinema; posters from her most recent hit, coyly titled *Slave of Love,* plaster the town. In the meantime, the White army, whose control of the region seems increasingly vulnerable, has been pursuing its enemies with increasing brutality as the Reds move closer. White-army cruelty is embodied in the local chief of intelligence, Captain Nikolai Fedotov. We first meet Fedotov storming into a movie theater, interrupting the show (of Olga's *Slave of Love*) to arrest a suspected Red underground activist. Fedotov reappears at critical moments, dropping in on the movie set, flattering Olga, and making everyone nervous, especially cameraman Viktor.

It turns out that Viktor has reason to be nervous. He has been using his camera (and depleting the limited supply of film stock) to capture White atrocities on film. Fedotov suspects something, but we don't know that right away. Olga suspects something, too. And in her curiosity and boredom she is drawn to Viktor for the diversion of a mystery and the male company. The rest of the narrative chronicles Olga's political and romantic seduction as the Reds circle the city and the Whites close in on Viktor.

Olga, patterned to some extent on Vera Kholodnaia, the exquisite film idol of the 1910s, whose popularity in life and death is discussed in Helena Goscilo's essay in this collection, is isolated by fame from reality and from the rest of humanity. She lives a pampered fantasy life, with people to wait on her every whim; her two children and her mother seem little more than props for an intermittent role as "mother" and "daughter." She seems more oblivious than everyone else of the political realities, which makes her both naïve and silly, but also emotionally pure. Or, rather, almost purely emotion—for which her millions of fans adore her. The other members of the crew also do not begin to understand what's happening around them, but at least they realize that the world they knew is gone. Near the beginning of the film the producer Iuzhakov laments that "we're like children forgotten in the nursery when the house is on fire." With a gentle irony, Kolyagin, the director, replies that when he was a child and got scared he kept his eyes closed. But these are men savvy about business and cinema; they are just completely taken by surprise by the destruction of the world as they know it. Olga, it seems, never even knew the old world.

Although Olga is isolated and infantilized by her inability to see, Viktor sees too much. Both his political commitment and his powers of observation—he is a man with a movie camera after all—isolate him from the rest of the troupe. We first notice him sitting in a privileged position above and apart from the set, gazing at Olga, who is throwing a minor tantrum. Later we realize that he alone, of all the positive characters, observes and understands what is happening in the world off the movie set.

But Victor is not entirely clear-sighted and rational, nor is Olga entirely clueless—and this is central to the structure of the film. Each step toward valorizing public political commitment is riddled with ambiguity and weighted with the tug of private pleasure. Each celebration of private life is shadowed by the suggestion that it is shallow and useless. Both Viktor and Olga confuse fantasy with reality, and private with public virtue. Viktor chooses Olga for conversion to the revolutionary cause because he mistakes the purity of feeling she conveys on screen for her own personal virtue. And like legions of revolutionaries before and after him, he imagines that conversion is a matter of rational persuasion. In fact, when commitment finally captures Olga, it takes the form of emotionally shattering *images.* Throughout the movie, representations of revolutionary politics/public commitment/dramatic heroism are played off against those of melodrama/private life/romantic love.

Mikhalkov pairs the personal with the political in a number of narrative threads that run through the movie. The joys of private, individual, bourgeois life that he presents are utterly seductive at the pastoral, sunlit villa of the film set, where the crew and their friends meet to work and wait in a replica of domesticity. Although Olga is painfully naïve and Iuzhakov is equally unbearable in his self-centered shallowness, their childlike simplicity and apparent harmlessness lends them a purity that lets us forgive them even as it prompts us to condescend to them. Although Kolyagin seems considerably more aware of what he is about to lose, he is equally bewildered by it. Early on we hear this most genial and gentle of men express his amazement that the Bolsheviks refer to people like him as "beasts in the jungle." The implicit irony that these idle makers of vapid melodramas might be class exploiters is brought home by the inarticulate and well-meaning sweetness of the chubby Kolyagin. And although we might share the bemused bewilderment of the film crew when subjected to the harsh revolutionary judgment, we also want to side with the challenge presented by the equally gentle heroism of our love-struck cameraman Viktor. We cannot help but agree with the characters who assert that their movies are frivolous and empty given the political transformation engulfing society. This ironic pairing of the danger and harmlessness in bourgeois self-absorption in the context of revolution is captured in one tiny moment (shown in extreme long shot) when one of Olga's legion of fans spots her, and in mad pursuit shouts that "her last film *rocked* society."

The revolution in *Slave of Love* is represented as a mysterious, incomprehensible force. It shows up as a kind of contagion when it turns out that Maksakov has embraced the revolution and has chosen to remain in Moscow—the other characters seem to think he has been infected by something beyond his control. Later, revolution appears as a force of nature: quite literally as winds of change blow Viktor's words away. It becomes less mysterious as we learn that revolutionary victories in the capitals have forced the film crew into southern exile and have nationalized their equipment and unleashed the civil war, but for the most part the revolution is coded as genuinely positive and heroic, a force for good for people who are good. It is depicted as offering an ideal of selfless social action, political commitment based on high-minded ideas, a necessary antidote to the evil of the White army, personified in the reptilian Fedotov. Its advocates are all sympathetic (including Mikhalkov in a small role) and are committed to sacrificing private pleasures for the dangers of public life for all the right reasons: to battle tyranny and poverty. The film's principal revolutionary, however, ends up dead.

Viktor seems an unlikely hero, and it is appropriate that his activism is motivated not by ideological commitment or a belief in class justice, but by the cruel atrocities committed by the local White army. When we first meet him he seems as dreamy and immobilized as anyone else on the set, mesmerized by the sunshine and Olga's silver-screen charm. His attempts to convert Olga are inarticulate and heartfelt, and like most intellectual adherents of revolution in the early years his politics are rooted more in a desire to effect change than in the specific ideology of change that the Bolsheviks represented. His early efforts are frustrated by Olga's willful transformation of everything she doesn't understand into more familiar images of melodramatic romance. When Viktor first tries to open her eyes to the changing reality, a sudden fantastically violent wind blows his words away. Olga composes herself as the wind dies down and, as if reverting to a well-known role, deflates him by cooing, "my dear, wonderful, incomprehensible Viktor, you're just jealous of Maksakov." Here in the first encounter between Viktor as revolutionary and Olga as melodramatic heroine, both seem slightly ludicrous. During the course of the film, the *words* of melodrama and revolution will be fleshed out by *images* of experience and action, acquiring positive if contrasting connotations.

Olga's political seduction takes place almost entirely in Viktor's car. Lost cars, broken-down cars, and inconveniently waylaid cars play a role in each of Mikhalkov's twentieth-century films. Presumably they represent Mikhalkov's take on Gogol's famous troika, an enduring symbol of Russia's unknown destiny. Gogol's troika, stampeding into the future, is here transformed into an image of Russia's history lost, halted, or *na remont,* in need of repair. In *Slave of Love,* only the producer's car is capable of performing its ordinary job of conveying him around town. Fedotov's car (and his soldiers' trucks) continually interrupt the action. Viktor's car carries Olga to enlightenment and Viktor to his encoun-

Olga's political education in Nikita Mikhalkov's *Slave of Love* (Mosfilm, 1975).

ters with Olga, and ultimately it takes him to his own truncated destiny. In three car rides with Viktor we see Olga's dawning awareness of the world around her, not through anything Viktor has said to her, but through her transformation of her experiences into new roles for her to play. She reenacts all of her experiences into melodramatic roles until events finally strip away her ability to play and she is forced to become authentic.

Olga approaches consciousness in a parody of Marxist stages of proletarianization: recognition, apprehension, and agency (*klass v sebe, klass o sebe, klass dlia sebia*). At the beginning of their first ride together, her attempt to banish melancholy with giddiness dissolves Viktor's will to talk about serious things. Romantic music rises in a song that turns out to be the film's theme: "I believe in dreams, I believe in love." Emotion drowns out idea, as Olga's self-involvement overwhelms Viktor's feeble attempt to bring up politics. But not completely. Suddenly Olga seizes the opportunity to assert some independence by seizing the wheel of the car—and careening off the road. Viktor guides her back on track and as they steer together, laughing, she gathers the courage to call him "a Bolshevik!"—which only makes them laugh harder. At this point we don't know what Viktor has been up to, so the accusation seems connected, ironically, to his radical driving habits alone. His own entirely disingenuous laughter persuades us that melodrama is ascendent and revolution in retreat. A flash of primitive independence on Olga's part followed by her reversion to flirtation is all it has taken to seduce Viktor, this time.

On their second ride in the car, in an utterance of supreme self-awareness (for her) Olga denounces the films they make as useless trash. In the meantime, since their last ride, the lyrical otherworldliness of sunny, bourgeois repose has been disrupted by a dose of harsh reality in the form of the train that finally arrives with the missing film crew. The passengers disembark after a prolonged, two-week journey across war zones, with nothing to eat (dog food is mentioned), with tales of a chaotic Moscow, and with evident relief at having arrived in a safer place. The disjuncture between one reality and another is highlighted by moments of mutual incomprehension, bleached out by the blinding sunshine, abundant bouquets, and nervous laughter. Eventually it becomes clear that the Muscovites have brought a miraculous supply of film stock, but no Maksakov. Olga's leading man has remained behind, having joined the revolution. The tales of starvation and violence make no impression on our Olga. Only the defection of Maksakov, her emotional support and link to the world, coming after Victor's political initiation, makes a dent in her cocoon.

By the time we find Olga and Viktor driving again we are prepared to share Viktor's impression that Olga's newfound awareness comes as a result of her lover's embrace of the revolution. Half-jealous and half-irritated at her stunning shallowness, Viktor accuses Olga of simply missing Maksakov and parroting what she imagines to be his ideas. She turns on him, balancing almost equally her familiar use of the melodramatic and her new understanding of the revolutionary. She accuses him of insulting her: "You're nothing but a wretched cameraman, . . . who do you think you're speaking to?" She demands that he stop the car so that she can take her message to the people. She runs down the steps to the plaza in front of the Soleil-Palace, the theater where her film has been playing, declaiming all the while. "People, listen" she cries, and a crowd immediately gathers around her. "The films we make are terrible, Maksakov is talentless and everything I do is cheap and vulgar. . . . Look around—there is hunger and poverty." But no one takes her seriously, no one even hears her words. With the joyful faces of fans happy to bask in the presence of their idol, they gaze at her with the kind of devotion that socialist realist filmmakers would depict in the eyes of those gazing at Stalin. The crowd that surges around Olga and showers her with love wants only to revel in the reflected glow of her famous smile. They shove flowers into her arms and pieces of paper for her to sign, which together with the brilliant sunshine and the soundtrack (another wordless version of "I believe in love," with an electric guitar now joining the violins) drain her resolve. Through tears and laughter she gives herself up to her fans, unable to adopt a new role or escape the old one.

Mikhalkov portrays Olga here in the kind of close-up that captures the claustrophobia of her public position. Overwhelmed by the flowers and fans that surround her, she can be nothing but an image, yet she barely inhabits the public persona that her fans seem to love. Viktor, despondent at both her own shallow response and the shallowness of her fans, looks on from his perch in the car. The sequence ends with Olga frozen in her role as melodrama film star, as the camera cuts from Viktor to a posed photo of Olga with her daughters in a fan magazine.

Decades of socialist realism in film cue us to read the crowd's response as the essence of bourgeois vacuity, as an image of people clinging to a superficial fantasy life unable to see or even to *feel* the weight of genuine social problems. But this conventional soviet portrait of the prerevolutionary bourgeoisie is challenged in this scene. Olga's popularity is represented as a symptom of bourgeois hollowness, but at the same time it becomes clear that she enjoys more authentic affection than any ideology or either political party. Eventually, we can't help but notice that all kinds of people are genuinely moved in her presence. The images of her that are everywhere in the town—on the walls, in the news, and on the screen—evoke authentic feelings of love and loyalty that neither side in the deadly civil war has managed to arouse (at least not here). Even the oily Fedotov testifies to Olga's extraordinary power when, on one of his visits to the set (following the scene in the plaza), he whispers that if it were not for her presence there he would long ago have had everyone else shot. To her credit, Olga responds with a look of horrified incredulity. This is the first time we see in Olga a sustained authentic reaction as her awakening awareness and the gravity of the whispered confidence come together. Mikhalkov brings the point home by reversing his previous use of long shots and close-ups (long and medium shots having been used earlier to establish a kind of familial public intimacy). We begin to see Olga's reaction in a medium shot as she emerges from behind the murmuring Fedotov. But then the camera zooms in to penetrate her surface reaction: the first psychological depth of character that we have seen is captured in the first psychologically revealing close-up. Olga's dawning consciousness, prodded by Fedotov's admiration, soon receives a harder shove.

Viktor tells Olga that he has been secretly shooting film that implicates Fedotov, and he enlists her to help protect him by hiding the film, because as Fedotov has just told her, she alone is "above suspicion." Olga carefully calls on her resources as an actress to retrieve the film and conceal it in her daughter's doll carriage, with a cleverness we had no reason to suspect previously. Driving together the next day, their third car ride, Olga, exhilarated by her courageous act, voices her admiration for Viktor's heroism and expresses her own longing to do something important, but she does so in a way that shows that heroism would be no more than another role for her. With stagy passion, she declares: "Oh! how *wonderful* to be involved in something for which one can be *imprisoned* or *killed*." Still, it is clear that she longs to take action and to live a life off the screen, "to exist the way a tree exists." With the perspective of a man in love, Viktor contradicts her: "But you do exist." Olga resists, however, in what may be her most perceptive line, as she says firmly: "No—I don't." She turns the conversation to Fedotov, at which Viktor, gambling on her new consciousness, invites her to a secret screening of the film he has been shooting. She vows her trustworthiness, but asks, "what should I wear?" Clearly, by the end of their third and last ride together Olga's conversion to decisive action and public commitment remains unfinished, but her instinct for melodrama and her desire for revolution have moved decisive steps closer together. The setting for the final stages of her transformation will move from the public intimacy of the car to that most private of public spaces—the movie theater.

If *Slave of Love* were nothing more than a nostalgic tribute to silent film makers and a meditation of the contest between reality and fantasy, public and private, it would still be a film worth watching. But Mikhalkov situates these contests in a tribute to the moving image itself. And he does this with extremely clever use of fabricated films within a film, representing a variety of cinema genres and theoretical positions. Taken together, the fabricated films within the film function as a counterpoint to the conflict between public and private by setting up a contrast between the frivolous and the serious, or "love" versus "revolutionary heroism," which in turn are represented by the melodrama (as a realm of emotion, private life, escapism, and fantasy) versus the drama of documentary (the realm of reason, public life, courage, and the "real"). This contest is never entirely resolved in the film. But one winner does eventually emerge from all these unsettled conflicts, and that is the moving picture, the filmed image.

Words, by contrast, are cheap in *Slave of Love.* They have none of the power that the cult of belles lettres in Russian literary history otherwise attributes to them. As in all Mikhalkov's films, this one contains one buffoon, viciously and gratuitously ridiculed. In *Burnt by the Sun,* it was the obese female agitprop worker, in *Slave of Love* it is the man of words—the screenwriter Benyamin Konstantinovich. As a writer on a silent film, his job is secondary at best, but as an intellectual and a Jew (and a crude caricature of both), Benyamin is pointedly marginalized on the set and treated with contempt by the key members of the crew. He is incapable of finishing the script, and he is seen repeatedly scratching out his words or crumpling up his pages, and hitting himself on the forehead, his frizzy hair askew. He is also the only actual emigrant that we see in the film. Everyone else talks about going to Paris, but we see Benyamin actually getting paid, saying his farewells, and leaving the motherland. The thirty rubles he was so pointedly offered at the beginning of the film foreshadow his betrayal of his homeland.

The writer's words, however, are not the only ones that have no power in *Slave of Love.* Olga's speech in the plaza is drowned out and, more important, Viktor tries in every way imaginable to *talk* to Olga about politics and social responsibility, but all in vain. As we have seen, his words are literally swept away by the wind and drowned out by music. Viktor's only instrument of persuasion is his ability to create images. It is the cameraman, not the writer, who is the true witness of the age and the one with the means to move us, to inspire us, and even to transform us. Mikhalkov makes his argument, so to speak, by taking us from the most conventional (and conventionally dismissed) images of early cinema, the domestic melodrama, through the harrowing documentary (the serious stuff), and ending with a scene that collapses the two, thereby collapsing the contests we've been following all along: between reality and fantasy, reason and emotion, revolution and love, and public and private.

In each interior film, elements of melodrama and revolutionary drama are implicitly juxtaposed. One of the things I like best about this movie is the way that Mikhalkov takes us back and forth from an ethereal realm of light comedy and light emotions into the arena of deadly politics and deeper feelings. Pacing, lighting, and acting make Mikhalkov a master of the light comedy, but *Slave of Love* is the only one of his films (I think) where his weightier themes come across with the same deft touch and balance.

To return to the beginning again, before catching up with Olga's political education, the film opens with lightness itself. Inside the Soleil-Palace movie theater, the fabricated melodrama *Slave of Love* starring our Olga and her Maksakov is a parody of the most conventional, theatrical, and least cinematic melodramas of early cinema. Anyone who has seen the films of Evgeny Bauer or any of the other early Russian melodramas (discussed by Louise McReynolds in her essay in this volume) can see that the *Slave of Love* within *Slave of Love* is a caricature of the form. The action occurs against a flat, obviously theatrical backdrop—the opposite of Bauer's innovative use of the deep-focus shot and imaginatively layered spaces. The camera is static and stagy, which produces a look that most film directors had long rejected by 1918. The fragment of a plot that we see is a caricature of the archetype: a blind Olga plays the violin for her husband while he sits nearby and takes a pretty servant onto his lap. A helpless woman, a duplicitous husband, a coquettish servant—these may have been the ingredients of the classic early cinema melodrama, but in Russia in the 1910s filmmakers tended to subvert or at least complicate these stereotypes. Bauer in particular gave women powerful roles, at least partially challenging gender hierarchies and revealing the impermanence of established social identities. But even this parody demonstrates the power of the image to evoke cathartic empathy. Cutting from the film to the audience of weeping women, Mikhalkov provides a foundation for the popular adulation that Olga receives whenever she steps out in public. Here at the beginning that adulation is coded almost entirely negatively. We are prompted to think: "silly film, silly women." Then when the screen fantasy is interrupted by political violence, we can only conclude that we are watching the fiddling while Rome burns.

Right at the beginning Mikhalkov uses the contrast between fantasy and reality to announce the film's thematic contest between private and public. The first thing we see is a medium shot of the piano player, and we hear the tinny piano of recordings from that era rather than the sound of live piano (establishing distance rather than verisimilitude).

We see the credits for the melodrama within—*Slave of Love* starring Olga Voznesenskaia and Ivan Maksakov—well before we see Mikhalkov's credits. Each of these images and the melodrama itself are shown in medium, stable camera shots. Then, before we have a chance to register much about the war between the sexes, the camera moves into action, panning, tracking, and zooming to convey visually the disruption of the narrative. The door to the theater is flung open, flooding the hall with light and abruptly halting the music. We find ourselves in the audience, lights up, with Captain Fedotov striding up to the screen trying to pacify the startled moviegoers while hunting for a Red spy among them, finding and seizing the Red as he tries to run. Fedotov takes him outside, camera tracking backward through the crowd, continuing our detached spectator's perspective, and zooming back and away to a shot that takes in the whole scene in front of the theater. As a murmuring crowd gathers, the camera zooms in on the first action to disturb our detachment. Fedotov unceremoniously smashes his captive against a shop window and orders him to be tossed into the back of a truck, which speeds away. "Go back to your movie," Fedotov shouts to the bystanders, and under his breath, "you sheep."

When Olga herself is finally converted to the cause, it is not an idea or even a charming cameraman who persuades her, but a film. Just when we start to accept the power of melodrama to move us, Mikhalkov shifts gears and presents us with an entirely different type of film: a documentary.[9] It turns out that the film Viktor is anxious to hide contains evidence of the White atrocities carried out by Fedotov, who is anxious to keep them secret. This is the film Viktor invites Olga to see. She is as thrilled to experience the revolution vicariously as her own fans are to experience her emotional life vicariously. Until she actually sees the film, though, she is still playing a role. She fusses that evening about what to wear and how to act the part of underground conspirator in love. Listening to her chatter on about her makeup while the world shatters around them, Olga's mother, packing in preparation to flee to Paris, quietly begins to sob for her daughter who manifestly does not seem to understand anything real.

But if Olga did not understand much before the screening, the images of poverty and brutality she sees on film finally break through to her. The result is shattering. She staggers out of the dark room, emotionally broken, unable to speak, unable to shed the tears she evokes in her own audiences. This is not secondhand emotion: stripped of all pretense, and of the ability to act, Olga has been forced to become real. The next time we see her she has resolved to return to Moscow, to join Maksakov and the revolution. Still unspeaking, still in the same clothes the following day, she is only dissuaded when Iuzhakov takes her children off the train, forcing her to stay in Crimea, on the set, and in character. "You've destroyed me," she whispers, "This is the end of me."

The fragmented images of Viktor's film—peasant refugees, homeless children, off-screen executions and beatings by Fedotov's men—are indeed disturbing. We have no trouble imagining such images as potent propaganda, more powerful than printed pamphlets of Marxist rhetoric for arousing revolutionary consciousness. But Mikhalkov also shows us here the important emotional component contained in revolutionary commitment. Rather than some heroic fiction it is the document of real events transformed into images on the screen that finally reaches Olga, but it reaches her in a deeply visceral way. Viktor's film leaves her transformed but wordless. She barely speaks again for the rest of the film.

However, Olga's newly discovered commitment to reality is, in some ways, no less a fantasy than her earlier roles of childish innocence. To return to Moscow can only seem suicidal or even murderous because she tries to drag along her mother and two little girls. This makes us wonder just what kind of transformation the filmmakers have in mind. Is this political consciousness? Certainly Olga seems more in touch with reality than before, but her state is entirely unrecognizable in serious political terms. She has been moved to make some kind of commitment by filmed images of real people, but only because she is moved emotionally to empathy. In this pivotal scene (both for Olga and for the narrative) the public and the private seem inseparable. But effective political action is still remote.

At the same time, Mikhalkov's images of political reality are politically tame. Ordinary, nonpathological people of every class are moved by images of homeless refugees and furtive executions. The men at the screening discuss retaliation, but they too are primarily moved by a desire to protect their children, rather than to protect the proletarian revolution against its class enemies. There is no class justice here, no indication of a specifically *political* consciousness, much less a socialist one. It is hard to say whether Mikhalkov's simple condemnation of violence against the innocent represents his own ideological views or whether he wants only to convey the essential humaneness necessary to any political ideology. He is certainly correct, though, in implying that most people who joined the revolution did so on the basis of only the foggiest notions of, and loosest of affiliations with, Bolshevik socialism.[10]

But despite its political weaknesses, at this point in *Slave of Love* the film document trumps the film melodrama. It shocks Olga and it moves us in a way that nothing else has done so far. Images of the real not only touch Olga but move her to action. Mikhalkov had shown us all the strengths of the melodrama and won us over with its appeal, only to reverse himself and reveal its essential limitations. Not that this is an unambiguous valorization of the real or the political. Just because images that convey the realities of poverty and warfare are powerful enough to move us to act does not mean that political action will eradicate them. When Olga and Viktor each try to act politically, their heroism is genuine but their efforts fail.

Despite our best efforts to live through films, some things really are real and love rarely triumphs. When Olga and Victor meet for the next (and last) time, he knows that his days are numbered. When Olga pledges to learn to love him, to escape into reality, he can only smile sadly in return—and leave the dangerous film canister with her. The existence of Victor's film has by now placed him in mortal danger. Fedotov either knows enough or is scared enough to kill the cameraman. Thus Olga's final conversion to the cause and her pledge of love is followed immediately by Viktor's shocking murder. Fedotov and his men gun Viktor down, in his car in the central plaza with Olga watching on in shock.

Shooting the cameraman doesn't quite end the movie, however. In fact the most interesting scene remains. The final sequence of *Slave of Love* recreates the revolution, to paraphrase Marx, first as farce and then as melodrama. The Red army is closing in on the town and order is disintegrating, symbolized by the dismantling of the film set after Viktor's murder, although it is not clear whether or not filming has been completed. Benyamin is paid off, stage hands run to and fro offering tea and cognac. Everyone is in shock, Iuzhakov noisily and insensitively, Kolyagin sorrowfully and pensively. Olga is nowhere to be found. Suddenly Fedotov shows up, drunk and looking for Viktor's film. No one wants to see Fedotov and the air is thick with the tension he always leaves in his wake. Mikhalkov handles the suspense perfectly in this scene. Fedotov drunkenly orders the filming to continue. Everyone is too frightened to resist so Kolyagin finds Olga and starts trying to give her character direction. He fumbles for words as always until he latches onto the only thing he can imagine—an image—that might help at that moment: he asks her to smile, just to smile. Kolyagin knows that Olga's smile won't bring back their lost world or the dead Viktor but it might, in fact, make everyone feel better, as it always had in the past. He continues trying to talk to her, but the words are swallowed by the melancholy theme music, as Olga offers us the most genuinely pitiful face. Patently unable to smile or to do anything else, she ruptures the murmuring, the music, and the mood—by shooting Fedotov. Bang. Silence. The smoke clears. The shot was a blank. Fedotov, shaken, tries to laugh it off as farce. But the next thing we know, the real drama begins.

Viktor's friends arrive (led by Mikhalkov), with real guns this time, to save the secret film, rescue the damsel in distress, and do away with the villain. Cinematically and thematically, in what is an ingenious echo of the two previous films within a film, Mikhalkov collapses the contest between revolutionary drama and melodrama. The friends cut the lights on the film set, so what follows is reduced to black and white in the flickering light of candles and ambient light, making the association with early cinema explicit. Yet the sequence remains within the framework of the real rather than within the discrete visual frame of a film within a film. Moreover, although the structure of the scene is pure melodrama, the events are quite unavoidably real. This revolutionary skirmish is fought with real bullets and people die: Fedotov first, and then his henchmen. The film crew becomes completely irrelevant now (and free to emigrate) as the revolutionaries spirit Olga away. Whether their intent is to rescue or to condemn her is unclear as they escape back outside into the full-color evening light mist.

The collapsing of categories in this revolution played as melodrama does not suggest that they cancel each other out. On the contrary, the last scene in particular reinforces the merging of principles that have been gradually evolving throughout the film. Love and politics, public and private, and reality and fantasy have no meaning apart from one another. To live honorably is to remember that at the heart of the political is the personal, but that private life without public responsibility is equally objectionable. When just minutes after Viktor has been mur-

Olga careening toward an ominous future in Nikita Mikhalkov's *Slave of Love* (Mosfilm, 1975).

dered Olga comes to the restaurant where one of the conspirators works to deliver the film canisters Viktor left with her, the conspirator refuses to let her in. She is in shock and the film places her in desperate danger, but in contrast to the display of cowardice before her, she radiates the self-possession of one who is acting out of both love *and* commitment.

But this being the dawn of soviet history, the future cannot be left so neatly wrapped up. Ambiguity returns in the final sequence as Olga, looking both hollow and aware at the same time, is left to ride off into the mist, all alone, on a trolley going who knows where. A company of White cavalrymen is gaining on her while the soundtrack rises with the theme song, "I believe in dreams, I believe in love." This trolley, like all the other lost cars of Mikhalkov's films, is last seen careening drunkenly toward an ominous future as the horsemen draw closer and the camera pans up to a blinding white sun, which threatens to obliterate both the private love and the heroic dreams.

Mikhalkov's use of the world of prerevolutionary melodramatic filmmaking to comment on the morality of private life in post-Stalinist society ignores many of the conventional features of the genre while it transforms others. Mikhalkov celebrates early cinematic melodrama's ability to move us emotionally, wordlessly, unintellectually, but he is less interested in the world represented by the slaves of love than he is in the ways people learned to live offscreen. Hence, the emotional excess and the psychoanalytical probing beneath the surfaces of the fin de siècle family and society play no role here. Nor does Mikhalkov seem to appreciate the ways in which turn-of-the-century melodrama valorized not only feeling and individuality, but specifically female experience. In *Slave of Love* (as in Mikhalkov's films generally), women remain very much objects of male desire and conjecture. The challenge to conventional gender roles, the issues of female virtue under assault, and the neurotic conflicts that tear at the fabric of Victorian bourgeois private life play no role in this film. On the other hand, Mikhalkov updates the genre to confront the murky moral issues of his own time in all their ambiguity, rejecting the Manichaean categories of the classic melodrama.

Jacky Bratton defines melodrama as a genre that "engages with and processes the complexity of modernity and the politics of cultural change."[11] In this she is referring to the period associated with the rise of modernism, but the changes she identifies are similar to those explored in *Slave of Love* and connected with the changes in late soviet culture. Revolutionary culture in the Soviet Union reproduced many of the tensions associated with challenges to bourgeois notions of private and public space and private and public morality. The Bolsheviks intensified the West's modern intrusion into private life and glorified the expansion of the public in official rhetoric. But while Mikhalkov's intimate portrait of the prerevolutionary filmmakers' world is an affectionate look back at a world that might have been his own, his nostalgia is ironic, critical, and multifaceted. The pleasure in this nostalgia is in the feeling itself, the imagining of a beautiful past or, for a filmmaker, the making of images of a past. Svetlana Boym writes of an ironic nostalgia that "puts the emphasis on the *algia,* longing, and acknowledges the displacement of the mythical place without trying to rebuild it."[12]

Symbolically, this nostalgic irony resides in the glorious Crimean sunlight, which may be warm and lush to experience but also blinds the eye and bleaches the color out of the world in this remembered past—the Muscovites in the film constantly complain about the heat. The pretty life of bourgeois ease—the beautiful clothes, the open-air cafes, the luxury cars that make the film so much fun to watch—is portrayed here as seductive but empty; tragically ephemeral, on the one hand, easily destroyed or sent into exile, and as farcically lightweight, on the other, easily carried away and no reason not to let it go. Mikhalkov engages us with nostalgia for an attractive past—he celebrates both the movies' power to move us and the appeal of the filmmakers' world—but, in thus seducing us, he exposes our reluctance to engage with the real world. No matter how tempting it is to escape into private pleasures, no matter how justifiable the defense of the right to a private life, especially after fifty years of soviet efforts to efface private life, at the heart of this affectionate look at both melodrama and revolution is a critique of the intelligentsia of both the 1910s and the 1970s for their failure to perceive the world in political terms. Although it valorizes and defends the right to a private life, *Slave of Love* does not let us forget that private fulfillment has its costs and that those costs are moral and political.

## Notes

1 Robert Lang, *American Film Melodrama: Griffith, Vidor, Minnelli* (Princeton: Princeton University Press, 1989), 50.

2 See Eric Naiman, *Sex in Public: The Incarnation of Early Soviet Ideology* (Princeton: Princeton University Press, 1997), for an excellent extended discussion of early soviet negotiations over public and private space.

3 Vera Dunham, *In Stalin's Time: Middle-Class Values in Soviet Fiction* (Cambridge: Cambridge University Press, 1976).

4 Andrei Tarkovsky, *Time within Time: The Diaries, 1970–1986* (London: Faber, 1994).

5 Susan Costanzo, "Slawomir Mrozek's 'The Emigrants' at the Moscow Theater-Studio 'Chelovek': Text and Context Again and Again," *Slavonic and East European Journal* 43, no. 1 (1999): 70.

6 *Raba liubvi,* dir. Nikita Mikhalkov, Mosfilm, 1975. All quotations and references are my transcriptions from the video version distributed in the United States by RCA/Columbia Pictures (1978). Screenplay by Andrei Konchalovsky-Mikhalkov and Fridrikh Gorenstein, cinematography by Pavel Lebeshev, art direction by Aleksandr Adabash'ian, music by Eduard Artem'ev, sound by V. Bobrovskii. Elena Solovei (Olga), Aleksander Kaliagin (Kolyagin), Rodion Nakhmetov (Viktor), Oleg Basilashvili (Iuzhakov), Konstantin Grigor'ev (Fedotov).

It may be somewhat misleading to call this Mikhalkov's film, because he was brought in as a replacement for the original director after the project had begun (and he did not write the screenplay). However, the film bears so many of the narrative concerns and technical signs of Mikhalkov's later work that it seems clearly to have been largely reshaped by him.

7 Svetlana Boym, *Common Places: Mythologies of Everyday Life in Russia* (Cambridge, Mass.: Harvard University Press, 1994), 338; Anna Lawton, *Kinoglasnost* (Cambridge: Cambridge University Press, 1992), 26; and E. Stishova, "Snimaetsia kino," *Iskusstvo Kino* no. 4 (1977): 101.

8 Peter Brooks, *The Melodramatic Imagination: Balzac, Henry James, Melodrama, and the Mode of Excess* (New Haven: Yale University Press, 1976): 14–15.

9 I use the word "documentary" loosely here. Viktor never had time to shape his material into a documentary narrative or even into a conventional newsreel. He was shooting on the go, trying to record events on film as evidence, as a "document."

10 This was not a position that could have been stated more directly or in academic or political settings, but it is worth noting that it could be explored at that time in the movies.

11 Jacky Bratton, "Introduction," in *Melodrama: Stage, Picture, Screen,* ed. Jacky Bratton, Jim Cook, and Christine Gledhill (London: British Film Institute,1994), 1.

12 Boym, *Common Places,* 284.

*Helena Goscilo*

# Playing Dead

## The Operatics of Celebrity Funerals, or,

## The Ultimate Silent Part

Dying is an art, like everything else.
—Sylvia Plath, "Lady Lazarus"

A single death is a tragedy, a million deaths is a statistic.
—Joseph Stalin, in conversation

### The Last Word in Graveside Traditions

In everyday life and in cultural categories such as literature, drama, and film, melodrama defines itself primarily in unflaggingly heightened emotions, intensity of moral claim, and extravagance of representation.[1] Funerals, which formally dispose of the dead in rituals shaped by the values of a given community, hyperbolize all three generic features. As a dramatic event, in the words of Donovan Ochs, death summons not "the forms of reasoned argument, but, rather, dramatic forms of narrative, poetry, and theater" that spotlight symbolically freighted gestures and carry unforgettable visual impact.[2] Whatever the variations dictated by culture-specific priorities and taboos, the last rite is by Roger Grainger's definition a "proclamation of meaning."[3] Accordingly, the conventions of funeral oratory mandate the deceased's metamorphosis into saint, hero/ine, martyr, or genius—and sometimes, especially in Russia, where the soviet intelligentsia haloed its famous representatives in a martyrological nimbus—all four simultaneously.[4] Because measured appraisals and allusions to character flaws violate the norms of the genre, valedictory speeches over the lifeless body inevitably present the latter in totalized summation as "*larger* than life" by dwelling exclusively on its owner's extraordinary personal qualities, peerless talent, exemplary deeds, and universal significance. This selective construction of an ennobling posthumous image initiates the process of monumentalization subsequently materialized in stone or marble structures erected at the grave or, in the case of celebrities, throughout the nation.[5]

The ostensibly contradictory imperatives of funereal glorification and gloom are reconciled through the logic of causality: *because* the unique virtues of the deceased were cause for rejoicing, their withdrawal from the world gives cause for lamentation. The pathos of loss played out at funerals—which require display—elevates the dead individual on the wings of martyrdom to personalized yet universal tragedy in terms codified by centuries of ritual mourning. Indeed, the graveside valediction may be traced to such ancient genres as elegy (from the Greek *elegeia,* meaning "lament"), threnody, lament, dirge, and epitaph, now classified as primarily literary, but rehearsed "live" during the actual burial of the dead.[6]

The widespread genre of literary dirge derives from the Greek *epikedeion,* a mourning song ceremonially sung over the dead, usually by their intimates but also by professional mourners.[7] Roman funeral processions likewise chanted the *nenia,* a song of praise for the departed that sometimes would be entrusted to professional wailing women (*praeficae*) specifically hired for the task.[8] Roman funerals differed from those of other ancient cultures in one notable respect: the dead body, normally burned on a pyre, remained shielded from view while assorted surrogates in the form of waxen images, for example, substituted for the actual corpse, symbolizing the individual's most admirable achievements.[9] This surrogate of inert matter proleptically signaled the symbolic process of petrification indispensable to a posthumous mythology implicated in the hyperbolic moral claims that Peter Brooks accurately identifies as melodrama's mode. The Russian version of installing static facsimiles entails the placement of a photograph on the grave, but during the burial ceremony the casket remains open and mourners line up to kiss the corpse, most often on the lips.

The Classical tradition of ceremonial grieving was preserved and modified in print when the posthumous summation of a life formulated according to the ethos of a community became the province of the literati.[10] Notable instances of literary threnodies include David's "Lament for Saul and Jonathan," Theocritus's "Lament for Daphnis," Milton's "Lycidas," Shelley's "Adonais," Tennyson's *In Memoriam,* and Auden's "In Memory of W. B. Yeats." Feofan Prokopovich's "Sermon on the Interment of Peter the Great," Derzhavin's philosophical "On the Death of Prince Meshcherskii," and Zhukovskii's highly visual, interpretive portrait on Pushkin's death, "He Lay Motionless," offer Russian variations within the canon. A purely oral, popular branch of the graveside genre surviving to this day is the formulaic folk lament invariably performed at funerals by professional mourners—an exclusively female occupation in ancient Greece and throughout Russia's history.[11]

Whether recorded as literature or merely recited once during the interment ceremony, the modern elegy commemorating the dead doubles as eulogy, for the interrelated immemorial functions of the genre (notwithstanding Marc Antony's disclaimer, "I come to bury Caesar, not to praise him") combine lamentation (the Greek *thrênoi*) with consolation and exaltation (the Greek *enkomia*).[12] Idealizing the "dear departed," apart from its pedagogical potential, both intensifies and legitimates the operatic enactment of tragic loss invited by the occasion.[13]

## Mortuary Melodrama

What brackets last rites with melodrama? As group spectacles, funerals are highly conventionalized, structured on contrasts, and profoundly paradoxical.[14] They spotlight the unavoidably, irreversibly silent passivity of the major "performer"—the corpse that has already become an approximate double for the individual about to enter familial or public history as a cultural monument in the making. The mute inertness of the key player who is no longer "herself" has two major consequences: it foregrounds visibility,[15] displacing attention onto the immobile body's physical *appearance*—a preview, in a sense, of the death mask and the monuments that may follow;[16] and it forces those relegated to secondary roles to act and speak for her, to create and begin immortalizing for posterity the persona of the "silent star." Their behavior lays the foundation for the image, the status of the deceased within her culture—just as the royal presence on stage relies on the behavior of those surrounding the king or queen to construct an aura of regality (*suita igraet korolia*). At funerals, that entourage doubles as both audience and participant, insofar as its members not only witness the permanent departure of the chief actor, but also regulate the terms of her passing and act out its implications.

This phenomenon of acting out links funerals with melodrama and silent cinema through their common reliance on bodily semiotics. As Brooks has noted, silent cinema must use the body in expressionistic ways as the vehicle of meanings that cannot be verbally conveyed. Similarly, melodrama's "simple, unadulterated messages must be made absolutely clear, visually present to the audience," an imperative that explains why "bodies of victims and villains must unambiguously signal their status."[17] If, as Brooks insists, acting out through the corporeal actions, gestures, and "sites of irritation and excitation" is essential for transmitting what otherwise remains under the "bar of repression,"[18] then funerals underscore the primacy of bodily signification through the melodramatic contrast between the chief player's inanimate form and the compensatorily hypereloquent physical activity of the "cast" congregated to mount the final interpretation of that player's life role—a last judgment of sorts that pinpoints the deceased's niche in the pertinent group's cultural history.

While these principles structure funerals in general, celebrity funerals magnify their specific elaborations, because the deceased's fame not only encourages an extravagant scale and cosmic moral claims, but also exerts a wider-ranging symbolic impact. The deaths of national figures—whose lives are ceaselessly exposed to public view and molded by public opinion—thus trigger mass spectacles executed in the hyperbolic register distinctive of melodrama. Such grand pageantry not only involves excess in scale and gesture, but also calls for a "restaging" of the deceased's life (distilled via carefully selected music, speeches, emblems, and symbolic gestures) that serves a triple function: it vouchsafes a public and recorded catharsis that unites, however briefly, the spectators performing the focal role of mourners; it maximizes the visibility of the "grief of the nation" as a measure of the deceased's purported greatness; and it permits the mourners to play a decisive part in their icon's last public appearance and the formation of her/his subsequent fate, which anniversary celebrations both reinforce and revise.[19] Although traditionally only heads of state and national military heroes (for example, the Duke of Wellington) have merited grand-theater funerals, more recently media celebrities have swelled the ranks of worthies.[20]

In the context of this generalized cultural paradigm, in this essay I examine the funerals of Vera Kholodnaia, Anna Akhmatova, Joseph Stalin, Vladimir Vysotsky, and Andrei Sakharov as national melodramas. Choreographed and preserved for posterity, these five performances scripted the posthumous reputations of the celebrities in question, adapting and magnifying those elements from their public biographies that responded to the sociopsychological needs and exigencies of the given political moment.[21] The notorious binarism of Russian culture ideally conforms to the requisite conditions for the enactment of melodrama:[22] a world, according to Brooks, "subsumed by an underlying manichaeism," its narratives implicated in the "moral occult, the domain of operative spiritual values which is both indicated within and masked by the surface of reality." Although not a metaphysical system, the moral occult is "the repository of the fragmentary and desacralized remnants of sacred myth."[23] Each of the five funerals discussed here revealed and made legible the basic desires and interdictions informing the national mythology of a society that has brooded for centuries over its ontological identity. That identity cohered around "the idea," which underwent myriad changes over decades—surfacing in the funerals in question—to confront its nullity in the postsoviet era.[24]

### From Screen to Street: Vera Kholodnaia (1893–1919)

A prerevolutionary star of the silent screen who had no professional training apart from a stint in a ballet school, Vera Kholodnaia reigned as the queen of celluloid melodrama from 1914 to 1919.[25] Her premature death of Spanish influenza at the age of twenty-six abruptly curtailed her spectacular career and extended the melodrama of her on-screen persona to her off-screen "exit." Equated throughout her career with spectacle, with the visibility of intense emotions—exaggerated on the silent screen where flamboyant gestures and overstated body language compensated for the absence of voice—Kholodnaia played heroines impaled on the horns of insoluble life-or-death dilemmas that usually entailed temptation and lust, poverty and luxury, betrayal and fanatical devotion, murder and self-destruction. Dusting, diapering, or folding the laundry never intruded on Kholodnaia's realm of on-screen concerns, for her persona dwelled in the overappointed mise-en-scène of self-indulgent, self-conscious capitalist excess.

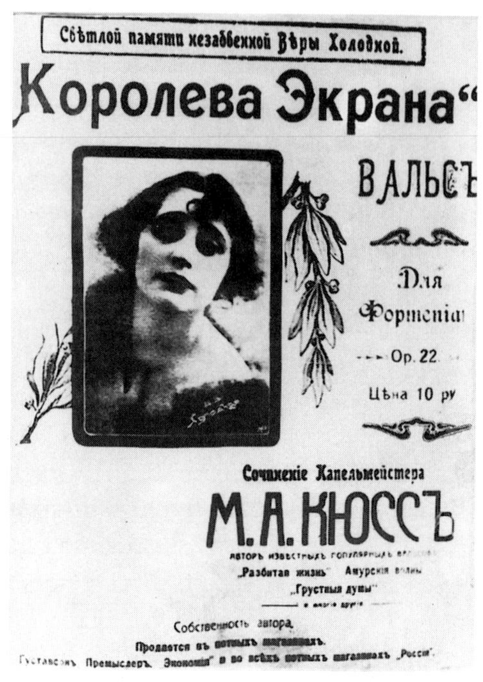


Cover to piano music of a waltz composed by M. A. Kiuss, dedicated "to the luminous memory of the unforgettable Vera Kholodnaia." From B. B. Ziukov, comp., *Vera Kholodnaia* (Moscow: Iskusstvo, 1995).

Despite her lack of acting experience, Kholodnaia starred in dozens of films that crystallized her celluloid personality as a beautiful (and beautifully melancholy) female victim, misunderstood or "done wrong" by circumstances and a society consisting of "tainted money, opulent restaurants, lavish champagne picnics, luxurious autos careening through the night, and illicit love ending in tragedy."[26] Her most memorable films include *The Song of Triumphant Love* (1914), based on Turgenev's "exotic" tale of mysterious psychosexual union; *Mirages* (1915); *A Life for a Life* (1916),[27] where her adulterous liaison with her adoptive sister's gambling husband ends when her adoptive mother shoots him; *The Chessgame of Life* (1916), which features Kholodnaia as a *demi-mondaine; The Live Corpse* (1918), which adapted Tolstoy's play of marital/sexual passions, complete with alcoholism, adultery, Gypsies, arrests, and fake and genuine suicide; *The Last Tango* (1918),[28] where she plays an Argentine heroine murdered by her jealous lover on a Paris dance floor; and *Be Still, My Grief* (1918). In short, the idea of woman as nondescript meek mouse could not be more remote from Kholodnaia's range of roles, and the Manichaean scheme structuring her films pitted the histrionically

Dressed for the last excess: the fatal knifing on the dance floor during *The Last Tango.* From B. B. Ziukov, comp., *Vera Kholodnaia* (Moscow: Iskusstvo, 1995).

paraded authenticity of her passion against the gloss of the world that inevitably doomed her.

With film still in its infancy and uninflected by the potential subtlety of verbal articulation, the dramatization of personal and social issues in these works perforce resorted to the black-and-white visual and moral polarization inherent in melodrama. Kholodnaia relied on a limited but, apparently, effective repertoire of physical signals that equated drastic with plastic: panting that tossed and heaved her generous bosom for impressively prolonged periods; hands clasped at breast or temples; drooping head (a favorite ploy of Garbo's); prolonged impassioned glances; abrupt sinking onto armchairs and sofas; and sudden immobility beside tables, columns, and doorways to project shock and devastation. The extent to which this heightened exteriorization of "women's experience" converted virtually all situations and decisions into crescendoes of affect may be gauged by the frequency with which the titles of Kholodnaia's films featured the word "life," with its ostensibly sole alternative—death—ominously hovering in the wings.

The emphasis on profound female suffering, imprinted on and expressed by the body, and the screen image of a beautiful female victim (glamorous or framed in glamorous surroundings) acquired special poignancy for audiences when Kholodnaia died "in the prime of

Significant looks that bear the weight of meaning, in P. Chardynin's *Fairy Tale of Dear Love* (*Skazka liubvi dorogoi,* 1918). From B. B. Ziukov, comp., *Vera Kholodnaia* (Moscow: Iskusstvo, 1995).

her beauty," as one soviet critic phrased it, substituting aesthetics for temporality.[29] The abbreviated film clip of Kholodnaia's funeral shows the cinema idol lying in an open coffin, "festooned with flowers"[30] and shrouded in lacy, white, gossamerlike material that eerily recalls the frothy peignoir in which she receives her adulterous lover, Prince Bartinskii, in the portentously titled melodrama *A Life for a Life.* Kholodnaia's premature death conjures an epilogue to the film—as though she had followed her murdered screen lover to the mysterious beyond. In a scene suggestively anticipating the milling masses in Eisenstein's *Potemkin* (and thus evoking national devastation), thousands crowded around the coffin carried down the streets of Odessa, some glancing over their shoulders to be captured on camera as the procession slowly wound its way through the city. Clearly, the public shared the opinion of Anatoly Lunacharsky, people's commissar of enlightenment, who just a few months earlier had announced: "Melodrama, simply as theatre, is superior to other dramatic genres."[31]

The newsreel of Kholodnaia's final silent role was released just three days after the funeral, enabling audiences to relive, via near-instant replay, the "national trauma" of her demise. Although panegyrics to the late actress flooded the Odessa press, bereaved fans acted out their

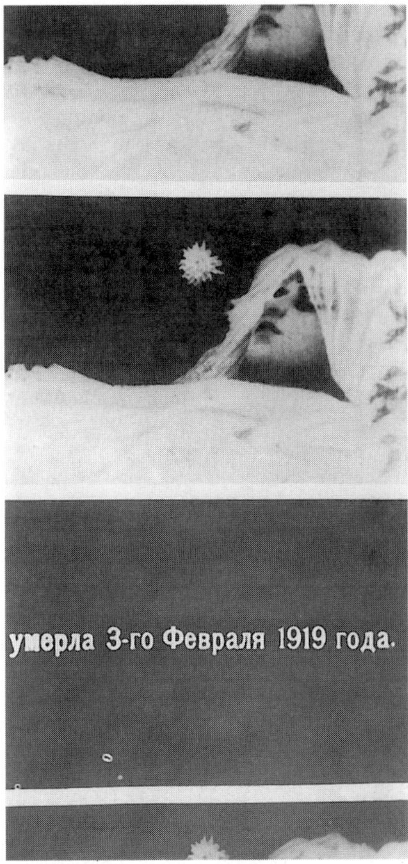


Dead beauty costumed for screenlike contemplation: Kholodnaia in her coffin. From B. B. Ziukov, comp., *Vera Kholodnaia* (Moscow: Iskusstvo, 1995).

grief in cynosural forms: "They read verses dedicated to the deceased, fainted, and sobbed; many had hysterics," and hordes rushed to view the corpse of the first Russian "queen of the screen."[32]

Shipped to Moscow, Kholodnaia's embalmed body, like that of Snow White, was placed in a glass coffin and installed in a chapel vault beside the remains of the Russian aviator Sergei Utochkin.[33] The real-life culmination of her on-screen misadventures as a lovely sufferer, Kholodnaia's funeral as immortalized on film and the posthumous exhibition of her body seemed to validate Edgar Allen Poe's notorious claim that "the death of a beautiful woman is, unquestionably, the most poetical topic in the world."[34] The public here assumed the role of the "bereaved lover" who realizes the goal of Samuel Richardson's Lovelace: to possess the beloved eternally by warding off the body's dissolution through

Enthralled spectators as grieving participants following Kholodnaia in her casket. From B. B. Ziukov, comp., *Vera Kholodnaia* (Moscow: Iskusstvo, 1995).

embalming.[35] Thereafter the public could enjoy two Kholodnaias as aesthetic objects of desire, both unchanging and eternally young: the perpetually mobile one on screen and the ever-immobile one displayed, like Lenin, under glass. The conjunction of death, femininity, and aesthetics that shaped Kholodnaia's cinematic career found its apotheosis in her spectacular final silent role.

Subsequent narratives of Kholodnaia's life and death, in fact, cast the incidents of her biography within the framework of theatrical genres. Operating on the worn assumption that all the world loves a lover, a 1995 study sentimentalizes her relationship with Vladimir Kholodnyi—a young lawyer whom she married at the age of seventeen—into "a model of exceptional love" (*obrazets iskliuchitel'noi liubvi*) and dubs the couple, who fell in love "at first sight," "the Russian Romeo and Juliet," minus, of course, the distracting complication of Tybalt and the double suicide in the family crypt at play's end.[36] In this hagiographic account Kholodnaia emerges as an icon of conjugal fidelity, devoted motherhood, social commitment, staunch nationalism, and professional largesse. The presumed incarnation of "the feminine ideal," Kholodnaia the "star" shines in orchestrated memory as a celestial entity, immortalizing the "idea" of fatal yet faithful beauty so dear to fin de siècle aesthetics.

### Words in Stone: Anna Akhmatova (1889–1966)

Anna Akhmatova's youthful public image both paralleled and contrasted with Kholodnaia's.[37] Physically striking, talented, "charismatic," and famous, both women reputedly emanated "romantic," "feminine" seductiveness. One of the few commentators to have noted the resemblance between the two icons of feminity, Solomon Volkov astutely observes that Kholodnaia's films, "like Akhmatova's poems, usually represented unrequited, duped, or humiliated love."[38] Both were picturesque martyrs of the heart. Unlike Kholodnaia, however, Akhmatova lived into old age, in the course of which her original image of a Lorelei lyricist underwent a radical sea change. During her final decades, the desexed, wheezing bulk of her body erased all traces of her former allure. Its torpid massiveness already previsioned her stature as cultural monument, as suggested by the reminiscences of her secretary, the poet Anatoly Nayman: "She held herself very erect, as if balancing her head, walked slowly, and even when she moved was like a sculpture, a massive, meticulously modelled—at some moments, it seemed, hewn—classical sculpture: a masterpiece of the art form. And what she had on, something threadbare and long, perhaps a shawl, or an old kimono, was reminiscent of the flimsy wrappings which are thrown over the finished piece in the sculptor's studio."[39] By then, Akhmatova's fame as fascinating charmer and love poet had ceded to that of preeminent poet laureate, national tragedienne, and noble survivor. She had become, as the cliché has it, a living monument—a historical work of art conceived by herself and "finished" by those who followed her cues for the work's completion. For the educated segment of Russian society, the demise of youthful beauty that tugged at the heartstrings of Kholodnaia's film-going mourners (that is, the aesthetic paradigm) paled beside the loss of Akhmatova as poetic spokeswoman for the spiritual values of her country and witness to its history (the soviet intelligentsia's ideological replacement).

Whereas Kholodnaia's reputation originated and grew amidst her on-screen muteness, Akhmatova's image depended decisively on her ability to wield words in a radically logocentric culture. Supremely adept at embellishing her role of leading female poet, Akhmatova invested tremendous energy in orchestrating her posthumous reputation, and she meticulously planned well in advance to ensure its appropriateness. Photographs and portraits of Akhmatova in her youth and middle age—the circulation of which, reports claim, she attentively monitored[40]—reveal her sophisticated understanding of self-presentation: grave poses, an undeviatingly thoughtful or melancholy expression, a skillfully draped shawl, deft "presentation" of her "remarkably beautiful hands," which she highlighted through manicures and rings ("her smoking was a ritual in itself"[41]), and so forth. This choreographed demeanor emphasized imperial uniqueness, self-possession, and an apartness from, as well as sense of superiority to, those surrounding her. Memoirs of the period, which transform the adjectives "regal," "imperious," and "majestic" into Homeric epithets for Akhmatova, evidence the startling degree to which people in her orbit assimilated and disseminated her carefully wrought self-image throughout her career.

If lyrics, love, and loveliness dominated Akhmatova's early years, after Nikolai Gumilev's (her husband) execution, the ravages of Stalinism, her son's protracted imprisonment, Nikolai Punin's (her lover) death, her failed marriages, physical deterioration, and the shift to such historical poems as *Requiem* and *Poem without a Hero,* Akhmatova in her sixties cultivated a new identity: that of ultimate literary arbiter and stoic epic sufferer—the genius-victim who, as witness and participant in the tragic fate of her country, had fearlessly recorded its depradations for posterity. Her protégé, Joseph Brodsky, sums up this trajectory as the mythic progression from "a Russian Sappho" in the 1910s, to "a Cassandra of the twenties and thirties," and a "Keening Muse for the rest of her life."[42]

According to Nayman, Akhmatova's whole life "was lived . . . under the sign *memento mori.*"[43] Inordinately preoccupied with her posthumous reputation, she began generating her own epitaphs relatively early in life. Claiming "I taught women how to write," she arrogated to herself the entire realm of women's verbal creativity; she declared herself an objective Akhmatova specialist whose self-commentary future scholars could ignore at their own peril;[44] and she embraced "the tragic image of herself as Cassandra" regarding Russia's fate.[45] Any version of her life that deviated from her own mythmaking she rejected out of hand.

The power of that myth manifested itself in full force on Akhmatova's death on March 5, 1966, marked by memorial ceremonies and not one but two funerals, one in Moscow and one in Leningrad.[46] In his speech over Akhmatova's body at the morgue in Moscow, Lev Ozerov pronounced: "Akhmatova! The name conjures up an entire epoch. . . . The great life of Anna Akhmatova has ended. And now immortality begins, has already begun."[47] Encomia accompanying subsequent rituals corroborated his words. Nadezhda Mandelshtam's recollections capture the concrete circumstances of the final rites: "Leningrad. The church. Funeral services. A crowd of thousands encircled the Church of Nikola Morskoi. Inside, people were crushed together. Movie cameras whirred, but the films were later confiscated. . . . The films were hidden away in some archives."[48] Details in a more emotional vein are supplied by Roberta Reeder, a faithful perpetuator of the Akhmatova legend as legislated by its deity: "Akhmatova lay in an open coffin . . . [Those saying farewell included] old ladies from Petersburg, . . . well-dressed young women, young men, the intelligentsia, workers. They kissed her forehead; some cried quietly, others lamented loudly. *Akhmatova's face was noble as it had been in life.* . . . Beggars chatting loudly [outside said]: "*She was pious, serious. . . . She always gave us something.*"[49] At the House of Writers, where the coffin was placed on a pedestal, the scenario resembled a rock concert or what today would qualify as a photo-op event: only ticket holders among the huge crowds congregated outside could gain entry. Wreaths and flowers decorated the room; Boris Tichenko played the *Requiem* he had composed specifically for Akhmatova: "Female poets with hair of various hues hysterically claimed allegiance to Akhmatova";[50] and Mikhail Alekseev intoned: "A famous poet has departed, *a poet of unprecedented strength, who glorified Russian verse far beyond the borders not only of her native city but of her entire land.*"[51] Kindred grandiose phraseology and sententious exaltation were sustained at the actual interment in Komarovo, and at the first evening in memory of Akhmatova organized at Moscow University on March 31. Lev Kopelev proclaimed:

> The poetry of Anna Akhmatova, her fate, her image is beautiful and magnificent—it embodies Russia in its most difficult tragic years of its one-thousand-year history. . . . "Anna of all Rus"—this is what Marina Tsvetaeva called her. Anna of all Rus. . . . The powerful elegant thought of the *scholar, the clairvoyance of the stern prophetess, . . . that wise self-control when a sorceress is herself bewitched by love,* by the breathing of the earth, by the magical harmonies of the magic word. *Anna of all Rus double-crowned—the crown of thorns and the starry crown of poetry. . . . She is as immortal as the Russian word.*[52]

Iteration and multiplication inflated discourse into the hyperbole and extravagant moral claims normally associated with melodrama: Akhmatova as prophetess and sorceress, as a female Christ, as the incarnation of charitable democracy, *the* supreme poet. The funeral paeans cementing the myth of Akhmatova that she had so assiduously propagated resonate in the videofilm by Semeon Aranovich and Elena Ignatova *The Personal Case of Anna Akhmatova* (1989; *Lichnoe delo Anny Akhmatovoi*); in Reeder's painstakingly detailed yet utterly uncritical hagiography; and in John Bayley's breathless review of Reeder's book, where Bayley dubs Akhmatova "the high priestess of Russian poetry."[53]

If the vast crowds and eulogies at the multiple funerary rituals consolidated Akhmatova's cultural identity as poet laureate, a frequently reproduced funeral photograph by B. Shvartsman clearly shows who inherited that laureateship at Akhmatova's death. The extensive network of people who in her last decade served as Akhmatova's unofficial secretaries, nurses, and servants included a quartet of young male poets, her "literary sons" Dmitry Bobyshev, Evgeny Rein, Anatoly Nayman (also her official secretary), and Brodsky. Although the photograph captures the last three "orphans" gazing down on Akhmatova's corpse, the camera focuses on the face of the youthful, stricken Brodsky, his hand clapped over his mouth. That symbolic gesture of grief, as if silencing *his* capacity for speech, mirrors *her* ever-stilled poetic voice. The visual drama uniting the two implies the transfer of the "thorny" and "starry" crown to Akhmatova's rightful heir, observing the funeral's traditional function of assuring continuity at the moment of separation.[54] In fact, Akhmatova not only had earlier singled out Brodsky out for future poetic fame, but during the "thorny" phase of his life when he was sentenced to exile for parasitism, she revealingly remarked: "What a biography they're making for our Ginger [Rusty]. As if he'd gone out

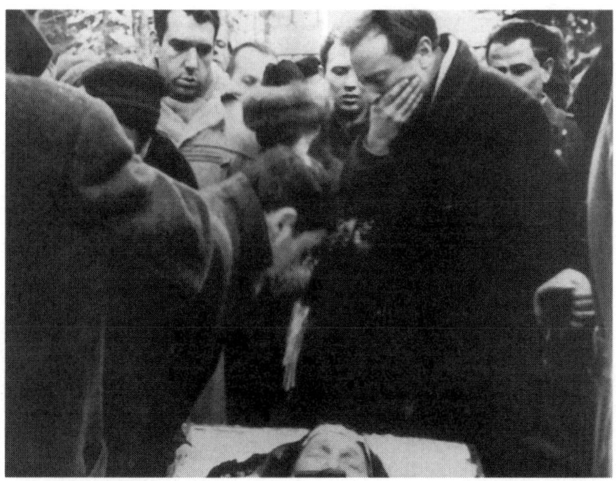

Keening muses: Akhmatova's funeral.
From Anatoly Nayman, *Remembering Anna Akhmatova* (London: Peter Halban, 1991), photo B. Shvartsman.

and hired someone to do it."[55] With her unparalleled self-consciousness and keen eye for posterity, Akhmatova fully grasped and exploited the value of suffering within the Russian poetic tradition ("Fate spared me nothing. My lot was to suffer everything it's possible to suffer").[56] Her death and funerals permitted others, notably members of the intelligentsia, to take over her task of heroicizing those sufferings for future generations.

## State and Stalin: An Optimistic Tragedy (1880–1953)

By an ironic coincidence March 5, the day of Akhmatova's death in 1966, coincides with Stalin's in 1953. The circumstances of Stalin's death are still partly shrouded in mystery: reportedly isolated behind his iron-cast door,[57] suffering from a brain hemorrhage that deprived him of speech and paralyzed the right side of his body, he slowly suffocated and, according to his daughter Svetlana, "died a difficult and terrible death."[58] The unrivaled expertise of the embalmers summoned to prepare his body for three days of public viewing transformed the seventy-three-year-old, decrepit, white-haired cadaver into a rosy-cheeked, dark-haired, robust man in his fifties. Smartly dressed in a brand-new uniform to remind Russians of his victorious military leadership during the Fatherland War, the "preserved" Stalin rested on hundreds of fresh-cut blooms that decoratively surrounded his body.[59] Just as photographers of the live Stalin had painstakingly removed his disfiguring pockmarks via airbrushing, now the rejuvenating skills of the state's cosmeticians perpetuated the illusion of the Father's immortal virility. The resulting work of art—a colorful, plastic "still life" of a man ostensibly in his prime—could only intensify the nation's bereavement. In that sense, Stalin died as he had lived. The illusion of visible verification allegedly had defined his public appearances within the Soviet Union: rumors had it that Stalin's doubles, perfected through plastic surgery and trained in his mannerisms, attended state funerals and sundry public functions, both to reduce his workload and to lessen the likelihood of his assassination.[60] Had Stalin not been sequestered in his room when he suffered the stroke that ultimately proved fatal, those "intimates" familiar with his reliance on doubles might reasonably have wondered whether the corpse was the real Stalin or one of his hired simulacra.

The pathos-steeped announcement over Radio Moscow on March 6 that "the heart of Joseph Vassarionovich Stalin . . . had stopped beating" was followed by repeated broadcasts of a communiqué intended to reassure the populace and of proclamations of Stalin's immortality. In a polarization typical of melodrama, the state combined celebration (of Stalin's "achievements" and heritage) with devastation (at the loss of the nation's Wise Father). Overnight the city metamorphosed into one gigantic funeral, accompanied by various symbols that historically have marked rituals of national tragedy and victory: lugubrious music blaring nonstop from loudspeakers; red flags with black crepe hanging from every lamp post; henchmen symmetrically flanking the bier (Khrushchev, Beria, and Malenkov at the head, Bulganin, Voroshilov, and Kaganovich at the foot) and wearing armbands of mourning; enormous photographs of Stalin appearing on every building; candles flickering in windows.[61] Tidal waves of mourners from across the country and torrents of poems and speeches lamenting the death of "the deathless Leader" washed over the capital, while old and young publicly wailed in schools, factories, offices, and the streets. As millions streamed to the Hall of Columns in the House of Trade Unions for a last glimpse of Stalin's body (by the third day the line stretched for six miles), hundreds perished, trampled to death in the stampede.[62] Their deaths,

Lining up outside the House of Trade Unions to view Stalin's body, March 1953. From Novosti of RIA.

ironically, literalized the bathetic metaphor of the countless Stalin dirges asserting that his "orphans" would not survive his demise.[63]

Throughout his rule Stalin had taken measures to imprint his presence on the visible landscape of the Soviet Union: publications on virtually every subject from agriculture to opera cited him as the final, unassailable authority; images of him in paintings, placards, photographs, postcards, busts, and monuments—some of mammoth size, like the thirty-six-foot bronze statue on the Volga-Don Canal that he had ordered in 1951—occupied central locations in cities, villages, and the open countryside.[64] Given the proportions of the Stalin cult during his life, the hyperbolization demanded by his funeral challenged the imagination. A partial solution was found in the unprecedented length, grandeur, and orchestration of symbolism during the burial ceremony: all work and all transportation from the Gulf of Finland to the Bering Sea came to a halt (the "heart" of the country ceased beating, along with

Stalin's); the interment took place at noon, just as the Kremlin clock struck twelve times; cannons roared; the red flag on top of the Kremlin tower was hoisted, while the standards of the Moscow Regiment dipped; and the Red army band of three hundred musicians played Chopin's funeral march.[65] Not only this meticulous choreography of sight and sound, but, above all, the place of interment signaled the import both of the historic moment and of Stalin's significance for Russian history. By placing Stalin's embalmed body next to Lenin's in the Red Square mausoleum, the funeral organizers specifically emphasized the ideological bloodline linking the two that Stalin had cannily advertised, and more generally observed the principle of continuity so critical to the funerary genre. Having presented himself throughout his career as "Lenin alive," in death Stalin became "one with Lenin." Even before his coffin, which rested on a catafalque atop a gun carriage pulled by six black horses, reached the tomb, Stalin's name was already carved in stone under Lenin's.[66]

The mass hysteria, violent deaths, and hundreds of arrests by the NKVD as part of the "mobilization plan"[67] accompanying Stalin's final silent part rendered it perhaps the single most melodramatic—and, fittingly, bloody—funeral in Russian history. Reactions on the international level succumbed to the same amplification that marked Russia's profound sense of a pivotal cosmic tragedy from which the nation would not recover. The *New York Times* equated Stalin's death with the end of an epoch in world history; the Swiss *Neue Züricher Zeitung* announced that Stalin's death had shaken the entire world; and the French paper *Figaro* questioned whether the Soviet Union would survive without its "Strong Hand." All the more startling, then, that a few short weeks after the mammoth spectacle of Stalin's funeral his name virtually vanished from the press, and in 1961 the Communist Party symbolically demoted him by relegating his corpse to a burial space shared by the cosmonaut Yuri Gagarin and the American revolutionary John Reed *beside* the mausoleum, *within* which Lenin would be exhibited thereafter in unique and solitary splendor.[68]

Yet, true to the principle that "memory is always life-giving. A return of the dead to the living," in the words of Jan Kott,[69] Stalin as cultural signifier—the quintessence of merciless, inflexible political power—enjoys a vigorous revival in postsoviet Russia's current nostalgia for the glorious past of empire. Wistful recollections of Stalin, materialized

Poster for Evgeny Evtushenko's film *Stalin's Funeral.*
From *Posmotri* no. 1, 1998.

in facsimiles of his embalmed body, videos with documentary footage, and busts and monuments that escaped the wholesale dismantling ushered in by desovietization, continue to nurture an empowering national identity among soviet diehards, while the quest for a New Russian Idea that would consolidate the nation, decreed by Yeltsin and earnestly pursued by the National Idea Search Commission, headed by Georgii Satarov (Weir), has culminated not in a unifying slogan of the sort in which the soviet regime excelled, but in an official confession of helplessness (packaged as an espousal of multiplicity).[70] Even Evgeny Evtushenko's film *Stalin's Funeral* and the second and third parts of Semeon Aranovich's documentary trilogy *I Was Stalin's Bodyguard* (1989–1990) and *I Worked for Stalin* (1989)[71]—all intended to expose the horrors of Stalinism—convey, instead, the contemporaries' widespread susceptibility to Stalin's fabled charisma.[72] Indeed, the year 1997 witnessed the battle over Stalin's body: in June, Grigor Oniani, the leader of the Stalin Society, called for the dictator's reburial in his native Georgia, guaranteeing full payment of all expenses.[73] Oniani's demand for the restitution of Stalin parallels Germany's thwarted efforts to recover *its* national treasures from Russia: both body and paintings symbolize part of the respective nations' past "glories." In his memoirs, Sergei Krasikov, a member of the elite Kremlin corps under Stalin, Khrushchev, and Brezhnev, unwittingly pinpoints self-reflection as the irreducible element in Russians' love of Stalin when he sighs admiringly: "[Stalin] was the greatest leader we ever had."[74] With the collapse of the soviet empire, the yearning for a vanished supremacy has led, predictably, to a resuscitation of Strong Hand heroes.

### Tripling the Tale-Telling Heart: Vladimir Vysotsky (1938–1980)

Stalin's apolitical counterpart in machismo, Vladimir Vysotsky, was one of Russia's major cultural luminaries during the late 1960s and 1970s, whose biography instantiated the melodramatic twinning of life and death. Born at the height of Stalin's purges, Vysotsky possessed colossal energy, an unquenchable thirst for immortality, and a versatile talent in three genres that during the 1970s drew gigantic audiences: theater, film, and bardic songs. Insatiable and driven, Vysotsky readily acknowleged his ambition to attain a permanent place in national memory (*chtoby pomnili, chtoby vezde puskali*),[75] and he cited dearth of time as the main drawback in life. Condensation of excess was his modus vivendi and his chosen route to immortality. Through the multitude of diverse personae he inhabited via song, stage, and screen he crammed countless assumed biographies into the forty-two years of his frenetic existence. In the words of film director Stanislav Govorukhin: "No run-of-the-mill person could cope with such a way of life, such a stressful schedule. . . . And his pace of life was maximally, incredibly accelerated" (*[t]akoi obraz zhizni, takaia nagruska—ne po silam obychnomu cheloveku. . . . i temp zhizni vzvinchil do nemyslimogo predela*[76]). Echoing that opinion, Iury Liubimov, the director responsible for first hiring Vysotsky at the Taganka Theater in 1964, compared him to a bolt of lightning with a strong electrical charge, one fated to burn out all too soon.[77] Like Achilles and other epic heroes, Vysotsky opted for "latitude" over "longitude," for vertical over horizontal: a brief, risk-laden life of glory instead of a lengthy but unremarkable career. And, true to the best traditions of Russian folk heroes, Vysotsky died three times; he survived two "clinical deaths," but not the third and final one that vouchsafed him the immortality he compulsively courted.[78] In both personal and professional spheres, Vysotsky challenged and thematized death, playing out the maximalist options innate to melodrama. In the romantic urban folklore that forged his posthumous identity, he died prematurely from having lived too intensely.

Acclaimed for his performance as Hamlet at the Taganka ("To be or not to be" became his existentialist calling card), Vysotsky also gained screen renown through more than two dozen different film parts and above all through his own verses, which at the time of his death numbered more than six hundred. Most of them he sang to a reverent audience of thousands at concerts and informal gatherings that generated unofficial cassette recordings disseminated among fans throughout Russia. Audiences fully identified Vysotsky with the protagonists he embodied in all three categories—poet, singer, and actor. If for Govorukhin "Hamlet *was* Vysotsky,"[79] for many who perceived the actor as an enigmatic brooder intent on exposing ugly truths, the reverse also held. Similarly, fan letters regularly attributed to him the criminal and war experiences that he popularized through his songs. His hoarse voice, tough looks, addiction to tobacco and alcohol, and preference for all-male company reinforced an image of machismo that Ernest Hemingway would have envied.

Vassily Aksënov justly called Vysotsky's position in soviet society "ambiguous": "unofficial," yet not "dissident."[80] His intimate knowledge of the quasicriminal world and the perceived glamour of his bohemian life—its aura of illicitness, his smoking, drinking, and reported use of drugs—constructed his image as a charismatic rebel-genius, despite his *priviligentsiia*-specific Mercedes, French filmstar wife, concerts abroad, and popularity with Leonid Brezhnev and the KGB. Although not prohibited from performing, Vysotsky was consistently denied access to both publishers and recording studios. His verses in music, which he himself accurately pegged as "thoroughly masculinist" and appealing chiefly to men,[81] circulated in cassettes taped by admirers at his performances. A high percentage of those songs deal with what Vysotsky himself characterized as extreme, life-threatening situations, the province of pilots, seamen, miners, and poets, who, according to Vysotsky's lyrics, "tread the razor's edge." In short, whatever the playfulness and humor of many Vysotsky lyrics, his principal passion was *mano a mano* confrontation with death.

Vysotsky's own death of a heart attack on 25 July 1980 seemed to confirm, if only metaphorically, widespread faith in his uncanny ability to divine the times, for he lost his final race against time just as Moscow was in the throes of hosting the Olympics. The melodrama of his funeral overshadowed Muscovites' involvement with official competi-

The bookplate designed by R. V. Kopylov, from Ekaterinburg (1994), wholly identifies Vysotsky with Hamlet, meditating on Yorick's skull.

R. V. Kopylov's bookplate (1994) condenses multiple aspects of the poet/singer/actor's personal and professional life, in symbolic and metonymical form.

Both images this page from V. Al'bertin, *Ekslibrisy posviashchennye V. S. Vysotskomy* (Moscow: "Moskva," 2000).

tive sports; his death triggered an outburst of adulatory sorrow that took a visually extravagant form. On the day of his burial, one hundred thousand people assembled at Taganka Square, where hundreds of police and *druzhinniki* were summoned to control the vast crowds, and where dozens of gigantic flower wreaths were propped up along with missives containing declarations of love and avowals of grief. Quite appropriately, the element of danger and conflict that typically suffuse many of Vysotsky's songs surfaced as the funeral procession left the square: attempting to clear the area, the police removed the portrait of Vysotsky displayed on one of the buildings (a modern analogue for Augustus's waxen funeral image and for the Orthodox icon). The crowds resisted, replacing the portrait with a larger one and maintaining vigil in the square until late that night, after Vysotsky's interment at Vagankovskoe Cemetery.

The occasion, in one journalist's words, was "one of the most remarkable events in the Soviet Union for decades" and resembled a spontaneous demonstration.[82] It corresponded to the extravagance with which Vysotsky had expended his seemingly limitless energy. And, in light of the repeated praise by fans of Vysotsky's "truth telling," by association it implied his heroic status as an uncompromised voice of truth raised in daring, solitary protest against the hypocrisy of official culture. Hence the epitaph engraved on the plaque above Vysotsky's grave cites his own lyrics from one of his best-known songs: "Poets walk on their heels on a knife's blade" (*poety khodiat piatkami na lezvii nozha*), uniting fans and the object of their veneration in their shared espousal of the myth that collapses creativity with kenoticism.

As Natalia Krymova, who was appointed the official secretary of Vystosky's literary estate in 1986, has remarked, "from the day of his funeral, Vysotsky's popularity entered a new phase."[83] The mythical Vysotsky, as Aksyonov puts it, was born. Although the press maintained a stubborn silence about his death, his grave became a site of pilgrimage, where hundreds gathered daily to leave flowers and commune with his "spirit."[84] His reputation as a seer, as one who penetrated and voiced a silenced truth, verged on canonization. And on the anniversary of his death Russians have continued to gather in hero-worship at the site of his bodily remains. During 1998, numerous magazines devoted to his memory celebrated what would have been his sixtieth birthday, with the usual cast of suspects testifying to his uniqueness and singular cultural role.

### "A Voice from the Chorus": Andrei Sakharov (1921–1989)

Vladimir Vysotsky's posthumous status (his popularity with the masses notwithstanding), like that of Anna Akhmatova, depended on the Soviet intelligentsia's ideologically driven penchant for making martyrs of its dead. As the theater director Stanislavsky remarked: "Melodrama has always risen when audiences were filled to the brim with lofty and noble feelings and needed ways to express them and find an outlet for their emotions."[85] The "beautiful sentiments" fueling the habit of martyrological funerary rituals became activated with a vengeance on the death of the soft-spoken Andrei Sakharov, who was revealingly dubbed by Russians as "the voice of the nation's conscience," or, in a western newsman's phrase, "the spiritual leader of the democratic forces in Russia."[86] Recalled by Gorbachev from his forced exile in Gorky (Nizhny Novgorod), the inventor of the hydrogen bomb—who later turned pacifist dissident—devoted himself to full-time political activity, especially to the repeal of Article 6 of the Soviet Constitution, which guaranteed the Communist Party a monopoly on official power. During perestroika, Sakharov's reputation as an oppositional force became advertised worldwide by a press that, in the spirit of *High Noon,* faithfully tracked the dramatic confrontations between Sakharov and his ostensibly benevolent opponent, Gorbachev, as well as his "villainous" ideological foes in the government.

Immediately upon Sakharov's death on December 14, 1989, the intelligentsia launched the standard process of martyred canonization, which enlisted such western journalists as David Remnick, the *New York Times* Moscow correspondent during perestroika and an impassioned advocate of *High Noon* versions of moral dilemmas. Casting Sakharov's role in Christological terms, the editor Vitaly Korotich resorted to the grandiloquence of polarized moral confrontation inseparable from melodrama:[87] "The totalitarian system had killed him . . . [but] before he died Sakharov dealt the system a mortal blow."[88] The Dostoyevsky scholar Iury Kariakin lamented that with Sakharov's death the country had lost its "perfect moral compass." Yeltsin reportedly declared: "Our duty is to Sakharov's name, to the persecution he suffered." For Remnick, Sakharov was a saint.[89] And, with the moralistic fervor typical of western liberals who during the soviet regime savored the defiant gestures, sufferings, and emotional funerals of Russian "political heroes," Remnick detailed how Muscovites instantly transformed the Sakharov/Bonner residence into a shrine: they heaped carnations on the doorstop; posted a photograph of Sakharov on the wall, bordering it with flowers and candles; and left messages of farewell, regret, and promises ("we will safeguard your memory"). These gestures, like Remnick's personalized account, enshrined *their* emotions, in the spirit of flaunted, pleasurable self-pity that funeral melodrama not only accommodates, but requires.[90]

Against the idyllic backdrop of mountains of flowers and rivers of mourners at the wake in the Palace of Youth, Lev Timofeev sublimated Sakharov and Elena Bonner into the by now familiar duo of ideal lovers: "they saw nothing except one another. . . . I felt like an interloper at a meeting of two lovers."[91] On the day of burial, five thousand people from all the soviet republics convened at Luzhniki to pay their final respects. Intimating an emotionally explosive parallel with Stalin's funeral and thereby accentuating the politico-moral contrast between him and Sakharov, Bonner publicly requested that the ceremony proceed in peaceful and safe fashion. The implications of that Manichaean contrast set the stage for the religious cast to the hyperbolic accolades that ensued: dubbed a saint, a holy man, and a prophet, Sakharov was lauded as "a citizen not only of our country, but of the whole world. . . . A man of the future." At Vostriakovskoe Cemetery just outside Moscow, nature harmonized with the atmosphere of dismal gloom, the falling sleet accompanying Chopin's *Funeral March,* tears, and two final kisses by the widow.[92]

Yet in one respect at least, Sakharov's posthumous standing eerily recalls Stalin's: both testify to the frailty of memory. Only a few years after Sakharov's funeral, enormous financial difficulties delayed Bonner's efforts to publish the Russian edition of her late husband's memoirs, which had appeared in the United States in 1990. Finally issued in a print run of five thousand copies by Human Rights Publishers, the two volumes encountered a mixed reaction among Moscow booksellers, who expressed doubts about the work's marketability. In the new era of entrepreneurship, even "holiness" could not afford to ignore sales potential.

Bonner's tribulations symptomatize the extent to which the official dissolution of the soviet regime has transformed the nature and stature of venerable cultural rituals, jeopardizing formerly sacrosanct genres. Reactions to the deaths of Sviatoslav Richter and Bulat Okudzhava, in August and June, respectively, of 1997, vividly confirm superficially minor but, in terms of the moral occult, profoundly significant changes in the melodrama of celebrity funerals. As a world-renowned pianist, Richter was buried in the prestigious Novodevichy Cemetery—the final home of Gogol, Chekhov, Eisenstein, Scriabin, Prokofiev, Shostakovich, Nadezhda Allilueva Stalin, Khrushchev, Andrei Tupolev, and Zoia Kosmodemianskaia[93]—to the customary chorus of aggrandizing pseudoepitaphs: "He wasn't just a performer, he was a great man" (the poet Bella Akhmadulina); "He was an exceptional man . . . on the same level as Michelangelo, with great power, soul, intellect, emotion, and will" (the artist Iury Libkhaber).[94] Yet the ceremonies connected with his burial were comparatively modest in scale, and media coverage of the events tended toward low-key, measured description, relatively free of emotionalism.[95] Reputedly a self-contained individual who shunned politics, publicity, and public pronouncements, Richter (who, incidentally, played at Stalin's funeral) performed in a nonverbal medium on which visibility rarely need impinge. One could argue, therefore, that, in contrast to Kholodnaia, Akhmatova, Stalin, Vysotsky, and Sakharov, Richter lived without taking his future epitaph into account, and thus forfeited the potential theatricality of his last public appearance. His unsuitability for instant posthumous monumentalization discouraged an enactment of scenarios articulating the moral occult.

Yet the case of the postwar bard Bulat Okudzhava suggests that additional and more complex factors have contributed to the modification of the funerary genre. Okudzhava's death near Paris elicited extreme and irrational responses, sanctioned by generic conventions, from his wife and his fellow literati—the *shestidesiatniki* (people of the 1960s) whose investment in the moral polarization of funerary melodrama exceeded that of any other constituency in the Soviet Union. Although Okudzhava died abroad from complications related to pneumonia and kidney failure, his widow fancifully cited "the psychological stress of loneliness" as the cause of death. On June 18, the day of burial at Vagankovskoe Cemetery, thousands of mourners filed down central Moscow's Arbat, immortalized by one of Okudzhava's best-loved songs, to catch a valedictory glimpse of the balladeer whose unpretentious, personal lyrics the intelligentsia had interpreted as a message of hope "for a more humane, liberal society" during the soviet era.[96] His intelligentsia cohorts observed the traditional fortieth day after his death by publishing a special thirty-two-page newspaper issue in memoriam, in a print run of forty thousand copies, devoted exclusively to copious photographs of Okudzhava, extracts from his songs, prose, and interviews, and reminiscences and elegies by friends and colleagues. Hagiographical testimonials included Egor Gaidar's stupefying claim that "a whole era has passed with him. Russia will never be the same again," and Iury Liubimov's assertion that Okudzhava was a "peaceful and wise man" (who, it bears remembering, had endorsed Yeltsin's decision in 1992 to shell parliament "into submission").[97] A physicist at the ceremony, Tatiana Leonteva, called Okudzhava "the most honest, frank and brave person I know," and compared him, tellingly, with Sakharov, adding: "I turned out to pay my respects to Sakharov and now to Okudzhava, but this is probably the last time I'll do this. There's nobody left now with their mentality and personality."[98]

Rather than witnessing the passing of an extraordinary individual, Leonteva in fact was bidding farewell to the moral occult of soviet-era celebrity funerals. Whereas the seventy-three-year-old Okudzhava was hardly the last surviving representative of the *shestidesiatniki* in Russia, the historical epoch that had elevated the former schoolteacher turned bard to a national hero *was* over. If, as Leonteva averred, Okudzhava was a "symbol of freedom" for her generation, desovietization has destabilized the Manichaeanized conditions enabling that symbolism. In postsoviet culture, canonization on the basis of genuine or perceived moral resistance to an official evil has become marginalized as a vestigial, anachronistic style specific to a pensioner-age interest group. Accordingly, amidst the hosannas to Okudzhava a dissonant note of restraint and common sense sounded in the unsigned "Last Page" (*Posledniaia stranitsa*) of the glossy macho magazine *Medved'*. With a matter of factness that violates all rules of celebrity elegies and that previously would have been roundly anathemized, the anonymous author punctures the extravagant rhetoric inflating farewells to Okudzhava: "No Pushkin could have dreamed of [achieving] what he did! . . . No other poet created such a number of authentic popular-folk works." In a stunning reversal of the values underpinning soviet intelligentsia myths, the anonymous author reasons: "He died at a time that's very difficult for our country, and *his departure wasn't a severe emotional blow for the majority. Our society has grown hardened:* people who early had time for poetry now think only of how to survive. Other deaths are heartrending. *In the context* of a thousand boys who have perished for nothing in Chechnia, *this loss is not very bitter.* The country did not shudder in pain. *The poet passed on* at a venerable age, cherished by the new order, *to a chorus of unrestrained praise.*"[99] This cool-headed assessment leaves little doubt that the most momentous funeral to have occurred during the 1990s is that of the intelligentsia as the unassailable source of an influential oppositional discourse. The very titles of Victor Erofeyev's controversial "Wake for Soviet Literature" (1989), announcing the demise of Soviet literature, and Masha Gessen's *Dead Again: The Russian Intelligentsia after Communism* (1997), which struggles to disprove its own title, perform postmortems on the sacred cows of the soviet era.[100] Of the manifold, far-reaching transformations within Russian society, not the least are the fact and the consequences of the intelligentsia's loss of status—a demotion that has divested of symbolic significance the demise of its more famous members. Since, *pace* Evtushenko, a poet is no longer "more than a poet," the death of a renowned writer or bard no longer represents depletion in the ranks of a moral army battling the dark forces of officialdom. Sense rules over sensibility, pragmatism over prophecy. Younger generations of Russians therefore perceive Okudzhava (if at all) as a mild, likable man whose songs warmed the heart, whereas the monopathic[101] eulogies of his fellow *shestidesiatniki* rely on the old black-and-white context of villainy versus noble self-sacrifice or, less floridly, them versus us. It is also inconceivable that the death of any political figure in Russia today would elicit the national frenzy of visible grief enacted during Stalin's burial ceremonies. In fact, Alla Pugacheva may be the only contemporary public persona likely to be accorded the "honor" of such graveside melodrama.[102] It is no accident that the recent funeral and burial of Raisa Gorbacheva at Novodevichy Cemetery reconceived one of the most despised First Ladies in recent memory not into a moral heroine, but into the modish female lead in a sentimental media romance, with Gorbachev the tearful Tristan to her Isolde. Not essence, but style—Gorbacheva's hallmark and the source of Russians'

Tombstone of local gangster Mikhail Kuchin in Uralmash, a northern suburb of Ekaterinburg. Photo by Samuel Hutchinson.

earlier implacable resentment, but now the cultural value of choice—provided her epitaph.

Fans of funerary histrionics may take heart, for the *Sturm und Drang* of last rites has not wholly disappeared in Russia, but merely "gone local." In a shift related to the country's comprehensive transition to crime-ridden privatization, the disproportionate gestures of national funeral melodrama have been co-opted by local mafioso clans. For instance, in Ekaterinburg (formerly Sverdlovsk), where gang wars have resulted in numerous fatalities, the beneficiaries of those who amassed vast fortunes in their brief lives have selectively improved on the symbolic excesses of these rites. Because acquisition of money defines the achievements of the late lamented, lavishness and scale suitably dominate in their immortalization. Lenin's embalmers from the Biological Research Institute preserve—or reconstruct—the body of the dear departed at the rate of fifteen hundred dollars for a day's work. Coffins range from the wooden "Al Capone" special in the shape of a cross (modeled after the prototype in the film *The Godfather*) to a twenty-thousand dollar glittering crystal showpiece, ideal for exhibition in a club or a casino. Rising as high as ten feet, gravestones of marble or malachite, some costing more than sixty thousand dollars, bear the condensed visual legend of the deceased's success: captured full-length, clad in Adidas sportswear and leather jacket, he holds a casual pose, the keys to his Mercedes in hand.

Gigantic expenditures mark not only funerals but also memorial services: relatives and friends in leather and furs arrive in limousines to gather at tables laden with imported champagne, vodka, caviar, assorted meats, pineapples, and other items of "the best that money can buy" as they pay respects to the man who, in a sense, proleptically footed the bill.[103] Gastronomical delights and luxurious clothes and appurtenances constitute the appropriate "currency of respect" for the deceased, paralleling the eulogies and quotations from their works uttered over the bodies of political and intelligentsia celebrities by their mourners in earlier times. Whether honoring martyrs of ideological discourse or youthful victims of a mafia-driven market, both groups operate in the medium of the deceased. If, as Brooks maintains, melodrama "has the *distinct value* of being about recognition and clarification,"[104] then the melodrama of Russian funerals, with its desacralization of soviet Manichaeanism, compels us to confront and acknowledge the *distinct transmutation of values* experienced by Russia in the 1990s.

## Notes

Affectionate thanks to Bozenna Goscilo, whose critical comments on an earlier draft of this essay eliminated some of its quirks; to Sabine Hake, who responded with brio to the topic and directed me to the article on mafioso burials; to Julie Buckler, whose commonsensical questions urged mental flab to firm into muscle; and to the editors of this volume, who combined kindness with a challenge to intellectual pistols at dawn.

1 Peter Brooks, *The Melodramatic Imagination: Balzac, Henry James, and the Mode of Excess* (New Haven: Yale University Press, 1976), ix.

2 Donovan J. Ochs, *Consolatory Rhetoric* (Columbia: University of South Carolina Press, 1993), 31.

3 Roger Grainger, *The Social Symbolism of Grief and Morning* (London: Jessica Kingsley, 1998), 105.

4 For an excellent treatment of this cultural move as it specifically relates to the operatic mezzo-into-soprano Evlaliia Kadmina, see Julie Buckler, "Her Final Debut: The Kadmina Legend in Russian Literature," in *Intersections and Transpositions: Russian Music, Literature, and Society,* ed. Andrew Baruch Wachtel (Evanston, Ill.: Northwestern University Press, 1998), 225–52.

5 If, as Arnold van Gennep and other anthropologists maintain, rites of passage have the tripartite structure of separation, marginalization, and aggregation, then monumentalization marks a key moment in the stage of separation. It captures the transition from the past—re-created during the eulogy that summarizes the deceased's "prior space in the community"—to the future, as the eulogy maps out the niche that will be occupied by the deceased thereafter ("we shall remember him/her as . . .") (Ochs, *Consolatory Rhetoric,* 30–31, 45).

6 In contrast to the grim solemnity of the other four genres, that of epitaph may be satiric or playful, as richly illustrated by Martial's epigrammatic exercises in the genre.

7 *Epikedeion* is distinguished from the more general *threnos,* which is not limited by time and place and could be sung on multiple occasions. For studies of the formal aspects of funeral oration, see Ochs, *Consolatory Rhetoric,* 81.

8 J. A. Cuddon, *A Dictionary of Literary Terms* (New York: Doubleday, 1976), 193.

9 Susan Walker, *Memorials to the Roman Dead* (London: British Museum, 1985), 7, 9.

10 This process entails what Bakhtin calls "finalization," and the image of the deceased created by it may dominate cultural memory for decades.

11 The gendering of ceremonial mourning in Russia has been noted by, among others, Iurii Sokolov, who wrote that "[funerary] chants, during the last few centuries, have been exclusively a genre of women's poetry" (Sokolov, *Russian Folklore* [Hatboro, Pa.: Folklore Associates, 1966], 225–34). Annette Michelson also notes: "The work of mourning is women's work"; its most famous practitioners are Irina Andreevna Fedosova and Nastasia Stepanovna Bogdanova (Michelson, "The Kinetic Icon and the Work of Mourning: Prolegomena in the Analysis of a Textual System" in *The Red Screen: Politics, Society, Art in Soviet Cinema,* ed. Anna Lawton [London: Routledge, 1992], 125–26). The practice of engaging profes-

sionals to perform laments was prevalent among the Chinese, Egyptians, and Romans and survives today among the Greeks and other Balkan peoples and in Asia Minor and in Spain. See Margaret Alexiou, *The Ritual Lament in Greek Tradition* (Cambridge, Eng.: Cambridge University Press, 1974), 10.

12 For more on the history and function of funereal elegies, see Alex Preminger and T. V. F. Brogan, eds., *The New Princeton Encyclopedia of Poetry and Poetics* (Princeton: Princeton University Press, 1993), 322–25.

13 For a thorough treatment of ancient Greek funerary conventions and legislation and their evolution, see Alexiou, *The Ritual Lament.*

14 The deceased is still, silent, and singular, whereas the mourners are highly mobile (a moving parade), voluble (speeches, weeping, lamentations), and collectively massed (the community, the collective). On the polarization of the contrasts between the dead body and the living who ritualize its departure, see Ochs, *Consolatory Rhetoric,* 48, 99.

15 Moreover, as Ochs rightly contends, in a spectacle symbolic codes and the sense of sight are predominant (Ochs, *Consolatory Rhetoric,* 96).

16 Zhukovskii's elegy on Pushkin's death, for instance, strives for a verbal rendition of the poet's visual portrait at death.

17 Peter Brooks, "Melodrama, Body, Revolution," in *Melodrama: Stage, Picture, Screen,* ed. Jacky Bratton, Jim Cook, and Christine Gledhill (London: British Film Institute, 1994), 11, 18.

18 Ibid., 19.

19 For an incisive, copiously documented analysis of the role played by anniversary celebrations in cult formation, and specifically the Soviet cooptation of Pushkin as icon, see Marcus Levitt, *Russian Literary Politics and the Pushkin Celebration of 1880* (Ithaca: Cornell University Press, 1989).

20 On the first day that the public could view the Duke of Wellington's body lying in state at the Chelsea Hospital, three people were killed in the crush. On the majestic nature of Wellington's funeral, see Crowley, 124–26.

21 For an examination of funerals in Russian political culture, see Thomas T. Trice, "The 'Body' Politic: Russian Funerals and the Politics of Representation, 1841–1929," Ph.D. diss., University of Illinois at Champaign-Urbana, 1999.

22 For a formal analysis of the pervasive dualism structuring Russian culture, see Iurii Lotman, "Binary Models in the Dynamics of Russian Culture," in *The Semiotics of Russian Cultural History: Essays by Iurii M. Lotman, Lidiia Ia. Ginzburg, Boris A. Uspenskii,* ed. Alexander Nakhi-

movsky and Alice Stone Nakhimovsky (Ithaca: Cornell University Press, 1985), 30–66.

23 Brooks, *The Melodramatic Imagination,* 4–5.

24 As the "unacknowledged legislators," to borrow Shelley's phrase, of "the Russian idea" for two hundred years, since the collapse of the Soviet Union the intelligentsia has lost its sense of self and mission. In fact, the commission appointed by Yeltsin to forge a new idea of Russia's identity acknowledged its inability to define any unifying national ethos.

25 Richard Stites, *Russian Popular Culture: Entertainment and Society since 1900* (Cambridge, Eng.: Cambridge University Press, 1992), 33.

26 Stites, *Russian Popular Culture,* 29. This social world has its American analogy in F. Scott Fitzgerald's *The Great Gatsby,* which, not incidentally, contains a highly revelatory funeral.

27 Evgeny Bauer (1865–1917), the director of *Life,* during the five years spanning his film career, attained fame as the director of psychological salon dramas and women's films—both identified with melodrama. See the essay by McReynolds in this volume.

28 Stites lists the date as 1919 (Stites, *Russian Popular Culture,* 21).

29 Neia Zorkaia, *The Illustrated History of Soviet Cinema* (New York: Hippocrene Books, 1989), 46.

30 Ibid., 47.

31 Daniel Gerould, "Melodrama and Revolution," in Bratton et al., eds., *Melodrama,* 192.

32 B. B. Ziukov, comp., *Vera Kholodnaia* (Moscow: Iskusstvo, 1995), 82.

33 Zorkaia, *The Illustrated History of Soviet Cinema,* 47.

34 Edgar Allan Poe, "The Philosophy of Composition," in *Essays and Reviews* (New York: Literary Classics of the United States, 1984), 19.

35 Elisabeth Bronfen, *Over Her Dead Body: Death, Femininity, and the Aesthetic* (New York: Routledge, 1992), 95–96.

36 Ziukov, *Vera Kholodnaia,* 13.

37 Kholodnaia's hagiographer Ziukov intimates an analogy between the two celebrities on the flimsy basis of their both having married in 1910 (Ziukov, *Kholodnaia,* 13). Unlike the Kholodnye's marriage, however, Akhmatova's marriage to Gumilev proved to be short-lived. A more substantial basis for comparison is the theatrical nature of Kholodnaia's on-screen and Akhmatova's off-screen behavior.

38 Ibid., 183.

39 Anatoly Nayman, *Remembering Anna Akhmatova* (London: Peter Halban, 1991), 3.

40 Polivanov, 128.

41 Ibid., 171.

42 Nayman, *Remembering Anna Akhmatova,* xii.

43 Ibid., 217.

44 Ibid., 81.

45 I. Berlin, "Anna Akhmatova: A Memoir," in *The Complete Poems of Anna Akhmatova,* vol. 2, trans. J. Hemschemeyer (Somerville, Mass.: Zephyr Press), 38.

46 For a detailed account of the events following Akhmatova's death, see Roberta Reeder, *Anna Akhmatova: Poet and Prophet* (New York: St. Martin's Press, 1994), 503–6.

47 Ibid., 504.

48 Polivanov, 111. In fact, the video *Delo Anny Akhmatovoi* uses part of the footage.

49 Reeder, *Anna Akhmatova,* 505; emphasis added.

50 Polivanov, 111–12.

51 Reeder, *Anna Akhmatova,* 505; emphasis added.

52 Ibid., 506; emphasis added.

53 For a concerted decrowning of this myth, see Catriona Kelly, *A History of Russian Women's Writing, 1820–1992* (Oxford: Clarendon Press, 1994); and especially Alexander Zholkovsky, "The Obverse of Stalinism: Akhmatova's Self-Serving Charisma of Selflessness," unpublished paper.

54 Ochs, *Consolatory Rhetoric,* 45.

55 The Russian "Ryzhik" would be rendered as "Ginger" by the British, but Americans would translate the name as "Rusty." Nayman, *Remembering,* 5.

56 Polivanov, 76.

57 According to Edvard Radzinsky, Stalin died not at the Kremlin but at one of his dachas. Radzinsky's account diverges significantly from all earlier ones, but what matters here remains unchanged: no one dared enter Stalin's room for six hours, according to one of Radzinsky's interviewees. For a detailed account of the circumstances surrounding Stalin's death and Radzinsky's speculations about it, see Edvard Radzinsky, *Stalin,* trans. H. T. Willetts (New York: Doubleday, 1996), 566–82.

58 Svetlana Alliluyeva, *Twenty Letters to a Friend,* trans. P. J. McMillan (New York: Harper Books, 1967). Her account of his last gesture, "incomprehensible and full of menace, . . . he suddenly lifted his left hand as though he were pointing to something above and bringing down a curse on us all" (10), is the very stuff of melodrama and has been quoted and summarized by virtually all subsequent biographers.

59 Stuart Kahan, *The Wolf of the Kremlin* (New York: William Morrow, 1987), 279. Sergei Prokofiev also died on March 5, and his widow was

unable to buy any flowers for the composer's coffin because all the stores were closed to honor Stalin's death (see Radzinsky, *Stalin,* 579).

60 Mark Franchetti, "Kremlin Confessions of a Top KGB Minder," *Sunday New York Times,* 1 June 1997.

61 Kahan, *The Wolf,* 277.

62 Ibid., 279. See also Evgenii Evtushenko's film *Stalin's Funeral,* which conveys the chaos and crazed reactions of the populace at the leader's death and burial.

63 Poems on Stalin's death penned by Margarita Aliger, Nikolai Aseev, Ol'ga Bergol'ts, Nikolai Gribachev, Evgenii Dolmatovskii, Mikhail Isakovskii, Semen Kirsanov, Konstantin Simonov, Sergei Smirnov, Aleksandr Tvardovskii, and Nikolai Tikhonov, among a host of others, are collected in *Sto stikhotvorenii o Staline* (Moscow: Vasanta, 1993), which prefaces the poetry by two citations from the Gospels! The majority yoke sorrow with rapture at Stalin's glorious deeds, which have rendered him "eternal" (the words *vechno* and *bessmertno* recur repeatedly in both Russian and non-Russian lyrics commemorating the momentous occasion).

64 Arthur M. Schlesinger Jr., *Joseph Stalin* (New York: Chelsea House, 1985), 100.

65 Kahan, *A Wolf,* 281.

66 Ibid., 280.

67 Roy Medvedev, *Let History Judge* (New York: Knopf, 1972), 559.

68 Few phenomena attest so eloquently to the weighty symbolic and ideological significance of dead bodies than the protracted battle over Lenin's embalmed remains, which allowed Yeltsin no peace. As vampire literature and films, as well as the specific cases of Lenin and Stalin, dramatize, burial brings no guarantee of "eternal rest" and oblivion. Ernst Kantorowicz's paradigm of the "king's two bodies," consisting of a visible, corporeal, mortal body, on the one hand, and an invisible, ideal "body politic" on the other, finds potent confirmation in the relentless "resurrection" of both soviet leaders (Kantorowicz, *The King's Two Bodies: A Study in Mediaeval Political Theology* [Princeton: Princeton University Press, 1957], 409).

69 Jan Kott, "Kantor, Memory, and Mémoire (1915–90)," in *The Memory of the Body* (Evanston, Ill.: Northwestern University Press, 1992), 55.

70 Semen Shatskoi, "Poisk national'noi idei," *Nezavisimaia gazeta,* August 9, 1997, 2.

71 *The Case of Anna Akhmatova* comprises the first segment of the trilogy.

72 Fazil Iskander's "Balshazzar's Feasts," from the novel *Sandro from Chegem,* vividly captures Stalin's appeal, intimating its sexual aura. As Tenghiz Abuladze's perestroika film *Repentance* suggested, laying Stalin

as cultural sign to final rest may be possible only with the advent to power of the postsoviet generation.

73 For more on the controversy of Stalin's reburial and the burial of Lenin, see Paul Goble, "Reburying the Past," *Radio Liberty*, June 18, 1997.

74 Franchetti, "Kremlin Confessions."

75 A. S. Epshtein, comp., *Vladimir Semenovich Vysotskii: Bibliograficheskii spravochnik (1960–1990)* (Kharkov: Studiia-L, 1992), 379.

76 V. T. Kabanov, ed. *V. Vysotskii: Ia, konecho, vernus'* (Moscow: Kniga, 1988), 63.

77 Samuel Rachlin, *A Voice from Russia: Vladimir Vysotsky*, video, 1983.

78 Kabanov, *V. Vysotskii*, 87. The number three, which is a topos in Russian folklore, figured centrally in Vysotsky's life: three wives, three professions, three deaths.

79 See the volume of reminiscences issued after Vysotsky's death (Kabanov, *V. Vysotskii*, 87).

80 Rachlin, *A Voice from Russia.*

81 Epshtein, *Vladimir Semenovich Vysotskii*, 389.

82 Rachlin, *A Voice from Russia.*

83 Ibid.

84 Ibid.

85 Gerould, "Melodrama and Revolution," 196.

86 David Remnick, *Lenin's Tomb: The Last Days of the Soviet Empire* (New York: Random House, 1993), 282.

87 Brooks, *The Melodramatic Imagination*, 25.

88 Remnick, *Lenin's Tomb*, 282.

89 Ibid., 283, 279, 284.

90 Brooks, *The Melodramatic Imagination*, 12.

91 Remnick, *Lenin's Tomb*, 285–86.

92 Ibid., 288–89.

93 John Francis Marion, *Famous and Curious Cemeteries* (New York: Crown, 1977), 48–49. Both the prestige of Novodevichy and the barriers facing those eager to join the elite, if only in death, emerged clearly in November 1996, when Paul Tatum, an American businessman from Oklahoma and part owner of the Radisson Slavianskaia hotel, was slain. His friend Natal'ia Bokadorova fought for nine months to honor his wish to be buried in Novodevichy, but finally, in August 1997, she had to settle for the humbler Kuntsevo Cemetery west of Moscow. Bokadorova reportedly plans to erect a red granite headstone for Tatum, "to symbolize the blood he shed in Russia" (Bronwyn McLaren, "Tatum's Ashes Find Resting Place at Last," *Moscow Times*, 13 August 1997, 1–2).

94 McLaren, "Tatum's Ashes," 3.

95 An exception was the short elegiac piece by Leonid Gakkel', "XX vek proshchaetsia s Rikhterom," which appeared in *Literaturnaia gazeta,* August 6, 1997, 6.

96 See Gareth Jones, "Russians Bid Farewell to Legendary Bard Bulat Okudzhava," *Reuters,* June 18, 1997; and Michael Specter, "Bulat Okudzhava, 73, Poet of Dissent in 1950s Russia," *New York Times,* 14 June 1997.

97 Jones, "Russians Bid Farewell."

98 Ibid.

99 *Medved'* no. 8 (1997): 144; emphasis added.

100 Organic metaphor, however, can neither naturalize nor disguise slippage. Gessen's conclusion contradicts her own title, hailing, as it does, a "new vintage" of the intelligentsia. See Masha Gessen, *Dead Again: The Russian Intelligentsia after Communism* (London: Verso, 1997), 202.

101 In his study of tragedy and melodrama, Robert Heilman coins the term *monopathy* to denote "the singleness of feeling that gives one the sense of wholeness." The chief usefulness of the term resides in its stress on the subjective provenance of what might otherwise appear as objective or circumstantial unity (Heilman, *Tragedy and Melodrama: Versions of Experience* [Seattle: University of Washington Press, 1968]).

102 Pugacheva's undiminished appeal to a broad range of fans (young and old, apolitical and politically engaged, rich and poor, et cetera) accounts for the startling popularity of her biography, which in 1997 was, with A. Korzhakov's memoirs, the top best-seller in the country.

103 Samuel Hutchinson, "Whacked but Not Forgotten," *New York Times Magazine,* 13 April 1997, 52. Hutchinson's brief, excellent note, explicating the specific significance of symbolic acts to Ekaterinburg mafioso funerals, underscores the universal reliance of funerary rituals on symbols.

104 Brooks, *The Melodramatic Imagination,* 206; emphasis added.

# Suggested Reading

## Secondary Sources for the Study of Russian Melodrama


Arvin, Neil Cole. *Eugène Scribe and the French Theatre 1815–1860.* Cambridge, Mass.: Harvard University Press, 1924.

Booth, Michael R. "The Drunkard's Progress: Nineteenth-Century Temperance Drama." *Dalhousie Review* 44, no. 2 (summer 1964): 205–12.

———. *English Melodrama.* London: Herbert Jenkins, 1965.

———, ed. *Hiss the Villain: Six English and American Melodramas.* New York: Benjamin Blom, 1964.

Bratton, Jacky, Jim Cook, and Christine Gledhill, eds. *Melodrama: Stage, Picture, Screen.* London: British Film Institute, 1994.

Brooks, Peter. *The Melodramatic Imagination: Balzac, Henry James, Melodrama, and the Mode of Excess.* New Haven: Yale University Press, 1976.

Bronfen, Elisabeth. *Over Her Dead Body: Death, Femininity and the Aesthetic.* New York: Routledge, 1992.

Carlson, Marvin. *Theories of the Theatre: A Historical and Critical Survey from the Greeks to the Present.* Ithaca: Cornell University Press, 1984.

Cavell, Stanley. *Contesting Tears.* Chicago: University of Chicago Press, 1996.

Chester, Pamela, and Sibelan Forrester, eds. *Engendering Slavic Literature.* Bloomington: Indiana University Press, 1996.

Corrigan, Robert W., ed. *Tragedy: Vision and Form,* 2nd ed. New York: Harper and Row, 1981.

Davies, Robertson. *The Mirror of Nature: The Alexander Lectures, 1982.* Toronto: University of Toronto Press, 1983.

Disher, M. W. *Blood and Thunder: Mid-Victorian Melodrama and Its Origins.* London: Muller, 1945.

———. *Melodrama: Plots That Thrilled.* New York: Macmillan, 1954.

Doane, Mary Ann. "Melodrama, Temporality, Recognition: American and

Russian Silent Cinema." *East-West Film Journal* 4, no. 2 (June 1990): 69–89.

Gerould, Daniel, and Julia Przybos. "Melodrama in the Soviet Theater 1917–1920: An Annotated Chronology." In *Melodrama,* ed. Daniel Gerould. New York: New York Literary Forum, 1980, 75–92.

Gledhill, Christine, ed. *Home Is Where the Heart Is: Studies in Melodrama and the Woman's Film.* London: British Film Institute, 1987.

Grimsted, David. *Melodrama Unveiled: American Theater and Culture, 1800–1850.* Chicago: University of Chicago Press, 1968.

Hadley, Elaine. *Melodramatic Tactics: Theatricalized Dissent in the English Marketplace, 1800–1885.* Stanford: Stanford University Press, 1995.

Hays, Michael, and Anastasia Nikolopoulou, eds. *Melodrama: The Cultural Emergence of Genre.* New York: St. Martin's Press, 1996.

Heilman, Robert B. *Tragedy and Melodrama: Versions of Experience.* Seattle: University of Washington Press, 1968.

———. *The Iceman, the Arsonist, and the Troubled Agent: Tragedy and Melodrama on the Modern Stage.* Seattle: University of Washington Press, 1973.

Jensen, Margaret Ann. *Love's Sweet Return: The Harlequin Story.* Bowling Green, Ohio: Bowling Green State University Popular Press, 1984.

Kaplan, E. Ann, ed., *Psychoanalysis and Cinema.* New York: Routledge, 1990.

Klinger, Barbara. *Melodrama and Meaning: History, Culture, and the Films of Douglas Sirk.* Bloomington: Indiana University Press, 1994.

Landy, Marcia, ed. *Imitations of Life: A Reader on Film and Television Melodrama.* Detroit: Wayne State University Press, 1991.

Leyda, Jay. *Kino: A History of the Russian and Soviet Film.* 1960; Princeton: Princeton University Press, 1983.

Marcoux, J. Paul. *Guilbert de Pixérécourt: French Melodrama in the Early Nineteenth Century.* New York: Peter Lang, 1992.

Mason, Jeffery D. *Melodrama and the Myth of America.* Bloomington: Indiana University Press, 1993.

McConachie, Bruce A. *Melodramatic Explorations: American Theater and Society, 1820–1870.* Iowa City: University of Iowa Press, 1992.

Modleski, Tania. *Loving with a Vengeance: Mass-Produced Fantasies for Women.* Hamden, Conn.: Archon Books, 1982.

———. "Time and Desire in the Women's Film." *Cinema Journal* 23, no. 3 (spring 1984): 21.

———. "Melodrama and Memory." *Southern California Law Review* 65, no. 3 (March 1992): 1353.

———, ed. *Studies in Entertainment: Critical Approaches to Mass Culture.* Bloomington: Indiana University Press, 1986.

Neale, Steve. "Melodrama and Tears." *Screen* 27, no. 6 (November–December 1986): 6–22.

Petro, Patrice. *Joyless Streets: Women and Melodramatic Representation in Weimar Germany.* Princeton: Princeton University Press, 1989.

Przybos, Julia. *L'enterprise melodramatique.* Paris: Librairie José Corti, 1987.

Radway, Janice A. *Reading the Romance: Women, Patriarchy, and Popular Literature.* Chapel Hill: University of North Carolina Press, 1984.

Rahill, Frank. *The World of Melodrama.* University Park: Pennsylvania State University Press, 1967.

Redmond, James, ed. *Melodrama.* London: Cambridge University Press, 1992.

Robin, Régine. *Socialist Realism: An Impossible Aesthetic.* Trans. Catherine Porter. Stanford: Stanford University Press, 1992.

Segel, Harold B. *Twentieth-Century Russian Drama: From Gorky to the Present.* Updated ed. Baltimore: Johns Hopkins University Press, 1993.

Stites, Richard. *Russian Popular Culture: Entertainment and Society since 1900.* Cambridge: Cambridge University Press, 1992.

Usai, Paolo Cherchi, Lorenzo Codelli, Carlo Monanaro, and David Robinson, eds., with Yuri Tsivian. *Silent Witnesses: Russian Films 1908–1919.* London: British Film Institute, 1989.

Walkowitz, Judith. "Jack the Ripper and the Myth of Male Violence." *Feminist Studies* 8, no. 3 (fall 1982): 543–74.

Williams, Linda. "Melodrama Revisited." In *Refiguring American Film Genres: History and Theory,* ed. Nick Browne. Berkeley: University of California Press, 1998.

Zorkaya, Neia. *The Illustrated History of Soviet Cinema.* London: Hippocrene Books, 1989.

# Contributors

OTTO BOELE teaches in the Slavic Department at the University of Groningen, the Netherlands. He is the author of *The North in Russian Romantic Literature.* After spending a year as a visiting scholar at the University of California at Berkeley, he was awarded a fellowship by the Royal Dutch Academy of Sciences and Arts. Currently he is working on a book titled "The Myth of 'Saninism' in Russian Culture: Literature, Rumor, Sex (1907–1917)."

JULIE A. BUCKLER is Associate Professor of Slavic Languages and Literatures at Harvard University. She is the author of *The Literary Lorgnette: Attending Opera in Imperial Russia.* She is currently working on a book about St. Petersburg and the diverse types of writing that "mapped" the city during the eighteenth and nineteenth centuries.

JULIE A. CASSIDAY is Assistant Professor of Russian at Williams College. Her research focuses on the theater and theatricality in Russian culture in the nineteenth and early twentieth centuries. She has published a monograph devoted to early soviet show trials, *The Enemy on Trial: Early Soviet Courts on Stage and Screen,* and is currently researching the Russian professional theater of the pre-Pushkin era.

SUSAN COSTANZO is Associate Professor of History at Western Washington University. She is currently writing a book on amateur theater in the post-Stalin era, to be titled "Performing in the Wings: Amateur Theater and Alternative Culture in Post-Stalin Russia."

HELENA GOSCILO is UCIS Professor of Slavic Studies at the University of Pittsburgh. She has authored and edited more than a dozen books, including *Balancing Acts; Skirted Issues: The Discreteness and Indiscretions of Russian Women's Prose; Fruits of Her Plume; Lives in Transit: Recent Russian Women's Writing; Russia, Women, Culture* (with Beth Holmgren); *Dehexing Sex: Russian*

*Womanhood during and after Glasnost; TNT: The Explosive World of T. Tolstaya's Fiction;* and *Russian Culture in the 1990s.* She currently is working on a cultural study of the New Russians (with Nadezhda Azhgikhina) and on a volume about Russian book illustrators (with Beth Holmgren).

BETH HOLMGREN is Professor of Slavic Literatures at the University of North Carolina at Chapel Hill. Her research in Russian and Polish literatures and cultures focuses on women's cultural engagement and relations between high and popular commercial production. Her publications include *Women's Works in Stalin's Time: On Lidiia Chukovskaia and Nadezhda Mandelstam,* a coedited volume (with Helena Goscilo) *Russia, Women, Culture,* and *Rewriting Capitalism: Literature and the Market in Late Tsarist Russia and the Kingdom of Poland.* Her current scholarship examines Russian and Polish émigré culture in the United States.

LARS T. LIH has taught at Duke University and Wellesley College and now lives in Montreal, Quebec. He is the author of *Bread and Authority in Russia, 1914–1921* and is the American editor of *Stalin's Letters to Molotov.* A longtime interest in the narrative underpinnings of political doctrine is a central theme of a study he is now completing, titled "The Bolshevik Program."

LOUISE MCREYNOLDS is Professor of History at the University of Hawai'i. Her publications include *The News under Russia's Old Regime: The Development of a Mass-Circulation Press* and numerous articles on popular culture. She has translated Evdokia Nagrodskaia's *The Wrath of Dionysus* and coedited a collection of popular cultural materials, *Entertaining Tsarist Russia.*

JOAN NEUBERGER is Associate Professor of History at the University of Texas at Austin. She is the author of *Hooliganism: Crime, Culture, and Power in St. Petersburg, 1900–1914* and a series of articles on popular legal culture. She is currently at work on a study of the history and politics of Eisenstein's *Ivan the Terrible.*

ALEXANDER PROKHOROV is a doctoral student at the University of Pittsburgh, where is he writing a dissertation about soviet culture in the Khrushchev era, "Agonies: Cultural Conflicts in Literature and Film of the Thaw." Prokhorov's articles have appeared in anthologies published by the Institute of Linguistics and the Institute of Ethnology and Anthropology of the Russian Academy of Sciences. He also published several reviews and articles in *Russian Review, Slavic and East European Journal,* and *Studies in Slavic Culture.*

RICHARD STITES is Professor of History at the School of Foreign Service, Georgetown University. He is the author of *The Women's Liberation Movement in Russia; Revolutionary Dreams;* and *Russian Popular Culture.* He is currently at work on a book titled "Pleasure and Power in Imperial Russia: Life and the Arts, 1800–1861."

# Index

*Library of Congress Cataloging-in-Publication Data*

Imitations of life : two centuries of melodrama in Russia / edited by Louise McReynolds and Joan Neuberger.
p. cm.
Includes bibliographical references and index.
ISBN 0-8223-2780-5 (cloth : alk. paper) —
ISBN 0-8223-2790-2 (pbk. : alk. paper)
1. Melodrama, Russian—History and criticism. 2. Russian drama—19th century—History and criticism. 3. Russian drama—20th century—History and criticism. 4. Theater—Russia—History. 5. Popular culture—Russia. I. McReynolds, Louise, 1952– II. Neuberger, Joan, 1953–
PG3089.M44 I53 2001
891.72′309—dc21 2001051071